Ius Comparatum – Global Studies in Comparative Law

Volume 16

More information about this series at http://www.springer.com/series/11943

Académie Internationale de Droit Comparé
International Academy of Comparative Law

Gregor Thüsing • Gerrit Forst
Editors

Whistleblowing - A Comparative Study

Springer

Editors
Gregor Thüsing
Institut für Arbeitsrecht und Recht der Sozialen Sicherheit
University of Bonn
Bonn, Germany

Gerrit Forst
Hengeler Mueller
Partnerschaft von Rechtsanwälten mbB
Düsseldorf, Germany

ISSN 2214-6881 ISSN 2214-689X (electronic)
Ius Comparatum – Global Studies in Comparative Law
ISBN 978-3-319-25575-0 ISBN 978-3-319-25577-4 (eBook)
DOI 10.1007/978-3-319-25577-4

Library of Congress Control Number: 2016934050

Springer Cham Heidelberg New York Dordrecht London

Printed on acid-free paper

Springer International Publishing AG Switzerland is part of Springer Science+Business Media (www.springer.com)

Foreword

Whistle-blowing has become a topic of interest during the last decades, for practitioners, politicians, and academics likewise. While whistle-blowing legislation dates back more than a hundred years in some countries and it is likely that some form of behavior that we would describe as whistle-blowing today existed since the beginning of human civilization, only in recent years it has been identified as a potential weapon against corruption, mismanagement, and general noncompliance with legal obligations by a broader public. This was also the reason for the International Academy of Comparative Law to deal with the topic on their XIXth International Congress of Comparative Law (20 and 21 July 2014) in Vienna. This book is based on the preparations for and the outcomes of that convention.

The reasons for the gaining interest in whistle-blowing are diverse: Especially in the United States, the Enron and WorldCom accounting scandals triggered far-reaching legislation on whistle-blowing – the Sarbanes Oxley Act – that influenced legislators around the globe. That first wave of capital market-driven whistle-blowing was followed by a second wave in the wake of the global banking crisis, in the United States, namely, the Dodd Frank Act. However, other countries such as the United Kingdom have their own body of legislation which was not triggered by accounting scandals or economic considerations at all, but by human tragedy. In the United Kingdom, whistle-blowing was regulated and thereby introduced as a consequence of two catastrophes claiming many casualties – the Clapham Junction rail accident and the sinking of the MS Herald of Free Enterprise. In the United Kingdom, whistle-blowing seems to be used as an early warning system against all kinds of dangers in the first place. It comes hardly as a surprise on this canvas that opinions on what constitutes whistle-blowing are diverse. A common denominator is that a whistle-blower releases secret information to a third party with the aim to prevent or stop a maldoing or grievance.

There are countries in which whistle-blowing has been observed with a good deal of mistrust, based on historical experience with "informers" to the state.

In these countries (though not only in them), whistle-blowers are rather perceived as denunciators and troublemakers than as sponsors of public interests. A rather reserved approach to whistle-blowing can be observed throughout many countries of continental Europe especially. In Germany, the rule of National Socialism and, after 1945, the socialism of the former German Democratic Republic led to a deep mistrust against any kind of behavior that aimed at informing public authorities about the behavior of other people. In France, which had to suffer severely under the German occupation during WW II and the Vichy regime, similar reservations to whistle-blowing exist to the day. In addition to that, the European approach to data protection led to a rather restrictive approach to whistle-blowing during the last decade especially.

This tome tries to build bridges between the different points of view by giving authors from fourteen countries around the world an opportunity to present the legal situation on whistle-blowing as well as the cultural perception of whistle-blowing in their country. This, in itself, is a valuable source of information, as practitioners and legislators throughout the world may profit from insights into other countries' legislation when drafting new rules at home. In addition to that, the editors tried to combine the different perceptions of whistle-blowing and to name commonalities and differences between the legal orders with the aim to identify a general concept of whistle-blowing that distinguishes it from denunciation. The reader may judge whether the editors have been successful in this undertaking. We, however, want to express our deep gratitude to the International Academy of Comparative Law, all the authors of this book, and to all those people without whose help it could not have been completed.

Bonn and Düsseldorf
June 2015

Gregor Thüsing
Gerrit Forst

Contents

Contributors

Shawn Marie Boyne Indiana University Robert H. McKinney School of Law, Indianapolis, IN, USA

Katrin Deckert Associate professor at Paris Ouest Nanterre University and deputy secretary-general of the International Academy of Comparative Law. Studied law in different universities in France and Germany. Since 2009, holds a PhD in German and French law from Panthéon-Sorbonne University (Paris I, France) and the University of Hamburg (Germany). Research fellow at Pantheon-Sorbonne University (2001–2004), research and teaching assistant at Panthéon-Assas University in Paris (2004–2006), research assistant at the Max Planck Institute for Comparative and International Private Law in Hamburg (2007–2009), lecturer in German law at Paris-Est Créteil University (2008–2010), and senior research fellow at the Max Planck Institute for Comparative and International Private Law in Hamburg (2010–2011). Teaches and researches in German, French, and European civil, corporate, and capital markets law as well as in comparative law.

Paris Ouest Nanterre University, Nanterre, France

Paris, France

Raluca Dimitriu Labour law professor at the Bucharest University of Economic Studies, Law Department Bucharest, Bucharest University of Economic Studies, Romana P-ta no. 6, Bucharest, Romania.

Michael Doherty Department of Law, Maynooth University, Maynooth, Ireland

David Fabri Commercial Law Department, University of Malta, Msida, MSD 2080, Malta

Gerrit Forst Hengeler Mueller, Partnerschaft von Rechtsanwälten mbB, Düsseldorf, Germany

Júlio Gomes LLM (Columbia University), DPhil (Oxford), invited professor of law at the Portuguese Catholic University, member of the Católica Research Centre for the Future of Law, and judge at the Supremo Tribunal de Justiça (Portuguese Supreme Court).

Vila Nova de Gaia, Portugal

Constantinos Kombos Law Department, University of Cyprus, Nicosia, Cyprus

Rüdiger Krause Professor for civil law and labor law at the Georg-August-University of Göttingen (Germany). Director of the Institute for Labour Law. Director of the Sino-German Institute for legal studies of the Universities of Göttingen and Nanjing (PRC).

Institut für Arbeitsrecht, Juristische Fakultät, Georg-August-Universität Göttingen, Göttingen, Germany

Sandra Laleta Faculty of Law, University of Rijeka (Pravni fakultet), Rijeka, Croatia

John P. McEvoy Professor at the Faculty of Law, University of New Brunswick, Canada. Former president of the Canadian Association of Law Teachers. Presently president of the Canadian Comparative Law Association as well as a vice-chair of the New Brunswick Labour and Employment Board.

Faculty of Law, University of New Brunswick, Fredericton, NB, Canada

Jakub Morávek Jakub Morávek is a senior lecturer of the Department of Labour Law and Social Security Law at the Faculty of Law, Charles University in Prague. He works too as an advocate.

Jakub Morávek is an author or coauthor of numerous monographs and articles in the field of labor law.

University v Praze, Právincká Fakulta, Praha 1, Czech Republic

Darja Senčur Peček Associate professor at the Faculty of Law, University of Maribor, where she is teaching labor law and social security law. Head of the Labour Law Department and a head of the Institute for Employment Relations and Social Security at the Faculty.

Faculty of Law, University of Maribor, Maribor, Slovenija

Jan Pichrt Jan Pichrt is a head of the Department of Labour Law and Social Security Law at the Faculty of Law, Charles University in Prague. He has lectured in labor law more than 20 years.

Jan Pichrt decides disputes as an arbitrator entered into the list of arbitrators of the Arbitration Court attached to the Economic Chamber of the Czech Republic and Agricultural Chamber of the Czech Republic. He works too as an advocate.

Jan Pichrt is an author or coauthor of numerous monographs and articles in the field of labor law and a coauthor of a prestigious commentary on the Czech Labour Code and some textbooks on labor law.

University v Praze, Právincká Fakulta, Praha 1, Czech Republic

Björn Rohde-Liebenau Lecturer for integrity management and corruption prevention, Hochschule für Öffentliche Verwaltung, Bremen; founder of Risk Communication Concepts (RCC), ombudsman, mediator, and compliance counsel.

Hochschule für Öffentliche Verwaltung, Bremen, Germany

Desmond Ryan Trinity College Dublin, Law School, Dublin 2, Ireland

Dagmara Skupień Faculty of Law and Administration, University of Lodz, Łodź, Poland

Vanja Smokvina Faculty of Law, University of Rijeka (Pravni fakultet), Rijeka, Croatia

Morgan Sweeney Associate professor at the University of Paris Dauphine; specialized in national and European labor law, especially in discrimination law; and contributes to biannual reports on the French judiciary supreme court's implementation of European law. Also published an article on the European strategy to fight child poverty (in La symphonie discordante de l'Europe Sociale, L'aube, dir. N. KERSCHEN, M. LEGRAND, M.MESSU, 2013, p.265).

University of Paris Dauphine, Paris, France

Levallois Perret, France

Gregor Thüsing Professor for civil, labour, and employment law, Institut für Arbeitsrecht und Recht der Sozialen Sicherheit, Rheinische Friedrich-Wilhelms University of Bonn (Germany).

Abbreviations

about	Approximately
app	Appendix
Art/arts	Article/articles
c	Circa
C.F.R.	Code of Federal Regulations
Cass. soc	Cour de cassation
Cf	Confer
Ch	Chapter
Cons. const	Conseil constitutionnel
Dir	Directive
e.g.	For example
Ed/eds	Editor/editors
etc.	And other things/and so forth
f./ff.	And the following
fn	Footnote/footnotes
i.e.	That is
Ibid.	At the same place
n	number
No./Nos.	Number/numbers
p./pp.	Page/pages
para./paras	Paragraph/paragraphs
pt	Part (of statue)
Reg/regs	Regulation/regulations
s.	See
Vol/vols	Volume/volumes

Part I
General Report

Chapter 1
Whistleblowing Around the World: A Comparative Analysis of Whistleblowing in 23 Countries

Gregor Thüsing and Gerrit Forst

Abstract This chapter gives a general overview of whistleblowing around the world. Its purpose is to disclose commonalities and differences between several jurisdictions and to give a general idea of what constitutes whistleblowing. The chapter is based on the country reports published in this volume and on a number of additional country reports the essence of which is given account of in the tabula in Part III. This chapter is also an updated version of the general report presented to the International Academy of Comparative Law at the XIXth International Congress of Comparative Law in Vienna.

Introduction

Whistleblowing has become omnipresent during the last decade, touching on almost every field of the law.[1] Yet whistleblowing is much more than a topic of legal interest. It is an issue that raises the attention of the broader public: The stories of *Julien Assange*, *Bradley* (now *Chelsea*) *Manning* and *Edward Snowden* first hit the front

[1] *cf.* J Bowers, M Fodder, J Lewis, J Mitchell, *Whistleblowing: Law and practice*, 2nd edn, (OUP Oxford, 2012); A. J. Brown, D Lewis, R Moberly, *International Handbook on Whistleblowing Research*, (Cheltenham, Edward Elgar Publishing Ltd., 2014); R Calland, G Dehn, *Whistleblowing Around The World: Law, Culture and Practice* (Pretoria, IDASA Publishers, 2004); A von Kaehnel, *Whistleblowing – Multidisziplinäre Aspekte* (Bern, Stämpfli, 2012); K Leisinger, *Whistleblowing und Corporate Reputation Management* (Mering, Hampp Verlag, 2003); D Lewis, *A Global Approach to Public Interest Disclosure: What Can We Learn From Existing Whistleblowing Legislation and Research?* (Cheltenham, Edward Elgar Publishing Ltd., 2010); X Patier, *La*

G. Thüsing (✉)
Institut für Arbeitsrecht und Recht der Sozialen Sicherheit, University of Bonn,
Adenauerallee 8a, 53113 Bonn, Germany
e-mail: thuesing@jura.uni-bonn.de

G. Forst (✉)
Hengeler Mueller Partnerschaft von Rechtsanwälten mbB,
Benrather Str. 18-20, 40213 Düsseldorf, Germany
e-mail: gerrit.forst@hengeler.com

G. Thüsing, G. Forst (eds.), *Whistleblowing - A Comparative Study*,
Ius Comparatum - Global Studies in Comparative Law 16,
DOI 10.1007/978-3-319-25577-4_1

pages of newspapers around the globe and then led to a political aftermath. Notwithstanding the popularity of the topic, whistleblowing also raises several legal questions that have not yet been answered properly in every jurisdiction. The aim of the Vienna conference was and of this report is to allow researchers, judges and legislators around the world to learn from each other by comparing different approaches to whistleblowing and especially by presenting different legal solutions to real life problems that are basically the same everywhere on our planet. Comparative analysis may thus prove to be the "*Vorrat an Lösungen*" (stock of solutions) that German legal scholar and writer *Ernst Zitelmann* saw in it in 1900.[2]

A global comparison of different approaches to whistleblowing can be achieved successfully only in a team, as no single person is able to gather in-depth knowledge of more than 20 jurisdictions within a reasonable period of time. Therefore, we asked leading experts on whistleblowing from jurisdictions around the world to kindly help us in our task. At this point, we would above all like to express our gratitude to all contributors for their quantitatively and qualitatively impressing replies.

Before we start our survey, we would like to give an outline of our methodology: In preparation of this general report, we firstly sent a questionnaire of about 20 questions to the national experts.[3] Any statement on the situation in a specific country we make in this report is based on their country reports,[4] apart from Germany, which is our home jurisdiction and which we took the freedom to give additional comment on based on our own expertise. At this point, we would like to thank all national experts for their excellent contributions without which this report could not have been written. The structure of the questionnaire and the questions we asked are basically the same as the subheadings of this report. The exact wording and structure of our questionnaire can be derived from the tabula we attached to this report. Secondly, our task was to categorize the answers received to make them comparable. Therefore, we prepared the said tabula. It contains our questions and the answers we received. To allow for comparability, we did not take into consideration too much detail but tried to categorize the contributions. For instance, we used the term "good faith requirement" for limitations to whistleblower protection that stem from

---

prévention de la corruption en France (Paris, DL, 2013); W Vandekerckhove, *Whistleblowing and Organizational Social Responsibility: A Global Assessment* (Burlington, Ashgate, 2006).

[2] E Zitelmann, Aufgabe und Bedeutung der Rechtsvergleichung (1900), *Deutsche Juristen-Zeitung 5*: 329 (330) right column.

[3] The experts we consulted are: Daphne Aichberger-Beig (Austria), Daniel Cuypers (Belgium), Priscila Fichtner (Brazil), John P. McEvoy (Canada), Sandra Laleta (Croatia), Constantinos Kombos (Cyprus), Jan Pichrt with Jakub Morávek (Czech Republic), Merle Muda (Estonia), Jari Murto (Finland), Katrin Deckert (France), Rüdiger Krause (Germany), Maria Teresa Carinci (Italy I) and Edoardo Ales with Antonio Riccio (Italy II), Hiroyuki Minagawa (Japan), David Fabri (Malta), Björn Rohde-Liebenau (Netherlands), Dagmara Skupień (Poland), Júlio Gomes (Portugal), Raluca Dimitriu (Romania), Chandra Mohan (Singapore), Darja Senčur Peček (Slovenia), Sung-Wook Lee (South Korea), Owen Wamock (UK), Shawn Marie Boyne (USA).

[4] These shall become available at www.iacl2014congress.com/reports/ (as at 12.1.2015). To simplify matters, we will refer to "Country Report ..., p. ..." in this general report only.

either a whistleblower making allegations erroneously or his[5] motivation. We are perfectly aware that this categorization is quite imprecise and that the jurisdictions surveyed find quite different solutions to these legal challenges. However, we feel that this was the only way to achieve comparability at all. We tried to give more precise information on the solutions various jurisdictions opted for in this report. Also, at least some of the country reports we received are going to be published in a separate volume. Readers who are interested in the details of the answer a jurisdiction gives to a certain problem will hopefully be satisfied there.

In this report, we will at first take a look at the *status quo* of whistleblowing in the various jurisdictions (see below at section "Whistleblowing: a well-known phenomenon not yet fully understood"). Afterwards, we will commit ourselves to the following questions: Who is protected as a whistleblower? What kind of behaviour is protected? What is the level of protection offered? A summary concludes.

Whistleblowing: A Well-Known Phenomenon Not Yet Fully Understood

Professional Coverage of Whistleblowing

Whistleblowing is a well-known phenomenon in all the jurisdictions we surveyed. It has also been the topic of international consultations in relatively recent times, particularly by the United Nations, the Organisation for Economic Cooperation and Development, the G-20, the International Chamber of Commerce, the Council of Europe, the Organisation for Security and Cooperation in Europe and the International Labour Organisation.[6] Interest in the topic is massively gaining ground around the world. Several comparative legal analyses are already available.[7] This

[5] To improve legibility, we opted to use the masculine term only, although whistleblowers of course can be female or of another sex (a third sex is recognized e.g. in Australia, Germany and India) as well.

[6] *cf.* Art. 33 of the Convenction Against Corruption of the United Nations and Principle No. 10 of the UN Global Compact; Art. 9 of the Civil Law Convention on Corruption of the Council of Europe; G-20, Agenda for Action on Combating Corruption, Promoting Market Integrity, and Supporting a Clean Business Environment of 12.11.2010 (Annex III No. 7); ICC, Guidelines on Whistleblowing; OECD, Recommendation of the Council for Further Combating Bribery of Foreign Public Officials in International Business Transactions of 26.11.2009 as at 18.2.2010 (Annex II-A Abs. 11 lit. ii); OSCE, Best Practices in Combating Corruption, 2004; Art. 5 lit. c of ILO-Convention No. 158: Convention concerning Termination of Employment at the Initiative of the Employer of 22.6.1982.

[7] Amongst others: R Calland, G Dehn, *Whistleblowing Around The World: Law, Culture and Practice* (Pretoria, IDASA Publishers, 2004); J Düsel, *Gespaltene Loyalität: Whistleblowing und Kündigungsschutz in Deutschland, Großbritannien und Frankreich* (Baden-Baden, Nomos, 2009); D Lewis, *A Global Approach to Public Interest Disclosure: What Can We Learn From Existing Whistleblowing Legislation and Research?* (Cheltenham, Edward Elgar, 2010); D Imbach Haumüller, *Whistleblowing in der Schweiz und im internationalen Vergleich – ein Bestandteil*

development was originally triggered by the global fight against corruption in the wake of the early 2000s recession and particularly the US-American *Sarbanes-Oxley Act*, but attention increased in recent times due to the disclosures made by *Edward Snowden*. He revealed a global-scale intrusion into the privacy of citizens by secret services in a scale unheard of and virtually unimaginable before.[8] On this canvas, the professional discussion of whistleblowing has become much more sophisticated in the last couple of years in many countries.[9]

It comes hardly as a surprise that countries having special legislation on whistleblowing in force for quite a while now, such as Canada,[10] the Netherlands,[11] the UK[12] or the USA[13] also feature a notable body of case law and literature on the topic. Exceptions are Japan and South Korea: Although Japan may pride itself of a very sophisticated piece of legislation since 2004,[14] neither jurisprudence nor commentators seem to have paid much attention to whistleblowing up to date. Similarly, in South Korea two acts are in force since 2008 and 2011.[15] Nevertheless, there is still only a manageable amount of case-law and literature on the topic available.

On the other hand, professional coverage of whistleblowing has become much more intense in countries that were historically not much interested in the topic. Examples for this development are Austria, Belgium, the Czech Republic (discussing legislative proposals from about 2012 onwards), France (which established new rules on whistleblowing in 2013),[16] Germany (discussing the topic since the late 1990s and more intensely after several legislative proposals were made in 2009 and again in 2012), Italy and Malta (which enacted new rules on whistleblowing in 2013).[17] Nonetheless, whistleblowing is not yet fully understood and there is not yet an international consensus on what whistleblowing exactly is and how it should be treated.

---

einer effektiven internen Kontrolle? (Zürich, Schulthess, 2011); Rapporteur Omtzigt, in: *Parliamentary Assembly of the Council of Europe, Doc. 12006*: *The protection of* "*whistle-blowers*" (2009); Group of States Against Corruption in the Council of Europe (GRECO), Seventh General Activity Report (2006), 2007; W Vandekerckhove, *Whistleblowing and Organizational Social Responsibility*: *A Global Assessment* (Burlington, Ashgate, 2006).

[8] A first-hand insight into the facts of that case is given in No place to hide: Edward Snowden, the NSA, and the U.S. surveillance state, 2014 by the journalist Glenn Greenwald who supported Edward Snowden in making his revelations.

[9] *cf.* n 1.

[10] Public Servants Disclosure Protection Act of 2005, amongst others.

[11] Several statutes and decrees, *cf.* Country Report Netherlands, p. 1 f.

[12] Public Interest Disclosure Act (since 1998, amended in 2013, which equals Art. 43A ff. Employment Rights Act 1996).

[13] The first piece of legislation is the False Claims Act of 1863. Today, a large number of sector-specific legislation is in force, *cf.* Country Report USA, p. 3 ff.

[14] Whistleblower Protection Act.

[15] Act On The Prevention Of Corruption And The Establishment And Management Of The Anti-Corruption And Civil Rights Commission of 2008 and Protection of Public Interest Reporters Act of 2011.

[16] Art. L. 1161-1 Code du travail amongst others, *cf.* Country Report France, p. 2 ff.

[17] Protection of the Whistleblower Act.

The Legal Basis for the Protection of Whistleblowers

The legal basis for the protection of whistleblowers is quite heterogeneous: While in some countries special legislation on the protection of whistleblowers is in force, other countries do not know any legal protection of whistleblowers at all. In some countries, protection is granted by means of administrative procedures, while others rely heavily on the protection granted by the courts. The Netherlands take yet another approach in the private sector by relying on a non-binding code of conduct setting best practices for employers.

One of the most sophisticated acts on the protection of whistleblowers still is without doubt the Public Interest Disclosure Act, enacted by the UK in 1998 and amended in 2013. This act covers the public sector as well as the private sector. It contains detailed rules on what a whistleblower is allowed to report, how to report and whom to report to. The act also protects whistleblowers against unfair dismissal and other forms of detriment. Another very sophisticated statute is the Japanese Whistleblower Protection Act of 2004, resembling the British archetype in many ways, but going beyond it in some respect (e.g. the allocation of the burden of proof). Malta also established a high level of protection by enacting the Protection of the Whistleblower Act in 2013. This act also covers the public and the private sector. However, experience with the act is limited as it is still so new. South Korea has the Protection of Public Interest Reporters Act in force since 2011 (another act applying to the public sector is in force since 2008), which as well resembles the UK act in many ways. The UK act also has been the blueprint for special legislation in force in the Netherlands since 2001 in the public sector.[18]

Special legislation also is in force in Austria,[19] Belgium,[20] Canada,[21] France,[22] Germany,[23] Italy,[24] Malta,[25] Romania,[26] Singapore,[27] Slovenia[28] and the USA.[29] The scope of whistleblower protection legislation differs in these jurisdictions. A number of countries protect whistleblowers by means of special statutes in the public sector only. This includes Italy, the Netherlands, Romania and, in principle, Belgium and

---

[18] *cf.* n 11.

[19] Country Report Austria, p. 2.

[20] Country Report Belgium, p. 3 f.

[21] *cf.* n 10.

[22] *cf.* n 16.

[23] See above and Country Report Germany, p. 1.

[24] Country Report Italy I, p. 2 f. and Country Report Italy II, p. 1 f.

[25] *cf.* n 17.

[26] Country Report Romania, p. 3.

[27] Country Report Singapore, p. 1 f.

[28] Country Report Slovenia, p. 2.

[29] *cf.* n 13.

Canada. However, regional laws in Belgium (Flanders)[30] and Canada (Manitoba)[31] cover the private sector as well.

Several other countries do not draw a separation line between the public and the private sector but protect whistleblowers in certain situations only. France is a good example for this approach. Art. 1161 *Code du travail* (Labour Code) protects employees blowing the whistle. The act does not differentiate between employees employed in the private or in the public sector. Since 2013, French law additionally covers whistleblowing in the context of the protection of the environment as well as reports concerning a conflict of public interests. Similar legislation exists in Austria and Germany: Austria protects whistleblowers in the public sector (§ 53a *Beamten-Dienstrechtsgesetz* [Public Servants Act]) and persons reporting violations of laws protecting the environment (§°9b *Umweltinformationsgesetz* [Environmental Information Act]). Germany protects whistleblowers in the public sector (e.g. § 67 (2) Nr. 3 *Bundesbeamtengesetz* [Federal Public Servants Act]), persons reporting breaches of work place security standards (§°17 (2) *Arbeitsschutzgesetz* [Work Place Security Act]) and has whistleblower protection laws in force in public health care (§§°81a, 137d, 197a *Sozialgesetzbuch 5* [Social Security Code 5]).[32] In the USA, a piecemeal legislation on the protection of whistleblowers is in force, covering areas such as capital markets (Sarbanes-Oxley Act, Dodd-Frank Act), health services and consumer products. Although the USA established one of the first modern laws on the protection of whistleblowers, the False Claims Act of 1863, there is no general law on the protection of whistleblowers in force yet. However, the piecemeal legislation in force in the USA is extensive.[33] Singapore also features more than a dozen rules protecting whistleblowers in certain situations. In Slovenia, whistleblower protection legislation is part of an act on the prevention of corruption. Similar legislation is prevalent in Cyprus and in the public sector in South Korea.

In almost all the jurisdictions we surveyed, whistleblowers are protected by general laws to a certain extent. Often whistleblowing is perceived as behaviour falling into the scope of the fundamental right of freedom of expression (e.g. in Estonia, France, Germany, Italy, Poland and Portugal). This right is guaranteed by the Universal Declaration of Human Rights (Art. 19) as well as by the Charter of Fundamental Rights of the European Union (Art. 11), the European Convention on Human Rights (Art. 10) and by many constitutions. However, almost all jurisdictions surveyed balance this right against the legitimate protection of public interests or business secrets. Whistleblowers are often bound by a contractual or statutory duty of loyalty which limits their right to blow the whistle, as it obliges them to confidentiality to a certain extent. Some jurisdictions additionally protect whistleblowers by means of the fundamental right to equality (e.g. Poland).[34]

---

[30] Country Report Belgium, p. 3.

[31] Country Report Canada, p. 9.

[32] *cf.* G Forst, 'Whistleblowing im Gesundheitswesen' (2014), *Die Sozialgerichtsbarkeit 60*: 413–422.

[33] Country Report USA, p. 3 ff.

[34] Country Report Poland, p. 4.

In parts of Europe, whistleblowing is regulated by statutes on data protection as well (e.g. in the Czech Republic, Finland, France, Germany and Italy).[35] These statutes usually strike a balance between the right of the accused person to be informed of the source of information relating to them and the interest of the whistleblower to have his identity kept confidential. This kind of regulation is for instance known in the Czech Republic, Finland, France, Germany and Italy. It should be existent in other Member States of the EU as well, as the data protection legislation in these countries is based on the Data Protection Directive of the EU[36] that other Member States also have to implement according to Art. 288 (3) of the Treaty on Functioning of the European Union (TFEU).

The same applies to antidiscrimination legislation in the EU. According to the rapporteurs, several Member States protect whistleblowers reporting discrimination by means of domestic antidiscrimination legislation (e.g. France, UK). Rules of this kind should be prevalent in all of the Member States, as all of them have to implement the EU Directives on antidiscrimination.[37] The Directives allow persons discriminated against to complain to the employer about discrimination. They prohibit the employer to make use of any kind of retaliation following the complaint against the person complaining or persons supporting that person.[38] This mechanism can easily be qualified as a special kind of whistleblower protection in the field of antidiscrimination legislation.

In the fields of the prevention of money laundering, the protection of health and safety at work and of the environment, there are also EU Directives obliging certain persons to blow the whistle (see below at section "Is there an obligation to blow the whistle?").

In some countries, however, whistleblowers are primarily protected by administrative procedures. For instance, Brazil does not have special legislation on the protection of whistleblowers in force, but employees can report to the Labour Attorney's Office, which protects employees and can take action against employers in form of administrative fines or lawsuits. In France, the *Commission Nationale de l'Informatique et des Libertés* (CNIL) – the national data protection authority – issued several administrative decisions governing whistleblowing.[39] This action was triggered by the requirement of Section 301 (4) of the US-American Sarbanes-Oxley Act that subsidiaries of companies listed in the USA have to allow for anonymous whistleblowing by their employees. The CNIL decided that anonymous whistleblowing is permissible with respect to certain breaches of the law only and that

---

[35] For Germany, *cf.* G Forst, 'Whistleblowing und Datenschutz' (2013), *Recht der Datenverarbeitung 36*: 122–132.

[36] Directive 95/46/EC.

[37] Directives 2000/43/EC, 2000/78/EC, 2006/54/EC and 2010/41/EU.

[38] Art. 9 Directive 2000/43/EC, Art. 11 Directive 2000/78/EC, Art. 24 Directive 2006/54/EC.

[39] CNIL, Autorisation unique No. AU-004 – Délibération No. 2005-305 of 8.12.2005, amended by Délibération No. 2010-369 of 14.10.2010; Délibération No. 2011-345 of 10.11.2011 (concerning EDF), Délibération No. 2011-346 of 10.11.2011 (concerning Thales) and Délibération No. 2011-406 of 15.12.2011 (concerning Aggreko).

several other conditions have to be met to ensure that such a system is compatible with data protection law. This point of view was later, at least in principle, endorsed by the French *Cour de cassation* (Supreme Court).[40] In these French proceedings, data protection law turned out to be an ambiguous instrument, however: Although aiming at a protection of whistleblowers on the one hand, the CNIL also had to take into consideration the legitimate interests of the persons accused. Although it managed to strike a balance accepted by the *Cour de cassation* (Supreme Court), the outcome is highly problematic for subsidiary companies of companies being subject to the Sarbanes-Oxley Act. The situation in Italy seems to be very similar. The same could be true for other Member States of the EU, as the combined working group of Data Protection Authorities took a view similar to that of the CNIL in a working paper issued in 2006.[41]

The strong position of the *Cour de cassation* (Supreme Court) in the regulation of whistleblowing is not an exemption, but rather the rule: The courts generally play an important role in the protection of whistleblowers. Jurisdictions featuring special legislation on whistleblowing usually also have a substantial body of case-law interpreting the statutes. The UK is a good example for this.[42] Also in Japan, it was the courts that established whistleblower protection at first by means of general rules before the legislator took action in 2004. However, the existence of special legislation and supplementary case-law is not necessarily to the benefit of the whistleblower: In the USA, courts have shown a tendency to restrict the rights of whistleblowers by interpreting the legal bases of whistleblower protection restrictively.[43] The legislator therefore extended the scope of the relevant acts repeatedly to counterbalance this unwillingness of the courts to grant protection.

In jurisdictions not having special whistleblower protection in force, two patterns can be identified: In most jurisdictions of this kind, very little or virtually no case-law on whistleblowing seems to exist. This finding is to be treated with some caution, however, as whistleblowing is not always and everywhere given the same meaning and sometimes whistleblowing is not identified as such, e.g. in dismissal

[40] Cour de cassation (France), No. 08-17191, Judgement (Chambre sociale) of 8 December 2009.

[41] Art. 29 Working Group (the name refers to Art. 29 Directive 95/46/EC, the legal basis of the group), Opinion 1/2006 on the application of EU data protection rules to internal whistleblowing schemes in the fields of accounting, internal accounting controls, auditing matters, fight against bribery, banking and financial crime (Working Paper 117), available at www.ec.europa.eu/justice/data-protection/article-29/documentation/opinion-recommendation/index_en.htm (as at 12.1.2015).

[42] *cf.* England and Wales Court of Appeal, No. A2/2010/2919/EATRF, Case *NHS Manchester v Fecitt & Ors*, Judgement (Civil Division) of 25 October 2011; No. A2/2006/0402, Case *Bolton School v Evans*, Judgement (Civil Division) of 15 November 2006; No. A1/2003/2160, Case *Street v Derbyshire*, Judgement (Civil Division) of 21 July 2004; No. A1/2001/1241&B, Case *ALM Medical Services Ltd. v Bladon*, Judgement (Civil Division) of 26 July 2002; United Kingdom Employment Appeal Tribunal, No. UKEAT/0141/09, Case *BP v Elstone*, Judgement of 31 March 2010; No. UKEAT/0275/08/DA, Case *Hibbins v Hester Way Neighbourhood Project*, Judgement of 16 October 2008.

[43] cf. Supreme Court (USA), No. 07-214, Case Allison Engine Co. v United States ex rel. Sanders, Judgement of 9 June 2008; No. 04-169, Case Graham County Soil and Water Conservation District v U.S. ex rel. Wilson, Judgement of 20 June 2005.

cases. On the other hand, case-law is the bedrock of whistleblower protection in some jurisdictions not featuring special legislation on whistleblower protection or knowing special legislation of limited scope only. This seems to be the case e.g. in Austria, Canada (before special laws entered into force), Croatia, France, Germany and Italy. In Austria, courts balance the right to freedom of expression and the duty of loyalty of employees in dismissal cases.[44] Before various acts on whistleblower protection entered into force in Canada, the Supreme Court held that an employee was allowed to blow the whistle "up the ladder", i.e. that he was allowed to report the issue to his immediate superior.[45] In another case, the court struck a balance between the right to freedom of expression and the duty of loyalty of public sector employees.[46] In France, the *Cour de cassation* (Supreme Court) issued a judgement on a decision of the CNIL on anonymous whistleblowing. In this case, a French subsidiary of a company that was listed in the USA and that was thus subject to the Sarbanes-Oxley Act had implemented a whistleblowing system allowing for anonymous reports. The French subsidiary based the system on a decision of the CNIL that allowed whistleblowers to report, amongst other violations of the law, insider trading and infringements of antidiscrimination legislation.[47] The *Cour de cassation* held that such a system was in principle compatible with French law but that the scope of the system had to be limited to auditing, financial reporting and corruption.[48] A similar development can be observed in Italy, leading to calls for an amendment of data protection legislation in 2009. In Croatia as well as in Germany, judgements of the ECtHRs (ECtHR) played an important role in the development of whistleblower protection:

- In *Balenović v. Croatia*,[49] the applicant in 2000 alleged to have found out that her former employer, the national oil company of Croatia, lost about 20 million Euros a year to fraudulent haulage providers who transported petrol from refineries to petrol stations on behalf of the company. Moreover, she claimed to have discovered that the company would be able to make an additional profit of about 35 million Euros a year by running its own fleet of road tankers. On 19 January 2001, she reported these facts to her immediate superior. One day later the company issued a public call for tenders for haulage services. In reaction to this, the applicant sent a letter to the general director of the company, repeating her allegations. When she did not receive any reply, she complained to the chairman of the supervisory board. The chairman met her and listened to her allegations but

[44] Country Report Austria, p. 2.

[45] Supreme Court (Canada), No. 30090, Case *Merk v International Association of Bridge*, Structural, Ornamental and Reinforcing Iron Workers, Local 771, Judgement of 24 November 2005.

[46] Supreme Court (Canada), No. 17451, Case *Fraser v Public Service Staff Relations Board*, Judgement of 10 December 1985.

[47] CNIL, Autorisation unique No. AU-004 - Délibération No. 2005-305 of 8.12.2005, amended after the decision of the Cour de cassation by Délibération No. 2010-369 of 14.10.2010 and again by Délibération No. 2014-042 of 30.1.2014.

[48] Cour de cassation (France), No. 08-17191, Judgement (Chambre sociale) of 8 December 2009.

[49] ECtHR, No. 28369/07, Case *Balenović v Croatia*, Judgement (Chamber) of 30 September 2010.

did not do anything to improve the situation. In April 2001, a newspaper published a series of articles on the issue. The applicant was quoted in these articles, accusing some of the managers of the company of corruption and nepotism. Shortly after these articles had been published, the applicant was summarily dismissed. The courts of Croatia held that the dismissal was justified as the applicant had acted contrary to the interest of the employer, was not under a civic duty to report crimes and that she had violated internal rules of the employer concerning communication with the media. In May 2001, the applicant filed a criminal complaint with some of the managers of the company. However, she claimed in the proceedings at the ECtHR to have informed the police of the facts of the case as early as in February 2001. The applicant argued that Croatia had violated her rights under Articles 9 (freedom of thought), 10 (freedom of expression) and 14 (right to non-discrimination) as guaranteed by the *European Convention on Human Rights* (ECHR). The ECtHR held that whistleblowing was covered by the right to freedom of expression only. In assessing whether the applicant had suffered a violation of that right, the court found that the Croatian courts pursued legitimate aims by confirming the dismissal as lawful, namely the protection of the reputation and the rights of others (i.e. the managers and the company). The ECtHR then considered whether the dismissal was necessary in a democratic society, which is required by Article 10 ECHR to justify an interference with the right to freedom of expression. The court held that "the applicant's freedom of expression, in particular her right to publicise her criticism of the business policy of the national oil company, as well as to impart information on alleged irregularities within the company, and, more importantly, the right of the public to receive that information, must be weighed against the requirements of the protection of the reputation and the rights of others..." The ECtHR stresses that "that Article 10 [ECHR] does not guarantee wholly unrestricted freedom of expression and that the exercise of this freedom carries with it 'duties and responsibilities'. Therefore, whoever exercises that freedom owes 'duties and responsibilities', the scope of which depends on his or her situation, the (technical) means he or she uses and the authenticity of the information disclosed to the public." Assessing the facts of the case in the light of these parameters, the court concluded that the dismissal was not disproportionate to the legitimate aim pursued and thus could be regarded as being necessary in a democratic society. The complaint therefore was held inadmissible.

- In *Heinisch v. Germany*,[50] the applicant had been working as a geriatric nurse for her former employer, a state-owned company offering health care services. As an employee, she was working in a geriatric nursing home where the patients generally depended on special assistance. In 2002 and 2003, a supervisory authority, acting on behalf of the public health care system, detected serious shortcomings in the care provided as well as inadequate documentation of care, and accordingly threatened to terminate the service agreement with the applicant's employer. In 2003 and 2004, the applicant and her colleagues regularly indicated to the

[50] ECtHR, No. 28274/08, Case *Heinisch v Germany*, Judgement (Chamber) of 21 July 2011.

management of the employer that they were overburdened on account of staff shortages and therefore had difficulties carrying out their duties. They specified the deficiencies in the care provided and also mentioned that services were not properly documented. By the end of 2004, the applicant fell ill due to overwork and consulted a lawyer. The legal counsel wrote to the management of the employer, claiming that due to a lack of staff, the basic hygienic care of the patients could no longer be guaranteed for and that the management and the employees were risking criminal responsibility. The management rejected these accusations. In reaction to that statement, the lawyer lodged a criminal complaint against the management of the employer, also to avoid criminal responsibility of the applicant, claiming that the employer knowingly failed to provide the high-quality care announced in its advertisements and hence did not provide the services paid for (i.e. committed fraud) and was putting the patients at risk. In January 2005, the public prosecutor's office discontinued the preliminary investigations against the employer. Two weeks later, the employer dismissed the applicant with a notice period on account of her repeated illness. The applicant reacted by contacting her friends and her trade union. They issued a leaflet demanding the revocation of the notice. The leaflet also informed of the facts reported above. One of the leaflets came to the knowledge of the employer who only then learned that a criminal complaint had been lodged against him. In February 2005, after hearing the works council and the applicant, the employer summarily dismissed her on suspicion of having initiated the production and dissemination of the leaflet.[51] A new leaflet was subsequently issued reporting of this dismissal. Moreover, the whole situation was reported in a TV programme and in two articles published in different newspapers. Meanwhile, the public prosecutor's office had resumed preliminary investigations at the applicant's request. These investigations were again discontinued some months later. The applicant sought protection against the dismissals at the labour courts. The first instance held that the dismissal without notice had not been justified as the leaflet – the content of which was attributed to the applicant – was covered by her right to freedom of expression and did not amount to a breach of her duties under the employment contract. However, the appellate court as well as the *Bundesarbeitsgericht* (Federal Labour Court) and the *Bundesverfassungsgericht* (Federal Constitutional Court) held that the dismissal without notice had been justified, since the applicant had based the criminal complaints on facts that she could not prove. The applicant's reaction also was held to be disproportionate as she had not attempted to have the allegations investigated internally and as she had provoked a public discussion of the issue. The ECtHR held that there had

[51] The dismissal with notice period from January 2005 had not taken effect at this point, as the notice period had not expired yet. It is not uncommon for employers in Germany to dismiss employees several times for different reasons just in case that a dismissal should be rendered void by a court. The employee has to challenge each dismissal individually to make sure that none of them takes effect. In this case, however, the employer wanted to dismiss the applicant *summarily* with the second dismissal.

been an infringement of the applicant's right to freedom of expression but that this infringement had been prescribed by Section 626 *Bürgerliches Gesetzbuch* (Civil Code), i.e. the rule allowing for employees to be summarily dismissed. Nevertheless, the ECtHR concluded that the infringement had not been necessary in a democratic society: On the one hand, employees were under a duty of loyalty, reserve and discretion. According to the court, a disclosure therefore should be made in the first place to the person's superior or other competent authority or body. Only as a last resort, information could be disclosed to the public. On the other hand, the court considered whether the applicant had had any other effective means of remedying the wrongdoing which she intended to uncover. The ECtHR also weighed the authenticity of the information disclosed. A state was allowed to answer proportionately to defamatory accusations made in bad faith. Other factors to be included were the potential damage suffered by the employer if the information was revealed and the potential damage suffered by third parties or the public if it was not revealed. Finally, the motivation of the whistleblower had to be taken into account. Striking a balance between these factors, the court finally held that the interference with the applicant's right to freedom of expression was not "necessary in a democratic society".

The *Heinisch* case triggered a political discussion in Germany on whether to protect whistleblowers by a special statute or not. Although all political parties represented in the *Bundestag*, the federal parliament, agreed that whistleblowing could be a valuable instrument to fight corruption and to prevent harm to people and although the opposition parties made legislative proposals, no steps were taken by the governing coalition in the end. The German experience is similar to that of the Czech Republic, where legislative proposals were made in 2012 but also did not yield a statue. Also in Singapore, proposals to regulate whistleblowing were not pursued to the end.

Who Is Protected?

The first question legislators willing to improve their legal systems have to answer is who should profit of a statute, i.e. who should be protected as a whistleblower and whether a person should also be protected as a supporter of a whistleblower or as a witness proving his allegations.

Who Qualifies as a Potential Whistleblower?

There are huge differences between the jurisdictions we surveyed as to who qualifies as a whistleblower. These differences take their root in the legal basis of whistleblowing in the various jurisdictions. Legal systems that protect whistleblowers by fundamental rights – such as the right to freedom of expression – tend to protect everyone, at least in principle. However, as whistleblowing in many jurisdictions is governed first and foremost by labour legislation, employees are the group of persons who are mainly protected in most countries (e.g. Austria, Croatia, Estonia, Finland, France, Germany, Italy and Poland). But even in countries featuring special legislation, the personal scope of whistleblower protection varies. Some countries protect public sector employees and civil servants by means of special legislation only (e.g. Canada [with broader legislation in force in some provinces], Cyprus, Italy, the Netherlands, Romania), while employees in the private sector are not included or covered by general rules only. Legislation in the UK protects "workers",[52] which includes a broader range of persons than the term "employee" (e.g. agency workers, self-employed persons). A similar broad definition of "employee" is in force in Malta, including former employees and volunteers.[53] Japan takes an intermediate stance, as it features special rules for employees only, but extends protection to agency workers in the enterprise of the host employer insofar as they are allowed to report to him rather than to their contractual employer. As far as special legislation is applicable, some countries such as Singapore, Slovenia and the USA do not have any restrictions in force concerning the person that blows the whistle. South Korea even covers anyone by its 2011 act that at the same time covers a very broad range of situations.

The Protection of Supporters

Whistleblowers do not always operate on a stand-alone basis. Sometimes they have to cooperate with others to be able to make their disclosures. Whistleblowers working in a team for instance may have to retrieve information from colleagues to verify and/or prove a wrongdoing. Whistleblowers also may hesitate to disclose information and may need exhortation by others to pluck up their courage and finally blow the whistle. The *Heinisch* case reported above is a good example, as it was the friends of the whistleblower and her trade union who issued a leaflet that finally persuaded the whistleblower to insist on further investigations by the public prosecutor and to disclose information through the media. If supporters of a potential whistleblower are not protected, he may shy from a disclosure because he fears a detriment for his relatives or friends. Whistleblowing also might be suppressed on a preliminary stage because information a potential whistleblower requires to fully understand the facts of a case and to recognise a wrongdoing might never reach him.

Although the need for a protection of supporters of whistleblowers is rather obvious, legal response so far has been chastening. Hardly any of the jurisdictions we surveyed have special provisions for the protection of supporters of whistleblowers in force. A notable exemption is Belgium, which features a special rule for support-

---

[52] See 43 K Employment Rights Act 1996.

[53] Country Report Malta, p. 2.

ers of whistleblowers in the public sector.[54] In some jurisdictions (Brazil, Canada, Poland, private sector in Belgium) supporters of whistleblowers have to rely on the rather wobbly ground of any general rule applicable in their specific case. All the other jurisdictions we surveyed do not seem to deal with the problem specifically at all, with the exception of EU Member States having to implement antidiscrimination Directives that also protect supporters of persons reporting discrimination against retaliation by the employer (see above at II.2.) and South Korea that treats supporters and witnesses in principle just like the whistleblower.[55]

The Protection of Witnesses

This is all the more surprising as most of the jurisdictions surveyed protect persons who affirm a whistleblower's allegations, at least if this happens in court trials. If a person confirms the allegations disclosed by whistleblowing in a court trial (i.e. as a witness), this person is protected by the general laws protecting witnesses in most countries. However, this also reveals a gap in the protection of witnesses: Hardly any jurisdiction we surveyed expressively protects witnesses giving testimony not in a court trial, but in proceedings outside such a trial, e.g. an internal investigation conducted by the employer. Notable exemptions are – again – Belgium, which protects witnesses in the public sector, and South Korea, that protects supporters in general (see above at III.2.). France also expressively protects witnesses in this situation, at least if they give testimony on certain wrongdoings, including environmental and health and safety issues, corruption, or a conflict of interest in the public sector (Art. 1132-3 *Code du travail*). Canada also has special legislation in force for witnesses, at least in the public sector.[56] Some Canadian provinces extend this protection to the private sector as well.

What Kind of Behaviour Is Protected?

Once a legislator has established whom he wants to protect as a whistleblower, he needs to ask himself what kind of behaviour shall be protected. Again, the jurisdictions surveyed vary widely with respect to the facts a whistleblower may disclose and the circumstance under which a disclosure qualifies as a disclosure protected by the law.

---

[54] Country Report Belgium, p. 8.

[55] Country Report South Korea, p. 3.

[56] Country Report Canada, p. 25.

Should Anonymous Whistleblowing Be Permitted?

An especially ambiguous instrument is anonymous whistleblowing. Comparative analyses conducted earlier[57] have led to the conclusion that anonymous whistleblowing is considered by some to offer particularly strong protection for whistleblowers while others perceive it as an invitation to denunciators. Critics also point out that the protection of whistleblowers by anonymity is far from perfect as their identity could be revealed by the facts they disclose, which may be known to one person or very few people only. If the identity of the whistleblower is revealed, he also cannot be protected against retaliation properly, as he cannot prove that it was actually him who blew the whistle and that he is facing detriment in retaliation for the disclosure he made. The Article 29 Working Party also identifies obstacles to anonymous whistleblowing based on data protection legislation.[58]

Irrespective of these arguments, most of the countries we surveyed allow anonymous whistleblowing or at least do not prohibit it (Austria, Belgium, Brazil, Cyprus, Czech Republic, France, Germany, Italy, Romania, Singapore, Slovenia, UK, USA). However, many of these countries restrict anonymous reporting in some respect: In Austria, anonymous whistleblowing is not permitted or prohibited by law, but it is used by the public prosecutor's office since 2013. In Belgium, anonymous reporting is excluded in certain proceedings including an ombudsman, but it seems to be allowed in other situations. In France, anonymous whistleblowing is not forbidden, but according to the CNIL, anonymous whistleblowing may not be promoted, a company must encourage whistleblowers to reveal their identity and information gathered anonymously must be treated with special care, i.e. suspiciousness.[59] In Germany, anonymous whistleblowing is not prohibited, but an anonymous whistleblower will not be protected by the fundamental right to freedom of expression according to the Federal Labour Court,[60] as in the judges' eyes, expressing one's opinion necessarily includes revealing one's identity. In Romania, only disclosures of persons identifiable shall be inquired. However, exceptions apply to the labour inspection, which has to investigate facts disclosed anonymously as well. On the other hand, Section 301 (4) Sarbanes-Oxley Act (USA) expressively obliges companies to enable anonymous whistleblowing.

In some countries, the legal assessment of anonymous whistleblowing seems to be somewhat opaque (Croatia, Estonia, Japan, the Netherlands, Poland, Portugal). In Japan, anonymous whistleblowing is not expressively prohibited. However, an employer who has received a complaint is obliged to give the whistleblower within 20 days information on the measures he has taken to stop the reported wrongdo-

---

[57] GRECO, Seventh General Activity Report (2006), 2007, p. 12; Rapporteur Omtzigt, in: *Parliamentary Assembly of the Council of Europe, Doc. 12006*: *The protection of "whistle-blowers"* (2009), para. 116 lit. f.

[58] *cf.* n 41, p. 11.

[59] *cf.* n 47, Art. 2.

[60] Bundesarbeitsgericht, No. 2 AZR 235/02, Judgement (Second Senate) of 3 July 2003, para. 34.

ing.[61] This implies that the employer needs to be able to identify the whistleblower. In the Netherlands, anonymous whistleblowing is not expressively permitted or prohibited. However, it is accepted in practice in certain situations.

Some countries deny anonymous whistleblowers special protection (Canada, Malta, South Korea). In Canada, anonymous whistleblowing is seen as a breach of the whistleblower's duty to loyalty. In Malta, the law point-blank denies anonymous whistleblowers protection.[62] Nevertheless, a unit receiving an anonymous report is allowed to inquire the facts of the case. In South Korea, the authorities acting as addressees of a report are allowed not to inquire into anonymous reports.

Does Internal Reporting Prevail?

Needs a whistleblower to make use of internal reporting before he is allowed to report to third parties? The answer given to this question varies in the jurisdictions we surveyed: Some countries oblige the whistleblower expressively to report internally or at least such a duty is likely to be necessary to be recognised and protected as a whistleblower by the courts (Cyprus, Estonia, Malta). Some countries differentiate between whistleblowing in the public sector and in the private sector. It is not uncommon for jurisdictions to oblige public sector employees and civil servants to report internally, while no such rule exists for private sector employees. Regulations of this kind are to be found in Belgium, Canada, Croatia, Singapore and Slovenia. Some countries require whistleblowers to report internally at first in principle, but allow external whistleblowing in exceptional cases (Austria, Germany, Japan, UK). In the UK, the law stipulates that exceptions may apply for instance if the whistleblower has to fear retaliation, if evidence is likely to be destroyed following an internal complaint or if an earlier internal reporting did not yield any effect.[63] A very similar rule exists in Japan, where whistleblowers may also report to external instances directly if the life of a person is at danger.[64] The Netherlands also feature rules comparable to those in force in Japan and the UK. The ECtHR seems to endorse a similar view in the *Heinisch* case.[65] French law does not expressively require whistleblowers to report internally before appealing to third parties, but it encourages them to do so. Finally, there are countries that in principle do not require internal reporting (Brazil, Italy, South Korea, USA, also Romania, but in this country, work rules may oblige employees to report internally at first and the same seems to apply to Italy).

Especially controversial is whistleblowing via the media. Whistleblowers like *Edward Snowden* were not only criticised for the disclosures they made, but also for

[61] Country Report Japan, p. 4.

[62] Country Report Malta, p. 3.

[63] Country Report UK, p. 3.

[64] Country Report Japan, p. 3.

[65] ECtHR, No. 28274/08, Case *Heinisch v. Germany*, Judgement (Chamber) of 21 July 2011, para. 73.

the way in which they made these disclosures. If information is made public via the media, it is impossible to bring the genie back into the bottle – even for the whistleblower. An uncontrollable escalation of the situation then becomes likely. On the other hand, whistleblowing via the media is very effective as there is no way for officials or superiors to put a lid on a wrongdoing. In striking a balance between these considerations, only very few countries expressively ban whistleblowing via the media (Malta and Belgium, the latter only in the public sector). Some countries do not restrict whistleblowing via the media at all (Brazil, Croatia, Romania, also Slovenia, unless information is classified), while others acknowledge whistleblowing via the media in severe cases only (Canada, Germany, Finland, Japan, Poland, UK, also the Netherlands under the best practices applicable in the private sector and possibly also Italy, although the courts seem to take a generous position in this country towards whistleblowing via the media). The latter also seems to be the point of view endorsed by the ECtHR in the *Heinisch* case.[66] In some countries the legality of whistleblowing via the media is unclear (Austria, France, Portugal, USA). Nevertheless, in some of these countries it seems to be accepted de facto at least (Cyprus, Estonia, Singapore). In South Korea, whistleblowing via the media is not prohibited, but the protection of the whistleblower will not be granted by special legislation but by general rules of labour law – if applicable – only.

Who Bears the Risk of Misapprehension?

Another challenge legislators and judges around the world have to overcome is in how far a person should be protected as a whistleblower if the allegations turn out to be untrue. Two approaches to this problem can be identified in the various jurisdictions: Some countries deny whistleblowers protection if their allegations turn out to be false, irrespective of whether they acted in good faith, i.e. believed the facts to be true (Croatia, Portugal, probably also Belgium, although it precludes only "dishonesty" from whistleblowing in the public sector, indicating that the whistleblower must report false information intentionally). In Singapore, a whistleblower has to make proper inquiries to ensure that the information he reports is correct. Although such a rather restrictive regime is capable to prevent an abuse of whistleblowing systems and to guarantee a high quality of the information reported, most countries do not opt for this solution.

In most countries, whistleblowers are subject to what we wish to call a "good faith requirement", i.e. they have to make their allegations in good faith (Austria, Brazil, Canada, Germany, France, Italy, Japan, Malta, the Netherlands, Poland, Romania, Slovenia, South Korea, USA). The same was true for the UK up to amendments to the law taking effect in 2013, when the requirement to act in good faith was replaced by a requirement to act in the public interest.[67] So what does "good faith"

[66] ECtHR, No. 28274/08, Case *Heinisch v Germany*, Judgement (Chamber) of 21 July 2011, paras. 73 and 86.

[67] Country Report UK, p. 4.

respectively "the public interest" exactly mean? On the one hand, good faith/public interest may relate to the motivation of the whistleblower, the relevance of which we are going to investigate in the next chapter (see below at section "Is the motivation of the whistleblower relevant?"). In the context of misapprehension, a whistleblower lacks good faith/public interest if he reports false information although he should have known better. This does not generally preclude the erroneous reporting of false information from the scope of whistleblower protection, but it obliges potential whistleblowers to consider whether their allegations actually are correct. The difficulty now is to determine what a whistleblower must do to yield protection. The jurisdictions we surveyed use different criteria to draw a separation line, but the effect is comparable: In Brazil and Germany for instance, a whistleblower must not act intentionally (i.e. give false information away knowingly), but he may lose protection even if he only acts reckless or thoughtless.[68] Similarly, a whistleblower loses protection in Italy if he gives away false information because of gross negligence on his part.[69] Japan and the UK require the whistleblower to act in a "reasonable belief"[70] that the information he relays is actually true respectively in the public interest. South Korean legislation takes a similar position, although mere negligence seems to suffice to deny a whistleblower protection in this country. The ECtHR in the *Heinisch* case somewhat cryptic held that a whistleblower "who chooses to disclose information must carefully verify, to the extent permitted by the circumstances, that it is accurate and reliable."[71]

Is the Motivation of the Whistleblower Relevant?

Closely linked with, yet distinguishable from the "good faith requirement" is the motivation of the whistleblower. If a whistleblower tells the truth – not because he wants to stop a wrongdoing, but to harm the perpetrator for personal reasons (e.g. envy or hate) – should the law protect him? Only very few countries declare the motivation of a whistleblower as being irrelevant for the level of protection granted (Austria, Brazil and Belgium [public sector]).

Most of the other jurisdictions surveyed take the motivation of a whistleblower into consideration. In many jurisdictions, the motivation of a whistleblower is considered in establishing whether he acted in "good faith" (Belgium [private sector], Canada, Croatia, France, Italy, Japan, Malta, Poland, Portugal, Romania, Slovenia, Singapore, South Korea) respectively in "the public interest" (UK, since 2013). Motives recognised as harmful to whistleblower protection are, for instance, a striving for personal gain (Malta, South Korea), revenge (Portugal) or maliciousness

[68] *cf.* Federal Constitutional Court, case 1 BvR 2049/00, Judgement of 2 July 2001.

[69] Country Report Italy II, p. 6 f.

[70] Country Report Japan, p. 3; Country Report UK, p. 4.

[71] ECtHR, No. 28274/08, Case *Heinisch v Germany*, Judgement (Chamber) of 21 July 2011, para. 67.

(Singapore). Italy prohibits insulting comments and disclosure of information with the sole aim to harm the employer, but it protects satire as part of the right to freedom of expression.

However, the rule that the motivation of the whistleblower is to be taken into consideration is far from being self-evident: An argument can be made that it is irrelevant for which reason a whistleblower acts, as long as the information he discloses is correct or at least he was justly convinced that it is correct. The motivation of a whistleblower therefore can be seen as a barrier to abuse and denunciation at best, as a means to prevent the establishment of an Orwellian society. Nevertheless, it is hardly convincing to declare the motivation of a whistleblower to be the "predominant criterion" in judging whether a whistleblower deserves protection or not, as for instance the German Federal Labour Court did in 2003.[72]

The ECtHR takes an intermediate stance on the relevance of the motivation of a whistleblower in the *Heinisch* case:

> The motive behind the actions of the reporting employee is another determinant factor in deciding whether a particular disclosure should be protected or not. For instance, an act motivated by a personal grievance or personal antagonism or the expectation of personal advantage, including pecuniary gain, would not justify a particularly strong level of protection. It is important to establish that, in making the disclosure, the individual acted in good faith and in the belief that the information was true, that it was in the public interest to disclose it and that no other, more discreet means of remedying the wrongdoing was available to him or her.[73]

What Kind of Information May a Whistleblower Report?

Whistleblowing always verges on denunciation, i.e. the passing of information not to end a wrongdoing or a danger but to harm someone else. One way to limit the risk of such an abuse of whistleblowing systems is to limit the scope of such a system to certain wrongdoings or certain aspects of life.

Many of the jurisdictions we surveyed endorse such an approach. Three categories of jurisdictions can be identified:

- Countries belonging to the first group limit whistleblowing to illegal conduct (Brazil, Malta, Poland, Romania, Slovenia [covering "corruption", corruption being interpreted as any breach of the law], probably also Croatia and Cyprus, both covering "corruption", as well as Japan, that attaches a list of acts to the Whistleblower Protection Act the breaches of which a whistleblower may report [the list names about 400 acts at the time of the preparation of this report]). This means that only information relating to breaches of a law may be reported. Whistleblowers reporting unethical, but not illegal conduct are not protected in these jurisdictions.

[72] Bundesarbeitsgericht, No. 2 AZR 235/02, Judgement (Second Senate) of 3 July 2003, para. 29.

[73] ECtHR, No. 28274/08, Case *Heinisch v Germany*, Judgement (Chamber) of 21 July 2011, para. 69.

- Countries belonging to the second group allow whistleblowers to report certain breaches of the law and in addition to that also dangers that are not necessarily breaking any rules yet (France, the Netherlands, UK, USA). In France, for instance, the CNIL allows whistleblowers to report illegal conduct from the fields of accounting, finance, corruption and discrimination. Contrariwise, it does not accept whistleblowing systems that cover all forms of illegal activity.[74] However, certain groups of persons (works council, staff delegates) are also entitled by law to report dangers to health and safety or the environment. In the UK, the law protects whistleblowing with respect to breaches of the law, a miscarriage of justice, danger to the health and safety of an individual or the environment and the destruction of evidence relating to any of these issues.[75] Similar regulations exist in the USA, depending on which act is applicable. Italy also seems to belong to this group of countries.
- Countries belonging to the third group do not only allow whistleblowers to report illegal activity or dangers, but also to relay information on unethical behaviour or breaches of codes of conduct. Canada as an example allows the reporting of any illegal activity and of dangers to life, health and the environment. However, it also allows whistleblowers to report a misuse of public funds (which certainly is a nuisance to every taxpayer but not necessarily illegal) and even severe breaches of codes of conduct,[76] which usually do not have the quality and binding force of a law created by the state. Singapore has legislation in force that is similar to that of Canada, but it also allows whistleblowers to report unethical conduct.[77]

Another strategy to make an abuse of whistleblowing systems harder is to impose temporal restrictions to the facts that a whistleblower may report. Incidents that happened in the past do not have any effects in the present and are unlikely to happen again do not necessarily deserve the attention of internal investigators, public prosecutors or even the media. Nevertheless, only very few jurisdictions make use of this regulatory technique.

Most of the jurisdictions we surveyed do not impose any temporal limits on the whistleblower at all (Austria, Brazil, Germany, France, Italy, Malta, Singapore, UK, probably also Japan and the Netherlands). But there are exceptions: In Croatia, a whistleblower does not have the right to relay information on past incidents unlikely to happen again. In Canada, a whistleblower reporting mere dangers that were imminent in the past would possibly not qualify for protection. Also, in Canada, information on a reprisal of employees has to be disclosed within 60 days after the day on which the whistleblower knew, or ought to have known, that the reprisal was taken (Section 19.1 (2) Public Servants Disclosure Protection Act).

---

[74] *cf.* n 47, Art. 1.

[75] See 43B (1) Employment Rights Act 1996.

[76] Country Report Canada, p. 34.

[77] Country Report Singapore, p. 3.

Is There an Obligation to Blow the Whistle?

Protecting whistleblowers is the first step to a reporting-friendly legal environment. Obliging persons to blow the whistle means leaping ahead. There are only a handful of countries amongst those we surveyed that oblige persons to blow the whistle and all of them limit such an obligation to a rather limited number of persons or irregularities.

This does not really come as a surprise: Blowing the whistle often is a decision that requires careful consideration, a lot of courage and also a pure conscience. As there are still many wrongdoings that pass undiscovered or are discovered by other means than whistleblowing, one may assume that a lot of people refrain from blowing the whistle although they could do so. The causes for this may lie in a fear of retaliation, but sometimes people also have personal reasons not to report an incident. Especially in some continental European countries, whistleblowing is still perceived as denunciation, even if the behaviour that is reported is actually illegal. This is especially true for Germany, which had its fair share of state supported denunciation in the twentieth century: First in National-Socialist Germany, later in the German Democratic Republic. However, this phenomenon is by no means limited to Germany, as a line from the French literature proves: "*En France, dénonciation renvoie à Occupation*"[78] ("In France, denunciation evokes memories of occupation [by Germany]").

Bearing this in mind, there are still some countries obliging certain persons to blow the whistle. In Italy, for instance, certain civil servants are obliged to report criminal offences. In the private sector, Italy also allows employers to oblige employees to blow the whistle who are performing controlling tasks. Certain rules also exempt entities featuring legal personality from liability for criminal offences committed by their senior managers if there is a model in force obliging personnel to report irregularities to the body supervising the managers and if a failure to comply with this duty to blow the whistle can be sanctioned.[79] Cyprus, Estonia, the Netherlands and South Korea take a similar approach, obliging personnel working in the public sector to report corruption. Japan orders public servants to report crime related to their office and similar rules exist in Austria as well as Estonia. Germany obliges anyone to report to the responsible authorities intentions of others to commit a serious crime (e.g. murder) that becomes known to him. Noncompliance with the obligation constitutes a crime in itself (§ 138 *Strafgesetzbuch* [Penal Code]). A similar rule is in force in Estonia, the Netherlands and, although restricted to the most serious crimes against peace, humanity, state defence etc., in Poland.[80]

An obligation to blow the whistle is prevalent throughout the EU in specific situations, as a duty to report health and safety at work irregularities is to be found in a Directive of the EU.[81] According to that rule, every employee has a duty to report

[78] François Barrière, La Semaine Juridique Entreprise & Affaires 42 (2011), 1527 (1530).

[79] Country Report Italy II, p. 2 f.

[80] Country Report Poland, p. 5.

[81] Art. 13 (2) (d) Directive 89/391/EEC. In Canada, certain employees are also obliged to report breaches of health and safety at work standards.

any serious danger to and any severe irregularity concerning health and safety at work to the employer. Another Directive of the EU obliges certain persons conducting or counselling financial transactions to report to certain authorities if they suspect customers of laundering money.[82] A person putting the environment at an immediate danger of pollution is also obliged to inform the responsible authorities immediately so that they can take the necessary measures to prevent a damage under yet another EU Directive.[83] As the Member States of the EU are obliged to implement these rules according to Art. 288 (3) TFEU, similar obligations should exist in the domestic law of every Member State. Although ever more tesserae of that kind can be found in EU law, there is no general rule or general doctrine recognizable yet – the mosaic is still incomplete.

What Is the Level of Protection Offered?

In the preceding chapters, we sketched out who is protected by whistleblowing statutes and what kind of behaviour qualifies as protected disclosure. In the following chapter, we will discuss the level of protection offered. From a whistleblowers' point of view, a high level of protection is desirable of course. But also from an institutional perspective, the effectiveness of a whistleblowing system depends heavily on the level of protection granted, as a low level of protection will discourage whistleblowers and therefore will render the system ineffective.

The Kind of Reprisal Whistleblowers Are Protected Against

A first distinction can be made according to what kind of reprisal whistleblowers are protected against. In most jurisdictions (Belgium, Canada, Finland, France, Germany, Italy, Japan, Malta, the Netherlands, Poland, Romania, Slovenia, South Korea, UK, USA, possibly also Brazil), whistleblowers are protected against any kind of detriment, including discrimination, dismissal or any other disadvantage inflicted upon them because they reported a wrongdoing. Some jurisdictions differentiate, however: Cyprus protects whistleblowers in the public sector as just described, but it is unclear whether whistleblowers in the private sector are protected against reprisal in this country by means of civil law. They are protected by means of criminal law however, as an employer sanctioning a whistleblower may commit a crime.[84] In Singapore, protection is granted against unfair treatment.[85] Nevertheless, there does not seem to be a specific protection against dismissal in

[82] Art. 20 ff. Directive 2005/60/EC.

[83] Art. 5 (2) Directive 2004/35/EC.

[84] Country Report Cyprus, p. 5.

[85] Country Report Singapore, p. 4.

force in the Asian city-state. Some countries (Croatia, Estonia) lacking special legislation on whistleblowing protect whistleblowers against unfair dismissal only via the general rules applicable. A special case is Austria: In this country, protection by the courts so far has been granted against summary dismissals only. Given the Austrian system of dismissal protection, it is possible that a whistleblower is not protected against a retaliatory ordinary dismissal at all, subjecting him to the arbitrariness of his employer.[86]

The Burden of Proof in Dismissal Cases

Even the best theoretical protection against reprisal is of no use to a whistleblower if he cannot obtain legal protection in practice due to the distribution of the burden of proof, especially in a dismissal case. A whistleblower will hardly ever be able to establish positively in a court trial the he has been dismissed because he blew the whistle. Nevertheless, some jurisdictions (Brazil [allowing for a reverse of the onus of proof], Poland, possibly also the Netherlands) attribute the burden of proof to the whistleblower seeking protection.

Contrariwise, most jurisdictions put the employer for the reasons stated above under an onus of proof to establish that he did actually not dismiss a whistleblower in an act of retaliation for blowing the whistle (Canada, Croatia, Cyprus, Finland, France, Portugal, Romania, Singapore, Slovenia, South Korea, possibly also Italy). Some countries allow for a reversal of burden of proof though: In Germany for instance, the onus of proof that a dismissal was justified lies with the employer. He will usually bring forward in a court trial that he dismissed the whistleblower for reasons not related to the disclosure of information. The whistleblower then will have to challenge this claim.[87] In Malta, every party will have to prove whatever she alleges,[88] which in civil actions seems to be a principle of procedure law in most jurisdictions. Slightly different is the situation in the UK: In the UK, there is no onus of proof upon the claimant with the result that if the employer cannot prove that the dismissal was for some other reason, the tribunal is likely to conclude that the reason was whistleblowing.[89]

Japan takes a very sophisticated approach, differentiating between the addressees of a report: If a whistleblower reports internally, he will only have to prove that he acted having a reasonable belief of a wrongdoing. If a whistleblower reports externally, he will have to prove that all the requirements of the Whistleblower Protection Act are fulfilled.[90]

An intricate case is Belgium: In this country, it is possible for an ombudsman to start an inquiry and the result of this inquiry will mainly depend on what proof he

[86] Country Report Austria, p. 4.

[87] Country Report Germany, p. 3.

[88] Country Report Malta, p. 4.

[89] Country Report UK, p. 5.

[90] Country Report Japan, p. 4.

can find. In Flanders the burden of proof has been shifted under certain conditions to the employer by a special statue enacted in 2012. Outside the scope of this act, protection is especially strong for civil servants, as employers vis-a-vis them have to give a reason for any measures they take. A civil servant therefore should be able to establish quite easily that he was retaliated against for a disclosure he made – unless the employer gives false reasons, of course. However, this provision does neither cover contractual workers in the public sector nor employees in the private sector. In the private sector, the burden of proof in dismissal cases depends on whether the dismissal is without notice (onus of proof lies with the employer) or with notice (onus of proof depends on whether the whistleblower is a blue collar or a white collar worker). However, statutes protecting all employees against bullying may lead to a reverse in the burden of proof as well.[91]

Whistleblowing and Collective Action

Potential whistleblowers operating on a stand-alone basis can be more easily discouraged from whistleblowing than people who can rely on the support of a collective. Collectives of this kind can e.g. be trade unions, consumer protection groups or even collectives forming specifically for the purpose of supporting whistleblowing (such as *Whistleblowernetzwerk* [Whistleblower Network] in Germany, *Commissie Adviespunt Klokkenluiders* [Whistleblower Advice Centre] in the Netherlands or Public Concern at Work in the UK). Collective action needs not necessarily take the form of a suit filed on behalf of a whistleblower or even in the form of a class action. Collective action also would be e.g. supporting a whistleblower financially or by advising him. While many countries we surveyed allow trade unions, antidiscrimination organisations or employee representatives to support employees in court trials or even to sue on their behalf, none seem to have special laws in force yet that would improve the collective supporting of whistleblowers.

Financial Incentives for Whistleblowers?

While collective action may help whistleblowers to find the courage to blow the whistle knowing that they can rely on others, another promising way to improve whistleblowing is to set financial incentives for whistleblowers.[92] This is not a new concept: The US-American False Claims Act relied entirely on the financial interest of the whistleblower as early as 1863. If certain conditions are met, this act allows

[91] Country Report Belgium, p. 11 f.

[92] *cf.* H Fleischer, KU Schmolke, 'Financial Incentives for Whistleblowers in European Capital Markets Law? Legal Policy Considerations on the Reform of the Market Abuse Regime' (2012), *European Capital Markets Law* 9: 250–259.

anyone to charge a suit on behalf of the state against contractors committing fraud at the cost of the public. To encourage suits to the benefit of the public, the claimant is allowed to keep a part of the sum he is able to retrieve from the fraudulent contractor.[93] However, the US took another step ahead in setting financial incentives for whistleblowers in 2010. In this year, the Dodd-Frank-Act was signed. Section 922 Dodd-Frank Act allows the Securities and Exchange Commission (SEC) to award to a whistleblower who discloses information that leads to an SEC enforcement action 10–30 % of the sum the SEC recovers as sanctions, provided that the sanction exceeds US-$ 1 million. The act led to some spectacular disclosures. Especially well-remembered is the case of *Bradley Birkenfeld*: In 2009, he disclosed that the UBS, one of the giant Swiss banks, helped US citizens with tax evasion. The UBS faced a fine amounting to US-$ 780 million. In 2012, *Birkenfeld* received a reward amounting to US-$ 104 million.[94]

European countries in general are less willing to reward whistleblowers financially. Legislators in Europe seem to stress the downside of financial incentives: They do have the potential to encourage people to act solely for personal gain. Thus, they are able to create an atmosphere of mistrust, surveillance and denunciation that evokes memories of some of the gloomiest periods in European history. Nevertheless, the European Commission in 2011 decided to follow the example of the US. In Art. 29 (2) of its proposal of a "Regulation of the European Parliament and of the Council on Insider Dealing and Market Manipulation (Market Abuse)"[95] (MAR), the Commission suggested that the Member States of the EU should be allowed to set financial incentives for whistleblowers in the fields covered by the proposed regulation, i.e. financial services and markets. The provision that was finally adopted states: "Member States may provide for financial incentives to persons who offer relevant information about potential infringements of this Regulation to be granted in accordance with national law where such persons do not have other pre-existing legal or contractual duties to report such information, and provided that the information is new, and that it results in the imposition of an administrative or criminal sanction, or the taking of another administrative measure, for an infringement of this Regulation".[96]

Although there do not seem to be mandatory financial incentives prescribed in the jurisdictions of the Member States of the EU yet,[97] some Member States exist

[93] *cf.* U.S. Department of Justice, The False Claims Act: A Primer, available at www.justice.gov/sites/default/files/civil/legacy/2011/04/22/C-FRAUDS_FCA_Primer.pdf (as at 12.1.2015).

[94] On this case, see L Saunders, R Sidel, 'Whistleblower Gets §104 Million' (2012), *Wall Street Journal of 11.9.2012*, available at www.wsj.com/news/articles/SB10000872396390444017504577645412614237708?mg=reno64-wsj&url=http%3A%2F%2Fonline.wsj.com%2Farticle%2FSB10000872396390444017504577645412614237708.html (as at 12.1.2015).

[95] COM(2011)651.

[96] Art. 32 (4) Regulation (EU) No. 596/2014.

[97] Even the Financial Conduct Authority (FCA) of the UK – perceived by some as being the most likely institution to head for that way – decided against this instrument, *cf.* FCA, Financial Incentives for Whistleblowers, available at www.fca.org.uk/your-fca/documents/financial-incentives-for-whistleblowers (as at 12.1.2015).

that allow employers to oblige personnel to blow the whistle contractually (Czech Republic, France, Romania).

In lieu of monetary incentives, a different form of carrot is made use of in practice within the EU: Especially in the field of antitrust regulation, whistleblowers revealing cartels they were involved in themselves may expect to be treated as key witnesses and spared from at least the harshest sanctions. It comes as no surprise that the European Commission has a whistleblower system for this kind of disclosures available.[98] In Austria, a similar rule is to be found in the *Strafprozessordnung* (Code of Criminal Procedure) for certain crimes the whistleblower is involved in as well.[99] Although this kind of incentive has proven to be quite effective as well, the downside is that the whistleblower who acted illegally on his own is let off the hook.

Asian countries, on the other hand, seem to be even more reluctant to reward whistleblowers financially than European ones: Singapore, although being one of the hotspots of the global financial industry, does not know financial rewards for people reporting irregularities, notwithstanding that it has several acts on whistleblowing in force and therefore can be considered as featuring a quite advanced jurisdiction in this respect. Japanese legislation does neither allow nor prohibit financial incentives, but in practice, they do not seem to be used. An exemption is South Korea: Financial rewards are generally not permitted. However, they may be awarded by the responsible authorities to whistleblowers who prevented damage to public property or whose report helped to recover such property on the basis of the special legislation in force.[100]

Conclusion

Our comparison has shown that although whistleblowing is treated quite differently around the world in detail, some general patterns can be identified that are prevalent in many of the jurisdictions we surveyed. This refers to the personal scope of rules on whistleblower protection as well as to the facts that may be reported and the proceedings these facts may be reported in. Although the jurisdictions we surveyed feature a lot of differences in that respect, they also share a lot of commonalities. This does not really come as a surprise, as people around the globe are in the end – notwithstanding cultural peculiarities – just people and therefore everywhere quite similar. Therefore, the legal challenges to legislators and judges are quite similar everywhere in the world as well.

However, our report also reveals that the level of development of the legal order in the countries we surveyed is still very different. Leading jurisdictions are the UK, Japan and South Korea, which have very sophisticated statutes on whistleblowing in force since several years or even decades now. The USA, although being probably

[98] Available at www.ec.europa.eu/competition/cartels/leniency/leniency.html (as at 12.1.2015).

[99] Country Report Austria, p. 5.

[100] Country Report South Korea, p. 6.

the first nation to actively encourage whistleblowing by means of the False Claims Act of 1863, still lacks a generally applicable statute on whistleblowing, although the USA do have detailed acts in force covering many fields of life. Many EU jurisdictions made progress in establishing modern rules on whistleblower protection during the last years. This includes, amongst others, Italy, Malta and Romania. However, improvement is still possible and desirable in many other EU Member States. This is especially true for Germany. The German legislator has repeatedly proven to be unwilling or incapable of tackling the problem, leaving this difficult task to the courts. The courts, however, are not the right instance to regulate whistleblowing in a coherent manner, as they only have to decide the individual case at hand.

Finally, there is room for improvement even in the most advanced jurisdictions: Firstly, the protection of supporters and witnesses of whistleblowers can and should be improved. Although witnesses are protected if they give testimony in court trials in most jurisdictions, they are usually not protected if interviewed in private investigations or at least the legal situation is unclear. The protection of supporters is even less reliable. A notable and encouraging exception in this respect is South Korean legislation, which may serve as an archetype for other jurisdictions. Secondly, the role of collectives in the protection of whistleblowers needs to be clarified. In none of the jurisdictions we surveyed, collectives such as trade unions, consumer protection groups or even whistleblower associations such as Public Concern At Work are properly accounted for. Although at least trade unions do have certain rights in some jurisdictions, these rights are usually not awarded with special respect to whistleblowing, but as an acknowledgement of the role of trade unions in the field of employment in general. This situation needs to be improved, as collectives could be able to further improve the protection of whistleblowers and thus to encourage whistleblowing to the benefit of all. Thirdly, financial incentives for whistleblowers are a topic that requires attendance. The USA are leading in this respect, having centuries of experience with this regulatory technique and having refurbished it in the wake of the financial crisis by means of the Dodd-Frank Act. However, financial incentives for whistleblowers do have a downside as they increase the risk of denunciation for opportunistic reasons. A broad discussion of the desirability of financial incentives for whistleblowers is overdue and a clear decision needs to be made, as otherwise employers might opt for this instrument in a legal environment that is still very murky.

Bibliography

Barrière F (2011) *La Semaine Juridique Entreprise & Affaires* 42: 1527

Bowers J, Fodder M, Lewis J, Mitchell J (2012) Whistleblowing: Law and practice, 2nd edn, OUP Oxford

Brown AJ, Lewis D, Moberly R (2014) *International Handbook on Whistleblowing Research* Cheltenham, Edward Elgar Publishing Ltd.

Calland R, Dehn G (2004) *Whistleblowing Around the World – Law, Culture and Practice* ODAC and PCaW in partnership with the British Council Southern Africa, Cape Town

Düsel J (2009) *Gespaltene Loyalität: Whistleblowing und Kündigungsschutz in Deutschland, Großbritannien und Frankreich* Baden-Baden, Nomos

Fleischer H, Schmolke KU (2012) *Financial Incentives for Whistleblowers in European Capital Markets Law? Legal Policy Considerations on the Reform of the Market Abuse Regime* European Capital Markets Law 9: 250–259

Forst G (2013) *Whistleblowing und Datenschutz – Brauchen wir eine spezielle Regelung?* Recht der Datenverarbeitung (RDV) 29: 122–131

Forst G (2014) *Whistleblowing im Gesundheitswesen* Die Sozialgerichtsbarkeit 60: 413–422

Greenwald G (2014) *No place to hide: Edward Snowden, the NSA, and the U.S. surveillance state* Metropolitan Books

Group of States Against Corruption in the Council of Europe (GRECO) (2006) *Seventh General Activity Report* 2007

Imbach Haumüller D (2011) *Whistleblowing in der Schweiz und im internationalen Vergleich – ein Bestandteil einer effektiven internen Kontrolle?* Zürich, Schulthess

Leisinger K (2003) *Whistleblowing und Corporate Reputation Management* Mering, Hampp Verlag

Lewis D (2010) *A Global Approach to Public Interest Disclosure: What Can We Learn From Existing Whistleblowing Legislation and Research?* Cheltenham, Edward Elgar Publishing Ltd.

Omtzigt P (2009) *The protection of "whistle-blowers"* in: Parliamentary Assembly of the Council of Europe, Doc. 12006

Patier X (2013) *La prévention de la corruption en France* Paris, DL

Saunders L, Sidel R (11.9.2012) *Whistleblower Gets §104 Million* Wall Street Journal, available at www.wsj.com/news/articles/SB10000872396390444017504577645412614237708?mg=reno64-wsj&url=http%3A%2F%2Fonline.wsj.com%2Farticle%2FSB10000872396390444017504577645412614237708.html (as at 12.1.2015).

Vandekerckhove W (2006) *Whistleblowing and Organizational Social Responsibility: A Global Assessment* Burlington, Ashgate

von Kaehnel A (2012) *Whistleblowing – Multidisziplinäre Aspekte* Bern, Stämpfli

Zitelmann E (1900) *Aufgabe und Bedeutung der Rechtsvergleichung* Deutsche Juristen-Zeitung 5: 329

Gregor Thüsing Professor for civil, labour and employment law, Institut für Arbeitsrecht und Recht der Sozialen Sicherheit, Rheinische Friedrich-Wilhelms University of Bonn (Germany).

Part II
National Reports

Chapter 2
The Legal Response to Whistleblowing in Canada: Managing Disclosures by the "Up the Ladder" Principle

John P. McEvoy

Abstract Canadian law has generally adopted the "up the ladder" approach to whistleblowing in both public and private employment. This chapter addresses whistleblowing protection of employees at common law and civil law as well more recent legislative reforms to protect whistlebowers in relation to discrete matters invoking the principle of protection (such as children, the elderly and the environment).

Introduction

In the labour and employment law context, a whistleblower is an employee who discloses otherwise confidential information gained in the course of employment. The disclosed information may relate to "illegal, immoral or illegitimate practices"[1] undertaken by or on behalf of the employer such that its disclosure is detrimental to the employer's interests. An employee seeking corrective action typically makes the disclosure "to persons or organizations that may be able to affect action"[2] but disclosures are also made to the public at large through news and social media. Such disclosures risk the business reputation of the employer and may expose the employer to prosecution. Considered in this context, the legal position of a whistleblower depends on two competing interests: the private interest of the employer in the confidentiality of its information (the duties of loyalty, good faith, and confidentiality) and the public interest in disclosure of information about conduct detrimental to the public interest.

---

[1] Sean C. Doyle, "A Purposive Approach to Whistleblower Protection: A Comment on *Merk v International Association of Bridge, Structural, Ornamental and Reinforcing Iron Workers, Local 771*" (2007), 44 *Alberta Law Review* 903, at 903 quoting Terry Morehead Dworkin, "Whistleblowing, MNCs, and Peace" (2002), 35 *Vanderbilt Journal of Transnational Law* 457 at 461.

[2] ibid.

J.P. McEvoy (✉)
Faculty of Law, University of New Brunswick,
P.O. Box 4400, Fredericton, NB E3B 5A3, Canada
e-mail: mcevoy@unb.ca

G. Thüsing, G. Forst (eds.), *Whistleblowing - A Comparative Study*,
Ius Comparatum - Global Studies in Comparative Law 16,
DOI 10.1007/978-3-319-25577-4_2

Disclosure of workplace information is not a new phenomenon. It has probably existed since human beings started working together in a common endeavour. But, what has changed is the means of communication; technology has made disclosures easier and to a broader audience. Instead of a conversation with an outsider, an employee can more widely disseminate information using social media and the internet. Who hasn't received an otherwise confidential email from someone who inadvertently used the "reply all" option? Or, known of someone who posted information on a social media website in the mistaken belief that the website is private and available only to certain "friends"? Such disclosures may breach the employee's duties of loyalty, good faith, and confidentiality and may subject the employee to disciplinary action by the employer. But, such disclosures are not the disclosures by whistleblowers in the sense understood in this chapter.

A whistleblower makes an intentional disclosure of information to achieve a broader public purpose. A whistleblower is not engaged in gossip and personal complaints. A whistleblower generally believes that s/he acts for a higher purpose outside of the direct employment relationship or status. Notwithstanding this identifiable higher purpose, personal vendetta may or may not be a factor in an employee's decision to make a disclose disclosure.

Canada is a federal state consisting geographically of ten provinces and three territories.[3] Considered from a jurisdictional perspective, Canada consists of 14 law units: the 10 provinces, 3 territories, and national level of government. The legislative assemblies of the provinces exercise general legislative jurisdiction in relation to labour and employment matters "within the province" while the national Parliament exercises jurisdiction in relation to labour and employment matters as an exception to the provincial jurisdiction; that is, in relation to labour and employment in matters of national interest, such as interprovincial and international transportation, the federal public sector, and nuclear energy. The three territories exercise legislative jurisdiction similar to that of a province but with jurisdiction delegated to the territorial legislature rather than the constitutionally mandated jurisdiction exercised by the provinces.

Canada is bijural. Nine of the ten provinces and the three territories are common law jurisdictions. Quebec is a civil law jurisdiction with a *Civil Code* enacted in 1991[4] (in force in 1994) to replace the first code adopted in 1865. Statutes enacted by the national Parliament conform to both common law and civil law concepts.

Whistleblower protection is generally understood as an exception to the duties every employee owes to the employer particularly, the duty of loyalty – and is managed by the legal requirement that an employee first disclose wrongdoing through internal mechanisms – the "up the ladder" principle. Whistleblower protection has been the subject of legislation in most Canadian jurisdictions, reviewed in

---

[3] The ten provinces east to west are Newfoundland and Labrador, Prince Edward Island, Nova Scotia, New Brunswick, Quebec, Ontario, Manitoba, Saskatchewan, Alberta, and British Columbia. The three territories in northern Canada are Nunavut, the Northwest Territories, and the Yukon Territory.

[4] *Code civil du Québec*, L.Q. 1991, c. 64 ("*C.c.Q.*").

grievance arbitration awards and court cases, including the Supreme Court of Canada, and the subject of increasing scholarly attention. The number of cases and scholarly publications cannot be described as extensive. A check with legal databases for the period 2008–2013 reveals a mere 54 instances of Canadian tribunal decisions relevant to the whistleblower context, a mere 58 court cases, and no articles in scholarly journals.[5]

Just as the law has embraced the whistleblower, so have many employers who recognize that the disclosure of wrongdoing – at least, internally – accords with their long term business interests. As a result, private sector employers are increasingly adopting internal whistleblower policies to enable employees to make disclosures within the employment relationship. At the same time, commercial service providers have been quick to see a business opportunity and have established external whistleblower services which are provided to an employer for a fee.

The Legal Basis for Whistleblower Protection

Common Law and Civil Law

At both common law and civil law, an employee has duties of loyalty, good faith and confidentiality to the employer.[6]

The duties of loyalty and good faith are general in nature. In exchange for the payment of wages or salary, an employee is to perform assigned lawful duties in

---

[5] LexisNexis Quicklaw separate searches for tribunal and court decisions using the term "whistleblower" and the time period 01 January 2008 to 30 June 2013. Searches conducted on 24 October 2013. Note that the numbers include appeals of the same matter so the number of individual instances of whistleblowing under consideration is less. A search of the Canadian Index to Legal Literature on the same database and for the same time period identified a number of articles on the subject in magazines for the legal profession but not in scholarly journals.

[6] See Ontario Law Reform Commission, Report on Political Activity, Public Comment and Disclosure by Crown Employees (Toronto, Ministry of the Attorney General, 1986) at pp. 32–74; CL Dubin, Q.C. and J Terry, "Whistleblowing Study": Commissioned by Industry Canada (Industry Canada, Competition Bureau, 20 August 1997) and "Whistleblowing Study: Addendum" (30 September 1997); C Brunelle et M Samson, "La Liberté d'expression au travail et l'obligation de loyauté du salarié: plaidoyer pour un espace critique accru" (2005) 46 Cahiers de Droit 847; I Cantin and JM Cantin, La dénonciation d'actes répréhensibles en milieu de travail ou Whistleblowing (Cowansville, Les Éditions Yvon Blais, 2005); KP Swan, "Whistleblowing – Employee Loyalty and the Right to Criticize: An Arbitrator's Viewpoint" in W. Kaplan, J. Sack, and M. Gunderson, Labour Arbitration Yearbook 1991 (Vol. II) (Toronto, Butterworths-Lancaster House, 1991) at 191–198; J Carson, "The Need for Whistleblowing Legislation in Canada: A Critical Defence", paper presented to the Canadian Political Science Association Conference, June 2006 and accessible at the C.P.S.A. website at www.cpsa-acsp.ca/papers-2006/Carson.pdf (as at 29 July 2013); The Labour Law Casebook Group, Labour and Employment Law: Cases, Materials, and Commentary, 8th edn (Toronto, Irwin Law, 2011) at 992–94; M Mitchnick and B Etherington, Labour Arbitration in Canada, 2nd edn (Toronto, Lancaster House, 2012) at chapter 12 "Disloyalty and Breach of Trust", at 271–277.

good faith and with appropriate skill for the employer's benefit. This duty includes the obligation not to undermine the employment contract by acts of dishonesty and not to enter into relationships or conduct inconsistent with the interests of the employer; for example, by accepting secret commissions from third parties. The duty of loyalty also extends beyond the workplace so that, even in private conduct on the employee's own time, the employee is not to engage in conduct inconsistent with the reputation and good standing of the employer.

The duty of confidentiality is more specific. It may arise by contract or imposed by law. By contract, the duty of confidentiality may be expressed as a term of the contract of employment because of the nature of the duties undertaken by the employee; for example, a human resources officer or a financial advisor. At common law, the duty may be imposed when an employer shares confidential information with an employee on the understanding that the employee will keep it confidential unless and until told otherwise.

In Quebec civil law,[7] *C.c.Q.* article 2088 imposes similar duties on an employee:

> 2088. The employee is bound not only to carry on his work with prudence and diligence but also to act faithfully and honestly and not to use any confidential information he may obtain in carrying on or in the course of his work.

The *Commentaires du ministre de la Justice*,[8] a background document to explain the *C.c.Q.* to the public and jurists alike, describes article 2088 as reflecting the state of the jurisprudence and doctrine on an employee's obligation of loyalty to the employer in relation to confidential information obtained in the course of employment. The *Commentaires* also affirms that this duty of loyalty continues after termination of the immediate employment relationship for either a limited (reasonable) or unlimited period of time.

The *C.c.Q.* recognizes a specific exception to the duty of loyalty and confidentiality. In relation to a trade secret, *C.c.Q.* article 1472 specifically protects a person from liability for having disclosed a trade secret "by proving that considerations of general interest prevailed over keeping the secret and, particularly, that its disclosure was justified for reasons of public health or safety." In other words, by proving that the public interest supersedes the private employment interest.

The intersection of the legal duties of loyalty, good faith, and confidentiality and the concept of the justified whistleblower had its initial Canadian development in arbitral jurisprudence concerning employer discipline of perceived employee misconduct.

Wm. Scott & Co. and Canadian Food & Allied Workers, Local P16 (1976)[9] is considered a classic statement of the law. The employer fired an employee after a newspaper published negative comments attributed to her. The employee, who was also the union's financial secretary, had telephoned the newspaper to challenge a

---

[7] See I Cantin and JM Cantin, *La dénonciation d'actes répréhensibles en milieu de travail ou Whistleblowing* (Cowansville, Les Éditions Yvon Blais, 2005).

[8] Ministre de la Justice (Québec), *Commentaires du ministre de la Justice*, Les publications du Québec, Tome 1, at 1312–1313 (1993).

[9] *Wm. Scott & Co. and Canadian Food & Allied Workers, Local P16*, 1976 CLB 1780; [1976] B.C.L.R.B.D. No. 98; [1977] 1 C.L.R.B.R. 1; [1976] 2 WLAC 585.

statement it had published about her union's position on a matter of public interest. In a follow up article, the newspaper quoted her as having stated "you wouldn't believe the inefficiencies at the plant". The timing of this comment was not helpful because the employer and the union were already the subjects of public criticism in the media. An arbitration board dismissed the union's grievance and the Labour Relations Board of British Columbia dismissed the union's appeal. The Board a two step analytical approach asking first, if the employee engaged in conduct meriting discipline and, second, whether the discipline imposed by the employer was excessive in the circumstances. The Board answered these questions with a "yes" and a "no", respectively. It is to be observed that the employee did not first express her concerns to the employer before making a public statement.

Another now classic arbitral award, this time in the public sector, applied what is known as the "up the ladder" approach. In *Re Ministry of Attorney General, Corrections Branch and British Columbia Government Employees' Union* (1981),[10] two senior corrections officers grieved the termination their employment as being without just cause. The two employees expressed their personal concerns about conditions in the provincial penal institutions during radio, television and newspaper interviews and specifically criticized workplace policies of their employer. Their purpose, as presented by them, was to promote change for the better – they were, in brief, whistleblowers exposing matters of public concern and interest. After reviewing relevant arbitral decisions, the arbitrator addressed the duty of loyalty (fidelity):

> With respect to public criticisms of the employer, the duty of fidelity does not impose an absolute "gag rule" against an employee making any public statements that might be critical of his employer… However, the duty of fidelity does require the employee to exhaust internal "whistle-blowing" mechanisms before "going public". These internal mechanisms are designed to ensure that the employer's reputation is not damaged by unwarranted attacks based on inaccurate information. Internal investigation provides a sound method of applying the expertise and experience of many individuals to all problems that may only concern one employee. <u>Only when these internal mechanisms prove fruitless may an employee engage in public criticism of his employer without violating his duty of fidelity</u>. [emphasis added][11]

It is this "up the ladder" approach which informs Canadian law on whistleblower protection in the labour and employment context.

Special Statutes on the Protection of Whistleblowers: Public Sector Employees

In 1993, Ontario became the first Canadian jurisdiction to enact whistleblower protection legislation.[12] The Act established the office of Counsel to provide confidential advice to employees regarding their rights and obligations when considering

---

[10] Re Ministry of Attorney General, Corrections Branch and British Columbia Government Employees' Union (1981) 3 L.A.C. (3d) 140.

[11] ibid. at 162–163.

[12] *Public Service and Labour Relations Statute Law*, S.O. 1993. c. 38, Part IV "Whistleblowers' Protection".

disclosure of "serious government wrongdoing" – a phrase the Act defined as a breach of legislation, "gross mismanagement", "gross waste of money", "an abuse of authority", "a grave health or safety hazard… or a grave environmental hazard".[13] If and when an employee made a disclosure to the Counsel's office about "serious government wrongdoing", the Act authorized the Counsel (with the consent of the employee) to inform the appropriate head of the government department or agency about the disclosure and that person would then undertake an investigation and submit a report on the matter within 30 days. Subject to certain limitations, this report would be made public. The Act expressly protected an employee who followed its procedures in good faith from employer reprisal and protected the employee's identity.

Though enacted with good intentions, this Ontario statute was never proclaimed into law. With bad political timing, the governing political party lost the next provincial election and the new government decided not to implement its predecessor's legislative agenda.

Federal Legislation

Without legislative protection, whistleblowing employees in Ontario and elsewhere in Canada were subject to the protection available at common law or, in Quebec, civil law. Public pressure for legislative intervention grew as various government scandals came and went in the news media and public consciousness. One such matter became known as the "sponsorship scandal" over the misuse of federal funds intended to promote Canadian identity at approved cultural and other events. A public inquiry investigated the matter with extensive media coverage including daily television broadcast of the proceedings.[14] The federal government responded with the *Public Servants Disclosure Protection Act* ("*PSDPA*"), enacted by Parliament in 2005.[15]

The *PSDPA* requires the creation and adoption of codes of conduct for public sector employees. These codes are to be consistent with the good governance principle and require each department or agency of government to designate a "senior officer" to receive and deal with complaints of "serious government wrongdoing". Like the defunct 1993 Ontario statute, the 2005 *PSDPA* defines such "wrongdoing" in terms of a violation of federal or provincial laws, "misuse of public funds", "gross mismanagement in the public sector", "a substantial and specific danger to the life, health or safety of persons, or the environment", "a serious breach of a code of

[13] ibid. at s 28.13.

[14] For a brief backgrounder, see É Hurtubise-Loranger and R Katz, *Federal Public Sector Whistleblowing* (Ottawa, Library of Parliament Research Publications, 31 October 2008 and revised 26 June 2012).

[15] S.C. 2005, c. 46.

conduct" for the public sector, and "knowingly directing or counselling" the commission of any such wrongdoing.[16]

The *PSDPA* expressly permits a federal public sector employee to disclose information to the public in certain limited circumstances. Information may be directly disclosed if the employee has reasonable grounds to believe that the information relates to a "serious offence" under either federal or provincial law or involves "an imminent risk of a substantial and specific nature to the life, health and safety of persons or to the environment".[17] The limitation on such a disclosure is that it may only be done if "there is not sufficient time to make the disclosure" to a supervisor or senior officer as provided in the *PSDPA*.[18]

The *PSDPA* further requires that the identity of an employee making a disclosure be protected and that the disclosed information be kept confidential. However, if wrongdoing is found to have been committed, the information about the wrongdoing is to be disclosed to the public. The disclosure to the public may include information that might serve to identify the person who committed the misconduct but only if such information is "necessary to identify the wrongdoing".[19]

In terms of procedure, an employee covered by the *PSDPA* is authorized to disclose information to "his or her supervisor" or the designated "senior officer".[20] Such disclosure is not unrestricted as the *PSDPA* requires that an employee disclose "no more information than is reasonably necessary to make the disclosure" and that the employee "follow established procedure or practices for the secure handling, storage, transportation and transmission of information or documents".[21] Other restrictions apply to certain types of information – such as information subject to solicitor-client privilege and certain security information.[22]

The *PSDPA* established two administrative bodies to implement the procedures established by the Act and address the protections provided to whistleblowers. The first is the Office of the Public Sector Integrity Commissioner ("Integrity Commissioner") and the second is the Public Servants Disclosure Protection Tribunal ("Disclosure Protection Tribunal").

The Integrity Commissioner is a federal public officer appointed pursuant to resolutions adopted by the Senate and the House of Commons (the two Houses of Parliament) after consultation with the leader of each political party represented in either legislative body.[23] As a public officer appointed directly by Parliament, the Integrity Commissioner enjoys a level of independence from the executive government and from government departments and agencies.

---

[16] ibid. at ss 5, 8 and 10.

[17] ibid. s 16.

[18] ibid.

[19] ibid. at s 11.

[20] ibid. at s 12.

[21] ibid. at s 15.1.

[22] ibid. at ss 13 and 17.

[23] ibid. at s 39.

It is the role and function of the Integrity Commissioner to investigate a disclosure of wrongdoing and to report to Parliament the findings of the investigation.[24] These reports include recommendations on means to avoid such wrongdoing in the future and whether disciplinary action should be considered by the employer in relation to the wrongdoer.

The Integrity Commissioner is also responsible to investigate a complaint of reprisal against an employee and, if appropriate, to attempt to settle any such complaint by conciliation. This investigative process is available to both present and former employees who claim that they have been or may be subjected to disciplinary action in reprisal for a disclosure of information protected by the *PSDPA*. The limitation period for filing a reprisal complaint is 60 days after the complainant knew or ought to have known of the act of reprisal.[25] If, after completing the investigation, the complaint is not settled the investigator submits a report to the Commissioner who then decides whethesr to refer the matter to the Disclosure Protection Tribunal. For the purposes of the Act, the term "reprisal" is broadly defined in section 2(1) to include employment related action "because the public servant has made a protected disclosure or has, in good faith, cooperated in an investigation" commenced under the Act and specifically defines "reprisal" to mean:

(a) A disciplinary measure;
(b) The demotion of the public servant;
(c) The termination of employment of the public servant, including, in the case of a member of the Royal Canadian Mounted Police, a discharge or dismissal;
(d) Any measure that adversely affects the employment or working conditions of the public servant; and
(e) A threat to take any of the measures referred to in any of paragraphs (a) to (d).

It is this second body, the Disclosure Protection Tribunal, which conducts a formal adjudicative hearing to determine if the employee has indeed been subjected to reprisal and what remedy is appropriate in the circumstances. The remedial options include disciplinary action against the person responsible for the act of reprisal.[26] To ensure its institutional independence, members of the Tribunal are judges of either the Federal Court of Canada or of a provincial superior court and are each appointed for a term of 7 years.[27]

Provincial Legislation

Several provinces have enacted their own versions of public sector whistleblower protection legislation.

---

[24] ibid. at s 38(3.3)

[25] ibid. at s 19.1.

[26] ibid. at s 20.4.

[27] ibid. at s 20.7.

Nova Scotia acted first when, in 2004, it established whistleblower protection through a regulation under its public sector employment legislation.[28] In 2010, Nova Scotia became the first Canadian province to enact a distinct public sector whistleblower protection statute and issue a proclamation to have the statute enter into force as law.[29] Similar legislation now also exists in Manitoba, New Brunswick, Ontario, Saskatchewan, Alberta, and Newfoundland and Labrador under a title indicating "Public Interest Disclosure" either with or without the additional phrase "Whistleblower Protection".[30]

The provincial statutes follow the approach of the federal *Public Servants Disclosure Protection Act* in mandating both a disclosure procedure and employee protection from reprisal. These statutes require the selection of designated persons in government departments and units to receive information from employees seeking to disclose wrongdoing. The investigative role and functions of the Integrity Commissioner and the adjudicative role and functions of the Disclosure Protection Tribunal under the federal Act are assigned in the provincial statutes to the provincial Ombudsman and the provincial labour relations board, respectively, in the Nova Scotia, Manitoba, New Brunswick, and Newfoundland and Labrador legislation. In Ontario, Saskatchewan, and Alberta, the Integrity Commissioner and Disclosure Protection Tribunal roles and functions are assigned to a provincial Public Interest Commissioner whose authority includes investigating and reporting on a both a disclosure of information and a reprisal complaint. The statutes of Ontario, Saskatchewan, and Alberta provide for the possible future assignment of the provincial Commissioner's role to the provincial Ombudsman.

Like the federal statute, the statutes of three provinces – Nova Scotia, New Brunswick, and Manitoba – authorize an employee to make a direct public disclosure of information in limited circumstances. Such a disclosure may be made when an employee has information that reasonably concerns "an imminent risk of substantial and specific danger to the life, health or safety of persons or to the environment".[31] These statutes require an employee who intends to make such a disclosure to first disclose the information to an appropriate law enforcement officer or health agency, as appropriate; to follow the directions of that officer or agency

---

[28] *Civil Service Disclosure of Wrongdoing Regulations*, N.S. Reg. 205/2004 pursuant to the *Civil Service Act*, R.S.N.S. 1989, c 70, s 45.

[29] *Public Interest Disclosure of Wrongdoing Act*, S.N.S. 2010, c 42 replacing N.S. Reg.205/2004.

[30] *The Public Interest Disclosure (Whistleblower Protection) Act*, C.C.S.M. c P217 (w.e.f 2 April 2007); *Public Interest Disclosure Act*, S.N.B. 2007, c P-23.005 (w.e.f. 1 July 2008), now S.N.B. 2012, c 112; *Public Service of Ontario Act*, 2006, S.O. 2006, c 35, Sched. A "Part VI Disclosing and Investigating Wrongdoing" (w.e.f. 20 August 2007); *Public Interest Disclosure Act*, S.S. 2011, c P-38.1 (w.e.f 1 September 2011); *The Public Interest Disclosure (Whistleblower Protection) Act*, S.A. 2012, c P-39.5 (w.e.f. 1 June 2013); and *Public Interest Disclosure and Whistleblower Protection Act*, S.N.L. 2014, c P.37.2 (w.e.f. 1 July 2014). Note "w.e.f" means "with effect from" the date indicated which identifies when the statute came into effect.

[31] *Public Interest Disclosure of Wrongdoing Act*, above n 30, at s 8 (N.S.); *Public Interest Disclosure Act*, above n 30 ibid. at s 14 (N.B.); and *The Public Interest Disclosure (Whistleblower Protection) Act*, above n 30 at s 14 (Man.).

regarding the information to be disclosed in the public interest; and then, immediately after making the disclosure, to disclose the information to his or her supervisor or the designated officer in the department or unit.[32] The Alberta statute also permits an employee to make a disclosure in similar circumstances but limits the employee to making the disclosure to the Commissioner appointed under the statute.[33]

Both the Alberta and Saskatchewan statutes require that policies be established to address the procedures to protect confidentiality unless the information pertains to "an imminent risk of substantial and specific danger" to life, health, etc.[34] The Ontario and Newfoundland and Labrador statutes are silent on disclosures in such circumstances.

The statutes enacted by these provinces prohibit acts of reprisal being taken against an employee who, acting in good faith, sought advice pertaining to making of a disclosure, actually made a disclosure, or who cooperated in the investigation of a disclosure. The Ontario and Newfoundland and Labrador statutes specifically provide that an employee who engages in a reprisal action, or who directs another employee to engage in reprisal action, is subject to disciplinary action including suspension and dismissal.[35] The other provincial statutes do not include a similar disciplinary provision. The provincial statutes (except for New Brunswick and Newfoundland and Labrador) also make it an offence to take reprisal action against an employee and render a person convicted of such an offence subject to a fine – for example, in Nova Scotia, Manitoba and Saskatchewan, not exceeding $10,000; in Alberta, not exceeding $25,000 for a first offence and not exceeding $100,000 for a second offence; and in Ontario, not exceeding $5000.[36]

The provincial statutes contain other notable features. For example, the statutes of both Alberta and Saskatchewan declare that no civil cause of action "lies against a department, public entity or office of the Legislature, or an employee of any of them, for making a reasonable human resource management decision in good faith".[37] The Manitoba statute contains provisions extending protection against employment reprisal actions to private sector employees and persons contracting with the government.[38]

---

[32] ibid.

[33] *The Public Interest Disclosure (Whistleblower Protection) Act*, above n 30 at s 10(1)(f) (Alberta).

[34] ibid. s 5(1)(c) and *Public Interest Disclosure Act*, above n 30 at s 6(1) (Sask.).

[35] *Public Service of Ontario Act, 2006* above n 30 s 143 and *Public Interest Disclosure and Whistleblower Protection Act*, above n 30 at s 21(2) (N.L.).

[36] *Public Interest Disclosure of Wrongdoing Act*, above n 30 at s 35 (Nova Scotia); *The Public Interest Disclosure (Whistleblower Protection) Act*, above n 30 at s 33(4) (Manitoba); *Public Interest Disclosure Act*, above n 30 at s 40 (Saskatchewan); *The Public Interest Disclosure (Whistleblower Protection) Act*, above n 30 at s 49 (Alberta); and *Public Service of Ontario Act, 2006*, above n 30 at s 145(2) in combination with the *Provincial Offences Act*, R.S.O. 1990, c P.33, s 61 which establishes the general fine applicable when a statute does not otherwise express a specific fine or range of fines which is the situation with the *Public Service of Ontario Act, 2006*.

[37] *The Public Interest Disclosure (Whistleblower Protection) Act*, above n 30 at s 27 (Alberta) and *Public Interest Disclosure Act*, above n 30 at s 42 (Saskatchewan).

[38] *The Public Interest Disclosure (Whistleblower Protection) Act*, above n 30 at ss 30, 31 and 32 (Manitoba).

Although, as already mentioned, Newfoundland and Labrador in 2014 enacted general public whistleblower protection legislation similar to that of other provinces, that province first enacted disclosure protection legislation in response to the recommendations of an inquiry into the management of the provincial House of Assembly as Part VI of its *House of Assembly, Accountability, Integrity and Administration Act*.[39] The Act is, however, of limited application because it defines "wrongdoing" in terms of conduct by "a member, the speaker, an officer of the House of Assembly and persons employed in the House of Assembly service and the statutory offices".[40] Thus, the legislation is directed at the integrity of the democratic process and public administration in the House of Assembly itself. The Act implements a recommendation from a commission of inquiry into administrative and financial controls applicable to the provincial Legislature after a series of abuses were made public, including instances of abuse of member's allowances, inadequate record-keeping, and the purchase of items such as "magnets and rings and pins".[41] Not surprisingly, given its rather limited scope, the statute does not address disclosures in situations presenting a "substantial and specific danger" to the life, health, or safety of persons or to the environment.

The Newfoundland and Labrador legislation is a helpful reminder that the federal and provincial public interest disclosure statutes are not generally applicable to Parliament or the provincial Legislative Assemblies. This is because the definition of "public service" is typically defined with reference to government departments and agencies without mention of the legislative bodies. The reason for this exclusion is usually found in the separation of the legislative, executive, and judicial branches of government and the importance of maintaining the relative independence of each, particularly the historical privileges of a deliberative assembly.[42]

In Quebec, the relevant statue is the *Anti-Corruption Act* of 2011.[43] For the purposes of this statute, wrongdoing is defined as a breach of federal or provincial

[39] S.N.L. 2007, c H-10.1 (Bill 33).

[40] ibid. at s 54(1)(e). The *Act*, at s 2(r), defines the phrase "statutory offices" as referring to the Chief Electoral Officer, Commissioner for Members' Interests, Child and Youth Advocate, Information and Privacy Commissioner, Citizen's Representative, and "other offices of the House of Assembly, with the exception of the office of the Auditor General, that may be established under an Act".

[41] HJ Derek Green, Commissioner, *Rebuilding Confidence: Report of the Review Commission on Constituency Allowances and Related Matters* (St. John's, Government of Newfoundland and Labrador, 2007). The specific instances of abuse are referred to in the statement in the House of Assembly by Hon. Tom Marshall, Minister of Finance and President of Treasury Board, on second reading of Bill 33, above n 39. See: *House of Assembly Proceedings*, 45th General Assembly, 4th Session, Vol. XLV, No. 3 (Hansard) (14 June 2007) available at www.assembly.nl.ca/business/hansard.

[42] In the case of Newfoundland and Labrador, the provincial Assembly in the year 2000 had denied authority to the provincial auditor general to audit its accounts and decided to retain the services of external auditors for this purpose. But, in fact, it failed to do so and the accounts went unaudited for 2 years. See: second reading statement of Ms. E. Marshall in *House of Assembly Proceedings*, ibid.

[43] S.Q. 2011, c. 17; R.S.Q., c L-6.1 (the title of the Act in the French language is *Loi concernant la lutte contre la corruption*). On 23 September 2014, the Quebec National Assembly gave first read-

law that "pertains to corruption, malfeasance, collusion, fraud or influence peddling in, for example, awarding, obtaining or performing contracts granted, in the exercise of their functions, by a body or a person belonging to the public sector"; "misuse of public funds or public property or a gross mismanagement or contracts within the public sector"; and "directing or counselling" such misconduct.[44] This statute appears somewhat inspired by the model of the European Anti-Fraud Office, established in 1999.[45]

The *Anti-Corruption Act* establishes the positions of public officers known as the Anti-Corruption Commissioner and the Associate Commissioner. Public sector employees or, indeed, any person[46] may disclose "wrongdoing" to the Anti-Corruption Commissioner who then assigns Commission staff to examine and to investigate the information, as appropriate. The Anti-Corruption Commissioner issues two public reports annually and makes recommendations to government on any "wrongdoing" disclosed. Though the Anti-Corruption Commissioner is generally required to protect the identity of a person making a disclosure of information, the Act makes an exception to permit disclosure of personal identify information to the Director of Criminal and Penal Prosecutions if the disclosed information relates to criminal misconduct.[47]

The Act's specific emphasis on corruption in relation to the "awarding, obtaining or performing" of public sector contracts reflects concerns revealed by fairly recent scandals in Quebec, particularly in the construction industry. The Quebec statute is unique in conferring a proactive role on the Associate Commissioner who essentially directs teams of auditors to review public sector contracts.

The Quebec statute addresses whistleblowing and whistleblower protection from reprisal by making it an offence punishable by fines of up to $20,000, if the defendant is a natural person, and of up to $250,000, if a legal person (corporation).[48] While reprisal is not defined, a reprisal is presumed if it involves "the demotion, suspension, termination of employment, or transfer of a person… or any disciplinary

ing to Bill 192, *An Act to amend the Anti-Corruption Act as concerns protection of whistleblowers* which would broaden the protection of whistleblowers by enacting a scheme of protection similar to that in other jurisdictions in Canada. As a private member's Bill from an opposition party, it is not expected that Bill 192 will be enacted but it may foretell a future legislative initiative by government.

[44] ibid. Art 2.

[45] See Council Regulation (EURATOM) No 1074/1999 (25 May 1999) concerning investigations conducted by the European Anti-Fraud Office (OLAF).

[46] Above n 43 at Art. 26: "Any person who wishes to disclose a wrongdoing may do so by disclosing information to the Commissioner that the person believes could show that a wrongdoing has been committed or is about to be committed, or that could show that the person has been asked to commit a wrongdoing."

[47] Above n 24 at Art. 31. This disclosure of identity serves to facilitate the investigation and prosecution of criminal misconduct by the Director of Criminal and Penal Prosecutions.

[48] ibid. at Art. 33.

or other measure that adversely affects the employment or working conditions of such a person."[49]

Though the federal and provincial statutes impose obligations on persons to whom a disclosure is made to protect a whistleblower's identity, these obligations are not absolute. A public sector employee who wishes to protect his or her identity is generally not able to make a disclosure anonymously using the internal procedures provided by the public interest disclosure statutes. It is for this reason that the authors of a text on whistleblowing note the advantages of making a disclosure through the good offices of legal counsel.[50] The authors note that the standards of professional conduct applicable to lawyers can serve to protect the identity of a client and thus facilitate an anonymous disclosure of wrongdoing.[51]

General Statutes Including Protection of Whistleblowers

Criminal Law

Criminal law in Canada is a matter within the exclusive jurisdiction of Parliament; as a result, criminal law is uniform across Canada.

The *Criminal Code of Canada*, section 425.1 protects the whistleblower employee by making it an offence for an employer to "take a disciplinary measure against, demote, terminate or otherwise adversely affect the employment" of an employee in order to induce the employee not to disclose information that the employer has breached either federal or provincial law or, if the employee has made such a disclosure, to retaliate against the employee.[52] The prohibition is broadly

---

[49] ibid.

[50] I Cantin et JM Cantin, La dénonciation d'actes répréhensibles en milieu de travail ou Whistleblowing, above n 6, at 43.

[51] ibid. the authors quote M Proulx and D Layton, *Ethics and Canadian Criminal Law* (Toronto, Irwin Law, 2001) at 194:

> Where legal-professional privilege does apply, there is no doubt that a client's identity will be confidential within the meaning of professional conduct. The ethical rules in Canada go much further, however, placing a general obligation on counsel not to reveal the identity of a client or the fact of being consulted unless required by the nature of the matter.

Cantin et Cantin, then add, at p. 43, footnote 79: "Il nous semble que ce principe s'applique tant aux matière criminelles que civiles."

[52] *Criminal Code of Canada*, R.S.C. 1985, c C-46 as amended by An Act to amend the Criminal Code (capital markets fraud and evidence gathering), S.C. 2004, c 3, s 6 which inserted the following section:

> Threats and Retaliation Against Employees/Punishment
>
> 425.1 (1) No employer or person acting on behalf of an employer or in a position of authority in respect of an employee of the employer shall take a disciplinary measure against, demote, terminate or otherwise adversely affect the employment of such an employee, or threaten to do so,

expressed to apply to the employer and also to a "person acting on behalf of an employer or in a position of authority in respect of an employee". The retaliation offence arises when an employer acts after the employee has disclosed information to "a person whose duties include the enforcement of federal or provincial law" which obviously includes both police officers and persons with particular responsibilities; for example, in relation to environmental or health laws.

Parliament enacted these "compelling silence" and retaliation offences in 2004 as part of a package of legislative amendments addressing insider trading and the capital markets. The wording is not specific to insider trading and is obviously broad enough to apply to whistleblower employees generally. To date, there do not appear to have been any criminal prosecutions of employers for violating *Criminal Code*, section 425.1.[53]

Employment Standards

Federal, provincial, and territorial legislation establish minimum employment standards in relation to such matters as minimum wages, maximum hours of work, vacations and holidays, leaves of absence from work, sexual harassment, layoff, and termination of employment.[54] These statutes also prohibit an employer from taking reprisal action against an employee who makes a complaint that the employer has breached a minimum standard. In such instances, the complaint is personal in the

---

(a) with the intent to compel the employee to abstain from providing information to a person whose duties include the enforcement of federal or provincial law, respecting an offence that the employee believes has been or is being committed contrary to this or any other federal or provincial Act or regulation by the employer or an officer or employee of the employer or, if the employer is a corporation, by one or more of its directors; or

(b) with the intent to retaliate against the employee because the employee has provided information referred to in paragraph (a) to a person whose duties include the enforcement of federal or provincial law.

[53] No case reports of persons being charged with an offence under this section were identified in an electronic database search and a review of the commercially published annotated editions of the *Criminal Code*. Section 425.1 has been referenced in *Anderson v IMTT-Québec Inc.*, 2013 FCA 90 (CanLII); *Merk v International Association of Bridge, Structural, Ornamental and Reinforcing Iron Workers, Local 771*, [2005] 3 SCR 425; *Cadillac Fairview Corporation Ltd. v Standard Parking of Canada Ltd.*, 2003 CanLII 23598 (ON SC); and *El-Helou v Courts Administration Service*, 2011 CanLII 93945 (CA PSDPT). In *Anderson*, above, Mainville J.A. commented:

> – [44] The purpose of section 425.1 of the *Criminal Code* is not to allow an employee to make with impunity, reckless complaints to public authorities and without regard for the employer's internal mechanisms or respect for work colleagues. The provision does not allow an employee to avoid the consequences of a dismissal in progress by filing reckless complaints to public authorities against his or her employer and work colleagues. –

[54] At the federal level, such employment standards are found in the Canada Labour Code, R.S.C. 1985, c L-2, Part III "Standard Hours, Wages, Vacations and Holidays", ss 166–267. This statute only applies to employees in federally regulated employment, for example, persons engaged in interprovincial and international transportation, and to all private employees in the three northern territories.

sense that, by making a complaint, the employee acts in his or her self-interest in anticipation that it will result in an order that the employer comply with the standard and compensate the employee in respect of the standard.

Employment standards legislation protects employees who provide information or give evidence that an employer has breached the statutory standards. Typically, such information is provided to an inspector appointed under the statute and the evidence is presented before an administrative board with responsibility to adjudicate complaints. Thus, the protection is limited to that process.

The federal statute, the *Canada Labour Code*,[55] makes it an offence for an employer to retaliate against an employee who files a complaint or gives information or evidence and, upon successful prosecution, the employer is subject to a fine not exceeding 5000 dollars.[56] Territorial legislation follows the same approach.[57]

The provincial statutes generally take a different approach to enforcement. The prohibition on employer retaliation is itself an employment standard which can be made the subject of a complaint to be investigated and adjudicated. Generally, offence provisions become relevant, after final adjudication, if the employer fails to comply with the order for compliance or compensation issued by the administrative tribunal. In some provinces, such as Saskatchewan, offence provisions are used to invoke the jurisdiction of the provincial court (an inferior court) which, after trial, delivers a verdict on the specific charge(s) alleging that the employer breached one or more employment standards. Upon a conviction, the court is authorized to order civil remedies to the employee such as the payment of wages and, if discharged contrary to the statute, reinstatement.[58]

Three provinces – New Brunswick, Saskatchewan and Quebec – provide broader whistleblower protection in their respective employment standards statutes. For example, the New Brunswick Legislature amended the employment standards statute in 1988 to provide that "an employer shall not dismiss, suspend, lay off, penalize, discipline or discriminate against an employee if the reason therefor is related in any way to... (c) the giving of information or evidence by the employee against the employer with respect to the alleged violation of any Provincial or federal Act or regulation by the employer while carrying on the employer's business".[59] Thus, the protection is not restricted to a complaint of a breach of the employment standards statute itself. Saskatchewan amended its employment stan-

---

[55] ibid.

[56] ibid. s 256(1): "Every person who... (c) discharges, threatens to discharge or otherwise discriminates against a person because that person (i) has testified or is about to testify in any proceedings or inquiry taken or had under this Part, or (ii) has given any information to the Minister or an inspector regarding the wages, hours of work, annual vacation or conditions of work of an employee, is guilty of an offence and liable on summary conviction to a fine not exceeding five thousand dollars."

[57] e.g. *Labour Standards Act*, R.S.N.W.T. 1988, c L-1, s 68(b)(i).

[58] *Labour Standards Act*, R.S.S. 1978, c L-1, ss 87(1) and 89.

[59] *Employment Standards Act*, S.N.B. 1982, c E-7.2 as amended by S.N.B. 1988, c 59, s 9.

dards legislation to provide similar whistleblower protection in 1994 and Quebec did so in 2011.[60]

In 2005, the Saskatchewan employment standards statute came before the Supreme Court of Canada for interpretation in *Merk v. International Association of Bridge, Structural, Ornamental and Reinforcing Iron Workers, Local 771*.[61] The Saskatchewan statute protects an employee who has or proposes to disclose information "to a lawful authority" about an offence contrary to federal or provincial law.[62] In *Merk*, the bookkeeper and office manager of a local trade union disclosed instances of alleged financial misconduct by her immediate supervisors. She disclosed the information, not to the police, but to other members of the union local, including her father, a former president of the union local. These persons then disclosed the information to the president of the international union of which the local was an affiliate. In response, the international union sent a representative to investigate the matter. After release of the investigator's report, the employee herself wrote to the president of the international union concerning her complaint of alleged misconduct by her supervisors. The union local subsequently terminated her employment and the matter came before the courts as a prosecution against the employer for breach of the provincial statute.

The critical issue was the meaning of "lawful authority" for the purposes of the provincial statute. Should it be given a narrow interpretation as referring only to persons with authority to address the specific misconduct, such as the police? Or should it be given a broader interpretation to include representatives of the international union? The trial and appeal courts in Saskatchewan interpreted the phrase narrowly as referring to persons exercising public authority, such as the police, and not encompassing private authority such as that of the international union. The majority of the Supreme Court of Canada took a different approach. Referring to the general acceptance in labour and employment law of the "up the ladder" approach to reconcile the employee's duty of loyalty to the employer and the public interest in whistleblowing, the Court interpreted "law authority" expansively to include:

---

[60] See *Labour Standards Act*, R.S.S. 1978, c L-1, s 74 as amended by S.S. 1994, c 39, s 41 and *Loi sur les normes du travail*, L.R.Q., c N-1.1, art 122 as amended by L.Q. 2011, c. 17,art 56. The Quebec statute is expressly linked to disclosures of wrongdoing covered by the provincial anti-corruption legislation.

[61] *Merk*, above n 53.

[62] Above n 60 s 74:

Discrimination by employer prohibited

74(1) No employer shall discharge or threaten to discharge, take any reprisal against or in any manner discriminate against an employee because the employee:

(a) has reported or proposed to report to a lawful authority any activity that is or is likely to result in an offence pursuant to an Act or an Act of the Parliament of Canada; or

(b) has testified or may be called on to testify in an investigation or proceeding pursuant to an Act or an Act of the Parliament of Canada.

(2) Subsection (1) does not apply where the actions of an employee are vexatious.

> not only the police or other agents of the state having authority to deal with the activity complained of "as an offence" but also individuals within the employer organization who exercise lawful authority over the employee(s) complained about, or over the activity that is or is likely to result in the offence.[63]

Thus, the statutory whistleblower protection protected the employee when she disclosed information to the international union; she had complied with the "up the ladder" principle. Accordingly, termination of her employment constituted a prohibited act of reprisal.

Labour Relations

Federal, provincial, and territorial legislation on labour rights to collective bargaining expressly protect employees who "testify or otherwise participate in proceedings" under the statute from reprisal or discriminatory treatment by the employer.[64] Generally, an act of reprisal constitutes an unfair labour practice because the employees are normally engaged in their individual and collective rights to participate in the formation and management of a trade union. The legislation equally applies to trade unions which take reprisal action against employees who testify or otherwise participate in proceedings adverse to the interests of the trade union.

In addition to treating reprisal actions as an unfair labour practice, the federal legislation also makes such conduct an offence punishable by a fine not exceeding $5000.[65]

The relevant statute in Newfoundland and Labrador differs from that in other provinces and at the federal level by extending the testimonial protection from employer reprisal to employees who "testify or otherwise participate in proceedings under this Act <u>or another law</u>" [emphasis added].[66] The statute also protects an employee from reprisal because the employee made "a disclosure that he or she may be required to make in a proceeding under this Act or other law".[67]

---

[63] *Merk* above note 53 at para 38 (per Binnie J.). The Court rejected the argument that the statutory provision was penal in nature and should, therefore, be interpreted narrowly. Instead, the Court concluded that a plain meaning approach to interpretation should be informed by the labour relations nature of the statute and, thus, given a large and liberal construction. Between the date of the oral argument before the Supreme Court of Canada on 10 February 2005 and the date of decision on 24 November 2005, the Saskatchewan Legislature on 27 May 2005 amended the Act to define "lawful authority" to include "any person directly or indirectly responsible for supervising the employee". See: *An Act to amend The Labour Standards Act*, S.S. 2005, c 16 s 8.

[64] For example: *Industrial Relations Act*, R.S.N.B. 1973, c I-4, s 5(3); *Labour Relations Act, 1995*, S.O. 1995, c 1 Schedule A, s 87(1); *Labour Relations Code*, R.S.B.C. 1996, c 244, s 5(1); *Canada Labour Code*, R.S.C. 1985, c L-2, s 94(3)(iii) [re employer], s 94 [re trade union], s 147 [general prohibition], s 256(1) [offence provision].

[65] Canada Labour Code, ibid. s 256(1).

[66] *Labour Relations Act*, R.S.N.L. 1990, c L-1, s. 25(1)(a).

[67] ibid. s 25(1)(b).

Occupational Health and Safety

Canadian occupational health and safety legislation focusses on the mutual responsibilities of employers and employees to take positive measures to promote workplace health and safety. The legislation provides for the establishment of standards relating, for example, to the safe use of equipment, the use and storage of chemicals, and the establishment and duties of workplace health and safety committees and officers. An employee, faced with what is reasonably believed to be an unsafe working condition, is obliged to report the matter "up the ladder".

The first level of disclosure is to the employee's supervisor who, with the employee, is obligated to attempt to resolve the matter. If not resolved, the matter may proceed to further levels of internal review involving employee health and safety representatives and eventually health and safety officers appointed for the purposes of the Act. Pending resolution of the matter, an employee may refuse to operate equipment or refuse to undertake an assigned task if the employee reasonably believes the circumstances pose a danger to the employee or to another employee.

The legislation uniformly prohibits the employer from taking or threatening to take any disciplinary action (reprisal) because an employee has exercised rights or obligations declared by the legislation, including making a formal complaint; disclosed information to any person performing duties required by the legislation; or testifies at an inquiry or proceeding held for the purposes of the legislation. As expressed in the *Canada Labour Code*, Part II, "Occupational Health and Safety", section 147:

> 147. No employer shall dismiss, suspend, lay off or demote an employee, impose a financial or other penalty on an employee, or refuse to pay an employee remuneration in respect of any period that the employee would, but for the exercise of the employee's rights under this Part, have worked, or take any disciplinary action against or threaten to take any such action against an employee because the employee
>
> (a) has testified or is about to testify in a proceeding taken or an inquiry held under this Part;
> (b) has provided information to a person engaged in the performance of duties under this Part regarding the conditions of work affecting the health or safety of the employee or of any other employee of the employer; or
> (c) has acted in accordance with this Part or has sought the enforcement of any of the provisions of this Part.[68]

Similar employer reprisal provisions exist in the relevant provincial legislation.[69]

---

[68] Canada Labour Code, above n 64.

[69] For example, the Ontario *Occupational Health and Safety Act*, R.S.O. 1990, c O.1, s. 50(1) states:

> 50.(1) No employer or person acting on behalf of an employer shall,
>
> (a) dismiss or threaten to dismiss a worker;
> (b) discipline or suspend or threaten to discipline or suspend a worker;
> (c) impose any penalty upon a worker; or
> (d) intimidate or coerce a worker,

Environmental Protection

Environmental protection legislation has a logical connection with the contemporary whistleblower employee. Yet, the legislation in a number of provinces is silent on whistleblower protection. In many instances, the legislation is somewhat dated so that express inclusion of employee whistleblower protection may be expected in the future. But, notwithstanding the symbolic value of express whistle blower protection provisions in such legislation, it is also a reasonable inference that such provisions are considered unnecessary because of the protection provided at common law and civil law; the *Criminal Code*; in employment standards and occupational health and safety legislation; and the general whistleblower protections available to public sector employees.

Some Canadian jurisdictions include specific protection for whistleblower employees, particularly from employer reprisal. For example, the *Canadian Environmental Protection Act, 1999*, sections 16(4) and 96(4) prohibit an employer from taking reprisal action against an employee who discloses to an enforcement officer, or other such official, information relating to the release of a toxic substance into the environment.[70]

Ontario's legislation addresses the whistleblower employee in two statutes. First, the *Environmental Protection Act*,[71] section 174(2) protects from employer reprisal any employee who "has given or may give information to the Ministry or a provincial officer or has been or may be called upon to testify in a proceeding related to one of those Acts or a regulation under one of those Acts" (referring to named statutes listed elsewhere in the Act). An employee subjected to reprisal (dismissal, discipline, intimidation or coercion) may file a complaint with the Ontario Labour Relations Board for redress in the form of reinstatement to employment, if dis-

---

> because the worker has acted in compliance with this Act or the regulations or an order made thereunder, has sought the enforcement of this Act or the regulations or has given evidence in a proceeding in respect of the enforcement of this Act or the regulations or in an inquest under the *Coroners Act*.

For Quebec, see *Loi sur la Santé et la sécurité du travail*, L.R.Q., c S-2.1, art. 227 and for New Brunswick, see: *Occupational Health and Safety Act*, S.N.B. 1983, c O-0.2, s 24. The provisions in other provinces are similar.

[70] S.C. 1999, c 33, s. 96:

> 96. (1) Where a person has knowledge of the occurrence or likelihood of a release into the environment of a substance specified on the List of Toxic Substances in Schedule 1, but the person is not required to report the matter under this Act, the person may report any information relating to the release or likely release to an enforcement officer or to any person to whom a report may be made under section 95.
>
> (4) Despite any other Act of Parliament, no employer shall dismiss, suspend, demote, discipline, harass or otherwise disadvantage an employee, or deny an employee a benefit of employment, by reason that
>
> (a) the employee has made a report under subsection (1)....

[71] R.S.O. 1990 c E.19.

charged, or the payment of compensation. By section 174(10), the burden of proof rests with the employer to establish that it did not engage in an act of reprisal.

Second, the *Environmental Bill of Rights, 1993*,[72] Part VII, sections 103–116 similarly addresses the challenge of employer reprisals. Again, a complaint of reprisal is adjudicated by the Ontario Labour Relations Board which may order appropriate redress, i.e., reinstatement or payment of compensation. In section 104(s), the *Environmental Bill of Rights* identifies the conduct which motivated the employer reprisal as including that the employee did in good faith "4. Comply with or seek the enforcement of a prescribed Act, regulation or instrument"; "5. Give information to an appropriate authority for the purposes of an investigation, review or hearing related to a prescribed policy, Act, regulation or instrument"; or "6. Give evidence in a proceeding under this Act or under a prescribed Act".[73]

In essence, the federal and Ontario legislation mirror each other in prohibiting employer reprisal.

Miscellaneous

Statutory protection from employment related reprisal action is found in statutes of some provinces relating to vulnerable persons in society; for example, children, seniors, adults in need of protection, and foreign workers in vulnerable employment positions. These statutes prohibit employers from taking reprisal action because an employee has made a complaint in good faith about the care or condition of certain vulnerable persons in nursing homes, seniors' residences, child protection services, the care of health professionals, and vulnerable foreign workers employed as live-in care-givers.[74] Most provinces, however, have yet to enact such specific protections.

In 2011, the Legislature of Newfoundland and Labrador enacted specific whistleblower protection for employees who report that an adult person is in need of protection, sought advice about making such a report, or cooperated in an investigation of a report under the *Adult Protection Act*.[75] The adult person in need of protection would typically be a resident of a long term care or assisted living facility and the whistleblower would be an employee who became aware of a situation of concern. The provision prohibits any act of reprisal against such an employee and defines reprisal in the usual manner, applicable to employees, in terms of disciplinary action – i.e., demotion, termination, any measure that adversely affects employ-

[72] S.O. 1993, c 28.

[73] By regulation, a list of more than 20 provincial statutes are proscribed for the purposes of the *Environmental Bill of Rights*. See: *General Regulation* under *Environmental Bill of Rights* (1993) On. Reg. 73/94, s 3.

[74] For example: *Child, Family and Community Service Act*, R.S.B.C. 1996, c 46, s 101.1; *Nursing Homes Act*, R.S.O. 1990, c N.7, s 243; *Regulated Health Professions Act, 1991*, S.O. 1991, c 18, s 92.1; and *Employment Protection for Foreign Nationals Act*, S.O. 2009, c 32, ss 10, 24 and 41.

[75] *Adult Protection Act*, S.N.L. 2011, c A-4.01, s 31.

ment or working conditions, or a threat to take any such measure.[76] The statutory provision goes further and provides that a person taking a reprisal action is "subject to appropriate disciplinary action, including termination of employment".[77]

This more recent Newfoundland and Labrador whistleblower protection is in sharp contrast to that available to a person who discloses information about a child in need of protection in that province. The 2010 *Children and Youth Care and Protection Act*[78] merely states: "A person shall not interfere with or harass a person who gives information under this section." Express protection from employer reprisal would seem to enhance the position of both the whistleblower employee and the vulnerable child for the purposes of the statute.

Effectiveness of Whistleblower Protection Legislation

The effectiveness of federal and provincial whistleblower legislation is questionable particularly in its reliance on internal disclosure mechanisms, i.e., the "up the ladder" principle. To be truly effective, employees must have confidence in the confidentiality of the internal procedures established by the legislation or they will seek other venues such as, for example, an anonymous disclosure. Statistics gleaned from annual reports and the websites of official government agencies responsible to investigate and administer federal and provincial whistleblower legislation are informative.

The website of the federal Integrity Commissioner includes reports of investigations of disclosures of wrongdoing and of referrals of reprisal complaints to the Disclosure Protection Tribunal. There were two wrongdoing reports in 2012, five in 2013 and, to date, two in 2014.[79] Of these nine investigative reports, four involved alleged misuse of public funds, two involved alleged gross mismanagement, one concerned a breach of privacy, one concerned conflict of interest and inappropriate office behaviour, and one concerned alleged patronage in making employment decisions.

The four disclosures alleging abuse of public funds concerned: (1) a regional director of a government department who was revealed to have falsified travel claims and failed to keep proper financial records; (2) the director general of a government agency who used the employer's supplies and staff to conduct a private business during working hours; (3) two border control officers who, respectively, misused the employer's credit card for private purposes and breached the code of conduct by affiliating with persons known to be associated with crime and stating

[76] ibid. s 2(o).

[77] ibid. at s 31(2).

[78] S.N.L. 2010, c C-12.2, s 11(7).

[79] Website of the Public Sector Integrity Commissioner of Canada accessed on 28 November 2013 and 22 November 2014 at www.psic-ispc.gc.ca/eng under "Case Reports" and "Referrals to the Tribunal".

that he would not treat such persons objectively and professionally; (4) and a chief executive officer of a public corporation who was held responsible for the overpayment of retirement and severance allowances to two employees which wrongdoing was not determined to be gross mismanagement.

In two of the other reports, the disclosures of alleged wrongdoing were held not substantiated upon investigation. In the first, two managers had issued apprentice boat pilot licences to two persons who did not satisfy all the qualifications for the licence. The two managers issued the licenses because of problems recruiting employees to fill the vacant positions and in the knowledge that, as apprentices, the two license holders would be subject to supervision and training. In the second, a management level employee circulated to certain other employees a notice letter from the Integrity Commissioner advising of an investigation of a disclosure of alleged wrongdoing involving two named employees. The investigative report concluded the management level employee had failed in his duty to protect the identity of persons involved in the disclosure process, as required by the Act, but, instead of being a malicious act, it had been a faulty attempt to cooperate with the investigation. The report also noted that the matter was the subject of a separate complaint under the federal *Privacy Act*.[80] The remaining disclosure investigation report concerned allegations of gross mismanagement involving harassment and other abusive behaviour by the chairperson of an administrative tribunal against tribunal members and support staff. The report substantiated the allegations.

These reports include specific recommendations to improve practices and procedures to avoid similar acts of wrongdoing in the future but, as mentioned, do not necessarily include specific recommendations for specific employer responses to the wrongdoing employee (such as termination of employment). The published reports do indicate the employer's response to each recommendation and whether imposed that response included disciplinary action against the wrongdoer.

The federal Integrity Commissioner's website includes six instances in which reprisal complaints were referred to the Disclosure Protection Tribunal. Five of these referrals concerned termination of employment and one concerned the denial of security clearance. The Tribunal's website indicates that the five termination complaints were settled in mediation. The website identifies the security clearance matter as still an active file and that a preliminary hearing had been conducted on 31 August 2011. What the website does not report is that this matter was taken on judicial review to the Federal Court which quashed the Integrity Commissioner's decision and ordered the Commissioner to undertake further investigation.[81]

Nova Scotia, it will be recalled, was the first Canadian jurisdiction to establish whistleblower protection legislation for public employees. From 2004 to 2011 (when the provincial statute came into force to replace the previous regulation), the number of complaints to the Ombudsman far exceeded the number of internal dis-

[80] R.S.C. 1985, c P-21.

[81] Website of the Public Servants Disclosure Protection Tribunal accessed on 28 November 2013 and 22 November 2014 at www.psdpt-tpfd.gc.ca/Home-eng.html under "Cases". See also: *El-Helou v Courts Administration Service*, above n 53.

closures to the deputy department heads or their designates.[82] The Ombudsman received a total of 57 disclosures compared to 7 disclosures to the deputy department heads. These disclosures resulted in findings of only three instances of wrongdoing after investigations were completed.[83] In general, the deputy heads who received disclosures referred the matters directly to the Ombudsman – though in two instances, the deputy heads were able to resolve the matters themselves.

Interestingly, the 2007–2008 Annual Report on the Nova Scotia regulation reported the results of a survey of government employees concerning whistleblower protection under the then regulation and policies.[84] Sixty-six percent of employees who responded to the survey expressed awareness of the disclosure policy; 50 % were aware of the point of contact for making a disclosure; and 37 % responded that they would feel comfortable using the reporting process.[85] The annual report for the years following the survey showed relatively significant increases in the number of disclosures to the Ombudsman, from 1 in 2006–2007, to 15 in 2008–2009, to 23 in 2009–2010, and 26 in 2010–2011. Still, the numbers of disclosures remained relatively modest.

In New Brunswick, the statistical information about the 2007 provincial whistleblower statute (in effect from 2008) indicates a similar lack of use by public sector employees. Of 26 government departments and agencies listed on the government's main website, 8 addressed the statute expressly in its 2008–2009 annual report and 1 included the statute in the list of statutes for which the department or agency has responsibilities. Annual reports for 2011–2012 show an improvement with 11 departments or agencies addressing the statute expressly and 2 including it in the list of statutes. Eight of the 2011–2012 annual reports do not even mention the statute, including the Department of Health, the Department of Healthy and Inclusive Communities, and the Department of Justice and Consumer Affairs. One annual report, for the Department of Public Safety, reported that it had created an internal website to increase employee awareness about the whistleblower statute.[86] No departmental annual report, including those for 2012–2013, records any instance of an employee making any disclosure under the statute or referring any matter.

The annual reports of the office of the New Brunswick Conflict of Interest Commissioner for 2009 and 2010 reflect marginally greater interest in the disclosure legislation.[87] The Commissioner reported receiving 13 "queries/disclosures" in 2009 and 11 in 2010. Most of these "queries/disclosures" (13 of the 24 total) were

---

[82] Nova Scotia Public Service Commission, *Annual Report on the Civil Service Disclosure of Wrongdoing Regulation and Policy*, annually 2004–2005 to 2010–2011.

[83] ibid.

[84] Nova Scotia Public Service Commission, *Annual Report on the Civil Service Disclosure of Wrongdoing Regulation and Policy 2007–2008* at 4.

[85] ibid.

[86] Department of Public Safety, New Brunswick Emergency Measures Organization, *Annual Report 2009–2010* at 93.

[87] These annual reports are no longer available on the website of the Conflict of Interest Commissioner but were provided by the Commissioner's Office as email attachments.

reported as not relating to matters within the scope of the provincial *Public Interest Disclosure Act*; 8 of the 24 were described as "pending" in the sense of awaiting further information or referred to other procedures; 2 were simply general inquiries about the commissioner's role and function; and 1 was from a person who wanted to be anonymous and therefore declined to make a disclosure. In both annual reports, the Commissioner recommended that the Act be amended to provide for disciplinary sanctions to be made applicable to persons who take reprisal actions against an employee making a disclosure. In June 2011, the Ombudsman replaced the Conflict of Interest Commissioner's role under the statute and reported in its 2011–2012 annual report receiving four enquiries and one matter which was subsequently withdrawn in favour of an informal resolution.[88]

In Ontario, the annual reports of the Office of the Integrity Commissioner for the years 2008–2009 to 2012–2013 do not report substantial activity. The Ontario legislation requires the Commissioner to refer a disclosure of wrongdoing for investigation by a senior executive in the government department or agency concerned. The number of such referrals for investigation was seven in 2008–2009; three in 2009–2010; eight in 2010–2011; three in 2011–2012; and two in 2012–2013.[89] Many of these referrals resulted in findings of no wrongdoing which findings, on review, were accepted by the Commissioner. Nor, it should be noted, have the statutory prohibitions on reprisal resulted in significant work for the Labour Relations Board of Ontario in relation to employees governed by a collective agreement or the Public Service Grievance Board in relation to nonunionized employees.

A relevant decision of interest from the Public Service Grievance Board of Ontario is *Binda v. Ontario (Environment)*.[90] This 2011 decision addressed a preliminary objection to the adjudication of a reprisal complaint because of a claimed disclosure under the *Public Service of Ontario Act*.[91] The complainant, Binda, a senior manager in the Ministry of the Environment, considered himself harassed and discriminated against as a member of a visible minority. He felt that other employees received preferential treatment from the employer to the detriment of his career advancement. This was the very wrongdoing that he disclosed as violations of the provincial *Human Rights Code* and of the *Occupational Health and Safety Act*. Subsequently, a workplace discrimination and harassment complaint was brought against Binda himself. Before the Grievance Board, Binda asserted his belief that somehow the fact of his "disclosure" had become known to his supervisors and co-workers and that the workplace discrimination and harassment complaint brought against himself was an act of reprisal (along with other alleged discriminatory acts against him by other employees).

---

[88] Office of the Ombudsman, New Brunswick: *Annual Report 2011–2012* (May 2013) at 16. The 2012–2013 Annual Report is not yet available on the Ombudsman's website.

[89] See Office of the Integrity Commissioner of Ontario, *Annual Report*, available at www.oico.on.ca (accessed on 25 and 29 November 2013).

[90] *Binda v Ontario (Environment)*, 2011 CanLII 93306 (ON PSGB).

[91] Above n 30.

The Integrity Commissioner had declined to deal with Binda's reprisal complaint because it was essentially an employment matter that could be appropriately addressed through grievance proceedings before the Public Service Grievance Board or, as a human rights complaint, before the Human Rights Commission. In making this determination, the Commissioner characterized the matters as falling within one of the exclusions from her jurisdiction to review a complaint, being an employment matter subject to an existing dispute resolution mechanism (per section 117 of the *Act*).

When the matter came before the Grievance Board, it dismissed the employer's preliminary objection to the reprisal complaint. The employer had characterized Binda's reprisal complaint as, in substance, a general harassment complaint. The Grievance Board disagreed and held "that to the extent the complainant's disclosure to the Deputy Minister included allegations of breach of a statute such as the *Human Rights Code*, it qualifies as a disclosure of wrongdoing"[92] within the meaning of the whistleblower provisions of the *Public Service of Ontario Act*.

Though the *Binda* decision is certainly defensible, it and other decisions like it will undoubtedly lead to future amendments to provincial whistleblower protection legislation to avoid duplication of procedures in relation to what is essentially the same matter and thereby promote administrative efficiencies.

In Quebec, the annual report of the Anti-Corruption Commissioner for 2011–2012 states that the office received 146 corruption complaints and that, after review, it processed 38 complaints. Of these 38 complaints, it referred 17 for investigation, 16 for audit reviews, and 5 for review by external agencies.[93] As of the end of the 2011–2012 reporting period, the Commission's work had resulted in the arrest of 8 persons on 12 criminal charges relating to embezzlement, fraud, and intimidation.[94] The 2012–2013 annual report recorded a substantial increase in activity with the number of complaints rising to 500.[95] After review, 206 complaints were referred for investigation, 42 for audit reviews and 3 to external agencies. The annual report also records that the Commission's work in 2012–2013 resulted in 66 criminal charges (53 against persons and 13 against corporate bodies), 11 other charges, and the arrest of 56 persons.[96] As noted above, much of this activity relates to allegations of corruption in the public sector construction industry which is the subject of a much publicized commission of inquiry.[97]

---

[92] ibid. at para 22.

[93] *Le rapport annuel de gestion du Commissaire à la lutte contre la corruption 2011–2012* (Gouvernement du Québec, 2012) at 37. (The annual report is accessible online at www.upac.gouv.qc.ca).

[94] ibid.

[95] *Le rapport annuel de gestion du Commissaire à la lutte contre la corruption 2012–2013* (Gouvernement du Québec, 2013) at 38. (The annual report is accessible online at www.upac.gouv.qc.ca).

[96] ibid.

[97] The Commission of Inquiry on the Awarding and Management of Public Contracts in the Construction Industry, commonly known as the Charbonneau Commission after its chairperson, Judge France Charbonneau. The Commission was created on 19 October 2011 and resulted in the

Courts and Whistleblower Protection

As mentioned, Canadian courts have long accepted the "up the ladder" principle as an appropriate balance of an employee's duties of loyalty, good faith, and confidentiality to the employer and the public interest in disclosure of wrongdoing, particularly wrongdoing involving illegal and harmful activity.

On facts which arose before the coming into force of the *Canadian Charter of Rights and Freedoms* in 1982, the Supreme Court of Canada clearly affirmed the right of public sector employees to a measure of freedom to express themselves on government policies and practices in a manner consistent with their role as public sector employees. In *Fraser v. Public Service Staff Relations Board*,[98] an employee who worked as an auditor with a department of the federal government took exception to the government's plan to require use of the metric system in Canada. Obviously, the work performed by Fraser, as an employee, was unrelated to the policy he criticized. His public commentary began rather innocently with a letter to a local newspaper and advanced to the level of national media appearances. Over time, his public statements became intemperate to the point that he characterized the federal government, and the then Prime Minister, to the authoritarian and undemocratic regime of Nazi Germany. Eventually, the government employer had enough and dismissed Fraser from his employment. Fraser grieved his dismissal as unjust.

The Supreme Court of Canada, on appeal, sought to balance Fraser's individual right to freedom of expression in a free and democratic society with his duty, as a federal public sector employee, to exercise some restraint in such expression "in order to ensure that the public service is perceived as impartial and effective in fulfilling its duties".[99] The Court held that a public sector employee owes the same duty of duty of loyalty that is owed by every employee to every employer; the duty of loyalty, in the case of a government employee, being to the employer and not to the political party forming the government. In dismissing the employee's appeal, the Court recognized limits to that loyalty:

> in some circumstances a public servant may actively and publicly express opposition to the policies of a government. This would be appropriate if, for example, the Government were engaged in illegal acts, or if its policies jeopardized the life, health or safety of the public servant or others, or if the public servant's criticism had no impact on his or her ability to perform effectively the duties of a public servant or on the public perception of that ability. But, having stated these qualifications (and there may be others), it is my view that <u>a public servant must not engage, as the appellant did in the present case, in sustained and highly visible attacks on major Government policies</u>. In conducting himself in this way the appellant, in my view, displayed a lack of loyalty to the Government that was inconsistent with his duties as an employee of the Government.[100] [emphasis added]

---

resignations of the mayors of several communities in Quebec as well as the laying of criminal charges against a number of persons.

[98] *Fraser v Public Service Staff Relations Board*, [1985] 2 SCR 455.

[99] ibid. at para 30.

[100] ibid. at para 41.

Thus, public expression by public sector employees is considered by the courts in a contextual manner. Factors include the position held by the employee and the form and nature of the expression. Evidence of impairment of the employee's ability to perform the functions of his or her position is not always necessary if it is reasonable to infer such impairment. Given the very public and vociferous nature of Fraser's expression, the inference was held properly made in the circumstances.

Considering whistleblowing as a form of expression, Canadian courts generally protect the public sector whistleblower by considering factors similar to those applicable to private sector employees when applying the "just cause" standard. The significant difference between public and private sector employees in relation to the exercise of freedom of expression is that the *Canadian Charter of Rights and Freedoms* applies to the federal, provincial, and territorial governments acting as employer but does not apply to private sector employers (that is, employers that are not "government").[101]

In *R. v. National Post*,[102] the Supreme Court of Canada described the essential role of the whistleblower in modern democratic society:

> [28] It is well established that freedom of expression protects readers and listeners as well as writers and speakers. It is in the context of the public right to knowledge about matters of public interest that the legal position of the confidential source or whistleblower must be located. The public has an interest in effective law enforcement. The public also has an interest in being informed about matters of importance that may only see the light of day through the cooperation of sources who will not speak except on condition of confidentiality. Benotto J. accepted the evidence that many important controversies were unearthed only because of secret sources (often internal whistleblowers) including:
>
> 1. The tainted tuna scandal, that led to the resignation of the Minister of Fisheries in Canada.
> 2. The story that Airbus Industrie paid secret commissions in the sale of Airbus aircraft.
> 3. The book For Services Rendered about the search for a suspected KGB mole in the RCMP Security Service, and CBC's The Fifth Estate program on that mole, code-named "Long Knife".
> 4. Stories dealing with the City of Toronto's health inspection system for restaurants.
> 5. A story describing the operation of an illegal slaughterhouse that created a major health hazard.
> 6. Stories about the fall of Nortel Networks that contrasted optimistic public forecasts by Nortel executives with internal Nortel discussions warning of a potential devastating market downturn.
> 7. Stories about wrongdoing by members of the RCMP security service in early 1977, including a break-in to obtain documents from a left-wing news agency in Montreal, Agence Presse Libre du Québec, illegal wiretaps in Vancouver and pen-registers.

It is important, therefore, to strike the proper balance between two public interests – the public interest in the suppression of crime and the public interest in the free flow

[101] Section 24 of the *Charter* is the application section. It provides that the *Charter* applies to "the Parliament and government of Canada" and to "the legislature and government of each province" in relation to "all matters within the authority" of each. The *Charter* does not apply directly to private legal relations.

[102] *R. v National Post*, 2010 SCC 16, [2010] 1S.C.R. 477.

of accurate and pertinent information. Civil society requires the former. Democratic institutions and social justice will suffer without the latter.[103]

The Court's specific focus on the public interests at stake and the lack of any mention of an employee's duty of loyalty simply reflects the specific factual context of the case. A newspaper which had received documents from a "secret source", alleging misconduct by a senior public official, challenged a judicial order to disclose these documents to the police. The newspaper asserted immunity from disclosure because its investigative journalist had promised confidentiality/anonymity to the "secret source", described in the case as person "X". The judicial order that the original documents be disclosed had been granted to facilitate a police investigation which determined that the already publicly disclosed documents were, in fact, forgeries.

The immunity from disclosure asserted by the newspaper lay in the right guaranteed by the *Canadian Charter of Rights and Freedoms*, section 2(b) as "freedom of thought, belief, opinion and expression, including freedom of the press and other media of communication". In *R. v. National Post*, the Supreme Court of Canada acknowledged that, though freedom of expression applies to everyone, including whistleblowers, it was not appropriate to claim immunity from disclosure as a constitutionally protected right (negative freedom of expression) nor as a class immunity akin, for example, to solicitor-client privilege at common law. Instead, the Court adopted a contextual approach in which four elements must be established by the party asserting the privilege or immunity from a judicial order for disclosure. The four elements are:

> the communication must originate in a confidence that the identity of the informant will not be disclosed. Second, the confidence must be essential to the relationship in which the communication arises. Third, the relationship must be one which should be "sedulously [diligently] fostered" in the public good… Finally… whether in the instant case the public interest served by protecting the identity of the informant from disclosure outweighs the public interest in getting at the truth.[104]

In the instant matter, the Court concluded that the newspaper failed to satisfy the fourth element essentially because the disclosure sought by the judicial order was directed to real evidence of criminal conduct which would be essential to both the police investigation of serious crime and to any future prosecution of a person for that crime. Though certainly conscious of the freedom of expression arguments, the Court's analysis focussed primarily on the *Canadian Charter of Rights and Freedoms*, section 8 right to be "secure against unreasonable search or seizure". In context, the judicial order for disclosure was found to be reasonable.

Consistent with the decision in *Fraser*, the duty of loyalty at common law and civil law has been repeatedly held to be a reasonable limit on a public sector employee's constitutional right to freedom of expression.

Two Federal Court decisions, both known as *Haydon v. Canada*, illustrate this position. In a 2001 decision, *Haydon v. Canada*,[105] three employees challenged

---

[103] ibid. at para 28 (per Binnie J.).

[104] ibid. at para 53.

[105] *Haydon v Canada*, [2001] 2 F.C.R. 82, 2000 CanLII 16081.

reprimand letters imposed by the employer, the federal Department of Health, as a disciplinary response to public statements made by the employees in which they expressed concern about the drug review process, particularly in relation to approval of growth hormones and antibiotics. The three employees had expressed their concerns as guests on a nationally televised morning news and information programme. Unlike *Fraser*, these employees did not seek media attention until after attempting without success to bring their concerns to the employer's attention through internal means, including a request for the intervention of the Health Minister and of the Prime Minister, to support an external investigation. On an application for judicial review of the employer's decision to impose discipline, a decision made by an assistant deputy minister, the Court undertook a *Canadian Charter of Rights and Freedoms* analysis. On this analysis, the Court concluded that, while the disciplinary action infringed the employees' freedom of expression, the common law limitation was justified in a free and democratic society because, in part, it recognized the *Fraser* exceptions to an employee's general duty of loyalty in circumstances of a serious risk to the life, health or safety of members of the public. On the evidence, the employees had made their public disclosure after first attempting to "go up the ladder" through the internal management structures and their concerns were directly related to matters of health and safety. The Court considered that the employees had made a reasonable effort to resolve their concerns internally and expressly noted that they had no personal interests at stake other than the public interest.

The second *Haydon* decision is from 2005 and is known as *Haydon v. Canada (Treasury Board)*.[106] One of the employees involved in the 2001 case made another public disclosure to the media. The employee, a veterinarian, worked as a drug evaluator with Health Canada (the federal Department of Health) with expertise in relation to food-producing animals. In the context of a ban on the importation into Canada of beef from another country, due to concerns about exposure to B.S.E. ("mad cow disease"), the employee responded to a request for a comment from a journalist for national newspaper by stating, in effect, that the ban was not based on health concerns but was a political response due to another international trade issue between the governments of Canada and that other country. The employer responded to the employee's public comments by imposing discipline in the form of a letter instructing her to conform to internal policies regarding media contact. An arbitrator dismissed the employee's grievance of the employer's disciplinary action and the Federal Court of Canada dismissed her application for judicial review of the arbitrator's decision.

Before the Federal Court of Canada, the employee again argued that the employer's disciplinary action infringed her *Canadian Charter of Rights and Freedoms*, section 2(b) right to freedom of expression. The Court rejected the employee's characterization of herself as a whistleblower. The employee had not addressed a serious health and safety concern but had commented on the government's policy in relation to a trade matter specific to a foreign country. She had not taken steps to verify the accuracy of the information on which she based her opinion and had not first expressed her views internally so as to give the employer an opportunity to implement

[106] *Haydon v Canada*, [2005] 1 F.C.R. 511, 2004 FC 749 (CanLII).

corrective action, if appropriate. Thus, concluded the Court, the employee had engaged not in whistleblowing but in simple misconduct deserving of disciplinary sanction.

As reflected in the analysis and the result of the second *Haydon* decision, wrapping oneself in the whistleblower's cloak does not always immunize an employee from employer imposed discipline.[107]

Without statutory whistleblower protection, an employee may find arbitrators and courts reluctant to go beyond the common law and civil law duty of loyalty that the employee owes to the employer. That is the conclusion of a 2005 article published in *Les Cahiers de Droit*[108] in which the authors reviewed the legal regime in Québec and called for the "reconnaissance d'un espace critique accru en milieu de travail"/"recognition of accrued essential breathing space in the workplace"[109] consistent with recognition of the need to protect the greater public interest and freedom of expression in the whistleblower context. The authors consider that, in the modern context, freedom of expression is as fundamental in the workplace as minimum standards for hours of work though they acknowledge that the actual exercise of that expression by an employee must be subject to reasonable limits.[110]

The 2008 decision of the Commission des Relations du Travail in *Petitclerc c. Québec (Société immobilière)*[111] well illustrates the point. The government employer dismissed Petitclerc in response to statements he had made to a journalist, which were published in a newspaper, concerning the existence of asbestos in government buildings. At first instance, the grievance was argued on the basis that the employer had acted without just cause, particularly considering his position as a member of the union's health and safety committee. Petitclerc had argued that his public statements were justified as the acts of a whistleblower and as a union representative. The first instance commission member found that his published comments contained both exaggerated and inaccurate statements. Petitclerc had stated, in the absence of any proof to justify the statement, that the employer had done "next to nothing" in response to concerns raised by the union over a period of 15 years period and that the employer had challenged the validity of each concern. The commission member concluded that Petitclerc's alarmist statements had wrongly

[107] See also *Chopra v. Canada (Treasury Board)*, (2006), 354 N.R. 48 (F.C.A.) – employee critical of government policy to collect anthrax antibiotics after 11 September 2001 terrorist attacks on the United States but failed to attempt to resolve the matter internally and immediate disclosure not justified under urgent health and safety exception – and *Re British Columbia (Ministry of Public Safety) and B.C.G.E.U. (Kambo)* (2009), 186 L.A.C. (4th) 143 (Steeves) – supervisory employee held not justified for release of confidential information via email to media "tip lines" concerning health and safety matters at correctional facility, including identify and health status of an inmate.

[108] C Brunelle et M Samson, 'La Liberté d'expression au travail et l'obligation de loyauté du salarié: plaidoyer pour un espace critique accru' (2005), 46 *Cahiers de Droit* 847.

[109] ibid. at 847–848.

[110] ibid. at 902 and 904.

[111] *Petitclerc c. Québec (Société immobilière)*, 2008 QCCRT 302 (CanLII) dismissing review of the decision at first instance in *Petitclerc v Société Immobilière du Québec*, 2008 QCCRT 42 (CanLII).

created health concerns in the minds of both employees and other persons who visited the public buildings.

The appeal tribunal dismissed Petitclerc's appeal which he had grounded in his freedom of expression and his union position. The appeal tribunal agreed with the decision at first instance that Petitclerc had failed to satisfy the five conditions, applied in relevant jurisprudence, to be identified as a "whistleblower": (1) that the information communicated is true; (2) the disclosure is made in a reasonable and responsible manner; (3) internal remedies were exhausted; (4) the employer is a public institution; and (5) the matter is of public interest. On the evidence, Petitclerc was found not to have satisfied at least the first, second and third conditions.[112]

The courts and administrative tribunals have important contributions to make in relation to the interpretation and application of whistleblower protection legislation and of the development of the common law and civil law principles. The decisions to date have been relatively few but, as just discussed, they have been significant.

Specific Issues

Who Is Protected?

Scope of Protection: Employees and Self-Employed Persons

Common law and civil law recognize an employee's duty of loyalty, good faith, and confidentiality to the employer. The statutory provisions enacted at the federal and provincial levels of government generally reflect these common law and civil law principles but focus primarily on public sector employees. *The Public Interest Disclosure (Whistleblower Protection) Act* of Manitoba extends the scope of its protection from acts of reprisal by an employer to include private sector employees and those who contract with government.[113] Included in the group of protected persons who "contract with government" are self-employed persons who, as independent contractors, enter into a contract for services with a government department or agency.

The Quebec *Anti-Corruption Act* permits "any person" to make a complaint to the Anti-Corruption Commissioner and protects that person from reprisal action.[114] By using the phrase "any person" to identify those who may disclose "corruption" and be protected by the Act, the Quebec statute covers both employees and self-employed persons.

[112] ibid. at 2008 QCCRT 42, at para 67:

> [67] Finalement, la déclaration ne rencontre pas les cinq critères établis par la jurisprudence pour qualifier un geste de « whistleblowing » : 1) ce qui a été communiqué est vrai; 2) la critique est faite de façon raisonnable et responsable; 3) les recours internes ont été épuisés; 4) l'employeur est une institution publique; 5) la question est d'intérêt public.

[113] Above n 30 and text at n 38.

[114] Above text at nn 43–49.

As discussed above, the *Criminal Code of Canada*, section 425.1 expressly prohibits employer from taking acts of reprisal and from compelling silence by inducing an employee not to make a disclosure. These prohibitions apply generally regardless of the nature of the employment in either the public or private sectors.[115] Grounded in criminal law, the focus of the provision is the punishment of the employer for wrongdoing and not directly on the protection of the employee. That protection is really an indirect effect of the prohibition. Protection of an employee who disclosed a breach of federal or provincial law by his or her employer finds expression in the employment standards legislation of New Brunswick, Saskatchewan, and Quebec.[116]

Protection of Persons Helping or Encouraging Whistleblowers

Neither Canadian common law/civil law principles nor the statutory provisions on whistleblowers expressly address the situation of persons who help or encourage whistleblower employees. One may safely presume that, if such a person is also an employee and the whistleblower is found not to be making a disclosure in good faith, the helping or encouraging employee might also be subject to disciplinary sanction unless acting in good faith. An employee who helps or encourages a disclosure not made in good faith would probably be found to have acted in breach of his or her duty of loyalty to the employer.

Protection of Persons Who Affirm a Whistleblower's Allegations

Federal and provincial public sector disclosure legislation expressly protects persons who affirm a whistleblower's disclosure of alleged wrongdoing by including such affirmation in the definition of "reprisal".[117] To be protected, the employee must act in good faith and affirm the whistleblower's allegation in the course of an investigation under the Act. Thus, an affirming employee is not protected from sanction if the employee's affirming statements are made in the news media or other public forum because such an act would be contrary to the employee's own duty of loyalty to the employer.

In addition, the *Canada Labour Code* and the employment standards legislation in New Brunswick, Saskatchewan, and Quebec expressly protect an employee who gives "information or evidence… against the employer with respect to the alleged violation of any Provincial or federal Act or regulation… while carrying on the employer's business".[118]

The *Criminal Code* provision on employer retaliation (section 425.1) is probably broad enough to cover an act of reprisal by an employer against an employee

[115] Above text at n 52.

[116] Above text at nn 59 and 60.

[117] Above text following n 25 and text at n 35.

[118] Above text at n 56 and at nn 59–60.

because that employee "provid[ed] information to a person whose duties include the enforcement of federal or provincial law".[119]

In more limited circumstances pertaining to the legislation itself, federal and provincial legislation on labour relations, occupational health and safety, and some provincial environmental legislation protect employees from employer reprisal because the employee testified in proceedings under that legislation or, in some instances, provided information relating to a breach of that statute.[120]

It should also be noted, in this connection, that an employee who testifies at a hearing, pursuant to a lawful summons to testify, is justified in answering questions concerning employer wrongdoing. Such testimony would not provide just cause for any employer reprisal action.

The Kind of Behaviour That Is Protected

Anonymous Whistleblowing

Common law and civil law principles and the federal and provincial statutory whistleblower protection legislation are silent on the subject of the anonymous whistleblower. Doubtless, this is because such legislation is structured in a manner to "manage" the disclosure of information about wrongdoing through internal procedures. An anonymous disclosure of information is inconsistent with an employee's duty of loyalty to the employer.

The decision of the Supreme Court of Canada in the *National Post* case[121] should serve as a warning to an employee contemplating an anonymous disclosure that reliance on a confidentiality agreement with a journalist may not be sufficient to ensure anonymity. Even contemplation of sending a classic "brown envelope" to a journalist may not be sufficient protection of identity given modern forensic science. Disclosure through a lawyer may provide a solution because the lawyer is bound by professional ethics not to disclose the identity of a client.[122] (There are now commercial service providers who facilitate anonymous disclosures by employees – to be further discussed below).

Critically, anonymous disclosure of wrongdoing without first following internal procedures intended to bring the information to the employer's attention effectively deprives the employer an opportunity to take corrective action independent of public pressure to do so.

---

[119] Above text at nn 52–53.

[120] Above text at nn 64 ff.

[121] Above text at nn 102 ff.

[122] Above text at nn 50–51.

Use of Internal Reporting Systems Before a Whistleblower Is Allowed to Appeal to Third Parties

Whistleblower protection laws enacted at the federal and provincial levels in Canada require an employee to follow the internal reporting procedures within the employee's department or agency of government. In one sense, the integrity commissioners and their equivalents are within that very reporting structure. If considered external to the internal reporting procedures, the legislation foresees direct disclosure of information to such commissioners, particularly in relation to a reprisal complaint.

The "up the ladder" principle is, of course, also found in the arbitral jurisprudence reflecting the common law and civil law in relation to an employee's duties of loyalty, good faith, and confidentiality.

Turning to the Media in Extreme Cases

Federal and provincial whistleblower protection statutes permit a public sector employee to make a public disclosure – or at least to make a disclosure to an official who is then authorized to make such a disclosure – in extreme cases. For example, the federal *Public Servants Disclosure Protection Act* permits direct public disclosure of information when an employee has reasonable grounds to believe that the information relates to a "serious offence" under federal or provincial law or involves "an imminent risk of a substantial and specific nature to the life, health and safety of persons or to the environment". Such a direct disclosure is constrained to situations in which time is not sufficient to permit disclosure to a supervisor or other senior officer.[123]

Similar provisions are found in the statutory schemes enacted in Nova Scotia, New Brunswick, and Manitoba.[124] The statutes enacted in Alberta and Saskatchewan refer to the need to adopt policies to address such situations.[125]

Protection of the Erroneous Whistleblower

Federal and provincial public sector whistleblower protection statutes in Canada qualify references to an employee, contemplating making a disclosure or who has made a disclosure of information, by use of the phrases "good faith" and/or "reasonably believes". These phrases, it is suggested, are sufficient to impose a burden on such an employee to act in the contemplated good faith or reasonable belief by taking some step to ensure a level of accuracy of the information intended to be disclosed. An employee who discloses information, without having taken some steps to ascertain its authenticity and accuracy, cannot generally be characterized as

[123] Above text at nn 17 ff.

[124] Above text at n 31.

[125] Above text at n 34.

having acted in good faith or with a reasonable belief. More specifically, an employee not acting in good faith or with a reasonable belief will not find himself or herself protected from employer reprisal actions.[126]

The general law of defamation has developed a form of privilege which appears broad enough to protect the erroneous whistleblower. As explained by Raymond Brown in a leading Canadian text on defamation law:

> There are certain occasions on which a person is entitled to publish untrue statements about another, where he or she will not be liable even though the publication is defamatory. One such occasion is called a conditional or qualified privilege. No action can be maintained against a defendant unless it is shown that he or she published the statement with actual or express malice. A communication is protected by a qualified privilege if it is fairly made on a privileged occasion by a person in the discharge of some public or private duty, or for the purpose of pursuing or protecting some private interest, provided it is made to a person who has some corresponding interest in receiving it. The duty may be either legal, social or moral. The test is whether persons of ordinary intelligence and moral principle, or the great majority of right minded persons, would have considered it a duty to communicate the information to those to whom it was published.

A communication is protected on a privileged occasion where a person seeks to protect or further his or her own legitimate interests, or those of another, or interests which he or she shares with someone else, or the interests of the public generally.[127]

The description appears equally applicable to an employee who discloses employer or fellow employee misconduct, that impacts private and public interests. As with whistleblower protection generally, the privilege serves to balance the private interest in nondisclosure with the private and public interest in disclosure. The employee is protected.

Whistleblower Motivation

As just discussed, the employee making a disclosure is subject to a good faith and/or reasonably believes standard. The actual motive of the employee, altruistic or not, does not appear to be a relevant consideration unless it undermines or negates good faith or reasonable belief.

Kinds of Acts Reportable by a Whistleblower

The federal and provincial public interest disclosure statutes in Canada broadly define the type of "wrongdoing" which might prompt an employee to disclose information. Using the federal *Public Servants Disclosure Protection Act* to illustrate the concept of "wrongdoing", the federal *Act* refers to general categories of wrongdoing rather than a catalogue of specific actions; thus, the federal *Act* refers to a violation

---

[126] Above text at n 35.

[127] RE Brown, Brown on Defamation: Canada, United Kingdom, Australia, New Zealand, United States, 2nd edn, looseleaf (Toronto, ON: Carswell, 1999), vol. 3 at 135.

of federal or provincial law, "misuse of public funds", "gross mismanagement in the public sector", "a substantial and specific danger to the life, health or safety of persons, or the environment", "a serious breach of a code of conduct" for the public sector, and "knowingly directing or counselling" the commission of any such wrongdoing.[128]

In permitting an employee to make a direct public disclosure of information regarding a "serious offence" under federal or provincial law or "an imminent risk of a substantial and specific nature to the life, health and safety of persons or to the environment", the federal *Act* is implicitly concerned with current and pressing situations. Disclosure of information of a past incident which was thought at an earlier time to pose "an imminent risk of a substantial and specific nature" to the life or safety of persons, for example, would not qualify as a protected disclosure.

The only relevant time period applicable to a disclosure, under the federal *Act*, is the limit of 60 days for a making a reprisal complaint.[129]

The Quebec anti-corruption legislation is very much focussed on the awarding and performance of public sector contracts.[130]

Level of Whistleblower Protection

Protection Against Any Kind of Detriment or Against Dismissal Only

Federal and provincial whistleblower protection legislation plus the specific statutes applicable to such matters as employment standards, labour relations, etc. provide broad protection from virtually any employer reprisal action which detrimentally affects the employee.

Again, using the federal *Public Servants Disclosure Protection Act* to illustrate the point, section 2(1) of that *Act* defines "reprisal" as:

(a) A disciplinary measure;
(b) The demotion of the public servant;
(c) The termination of employment of the public servant, including, in the case of a member of the Royal Canadian Mounted Police, a discharge or dismissal;
(d) Any measure that adversely affects the employment or working conditions of the public servant; and
(e) A threat to take any of the measures referred to in any of paragraphs (a) to (d).[131]

The broader or more inclusive meaning appears to be that in (d) in relation to "any measure that adversely affects the employment or working conditions". In this

[128] Above text at n 16.

[129] Above text at n 25.

[130] Above text at nn 43–44.

[131] Above text following n 25.

regard, provincial statutes mirror the federal in taking an expansive approach to the concept of employer "reprisal".

Onus of Proof in Dismissal Cases

Canadian arbitral awards and practice in relation to discipline and dismissal grievances place the legal onus or burden of proof on the employer to demonstrate just cause for the sanction imposed.[132]

Though not expressly addressed in the federal and provincial whistleblower protection statutes, the *Ontario Environmental Protection Act* illustrates this approach to the legal burden of proof by expressly placing the burden squarely on the employer to prove that its action was not a reprisal within the meaning of that *Act*.[133]

Collective Protective Action by Certain Interest Groups (e.g. Trade Unions, Consumer Protection Groups)

The federal and provincial statutes on whistleblower protection are silent on the role, if any, of certain interest groups (e.g. trade unions, consumer protection groups) to take collective action to protect whistleblower employees.

There is no reason, on first principles, why an interest group could not take protective action in the form, for instance, of moral support such as an act of charity or more tangible support in the form of financial aid to cover the legal costs incurred by the employee.

Conclusion

The whistleblower employee is not a new phenomenon in Canadian labour and employment law. It is, however, a new phenomenon as a subject for legislative action by the federal Parliament and the provincial and territorial Legislatures.

The legislative action has been somewhat predictable. The enacted public sector employment statutes serve to manage rather than facilitate a disclosure of wrongdoing by governments and government employees. As such, the framework reflects the existing state of the arbitral jurisprudence and court decisions on whistleblower employees by imposing the "up the ladder" approach to disclosure. It is this approach which is consistent with the duties of loyalty, good faith, and confidentiality which every employee owes an employer, whether public or private sector. Exceptions are recognized in situations when the disclosure of information is necessary in the public interest to prevent serious risks of harm to persons or the environment.

---

[132] Mitchnick and Etherington, *Labour Arbitration in Canada*, above n 6 at 108.

[133] Above text following n 71.

Available statistical evidence does not demonstrate a significant use of federal and provincial whistleblower protection legislation. Greater effort by public sector employers is needed to instill a sense of confidence and trust in the statutory disclosure procedures. Most of all, there must be a sense of openness and willingness by public sector employers to address disclosed wrongdoing in a manner that appreciates the whistleblower rather than casting a negative light on their actions. These thoughts are well expressed in the 2007 report from Newfoundland and Labrador, *Rebuilding Confidence: Report of the Review Commission on Constituency Allowances and Related Matters*:

> A mechanism to promote good governance that has been developed in both the private and public sectors in recent years has been the notion of a "whistleblower" policy designed to encourage persons within an organization to report instances of behaviour of others in the organization that is considered improper, unethical or wrong. In the public sector, the policy is usually embodied in legislation and is often referred to by other names such as "public servants disclosure" or "public interest protection." The key elements of a whistleblower policy are: the provision of a well-publicized formal mechanism whereby a person concerned about the improper behaviour of another in an organization may express those concerns in confidence to another person who is regarded as independent; a process whereby those concerns will be investigated in a fair manner; and protection to the whistleblower against reprisals for having come forward. For the scheme to work, the policy must be communicated to all employees affected and key members of management should stress the importance of the policy. As well, potential whistleblowers must have confidence in the protections that are provided.[134]

It seems that, at least in the private sector, a good number of employers have responded to the need for confidentiality and confidence in the disclosure process by externalizing the requisite procedures. These employers have engaged commercial service providers to make available external reporting mechanisms which permit employees to make disclosures, even anonymous disclosures, to a service provider who then communicates that information to the employer for action, if needed.[135]

It is expected that the provinces and territories of Canada that have not yet enacted whistleblower protection statutes will do so in the not distant future. Finally, it is worth noting that, even though Canada is a state party to the *United Nations Convention against Corruption*,[136] the domestic legislation does not reference the *Convention* and it has not been invoked to support enactment of such legislation.

---

[134] Above n 41 at 5-47-48.

[135] Examples of such service providers are CanaGlobe Compliance Solutions Inc. (website www.canaglobecompliance.com) and ConfidenceLine by CKR Global HR Services (website www.confidenceline.net).

[136] UN General Assembly Resolution 58/4 of 31 October 2003. Canada signed the *Convention* on 21 May 2004 and deposited the instrument of ratification on 2 October 2007. The *Convention*, article 33 provides for domestic whistleblower protection legislation:

> Article 33. Protection of reporting persons
>
> Each State Party shall consider incorporating into its domestic legal system appropriate measures to provide protection against any unjustified treatment for any person who reports in good faith and on reasonable grounds to the competent authorities any facts concerning offences established in accordance with this Convention.

It is probably a safe bet that there will always be whistleblower employees and whistleblower laws to protect them. The extent of that protection is today in Canada somewhat tricky because of the "up the ladder principle" but it is to be expected that true whistleblower employees will find a way to protect their employment.

Bibliography

Brown RE (1999) *Brown on Defamation: Canada, United Kingdom, Australia, New Zealand, United States*, 2d ed., looseleaf (Toronto, Carswell, 1999), vol. 3.

Brunelle C, Samson M (2005) *La Liberté d'expression au travail et l'obligation de loyauté du salarié: plaidoyer pour un espace critique accru*, 46 Cahiers de Droit 847.

Cantin I, Cantin J-M (2005) *La dénonciation d'actes répréhensibles en milieu de travail ou Whistleblowing* (Cowansville, Les Éditions Yvon Blais)

Carson J (2006) *"The Need for Whistleblowing Legislation in Canada: A Critical Defence"*, paper presented to the Canadian Political Science Association Conference, June 2006 and accessible at the C.P.S.A. website at [cpsa-acsp.ca/papers-2006/Carson.pdf] (accessed 29 July 2013)

Commissaire à la lutte contre la corruption, Le rapport annuel de gestion du Commissaire à la lutte contre la corruption 2011–2012 (Gouvernement du Québec, 2012). https://www.upac.gouv.qc.ca. Accessed April 2015

Commissaire à la lutte contre la corruption, Le rapport annuel de gestion du Commissaire à la lutte contre la corruption 2012–2013 (Gouvernement du Québec, 2013). https://www.upac.gouv.qc.ca. Accessed April 2015

Doyle SC (2007) *A Purposive Approach to Whistleblower Protection: A Comment on Merk v International Association of Bridge, Structural, Ornamental and Reinforcing Iron Workers*, Local 771, 44 Alberta Law Review 903

Dubin QC, Charles L, Terry J (1997) *"Whistleblowing Study": Commissioned by Industry Canada*, (Industry Canada, Competition Bureau, 20 August 1997) and *"Whistleblowing Study": Addendum* (30 September 1997)

Green, Hon. J. Derek (2007) Commissioner, Rebuilding Confidence Report of the Review Commission on Constituency Allowances and Related Matters (St. John's, Government of Newfoundland and Labrador)

Hurtubise-Loranger É, Katz R (2012) "Federal Public Sector Whistleblowing" (Ottawa, Library of Parliament Research Publications, 31 October 2008 and revised 26 June 2012)

Ministre de la Justice (Québec), Commentaires du ministre de la Justice (Les publications du Québec, Tome 1, 1993).

Mitchnick M, Etherington B, *Labour Arbitration in Canada* (2nd Ed.) (Toronto, Lancaster House, 2012), chapter 12 "Disloyalty and Breach of Trust.

Morehead Dworkin, Terry, *Whistleblowing, MNCs, and Peace* (2002), 35 Vanderbilt Journal of Transnational Law 457.

New Brunswick Emergency Measures Organization, Annual Report 2009–2010 (Fredericton, Department of Public Safety, 2010).

Nova Scotia Public Service Commission, Annual Report on the Civil Service Disclosure of Wrongdoing Regulation and Policy (Halifax, Nova Scotia Public Service Commission, annually 2004–05 to 2010–11).

Nova Scotia Public Service Commission, Annual Report on the Civil Service Disclosure of Wrongdoing Regulation and Policy 2007–2008 (Halifax, Nova Scotia Public Service Commission, 2008).

Office of the Integrity Commissioner of Ontario, Annual Report. http://www.oico.on.ca. Accessed April 2015

Office of the Ombudsman, New Brunswick: Annual Report 2011-2012 (Fredericton, Office of the Ombudsman, 2013).

Ontario Law Reform Commission, Report on Political Activity, Public Comment and Disclosure by Crown Employees (Toronto: Ministry of the Attorney General, 1986).
Proulx M, Layton D (2001) *Ethics and Canadian Criminal Law* (Toronto, Irwin Law).
Swan KP (1991) *Whistleblowing – Employee Loyalty and the Right to Criticize: An Arbitrator's Viewpoint*, in Kaplan, W, Sack, J and Gunderson, M, Labour Arbitration Yearbook 1991 (Vol. II) (Toronto, Butterworths-Lancaster House).
The Labour Law Casebook Group, *Labour and Employment Law: Cases, Materials, and Commentary* (8th Ed.) (Toronto, Irwin Law, 2011)

John P. McEvoy Professor at the Faculty of Law, University of New Brunswick, Canada. Former president of the Canadian Association of Law Teachers. Presently president of the Canadian Comparative Law Association as well as a vice-chair of the New Brunswick Labour and Employment Board.

Chapter 3
The Protection of Whistleblowers in the Republic of Croatia

Sandra Laleta and Vanja Smokvina

Abstract This paper investigates the legal protection of whistleblowers in the Republic of Croatia. The first part of the paper presents an in-depth analysis of the legal framework (including both international and national sources of law), whereas the second part discusses settled case-law of national courts and of the ECtHRs. In conclusion the authors tackle the specific issue of whistleblowers within the public sector. To this end they analyse the results of a recently conducted study investigating the perception of whistleblowers in the public sector.

Introduction

Aware of the serious threat posed by corruption, Croatian authorities are taking conscious efforts to combat corruption. The latter are manifested in the form of strategic documents as will be elaborated hereinafter. Nevertheless, it appears that more could be done in this regard.

With this in mind the authors focus special attention to the legal and institutional framework of corruption regulation, while addressing pertinent issues of prevention, suppression, inter-agency and international co-operation and raising public awareness about the need for suppression of corruption by means of the Anti-Corruption Strategy. It should be noted that at the time of writing this paper, the Croatian Ministry of Justice opened a public debate about the ***Draft of the Anti-Corruption Strategy 2015–2020***. The proposed Strategy recognizes whistleblowers as "*having a great role in discovering and prosecuting corruption criminal offences, in giving a hand at making a higher level of transparency and greater political responsibility and those are reasons why a proper and effective legal protection should be given to whistleblowers.... According to the legislation in force and various cases regarding whistleblowers it is obvious that whistleblowers are facing a problem of reintegration in their labour relationship and that is indispensable to upgrade the legislative*

S. Laleta (✉) • V. Smokvina
Faculty of Law, University of Rijeka (Pravni fakultet), Hahlić 6, 51000 Rijeka, Croatia
e-mail: sandra.laleta@pravri.hr; vsmokvina@pravri.hr

G. Thüsing, G. Forst (eds.), *Whistleblowing - A Comparative Study*,
Ius Comparatum - Global Studies in Comparative Law 16,
DOI 10.1007/978-3-319-25577-4_3

framework with an aim of additional whistleblowers protection and the need of raising the level of transparency, ethics and integrity in the whole society."[1]

Non-Governmental Organizations (NGO-s) such as Transparency International Croatia, Association "Whistleblower",[2] GONG[3] and the Association for the Protection of Mobbing Victims,[4] provide valuable assistance in the fight against corruption. As regards investigation of corruption and malpractices, a number of different state institutions is responsible for investigating and prosecuting corruption: the Public Prosecutor's Office, the Office for Suppression of Corruption and Organized Crime (USKOK), National Council for Monitoring the Implementation of the National Program for the Suppression of Corruption, Anti-Corruption Unit, Ministry of Justice and the Commission for Conflict of Interests in the Exercise of Public Office.[5]

The following graph illustrates the ranking of the Republic of Croatia among 177 states on the corruption perception index (Fig. 3.1). This data was made available by

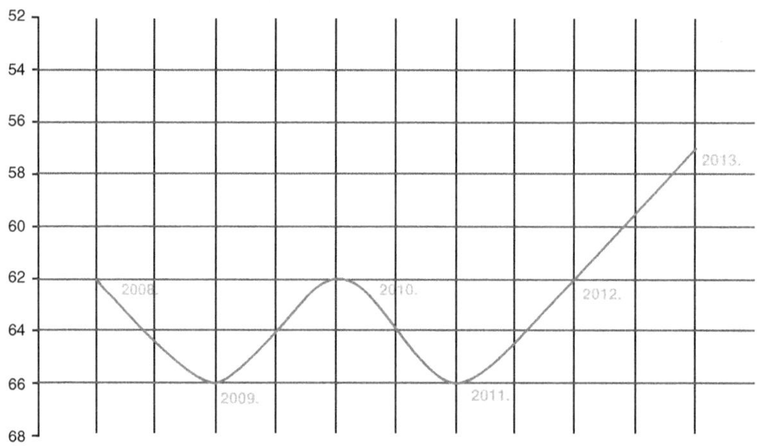

Fig. 3.1 Ranking of the Republic of Croatia on a world scale (2008–2013). Source: http://www.antikorupcija.hr/Default.aspx?art=1639. Accessed 10 Nov 2014

[1] Draft of the Anti-Corruption Strategy 2015–2020, Ministry of Justice of the Republic of Croatia, p. 17, available at www.mprh.hr/lgs.axd?t=16&id=4886 (as at 11 Nov 2014).

[2] Association "Whistleblowers" (*Udruga Zviždač*) provides a phone number for reporting corruption or malpractices. The Association was founded in April 2008 in Zagreb. In about 1 year, more than 1500 people have reported corruption or malpractices. In addition to providing advice to victims, the Association speaks out publicly about concrete cases.

[3] GONG is a non-governmental organization founded in 1997 with the view of promoting fundamental freedoms such as electoral rights, right of access to information, financing of political parties, prevention of conflicts of interests, freedom of speech, democratization, etc. See more at GONG official website, available at www.gong.hr/en/ (as at 11 Nov 2014).

[4] The Association for the Protection of Mobbing Victims, official website, available at www.mobbing.hr/. (as at 11 Nov 2014).

[5] S Vasiljević, *Tasks and challenges*: *Making whistleblowing work in Croatia* (2010) available at www.whistleblowing-cee.org/countries/croatia/research/#1 (as at 11 Nov 2014).

the Transparency International for the period from 2008 to 2013. Pursuant to the national Anti-Corruption Strategy of the Croatian Parliament (2008)[6] progress has been made as Croatia ranked 57th in 2013 which accounts for its best ranking in the last 10 years. By comparison, in 2009 Croatia had ranked 66th.

Sources of Whistleblowers Protection in the Republic of Croatia

With respect to legal sources of whistleblowers protection in the Republic of Croatia, distinction is to be made between international sources, mainly conventions and treaties that are legally binding for the Croatian legal system and the national sources, i.e. acts regulating whistleblowers protection. It is important to note that unlike in some other legal systems, Croatia does not have a special whistleblowers protection act. Instead, a variety of legislative acts regulate the protection of whistleblowers in the public and private sector (*infra* section "The Croatian legislative system").

International Sources Legally Binding for the Republic of Croatia

International sources (conventions, treaties) are legally binding according to the Croatian Constitution if they "*have been concluded and ratified in accordance with the Constitution, published and have entered into force. In such case they shall be a component of the domestic legal order of the Republic of Croatia and shall have primacy over domestic law*".[7] Provided the above requirement is fulfilled, international treaties or conventions in terms of legal hierarchy have primacy over other legislative acts, but are below the Constitution.

In this context we will first mention the ***United Nations Convention against Corruption***,[8] since its Art. 33 is of paramount importance for whistleblowing.[9] How

[6] Anti-Corruption Strategy of the Croatian Parliament, Official Gazette of the Republic of Croatia (hereinafter: OG), No. 75/2008.

[7] Constitution of the Republic of Croatia, OG, Nos. 56/1990, 135/1997, 113/2000, 28/2001, 76/2010, 5/2014.

[8] United Nations Convention against Corruption. For more visit the official UNODC webpage: www.unodc.org/unodc/en/treaties/CAC/ (as at 7 Nov 2014). Croatia transposed this Convention by an *Act on the ratification of the United Nations Convention against Corruption*, OG, International Treaties, Nos. 2/2005 and 1/2006. The Convention was signed by the Croatian representatives on 10-12-2003 and entered into force on 14-12-2005.

[9] Art. 33 of the United Nations Convention against Corruption, ibid.

and to what extent the Republic of Croatia has managed to implement Art. 33 of the Convention is elaborated under section "The Croatian legislative system".

Other anti-corruption instruments of the Council of Europe that are legally binding for Croatia are presented later in the paper. ***The Criminal Law Convention on Corruption***[10] is important in light of Art. 22 of the Convention which protects collaborators of justice and witnesses who report criminal offences and testify with respect to these offences.[11] As a party to the Criminal Law Convention on Corruption, the Republic of Croatia has the duty to provide protection to those persons who report corruption in good faith (whistleblowers). The latter are usually employed in state bodies or companies or may be other legal persons who first gain knowledge about corruption; in particular about the abuse of an official position or abuse of power by official or responsible persons. However, such persons are, despite their knowledge about corruption, mostly reluctant to report such illegal acts for fear of losing their job or facing other sanctions, even though the legislation provides for protection mechanisms.[12]

Article 9 of the ***Civil Law Convention on Corruption***[13] regulates employees' protection.[14] According to this Convention, Croatia is obliged to provide effective remedies for persons who have suffered damage as a result of acts of corruption. These remedies are ensured by means of general provisions of the ***Civil Obligations Act***[15] on the compensation of damage, as well as by provisions from other relevant legislation (see *infra* section "The Croatian legislative system"). Lastly, the ***Recommendation on Codes of Conduct for Public Officials*** (Recommendation No. R (2000) 10) is also of significant importance for the public sector.[16]

Although certain national law scholars[17] refer to the ***ILO 158 Termination of Employment Convention (1982)***,[18] as an important source not just for the public sector, but for all employees, the Republic of Croatia has not ratified this Convention

[10] Criminal Law Convention on Corruption (ETS No. 173, Strasbourg 27-1-1999). *Act on the ratification of the Criminal Law Convention on Corruption*, OG, International Treaties, No. 11/2000. Equally important is the Additional Protocol to the Criminal Law Convention on Corruption (ETS No. 191) and the *Act on the ratification of the Additional Protocol to the Criminal Law Convention on Corruption*, OG, International Treaties, No. 3/2005.

[11] Criminal Law Convention on Corruption, ibid., Art. 22.

[12] S Vasiljević, *Tasks and challenges: Making whistleblowing work in Croatia*, ibid.

[13] Civil Law Convention on Corruption (ETS No. 174, Strasbourg 4-11-1999). Act on the ratification of the Civil Law Convention on Corruption, OG, International Treaties, No. 6/2003.

[14] Civil Law Convention on Corruption, ibid., Art. 9.

[15] Zakon o obveznim odnosima (*Civil Obligations Act*), OG, Nos. 35/2005, 41/2008, 125/2011.

[16] Recommendation on Codes of Conduct for Public Officials (Recommendation No. R (2000) 10) by the Committee of Ministers to Member States, 11-5-2000. Art. 12.

[17] A Rajko, 'Zaštita "zviždača" – pravni izvori u hrvatskom pravnom poretku' (2011a), *IUSINFO*, available at: www.iusinfo.hr/Article/Content.aspx?SOPI=CLN20V01D2011B418 (as at 10 Nov 2014).

[18] See MĐ Učur, S Laleta, *Konvencije Međunarodne organizacije rada s komentarima*, Zagreb, TIM press, Pravni fakultet u Rijeci, p 100-103, p 375-383.; B Buklijaš, A Bilić, *Međunarodno radno pravo* (2006), Split, Pravni fakultet u Splitu, p 264–271.

by notification of succession, wherefore it is not legally binding for Croatia.[19] Former Yugoslavia was a signatory party and has ratified the Convention, whereas Croatia is the only former Yugoslav country which has not ratified the Convention. Nevertheless, the Convention is fully implemented in the Croatian labour law legislation, except for Division E: Severance allowance and other income protection, which is regulated differently in Croatia.

The Croatian Legislative System

General Remarks

Although the Republic of Croatia is a party to all main international legal instruments aimed at combating corruption as elaborated above, no attempts have been made to adopt specific legislation in order to protect whistleblowers.[20] In this respect it appears justified to characterize the regulation of whistleblowers protection in Croatia as rather fragmented and partial, and hence inefficient.

Furthermore, whistleblowing is protected by single provisions of several general statutes (acts), covering the field of employment law (in private and public sector), data protection, access to information, trade law and criminal law; indirectly, protection is guaranteed by acts regulating the criminal procedure and the media. Within Croatian employment law as the most important field for the protection of whistleblowers, whistleblowing remains a fringe notion as the notable lack of not only extensive literature on this matter, but also of case-law indicates.

The fundamental right of freedom of expression is guaranteed under Art. 33 of the **Croatian Constitution**.[21] Since whistleblowing represents "*behaviour falling into the scope of the fundamental right of freedom of expression*" it is extremely important that it is protected as a constitutional right, and that the breach of those rights can in turn be remedied by the Constitutional Court.

---

[19] ILO 158 Termination of Employment Convention (1982), available at www.ilo.org/dyn/normlex/en/f?p=NORMLEXPUB:12100:0::NO::P12100_ILO_CODE:C158 (as at 10 Nov 2014).

[20] S Vasiljević, *Tasks and challenges: Making whistleblowing work in Croatia*, ibid.

[21] Constitution of the Republic of Croatia, ibid., Art. 33:

1. "Freedom of thought and expression shall be guaranteed.
2. Freedom of expression shall particularly encompass freedom of the press and other media, freedom of speech and public opinion, and free establishment of all institutions of public communication.
3. Censorship shall be forbidden. Journalists shall have the right to freedom of reporting and access to information.
4. The right of access to information held by any public authority shall be guaranteed. Restrictions on the right to access to information must be proportionate to the nature of the need for such restriction in each individual case and necessary in a free and democratic society, as stipulated by law.
5. The right to correction is guaranteed to anyone whose constitutionally and legally established rights have been violated by public communication."

We will now mention acts of different branches of law that guarantee protection of whistleblowers. These are as follows: Labour Act,[22] Civil Servants Act,[23] Act on Employees and Servants in a Local and Regional Self-Government,[24] Act on the Public Sector Internal Financial Auditing System,[25] Trade Act,[26] Act on Data Secrecy Protection and Data Secrecy Act,[27] Law on the Right of Access to Information,[28] Criminal Act[29] (as a general statute on criminal offences), Criminal Procedure Act,[30] and Act on Media.[31]

Overview of Different Acts Regulating Whistleblowing

According to Art. 117 para. 3 of the **Labour Act** an employee's recourse to the responsible persons or competent public bodies based on his/her reasonable suspicion about corruption or filling *a bona fide* (good faith) application with these persons or bodies shall not be deemed as just cause (i.e. a valid reason) for the termination of an employment contract.[32] It is important to note that Labour Act represent the general statute governing (individual and collective) employment relationships in both the private and public sector.

Based on this general protection clause, the **Civil Servants Act**, as *lex specialis* that governs the employment relationship in the public sector, provides similar protection for a civil servant who reports suspicion about corruption in its Art. 14.a (Right to protection of civil servant who files an application based on suspicion about corruption) against termination of his/her civil service. Compared to the general clause of Art. 117 para. 3 of the Labour Act, the wording of this provision is

[22] Zakon o radu (*Labour Act*), OG No. 193/2014.

[23] Zakon o državnim službenicima (*Civil Servants Act*), OG Nos. 92/2005, 140/2005, 142/2006, 77/2007, 107/2007, 27/2008, 34/2011, 49/2011, 150/2011, 34/2012, 38/2013, 37/2013.

[24] Zakon o službenicima i namještenicima u lokalnoj i područnoj (regionalnoj) samoupravi (*Act on Employees and Servants in a Local and Regional Self-Government*), OG Nos. 86/2008, 61/2011.

[25] Zakon o sustavu unutarnjih financijskih kontrola (*Act on the Public Sector Internal Financial Auditing System*) OG No. 141/2006.

[26] Zakon o trgovini (*Trade Act*), OG Nos. 87/2008, 96/2008, 116/2008, 116/2008, 76/2009, 114/2011, 68/2013, 30/2014.

[27] Zakon o zaštiti tajnosti podataka (*Act on Data Secrecy Protection*), OG Nos. 108/96, 79/2007; Zakon o tajnosti podataka (*Data Secrecy Act*), OG Nos. 79/2007, 86/2012.

[28] Zakon o pravu na pristup informacijama (*Act on the Right of Access to Information*), OG No. 25/2013.

[29] Kazneni zakon (*Criminal Act*), OG Nos. 125/2011, 144/2012.

[30] Zakon o kaznenom postupku (*Criminal Procedure Act*), OG Nos. 152/2008, 76/2009, 80/2011, 91/2012, 143/2012, 56/2013, 145/2013.

[31] Zakon o medijima (*Act on Media*), OG Nos. 59/2004, 84/2011, 81/2013.

[32] This provision was introduced in the Labour Act via amendments of 2003, in order to guarantee stronger protection for whistleblowers. Ž Potočnjak, 'Prestanak ugovora o radu' (2007) in Potočnjak Ž (ed) *Radni odnosi u Republici Hrvatskoj*, Zagreb, Pravni fakultet u Zagrebu, Organizator, p 394.

almost identical, but for the *bona fide* requirement, as the application does have to be made in good faith. Moreover, the Civil Servants Act not only protects the whistleblower's anonymity, but also protects whistleblowers from denial or restriction of the rights provided by this Act, as well as protection from any type of harassment.

The same level of protection (with identical wording) is guaranteed to the servants and employees in local (and regional) government by another statute, namely the **Act on Employees and Servants in a Local and Regional Self-Government** (Art. 32 paras 1, 2).

With respect to the public sector the **Code of Ethics for Public Servants**[33] is an important legal source.[34] Though it is to a great extent consistent with the ***Recommendation on Codes of Conduct for Public Officials***,[35] the Code fails to address the pertinent issue of reporting (Art. 12 of the Recommendation). Not only is there no clear obligation for a public servant to report corruption or other forms of irregularities, but there are also no provisions regulating the public servants protection. This being a cause for considerable concern, the authors urge to amend this in the future.[36] Provisions that may be singled out in this respect are *protection of personal reputation and the reputation of public service* (Art. 7) and *the conduct of public servants in public expression* (Art. 8), though these do not deal with whistleblowing.

The Trade Act as a general act regulates trade activity. In so far it protects whistleblowers-workers employed in the field of trade, guaranteeing not only the basic protection of employment contract against dismissal, but also protection of anonymity for this category of workers; protection from denial or restriction of his/her employment rights and protection from any type of harassment (Art. 57 paras. 4 and 5).

In keeping with the practice of some European countries,[37] whistleblowing is also partly regulated by the Croatian data protection legislation. Art. 25 of the **Act on Data Secrecy Protection** provides that the disclosure of a person who is acquainted with a business secret information in reporting a criminal offence, economic offence and offence made to a competent body, as well as disclosure to a

---

[33] Etički kodeks državnih službenika (*Code of Ethics for Public Servants*), OG Nos. 40/2011, 13/2012.

[34] Even though the provisions of the code of ethics did not use to be regarded as legal, nor connected with a legal sanction and the Constitutional Court did not deliberate about the constitutionality and legality of the ethical rules, Potočnjak believes that the ethical rules are now transforming into legal norms. See Ž Potočnjak, 'Radni odnosi državnih službenika' (2007b), in Potočnjak Ž (ed) *Radni odnosi u Republici Hrvatskoj*, Zagreb, Pravni fakultet u Zagrebu, Organizator, p 843.

[35] See above.

[36] As regards the Code of Ethics for public servants see: MĐ Učur, 'Etički kodeks državnih službenika – heteronomni izvor prava sa specifičnim nomotehničkim karakteristikama' (2012), *Radno pravo, 33*, pp 40-50; D Juras, 'Etički kodeks državnih službenika' (2011), *Hrvatska pravna revija*, 6, pp 46-49

[37] G Thüsing, G Forst, *Whistleblowing Around The World – A Comparative Analysis of Whistleblowing in 23 Countries* (2014) (pdf material), p. 5.

controlling body in order to fulfil his/her employment rights, is not considered a breach of duty to keep the business secret confidential. What is needed thus is to strike a proper balance between the right of freedom of expression and legitimate protection of business secrets.

Pursuant to Art. 35 para. 2 of the **Act on the Right of Access to Information** a person in charge of providing information cannot be held accountable, in custody or sanctioned for the expressed opinion and actions done in his/her sphere of activity (work), unless he/she violates the law which constitutes a criminal offence.

The Act on the Public Sector Internal Financial Auditing System guarantees the protection of identity and acquired employment rights of internal auditors, persons involved in financial management and control, and other employees, who inform their chief and the person entrusted with the abusive activities about their suspicion concerning fraud and other findings about abusive activities (Art. 36). Likewise, it protects internal auditors from dismissal and job-shift (Art. 23 para. 1).

The new **Criminal Act** of 2011 protects whistleblowers in its Art. 131 para. 1 (Violation of the Right to Work). The provision in question reads as follows: "*whoever terminates an employment contract with a worker because he/she turned or reported in good faith and on justified suspicion of corruption to the competent persons or state authorities shall be sentenced to imprisonment for a term of up to three years.*"

It should be noted that the Criminal Procedure Act and the Act on Media guarantee indirect protection only. Arts. 204 and 205 of the **Criminal Procedure Act** (Criminal report), regulate the duty of every person who gained information about a criminal offence whose perpetrator is prosecuted *ex offo* to denunciate it to the competent public prosecutor. According to the **Criminal Act**, a person who under certain requirements does not denunciate a criminal offence commits a criminal offence herself (Art. 302). Another form of indirect protection of whistleblowers is found in Art. 30 of the **Act on Media**, which regulates the protection of the source of information published (or intended to be published) by a journalist (as well as the editor in chief, editors and authors of published materials who are not journalists). In general, a journalist has no duty to divulge the source of information. Exceptionally, the Office of the Public Prosecutor may request the competent court to order the journalist to reveal his/her source of information, if it is deemed necessary for the protection of public security, territorial integrity and health (Art. 30 par. 4).[38]

---

[38] Act on Media, ibid., Art. 30 para. 5: "The court may order to a journalist to give data about the source of the information he/she made public or about the information which he/she intends to make public, if it is necessary for the protection of public interest and it is about extremely important and serious circumstances and it is determined without doubt:

There is no rational optional measure for revealing the data about the source of the information, or that the competent body from the para. 4 of this Article has already used such a measure and that the public interest based on law for revealing the data about the source of the information clearly prevails over the interest of protection of the source of information."

Art. 30 para. 6: "The court will, bearing in mind the circumstances of the case, exclude the public during the course of the procedure and warn the present persons that they are obliged to

Finally, the last act to be considered in the context of whistleblowers is the **Occupational Health and Safety Act**.[39] Its Art. 69 para. 3 reads as follows: "*the worker shall inform without delay its employer, a designated authorised officer, an employed occupational health and safety specialist or occupational health and safety commissioner service about any fact that represents a direct risk for the occupational health and safety, along with any other fault in the system of occupational health and safety at work.*"

Protection of Whistleblowers: An Analysis of the Croatian Legislation

This chapter analyses the Croatian legislation governing whistleblowing, departing from the methodology used by professors Thüsing and Forst in the questionnaire that was part of a comparative analysis of whistleblowing that encompassed 23 countries.[40]

Personal Scope of Protection

In view of the fact that there is no general act covering whistleblowing, protection is guaranteed to workers in general. According to the **Labour Act**, the term 'worker' includes different categories of employees, such as clerks and civil servants, i.e. every natural person who performs work for the employer in an employment relationship (Art. 4 para. 1). The Labour Act as a general act regulates employment relationships in the Republic of Croatia, unless prescribed otherwise by another act or international treaty that was signed and ratified in accordance with the Constitution of the Republic of Croatia (Art. 1).

As mentioned in the previous chapters, several acts belonging to different fields of law guarantee the protection of whistleblowers. While it is true that they add a number of different elements to the general frame of protection, whether or not they introduce important novelties in this area is questionable. It appears as if the intention of the legislator was to underscore the protection of certain categories of workers protected by those acts: public sector employees, internal auditors, workers employed in trade, etc.[41]

keep as a secret whatever they have heard in course of the procedure and about the consequences of revealing the secret."

[39] Zakon o zaštiti na radu (*Occupational Health and Safety Act*), OG, Nos. 71/2014, 118/2014, Art. 69 para. 3.

[40] G Thüsing, G Forst, *Whistleblowing Around The World*, ibid.

[41] *cf.* for the Civil Servants Act; A Rajko, 'Zaštita "zviždača" u državnoj službi' (2008), *IUSINFO*, p 3, available at www.iusinfo.hr/Article/Content.aspx?SOPI=CLN20V01D2008B27 (as at 10 Nov 2014).

In this context it is fitting to mention that Croatian legislation does not protect a person who helps or encourages whistleblowers. What more, a person who as a witness confirms the allegations of the whistleblower before the court (in a trial) does not enjoy any special protection in Croatian law. Instead, the provisions of the **Criminal Procedure Act** (Chapter XVIII. Taking of evidence, 4. Questioning of witnesses, Arts. 283–300) as the general act governing the protection of witnesses, apply to such persons as well. Therefore, under the conditions prescribed by this Act[42] a whistleblower could be a protected witness.[43]

On the other hand, the exemption from the duty to testify provided for journalists in Art. 285. para. 1/6 of this Act could indirectly facilitate the position of a whistleblower. By virtue of this provision, journalists and their editors in the media are exempted from the duty to testify as to sources of information and data which becomes accessible to them in the performance of their professional activities. This exemption applies if their sources were used in the editorial process, with the exception of criminal proceedings for offences against honour and reputation that were committed by means of the public media, as well as in cases regulated by special law. Moreover, the above mentioned protection of journalist's information greatly assists the whistleblower (with some exceptions) (**Act on Media**).[44]

Consequently, an important aspect of protection is missing, namely the protection of persons giving testimony on whistleblowers' allegations outside the scope of a trial, i.e. in an internal investigation conducted by the employer.[45]

Protected Behaviour

This section examines "the circumstances under which a disclosure qualifies as a disclosure protected by the law" and the "facts a whistleblower may disclose". In this context the following issues are addressed: characteristics of behaviour, anonymity of whistleblower, duty of internal report, *bona fide* request and type of information that may be disclosed.

---

[42] M Habazin, 'Zaštita "zviždača"' (2010), *Hrvatska javna uprava*, 10(2), p. 344.

[43] "Criminal Procedure Act provides protection of witnesses (Arts 294–299) if it is likely that by giving a testimony or by answering any individual question, a witness might expose himself or any other person close to himself to a serious danger to life, health, physical integrity, freedom or property of considerable volume (threatened witnesses)." See more: M Škorić, 'Croatia' in K. Roach (ed) *Comparative Counter-Terrorism Law*, Cambridge University Press, 2015

[44] A Rajko, 'Zaštita "zviždača" u državnoj službi', ibid., p. 2.

[45] G Thüsing, G Forst, *Whistleblowing Around The World*, ibid., p. 14.

Behaviour

According to the general provision of **Labour Act** the worker-whistlerblower is protected if he/she: (a) recourses to (based on a reasonable suspicion about corruption) or files (in good faith) application to the responsible persons or competent public bodies (the latter being same pursuant to the **Civil Servants Act** and **Act on Employees and Servants in a Local and Regional Self-Government**). This means that the redress can be oral (and therefore informal) or made in writing (formal), either to the responsible persons or competent public bodies.

Croatian public bodies competent for criminal matters including corruption, are the police (Ministry of Interior), the Public Prosecutor's office, USKOK,[46] and PNUSKOK.[47]

The question arises as to who are the responsible persons to whom a whistleblower can recourse. As the laws do not specify this, these responsible persons can be described in general terms as persons employed by the same employer and in charge of managerial duties, e.g. superiors or higher-ranking employee (public servant, clerk), chief officers etc. In this regard the authors point to the issue of the breach of the employee's duty when providing information concerning potential criminal offences by the employer to the media, rather than first informing the competent public bodies and waiting for their criminal prosecution (see *infra* section "Case-law").

A detailed prescription of the internal procedure and the chain of responsible persons is provided for by the **Act on the Public Sector Internal Financial Auditing System**. Persons protected as whistleblowers, i.e. internal auditors and persons involved in financial management and control (but also other employees), have to inform at the same time two persons who have responsibilities concerning abusive activities: the chief and a person entrusted with the abusive activities. The chief is an employee of the budget beneficiary (public sector employer) who is responsible for the prevention of risk and for protective measures against abusive activities and frauds (Art. 36 para. 1). He/she may assign this duty to another person, wherefore he/she has to nominate a person in charge with the abusive activities. In consequence, this person has a duty to receive information on abusive activities and suspicion about fraud or to independently undertake measures in order to combat such activities.

The internal auditor has to inform the chief of the internal revision unit in case he/she during audict suspects that fraud was committed. Accordingly, the chief has a duty to stop the auditing and submit a written report to the director of the public beneficiary (public sector employer) as well as to the person in charge of abusive activities. The director or the latter person has to inform the Public Prosecutor's

---

[46] USKOK (Ured za suzbijanje korupcije i organiziranog kriminaliteta) – *Office for the Suppression of Corruption and Organized Crime, Law on the Office for the Suppression of Corruption and Organized Crime of the Republic of Croatia*, OG Nos. 76/2009, 116/2010, 145/2010, 57/2011, 136/2012, 148/2013, (Hereinafter: Act on USKOK).

[47] PNUSKOK (Policijski nacionalni ured za suzbijanje korupcije i organiziranog kriminaliteta) – *Police National Office for the Suppression of Corruption and Organized Crime, Regulation on the internal organisation of the Ministry of the Interior*, OG Nos. 70/2012, 140/2013, 50/2014.

Office of the Republic of Croatia, as well as the competent public authority (for abusive activities and fraud) of the Ministry of Finance. Moreover, he/she has to inform the person who warned of abusive activities or fraud, within 15 days following the information receipt, except when the recourse is anonymous. If the person who warned of those activities does not receive information that appropriate measures have been undertaken, he/she has to inform the competent bodies of the Ministry of Finance.

A somewhat complex procedure and chain of responsibility in this field is the result of harmonization of domestic legislation with the European Union (hereinafter: EU) *acquis*. The underlying purpose of EU principles on the integral system of internal financial auditing is to achieve good management over public financial resources.

A person privy to a business secret that is subject to protection under the **data protection** legislation (Art. 25) cannot be sanctioned for a breach of duty for a disclosure in the form of denunciation of a criminal offence, economic offence and offence to a competent body. Likewise, disclosing information to a controlling body in order to fulfil one's employment rights is not considered a breach of the duty to keep business-related information confidential. A person privy to secret business information is a person (or a special body) authorized to gain and keep such secret information, and decide about the authorization of the employees who are to gain knowledge of secret information, and about third persons to whom the information may be revealed (Art. 21 para. 3).

According to Art. 35 para. 2 of the **Act on the Right of Access to Information**, the person in charge of providing information (commissioner)[48] enjoys protection, i.e. he/she cannot be held accountable, in custody or sanctioned for opinions expressed and actions done in his/her sphere of activity (work), unless he/she breaks the law by committing a criminal offence. The commissioner is a functionary of the state and head of the Department of Commissioners. The provisions of the Civil Servants Act apply to the employment status of persons employed in this Department, while the Data Protection Act applies with respect to the duty of Commissioner and employees of the Department to keep secret all personal and other confidential information of which they gain knowledge in performing their activities (work).

Anonymous Whistleblowing, Internal Report and Report via the Media

Croatian legislation allows for **anonymous whistleblowing**. The **Act on Civil Servants** (Art. 14a) and the **Act on Employees and Servants in a Local and Regional Self-Government** (Art. 32) guarantee the protection of civil servant's,

[48] Person in charge of providing information ("*povjerenik za informiranje*") protects, controls and promotes the right of access to information guaranteed by the Constitution of the Republic of Croatia, Art. 38 para. 3. Croatian Parliament (*Hrvatski Sabor*) elects the commissioner on a five-year mandate, with the possibility of re-election. He/she is autonomous and independent in performing his/her duties and answers to the Parliament. (Art. 35 para. 1, Art. 36).

servant's and white-collar employee's anonymity if the competent public authority has assessed that the alleged corruptive act was serious. Anonymity is guaranteed to the internal auditors, persons involved in financial management and control and other employees, pursuant to the **Act on the Public Sector Internal Financial Auditing System**. In addition, the **Trade Act** prescribes anonymity for the worker who blows the whistle, so that employees who work in the field of trade also enjoy specific protection. Yet, considering that the content of the protection of anonymity is not regulated and hence remains unclear, one can only speculate about its efficiency.

Under Croatian law there is no general duty for whistleblowers to first make internal reports, prior to reporting to third parties. However, the **Act on the Public Sector Internal Financial Auditing System** prescribes this requirement when the internal auditor suspects that fraud was committed (*supra*, section "Behaviour").

There are many controversies in connection to whistleblowing via the media.[49] This is illustrated by the most famous national *case Balenović*, which is discussed in detail in chap. 4. At this point it should only be pointed out that Mrs. Balenović used the media to make her disclosure, without previously duly exhausting the employer's internal procedure and properly applying to the competent State authorities. This, as we shall see, led to a negative decision of the ECtHRs.

It is important to note that new Croatian **Act on the Right of Access to Information** of 2013 repealed an earlier provision that explicitly allowed a servant responsible for providing information (this function has been cancelled as well) to inform the public. Acting outside his/her competences the servant was thus able to – without being held accountable (except in some cases, Art. 8), enable access to certain information, if this was done in good faith and in order to provide true and complete information to the public (Art. 23).

Good Faith Requirement

Under the general rule (**Labour Act**) whistleblower enjoys protection if he/she acts in good faith and on a reasonable suspicion.

In contrast, the **Act on the Public Sector Internal Financial Auditing System** requests internal auditors and persons involved in financial management and control, as well as other employees in this sector, to blow the whistle if they have a "suspicion" (not necessary 'reasonable suspicion').

While the provisions of the **Civil Servants Act** (and the **Act on Employees and Servants in a Local and Regional Self-Government**) require that the whistleblower acts on reasonable suspicion about corruption, he/she need not to act in good faith.[50] However, the *bona fide* request and motivation of the whistleblower seem to

[49] G Thüsing, G Forst, *Whistleblowing Around The World*, ibid., p. 17.

[50] According to the explanation of this provision given in the Proposal of the Act on Changes and Amendments to the Civil Servants Act, in 2008, "for the protection of "whistleblowers" the existence of reasonable suspicion about corruption or filing of the application about that suspicion in good

be relevant in the public sector too. For the abuse of the civil servants' duty to file an application on reasonable suspicion about corruption represents a heavy breach of the professional duty (Art. 14a para. 4 Civil Servants Act; Art. 32 Act on Employees in a Local Self-Government).[51]

It should be noted that from the criminal law point of view, whistleblower who doesn't act in good faith risks to be accused of defamation (Art. 149) and of harming someone's reputation (Art. 148).

Type of Information Reported by Whistleblower

Croatian legislation allows whistleblowers to report corruption and other forms of illegal conduct.[52] According to the **Labour Act** whistleblowers may report 'corruption'; under the **Civil Servants Act** (and the **Act on Employees in Local Self-Government**) 'corruption' and 'heavy form of corruption', whereas under the **Act on the Public Sector Internal Financial Auditing System** 'fraud' and 'abusive activities' as relevant "breaches of law".[53] Similarly, **data protection legislation** allows a person who has knowledge of secret information to report a criminal offence, economic offence and offence to competent bodies.

The key question is which activities are denoted by the term '**corruption**'? The Criminal Act does not define corruption as a single criminal offence. Therefore, a definition of the 'corruptive criminal offences' described in the **Act on USKOK**[54] is used as the delineation criterion. In this sense corruptive criminal offences cover: misuse in insolvency proceedings, unfair competition in foreign trade operations, misuse in performing government duties, illegal intercession, accepting bribe, accepting a bribe in economic business operations, offering bribe, offering bribe in economic business operations etc.[55]

Furthermore, it remains unclear which meaning the legislator intended to attribute to the term 'heavy form of corruption' that accounts for the main criterion in granting anonymity to whistleblower–civil servant (as well as to a servant in local government, employee in trade) (Art. 14a para. 2 Civil Servants Act; Art. 32 para. 2 Act on Employees in Local Self-Government; Art. 57 para. 5 Trade Act).[56] If the intention was to cover a serious form of criminal offence in the criminal law sense, this should be regulated *de lege ferenda* referring to criminal law.

---

faith is needed [...] from the protection are excluded "whistleblowers", who make false applications, without reporting appropriate circumstances or submitting proof about it."

[51] About the duty to file an application see more in the following paragraphs.

[52] A Rajko, 'Zaštita "zviždača" u državnoj službi', ibid., p. 3.

[53] See G Thüsing, G Forst, *Whistleblowing Around The World*, ibid., p. 19.

[54] Act on USKOK, ibid., Art. 21.

[55] V Grozdanić, M Škorić, I Martinović, 'Kaznenopravna zaštita radnika prema odredbama novog Kaznenog zakona' (2012), *Hrvatski ljetopis za kazneno pravo i praksu*, 19(2), p. 497.

[56] A Rajko, 'Zaštita "zviždača" u državnoj službi', ibid.

An internal auditor can report about 'fraud' and 'irregularities'. While 'fraud' is defined in the **Criminal Act**, the term 'irregularities' is not defined in the **Act on the Public Sector Internal Financial Auditing System**, wherefore its meaning remains unclear. The provision of Art. 22 para. 1 of this Act can serve as a guideline for its interpretation, for it prescribes that internal auditors perform their work expert-wise and professionally "applying the methodology based on international standards for revision (auditing)".

In light of the above raised considerations we can conclude that Croatian legislation is still far from a progressive system of whistleblowing protection known in comparative law. The latter system protects not only breaches of law, but also other wrongdoings or aspects of life, such as dangers and not necessarily breaking of any rules, or unethical behaviour or breaches of codes of conduct.[57]

The Obligation to 'Blow the Whistle'

Croatian law recognizes several "levels" of the obligation to "blow the whistle". First, certain categories of civil servants and employees are obliged to blow the whistle. As already mentioned, pursuant to the **Act on the Public Sector Internal Financial Auditing System** civil servants and "other employees", i.e. every person employed by an employer – budget beneficiary have this duty.

Secondly, this obligation is imposed on the commissioner for information who files the application and issues a warrant for established minor offences (**Act on the Right of Access to Information**).

Thirdly, certain persons have this duty under circumstances regulated by the **Criminal Act** and the **Criminal Procedure Act**, as previously analysed.

According to the **Occupational Health and Safety Act** a worker has a duty to inform of any fact representing a direct risk for the occupational health and safety, as well as any other fault in the system of occupational health and safety at work.

Level of Protection

Croatian legislation protects all whistleblowers against dismissal, as provided for in a general rule of the **Labour Act**. Moreover, general rules on anti-discrimination protection concerning employment, working conditions and protection of worker's dignity apply to each 'worker' (Labour Act, Art. 7 para. 4 and 5).

In addition, the protection of anonymity is guaranteed for civil servants in general and servants in the local government; servants employed by the budget beneficiary (public sector employer) and employees in trade.

The Civil Servants Act has introduced additional protective elements for civil servants, i.e. protection from denial or restriction of the rights provided by this Act, as well as protection from any sort of harassment. This guarantee of protection is

---

[57] See G Thüsing, G Forst, *Whistleblowing Around The World*, ibid., pp. 19–20.

strengthened by the duty of the head of the state body, who has to initiate disciplinary procedure against the high official who has violated the above-mentioned duty of protection, thus committing a heavy breach of official duty (Art. 14a para. 3). As observed in the literature, a whistleblower could suffer harassment or his identity could reveal another person, not necessarily a high official.[58] Likewise, the same level of protection is enjoyed by servants and other employees in local government.

Finally, it is worth noting that in dismissal cases based on whistleblowing Croatian law places *onus probandi* on the employer.[59]

Case-Law

International Case-Law (Case Balenović Before the ECtHRs)

This chapter discusses the *Balenović Case*,[60] that represents the most famous whistleblower case in the recent Croatian history. The case was finally resolved by the ECtHRs. The argumentation of the judgment is extremely important not just for future conduct of official State organs in 'whistleblowers' issues, but also in educating the general and professional public about whistleblowers. What more, the judgment has an important labour law impact, especially with respect to the termination of employment contract.[61] As Potočnjak rightly points out, the decision of the Constitutional Court of the Republic of Croatia is equally important because it declared that "*a breach of an employee's duties towards an employer cannot be justified by the right to express a personal opinion*".[62]

---

[58] A Rajko, 'Zaštita "zviždača" u državnoj službi', ibid., p. 3.

[59] "In case of a dispute relating to putting an employee at a disadvantaged position compared to other employees as a result of an action taken on account of a founded suspicion of corruption or a report on such suspicion addressed by such employee to responsible persons or competent public authorities, which led to a violation of any of the rights of employees arising from the employment relationship, if such employee establishes facts from which it may be presumed that he or she has been treated less favourably and that his or her rights arising from the employment relationship have been violated, the burden of proof shall be shifted to the employer who must prove that the employee has not been put at a disadvantaged position compared to other employees or that no right arising from the employment relationship has been violated with regard to such employee" (Labour Act, Art. 135 para. 2).

[60] ECtHR, First Section, 30-09-2010, Application no. 28369/07 Vesna BALENOVIĆ against CROATIA, available at: www.sljeme.usud.hr/usud/prakESen.nsf/94b579567876f9fcc1256965002d1bf4/d38dcb5903ff80e3c12579f20047af30/$FILE/BALENOVIC%20v.%20CROATIA.doc (as at 12 Nov 2014).

[61] A Rajko, '"Zviždanje" iz perspektive slučaja Balenović protiv Hrvatske' (2011b), *Radno pravo 2, pp. 27–36.*

[62] ŽPotočnjak, 'Prestanak ugovora o radu', ibid., p. 394.

Facts of the Case

The applicant had been working for the joint-stock company INA – Industrija nafte d.d. (hereinafter "INA" or "the company") from 17 June 1983 to 18 April 2001, when she was dismissed. In the course of her work the applicant analysed issues relating to losses of petrol during transport from refineries to petrol stations. She came to the conclusion that in 2000 the value of petrol lost during transport amounted to 25,872,208.97 HRK, of which only 5,056,818.86 HRK had been compensated by the hauliers. Her findings suggested that the relevant persons in INA had shown considerable laxity as regards claiming compensation for the remaining losses. In the course of 3 months, the applicant informed her immediate superior INA's general director and the INA's supervisory board of her findings and submitted all the relevant documentation to them. After her continuous sending of letters to her superiors did not yield any results, a newspaper published articles about the INA case and included the contents of the letters sent by the applicant to her superiors. The articles in question also included interviews with the applicant. On 2 May 2001 the applicant lodged a request for the protection of her employment-related rights ("*zahtjev za zaštitu prava*") in response to the decision to dismiss her. On 14 May 2001 INA dismissed the applicant's request.

Case Balenović Before Croatian Courts

On 23 May 2001 the applicant brought civil action against INA before the Zagreb Municipal Court (*Općinski sud u Zagrebu*) challenging her dismissal. She sought reinstatement and salary arrears, however, the Court dismissed the applicant's action by its decision of 10 December 2002.[63] On 11 November 2003 the Zagreb

[63] Judgement of the Zagreb Municipal Court, Pr-2631/01-43, 10-12-2002, relevant part: "In the opinion of this court, irrespective of whether the plaintiff disclosed a business secret or financial or other information which does not represent a business secret, she acted contrary to the interests of the employer [...], regardless of the employer's ownership structure and the accuracy of the published information, in that she made extremely negative statements in the media, as a result of which she primarily harmed the reputation of the employer. By making public statements in this way, the plaintiff acted contrary to the [internal regulations] on business correspondence in INA [...], Rule 7 of which provides that the authority to conduct business communications and correspondence and provide information to the media lies exclusively with the general director and the director of the sector of promotional activities [...], and Rule 10 of which provides that non-observance constitutes a breach of the employee's duty, with the resultant consequences. Each of the above-mentioned breaches is, in the opinion of this court, [in itself] a sufficient reason allowing the respondent to lawfully dismiss the plaintiff [...] because [she] committed particularly serious breaches of employment-related duties, as a result of which, taking into account all the circumstances and the interests of both parties, the continuation of the employment relationship is no longer possible. It is to be noted that this court cannot find a 'civic duty' in, or deriving from, any existing legal provision, apart from the Criminal Procedure Act, which provides that the plaintiff, as a citizen, must file a criminal complaint against the perpetrator if she considers that a criminal offence has been committed. The civic duty is thereby discharged and the competent State authorities then proceed with the investigation of the criminal offence and identification of the perpetrators.

County Court (*Županijski sud u Zagrebu*) as the second-instance court dismissed the applicant's appeal and upheld the first-instance decision. The County Court held that the relevant provisions of the Labour Act protected employees from dismissal only in cases where they turned to the State authorities with a view to enforcing their rights or reporting a suspicion of corruption, but not in cases where they sought to do so through the media.[64]

On 24 May 2005 the Croatian Supreme Court (*Vrhovni sud Republike Hrvatske*) dismissed a subsequent appeal by the applicant on points of law.[65] The applicant

---

It is also to be noted that the Data Protection Act, in particular section 25, provides that revealing a business secret in a criminal complaint or when reporting an administrative offence to the competent authority or to the supervisory authority in the exercise of one's own employment-related rights – but not to the public – is not to be treated as disclosure of a business secret."

[64] Judgement of the Zagreb County Court, Gžr-176/03, 11-11-2003, relevant part: "[The first-instance court] established that the plaintiff, in her public statements in the daily newspaper Slobodna Dalmacija on 3, 4, 5, 6, 7 and 11 April 2001, expressed a whole series of negative comments and serious but flippantly made allegations about the business activities and management of the respondent, and in doing so acted contrary to the interests of her employer, and jeopardised and harmed the business reputation of the respondent[…]. Here it has to be mentioned that the first-instance court did not examine whether the plaintiff's comments were made competently [i.e. expertly], because that is outside the scope of this labour dispute. Those are questions relating to how a company runs its business, a matter within the exclusive competence of the management board, whereas the supervisory role is exercised by the supervisory board, and not an individual employee. In this connection it has to be noted that under Art. 108 para 2. [now Art. 117 para. 2] of the Labour Act, recourse by an employee to the [competent] executive authorities does not constitute a justified reason for [his or her] dismissal[…]. [U]nder Art. 108 para 3. [now Art. 117 para. 3], recourse by an employee to the competent State authorities on account of a reasonable suspicion of corruption, or the filing by an employee of a criminal complaint in good faith on the grounds of that suspicion, does not constitute a justified reason for dismissal […]. [I]t follows that the law protects an employee only when applying to the competent State authorities, and not in respect of the media. Hence, if the plaintiff wanted to inform the public of the existence of possible irregularities and illegalities in the respondent's operations, she could have done so by applying to the competent State authorities, which would then, pursuant to section 5 of the Media Act, be bound to make that information available to journalists…Therefore, the first-instance court correctly established that the plaintiff's unauthorised statements in the press constituted … an important fact justifying [her dismissal]. Lastly, the plaintiff also made publicly available various financial data, data concerning the course and content of preliminary negotiations on business cooperation etc., which are mentioned in the published articles, which she was not authorised to do, and in doing so seriously breached her employment-related duties within the meaning of Rule 31 of the respondent's [internal employment regulations]."

[65] Judgment of the Croatian Supreme Court, Revr-215/04-2, 24-05-2005, relevant part: "In the contested decision on summary dismissal of the plaintiff, […], the respondent, as the employer, refers, as the justified reason for dismissal, to the statements by the plaintiff in the daily newspaper Slobodna Dalmacija on 3, 4, 5, 6, 7 and 11 April 2001. It was established in the proceedings that in these statements the plaintiff made: extremely negative comments about the respondent's business activities and the management of resources, and allegations of conduct such as manipulations and machinations in the respondent's business affairs, as well as the covering up of crime on the part of the respondent's administration and management. The lower-instance courts found that this kind of behaviour on the part of the plaintiff constituted a justified reason for dismissal within the meaning of Art. 107, para. 1 [now Art. 116, para 1], of the Labour Act […]. In this case, answering the following question of principle is of decisive importance: What are the repercussions of the

then lodged a constitutional complaint against the Supreme Court's judgment, alleging infringements of her constitutional rights to equality, equality before the law, work and freedom of expression. On 18 October 2006 the Constitutional Court of the Republic of Croatia dismissed the applicant's constitutional complaint. Replying to the applicant's argument that she had been dismissed despite the fact that she had merely been fulfilling her statutory duty to report criminal offences, the Court underlined the fact that the applicant had filed her criminal complaint (against INA's responsible persons) only after having made the statements in question to the media.[66]

---

public statements of an employee, in which extremely negative comments about the business activities and management of resources of an employer were made, both for the employment contract and for the employment relationship between the employee and the employer? And also: What is the significance of the plaintiff's public statements in the present case? It should be noted that, in principle, public statements of this kind by an employee may have repercussions for the employment relationship, as a particularly important fact, as a result of which, while taking into account all the circumstances and interests of both parties, the continuation of employment is not possible.

In this particular case, the aforementioned statements by the plaintiff evidently damaged the reputation of the respondent, since an employer whose leadership structures tolerate and encourage criminal activities certainly cannot have a good reputation and be trusted in the business world. Therefore, this kind of behaviour on the part of the plaintiff has significant repercussions for the employment relationship between the parties and gives the employer a justified reason for termination of the employment contract, within the meaning of Art. 107 para. 1. [now Art. 116, para 1], of the Labour Act. This precisely, having regard to the given circumstances, constitutes a particularly important fact, as a result of which the continuation of employment is not possible.

[...] In the present case, the depiction of the employer's business activities in an extremely negative light in the media by the employee constitutes a particularly important fact of this kind, which gives the employer a justified reason for termination of the employment contract.

The plaintiff's reliance on her 'civic duty' is unfounded. In this regard the assessment of the second-instance court to the effect that the plaintiff could realise her 'intention to prevent damage and protect the property of the respondent' only by turning to, and lodging a complaint with, the competent State authorities, which would have resulted in that information being available to the press and other media – and could not have served as a reason for dismissal – is correct.".

[66] Judgment of the Croatian Constitutional Court,U-III-3121/2005, 18-10-2006, OG No. 123/2006, relevant part: "As regards the complainant's criticism directed against the part of the first-instance judgment referring to the notion of a 'civic duty', the Constitutional Court points out that the part of the reasoning in which the first-instance court notes that 'this court cannot find a civic duty in, or deriving from, any existing legal provision, apart from the Criminal Procedure Act [...]' is [rather] unfortunately worded. This does not, however, affect the validity of that court's legal view regarding the 'civic duty' of the complainant as an employee, according to which the complainant – if she considered that her employer had committed a criminal offence – should, as a citizen, have filed a criminal complaint against the perpetrator, whereupon the competent State authorities would have proceeded to investigate the criminal offence and identify the perpetrators [...]. The Constitutional Court notes that the complainant justifies her conduct towards the employer (that is, her statements in the media), for which the employer dismissed her, by claiming that 'she expressed her personal opinions primarily as a citizen', and as an employee in the part where she objected to the 'appropriation of State property'.

The Constitutional Court notes in this connection that a breach of an employee's duties towards an employer cannot be justified by the right to express a personal opinion in the manner presented by the complainant in her constitutional complaint."

ECtHRs' Judgment: Balenović Case

The applicant complained under Arts. 9 and 10 of the Convention about her dismissal and the refusal of the domestic courts in the ensuing civil proceedings to reinstate her.[67] She also complained under Art. 14 of the Convention that she had been discriminated against for expressing her opinion. The applicant further complained under Art. 6 § 1 of the Convention about the outcome of the above-mentioned civil proceedings and the lack of impartiality of the Constitutional Court that had adjudicated the case at the last instance. Lastly, the applicant complained that she had not had an effective remedy to protect her freedom of expression.

The findings of the Court can be summarized as follows:

(a) The Court notes at the outset that in a number of cases involving freedom of expression of civil or public servants, it has held that Art. 10 applied to the workplace in general and that therefore civil servants in particular also enjoyed the right to freedom of expression (see, for example, *Guja v. Moldova* [GC], no. 14277/04, §§ 52 and 70,[68] ECHR 2008-…; *Kudeshkina v. Russia*, no. 29492/05, § 86, 26 February 2009; and *Vogt v. Germany*, 26 September 1995, § 53, Series A no. 323). Although in the present case the applicant was working for a Croatian national oil company, of which the State was the sole stockholder at the time, she was not a civil servant. Nonetheless, the Court reiterates that Art. 10 of the Convention also applies when the relations between employer and employee are governed by private law and that the State has a positive obligation to protect the right to freedom of expression (see *Fuentes Bobo*, cited above, § 10). It therefore considers that the applicant's dismissal on account of her statements to the press constituted interference with her right to freedom of expression, as guaranteed by Art. 10 § 1 of the Convention (ibid.). The Court notes that, according to the decision on the applicant's dismissal of 18 April 2001, she was dismissed: (a) because in her statements to the press she had criticised certain aspects of INA's business policy and made serious accusations against members of the company's management, thereby harming INA's business reputation; and (b) because she had allegedly disclosed information classified as a business secret.

The domestic courts considered her dismissal lawful regardless of whether the disclosed information had constituted a business secret or not. They found that the applicant's dismissal was valid because she had harmed the reputation of INA by her negative statements in the press and had acted contrary to the interests of her employer by disclosing certain inside information without authorisation. She had thereby committed a serious breach of an employment-

[67] ECtHR, First Section, Vesna BALENOVIĆ against CROATIA, ibid.

[68] In this regard see J Omejec, *Konvencija za zaštitu ljudskih prava i temeljnih sloboda u praksi Europskog suda za ljudska prava – Strasbourški acquis* (2014), Zagreb, Novi informator, pp. 485-486.

related duty, which constituted a ground for summary notice under Art. 107 para. 1 [now Art. 116 para. 1] of the Labour Act.

The Court therefore accepts that the interference was prescribed by law and that it pursued legitimate aims as it intended to protect the reputation or rights of others, namely the business reputation and interests of INA (see *Fuentes Bobo*, cited above, § 45; *De Diego Nafría v. Spain*, no. 46833/99, § 31, 14 March 2002; and *Jacubowski v. Germany*, 23 June 1994, § 25, Series A no. 291-A). That being so, the Court also considers that, contrary to the Government's view, the present case is, as regards the legitimate aim, to be distinguished from the case of *Guja v. Moldova* (cited above). In that case the applicant, a civil servant, was dismissed because he had publicly disclosed confidential information. For that reason, the Court was ready to accept that the legitimate aim pursued by the interference was the prevention of the disclosure of information received in confidence (see *Guja*, cited above, § 59), whereas in the present case the legitimate aims sought to be achieved by the applicant's dismissal were the protection of the reputation and the rights of others.

Seeing that the interference with the applicant's freedom of expression in the present case was lawful and pursued legitimate aims, the only question for the Court to determine is whether that interference was "necessary in a democratic society".

The Court considers that it could be argued that the issues raised by the applicant were of legitimate public concern (see, *mutatis mutandis*, *Wojtas-Kaleta*, cited above, § 46, and *Fuentes Bobo*, cited above, § 48). On the other hand, the Court also considers that at least part of the applicant's statements, in particular those containing allegations of fraud, were certainly prejudicial to INA's business interests and were harmful to its business reputation. In this respect the Court shares the view of the Croatian Supreme Court, as expressed in its judgment of 24 May 2005, that a company whose management tolerates and encourages criminal activities certainly cannot have a good reputation and be trusted in the business world. The Court is also mindful of the Government's argument that the applicant made her statements to the press at a sensitive moment when the privatisation process in respect of INA had just begun. Therefore, in the instant case the applicant's freedom of expression, in particular her right to publicise her criticism of the business policy of the national oil company, as well as to impart information on alleged irregularities within the company, and, more importantly, the right of the public to receive that information, must be weighted against the requirements of the protection of the reputation and the rights of others, that is, the business reputation and interests of INA.

The Court reiterates in this connection that Art. 10 of the Convention does not guarantee wholly unrestricted freedom of expression and that the exercise of this freedom carries with it "duties and responsibilities". Therefore, whoever exercises that freedom owes "duties and responsibilities", the scope of which depends on his/her situation, the (technical) means he/she uses and the authenticity of the information disclosed to the public. Thus, in the present case there are three factors to be taken into account. The first concerns the applicant's situation as an employee, the second the nature of the means she used in making her statements (see *Handyside v. the United Kingdom*, 7 December 1976, § 49, Series A no. 24, and *Haseldine v. the United Kingdom*, no. 18957/91, Commission decision of 13 May 1992, Decisions and Reports (DR) 73, pp. 225 and 231) and the third the authenticity of the information disclosed (see *Wojtas-Kaleta*, cited above, § 50).

With regard to the first factor, the Court notes that the applicant was not a journalist – whose role is to inform and alert the public and impart information and ideas on matters of public concern – but an employee, who owes her employer a duty of loyalty, reserve and discretion (see, for example, *Wojtas-Kaleta*, cited above, § 43; *Guja*, cited above, § 70; and *Pay v. the United Kingdom* (dec.), no. 32792/05, 16 September 2008).

With regard to the second factor, the Court notes that the applicant, in expressing her opinions, used a means which has a broad and immediate impact, namely a daily national newspaper with wide circulation (see, *mutatis mutandis*, *Haseldine*, cited above).

With regard to the third factor relevant for the balancing exercise, the Court reiterates that it is open to the competent State authorities to adopt measures intended to react appropriately and without excess to defamatory accusations devoid of foundation or formulated in bad faith (see *Castells v. Spain*, 23 April 1992, § 46, Series A no. 236, and *Guja*, cited above, § 75). In such cases a distinction needs to be made between statements of fact and value judgments. While the existence of facts can be demonstrated, the truth of value judgments is not susceptible of proof even though there must be a sufficient factual basis to support them, failing which they may be excessive (see, for example, *Pedersen and Baadsgaard v. Denmark* [GC], no. 49017/99, § 76, ECHR 2004-XI).

The applicant, however, provided no evidence whatsoever in support of her allegations of criminal conduct on the part of INA's executives. This was confirmed by the Public Prosecutor in its decision of 22 September 2004, whereby it dismissed the applicant's criminal complaint against the named members of INA's management board and supervisory board. In particular, the Public Prosecutor found that the applicant had not provided any evidence giving rise to a reasonable suspicion that the criminal offences defined in Art. 292 (abuse of authority in business operations) and Art. 294 (concluding a prejudicial contract) of the Criminal Act had been committed and that there was no proof that any unlawful pecuniary gain had otherwise been obtained at INA's expense.

The content and the tone of her statements to the press, coupled with the lack of any factual basis for her most serious allegations (see, *mutatis mutandis*, *Morissens v. Belgium*, no. 11389/85, Commission decision of 3 May 1988, DR 56, pp. 127 and 136), suggest that they were a petulant reaction to the behaviour of INA's management, which ignored her business proposals. This finding is further corroborated by the fact that the applicant's serious accusations against certain members of INA's management were first made in the press, and that only on 9 May 2001 – that is, after she had been dismissed on that account – did she file a criminal complaint against them with the Public Prosecutor's Office.

Therefore, even though the applicant's dismissal was a severe sanction for her behaviour (see *Guja*, cited above, § 95, and *Pay*, cited above), the above considerations are sufficient for the Court to conclude that the interference complained of was not disproportionate to the legitimate aim pursued and thus may be regarded as "necessary in a democratic society" within the meaning of para. 2 of Art.10 of the Convention. It follows that this complaint is inadmissible under Art. 35 § 3 as manifestly ill-founded and must be rejected pursuant to Art. 35 § 4 of the Convention.

(b) The applicant further complained that she had been discriminated against for expressing her opinions. She relied on Art. 14 of the Convention. The Court refers to its above finding to the effect that the applicant's complaint under Art. 10 of the Convention is inadmissible as manifestly ill-founded. The Court has found no reason to conclude that her dismissal was based on any discriminatory elements. It follows that her related complaint under Art. 14 is also inadmissible under Art. 35 § 3 as manifestly ill-founded and must be rejected pursuant to Art. 35 § 4 of the Convention.

(c) The applicant also complained about the outcome of the civil proceedings in her case and alleged that the Constitutional Court had lacked impartiality when examining her case. The Court notes that the applicant complained about the outcome of the proceedings, which, unless it was arbitrary, the Court is unable to examine under Art. 6 § 1 of the Convention. In the light of all the material in its possession, the Court considers that in the present case the applicant was able to submit her arguments before courts which offered the guarantees set forth in Art. 6 § 1 of the Convention and which addressed those arguments in decisions that were duly reasoned and not arbitrary. In particular, the Court considers that the relationship between the Constitutional Court judge A.R. and the president of INA's supervisory board, S.L., to which the applicant referred, was so distant and remote that it could not justify her concern that the Constitutional Court lacked the impartiality required by Art. 6 of the Convention. Moreover, the applicant provided no evidence to suggest, and there is no indication of, any personal bias on Judge A.R.'s part. It follows that this complaint is inadmissible under Art. 35 § 3 as manifestly ill-founded and must be rejected pursuant to Art. 35 § 4 of the Convention.

(d) Lastly, the applicant complained of the lack of an effective remedy in respect of her complaint under Art. 10 of the Convention. She relied on Art. 13 of the Convention. The Court refers to its above finding to the effect that the applicant's complaint under Art. 10 of the Convention is inadmissible as manifestly ill-founded. It follows that her related complaint under Art. 13 is also inadmissible under Art. 35 § 3 as manifestly ill-founded and must be rejected pursuant to Art. 35 § 4 of the Convention.

Croatian Case-Law

In the next section we will briefly mention other important cases of whistleblowing in Croatia.[69]

The first whistleblower to gain media attention in Croatia was **Ankica Lepej**, an employee of the Zagrebačka Bank, who disclosed that Ankica Tuđman, the wife of the late Croatian president Franjo Tuđman, had made a 239,000 German Marks deposit and that her husband, Franjo Tudjman, had not disclosed this money in his property report. Subsequently, Mrs. Lepej was fired from the company. In 2002 police officer **Krešimir Mišić** pulled over Zagreb's Mayor Milan Bandić for driving under the influence of alcohol. Mišić was also fired after his police report leaked to the media. He was however reinstated 3 years later.

Another case worth mentioning involves **Stipe Mesić**, the former Croatian president who during his mandate in 1990s as the president of the Croatian parliament had anonymously delivered documents on the murder of the Zec family, i.e. Croatian Serbs murdered by the Croatian military officers and reports from court hearings during which the accused officers admitted committing the said criminal offence. A journalist of the Croatian magazine 'Globus' has discovered that Mr. Mesić delivered these documents. At this point Mr. Mesić was acting as the President of the Republic of Croatia and accused the journalists who decided to disclose this information to the public of being non-ethical. Needless to say, his reaction appeared justified in light of the fact that a journalist should keep his/her source anonymous, unless the source wishes to be identified. The journalist tried to justify his intention by using the public interest argument and the fact that president Mesić was no longer in danger. Nevertheless, it was up to Mr. Mesić to decide whether he wants to make this information public or not.

Other accounts of whistleblowers' experiences in Croatia are less fortunate. Viso Veraja, Dražen Keleminec, Božidar Lujanac and **Igor Rađenović** as the last victim are only some of those who were ambushed and violently beaten. Rađenović was the first who dared to call upon the some politics members and their involvement in the road company "Zagrebačke Ceste", after which he was attacked in May 2008 in the middle of the day. To date, his offenders remain unknown.

The existing legal and institutional framework in Croatia appears to fall short in terms of providing complete protection to whistleblowers. This was illustrated by the above discussed cases. The shortcomings of the protection system have resurfaced in a recent case in which two police officers who reported alleged corruption within the Ministry of the Interior, were not relocated and protected by the management of the Ministry. Instead, they were kept in the very same groups they reported against, which resulted in harassment and other disruptive behaviour. In another case, the workers' representative on the supervisory board of the Institute of Immunology in Zagreb and a member of the works council was suspended from

[69] These cases are referred to in more detailed in the study Vasiljević, *Tasks and challenges*: *Making whistleblowing work in Croatia*, ibid.

work and banned from entering the Institute's premises after denouncing the Institute's decision-making regarding a purchase of *swine flu vaccine* for a lack of transparency.[70]

As we recall from previous chapters, if an employee addresses a *bona fide* complaint to the person in charge or files one with the competent State authorities on grounds of a reasonable suspicion of corruption, this shall not constitute a justified reason for dismissal.[71] In one case the Supreme Court of the Republic of Croatia declared that the employee is in fact unlawfully basing his/her conduct upon his/her *civic duty*, if he/she first informs the media about potential irregularities. Sending letters to the media is not and could not be considered as addressing complaints to competent State authorities.[72]

The Supreme Court's case-law states that, "*if employee's statements have the character of informing the public about irregularities in the employer's work, even objectively offensive, but given in a public interest and bona fide and with the character of value judgements, in such case it is not a question of particularly serious breaches of employment-related duties, so there are no assumptions for delivering a decision on the termination of employment contract – extraordinary notice towards an employee who reacts with a public statement*."[73]

In short, whether or not the conditions for dismissal of an employee based on the fact that he/she approached the media are fulfilled is to be analysed on a case-to-case basis.[74]

Whistleblowing in the Croatian Public Sector: A Study of the Ministry of Justice

In this Chapter we will refer to an anonymous survey conducted by the Ministry of Justice of the Republic of Croatia in May 2013. By means of a questionnaire it surveyed the perception of civil servants employed[75] in the Ministry of Justice about effective protection of "whistleblowers".[76] The following table presents the results of the survey (Table 3.1):

---

[70] European Commission, Croatia to the EU Anti-Corruption Report, COM (2014) 38 final, Annex 11, p. 11–12.

[71] Labour Act, ibid., Art. 117 para. 3.

[72] See Balenovic case – Judgement of the Supreme Court of the Republic of Croatia, Revr-215/04 and the Judgement of the Constitutional Court of the Republic of Croatia, U-III-3121/2005.

[73] Judgment of the Supreme Court of the Republic of Croatia, Revr-700/06, 3-10-2007, in Crnić, I (2013) *Otkaz ugovora o radu*, Zagreb, Organizator, p. 185.

[74] Judgment of the Supreme Court of the Republic of Croatia, Revr-545/12, 19-6-2012.

[75] For employment relationship of civil servants see Ž Potočnjak, *Radni odnosi državnih službenika* (2013) Zagreb, Pravni fakultet Sveučilišta u Zagrebu, Studijski centar za javnu upravu i javne financije

[76] Anonymous questionnaire about the perception of civil servants employed in the Ministry of Justice. The questionnaires were sent by e-mails to 289 addresses, while 78 persons answered anonymously in an electronic or paper version, available at www.antikorupcija.hr/istrazivanja (as at 7 Nov 2014).

Table 3.1 Results of the anonymous survey of the Ministry of Justice of the Republic of Croatia about the perception of effective protection of "whistleblowers"

<table>
<tr><th>Question:</th><th>Yes</th><th>No</th><th>Don't know/made an unclear statement</th></tr>
<tr><td>1. Are you familiar with the term "whistleblower"?</td><td>77</td><td>1</td><td></td></tr>
<tr><td>2. Do you think that "whistleblowers" are adequately protected by the Croatian legal system?</td><td>6</td><td>71</td><td>1</td></tr>
<tr><td>3. As Ministry of Justice's employers have you been in touch with corruption?</td><td>20</td><td>57</td><td>1</td></tr>
<tr><td>4. In case you were aware of corruption, would you report it?</td><td>46</td><td>31</td><td>1</td></tr>
<tr><td>5. Do you think that in case you did report corruption, you would face harmful consequences (e.g. be dismissed)?</td><td>55</td><td>21</td><td>2</td></tr>
<tr><td rowspan="5">6. Name reasons why you would not report corruption.</td><td colspan="3">1. Nothing would change: 29</td></tr>
<tr><td colspan="3">2. The whole system is corrupted: 21</td></tr>
<tr><td colspan="3">3. I am afraid of mobbing: 34</td></tr>
<tr><td colspan="3">4. I am afraid of losing my job: 30</td></tr>
<tr><td colspan="3">5. It is not my problem: 1</td></tr>
<tr><td rowspan="2">7. What can be done to encourage potential "whistleblower"?</td><td colspan="3">1. Protection of anonymity: 72</td></tr>
<tr><td colspan="3">2. Receiving compensation: 59</td></tr>
<tr><td colspan="4">From 1 (non acceptable) to 5 (totally acceptable) rank the statements according to their importance:</td></tr>
<tr><td>Protection of anonymity:</td><td colspan="3">5–90 % of persons (of 72)</td></tr>
<tr><td>Receiving compensation:</td><td colspan="3">1–50 % of persons (of 59)</td></tr>
<tr><td rowspan="7">Suggestions made by employers for encouraging "whistleblowing":</td><td colspan="3">1. More effective prosecution and condemnation of criminal offenders</td></tr>
<tr><td colspan="3">2. Giving back the faith to people that making good is worth it</td></tr>
<tr><td colspan="3">3. Better legislative protection of "whistleblowers"</td></tr>
<tr><td colspan="3">4. Better information transition between organisation units in the Ministry of Justice would contribute to more transparency and to a direct information flow which would eliminate suspicion of corruption</td></tr>
<tr><td colspan="3">5. Legal support and help in potential cases before courts for reporting corruption</td></tr>
<tr><td colspan="3">6. "I am of the opinion that giving compensation is not a good option because it would also encourage false reporting"</td></tr>
<tr><td colspan="3">7. Quicker and more effective prosecution of corruption in procedures before courts</td></tr>
</table>

In response to the results of this survey the Ministry of Justice of the Republic of Croatia is to search for the most appropriate model to facilitate corruption reporting and to enable stronger "whistleblowers" protection. Such a model could be endorsed by other state organs and the entire public sector.[77] We should point out that this survey is in conformity with the general perception of whistleblowing protection. Namely, according to the UNODC study, more than half of all Croatians think that people who report corruption are likely to regret it, and that nothing constructive will come of reporting it.[78]

Conclusion

Corruption represents one of the biggest problems of the Croatian society. The legislation regulating the protection of whistleblowers has thus an important role in the prevention and fight against corruption.

As has been demonstrated, the protection of whistleblowers is fragmented, since it is regulated by several acts that belong to different fields of law (employment law in private and public sector, data protection, access to information, trade law and criminal law), and indirectly by acts regulating criminal (both substantive and procedural) law and media.

Despite this fragmented nature of the legislative protection, Croatian employment legislation guarantees general protection against dismissal to a worker–whistleblower who reports corruption. Specific categories of workers – mainly in the public sector (public servants and servants) – enjoy additional protection regarding whistleblowing such as the protection of anonymity, protection from denial or restriction of the rights provided by law, protection from any sort of harassment as a consequence of whistleblowing. The purpose behind this is to guarantee stronger protection mainly for whistleblowers among public servants and servants, considering that the public sector is the most fertile ground for corruption. Nevertheless, it is difficult to say whether these rules introduce important novelties in this area, especially since some of them are rather vague. As regards the issue of anonymity of whistleblowers, it is not clear just how it should be obtained, wherefore, although it is prescribed by the law, its implementation in practice remains questionable.

The intention of the legislator appears to have been merely to underscore the protection of certain categories of workers addressed by those acts: public sector employees, internal auditors and workers employed in trade. However, this protection is not efficient, and in urgent need of improvement by means of introducing more precise rules. For instance, since the law fails to specify the responsible persons to whom whistleblowers could report if they have a reasonable suspicion about corruption, our proposal *de lege ferenda* is to appoint an employee as the responsible person in charge of this issue.

Although whistleblowing is of vital importance for the employment relationship, it also affects other relationships. Likewise, since the whistleblower issue is rather

---

[77] At the time of writing of paper such a model was still not presented.

[78] European Commission, Croatia to the EU Anti-Corruption Report, COM (2014) 38 final, Annex 11, p. 12.

complex and covers a range of different sectors (from employment relationship, civic duty, environment protection etc.), it would be extremely useful to adopt a general act on whistleblowers with a view of regulating this issue in a more detailed and systematic way. Such an act would guarantee better protection to all those who expose themselves by 'blowing the whistle'.

Bibliography

Buklijaš B, Bilić A (2006) *Međunarodno radno pravo*, Split, Pravni fakultet u Splitu

Crnić, I (2013) Otkaz ugovora o radu, Zagreb, Organizator

Grozdanić V, Škorić M, Martinović, I (2012) 'Kaznenopravna zaštita radnika prema odredbama novog Kaznenog zakona', *Hrvatski ljetopis za kazneno pravo i praksu*, 19(2), pp. 437–499

Habazin M (2010) 'Zaštita "zviždača"', *Hrvatska javna uprava*, 10(2), pp. 331–348

Juras D (2011) 'Etički kodeks državnih službenika', *Hrvatska pravna revija, 6*, pp. 46–49

Omejec J (2014) *Konvencija za zaštitu ljudskih prava i temeljnih sloboda u praksi Europskog suda za ljudska prava – Strasbourški acquis*, Zagreb, Novi informator

Potočnjak Ž (2007a) 'Prestanak ugovora o radu' in Potočnjak Ž (ed) *Radni odnosi u Republici Hrvatskoj,* Zagreb, Pravni fakultet u Zagrebu, Organizator, pp. 375–494.

Potočnjak Ž (2007b) 'Radni odnosi državnih službenika' in Potočnjak Ž (ed) *Radni odnosi u Republici Hrvatskoj,* Zagreb, Pravni fakultet u Zagrebu, Organizator, pp. 803–876.

Potočnjak, Ž (2013) Radni odnosi državnih službenika, Zagreb : Pravni fakultet Sveučilišta u Zagrebu, Studijski centar za javnu upravu i javne financije

Rajko A (2008) 'Zaštita "zviždača" u državnoj službi', *IUSINFO*, available at www.iusinfo.hr/Article/Content.aspx?SOPI=CLN20V01D2008B27

Rajko A (2011a) 'Zaštita "zviždača" – pravni izvori u hrvatskom pravnom poretku' *IUSINFO*, available at: www.iusinfo.hr/Article/Content.aspx?SOPI=CLN20V01D2011B418

Rajko A (2011b) '"Zviždanje" iz perspektive slučaja Balenović protiv Hrvatske', *Radno pravo, 2,* pp.27–36

Škorić M (2014) 'Croatia' in K. Roach (ed) *Comparative Counter-Terrorism Law,* Cambridge University Press, 2015

Thüsing, G, Forst, G (2014) Whistleblowing Around The World – A Comparative Analysis of Whistleblowing in 23 Countries.

Učur MĐ (2012) 'Etički kodeks državnih službenika – heteronomni izvor prava sa specifičnim nomotehničkim karakteristikama', *Radno pravo,* 3, pp. 40–50

Učur MĐ, Laleta S (2007) *Konvencije Međunarodne organizacije rada s komentarima,* Zagreb, TIM press, Pravni fakultet u Rijeci

Vasiljević S (2010) *Tasks and challenges: Making whistleblowing work in Croatia*, available at www.whistleblowing-cee.org/countries/croatia/research/#1

Chapter 4
Protection and Support for Whistleblowers: The Cypriot Experience

Constantinos Kombos

Abstract The concept of whistleblowing in the legal order and social community of the Republic of Cyprus is mostly influenced by its European dimensions originated from the Council of Europe, the EU and the Council's Group of the States Against Corruption (GRECO). From a conceptual perspective, in Cyprus there is a considerable protection for internal whistleblowers working mostly in the public sector followed be a weaker protection of whistleblowers of private sector and even weaker protection for external whistleblowers that do not satisfy the employee criterion. The dichotomy of protection between public and private sector seems to be unnecessarily and unjustifiably overlooked. Whistleblowing in Cyprus is mostly connected with bribery and corruption while at the same time the small size, population and closeness of the Cypriot society must be taken into account. From the methodological perspective, there is almost absolute lack of sources in Cyprus regarding whistleblowing. The legal framework lacks a specific legislation offering independent protection to whistleblowers, a choice made by the State as regards the method of compliance with its international and European legal obligations and undertakings. In the case of Cyprus there has been no study or statistics exploring the public or intra-institutional attitude towards whistleblowers.

Introduction

The analysis of the concept of whistleblowing as can be observed in the legal order and the social community of the Republic of Cyprus, can not be conducted in isolation from the European dimension. The combined influence originating from the

C. Kombos (✉)
Law Department, University of Cyprus, Nicosia, Cyprus
e-mail: c.c.kombos@ucy.ac.cy

G. Thüsing, G. Forst (eds.), *Whistleblowing - A Comparative Study*,
Ius Comparatum - Global Studies in Comparative Law 16,
DOI 10.1007/978-3-319-25577-4_4

Council of Europe,[1] the EU[2] and GRECO[3] has been instrumental in reshaping the legal status of the protection afforded to individuals disclosing sensitive information about wrongdoings within different organizations. The European impact has been instrumental in defining in more detail and clarity the phenomenon of transparency and accountability, thus raising awareness for the useful role that can be performed through whistleblowing for promoting an ethos of openness and legitimacy. However, it must be pointed out that the positive changes have been apparent predominantly in the legislative level and much less in the social perception level. Put differently, the debate about issues relating to the specific protection of whistleblowers has not entered in the public forum and the established perception is that external sources, in this case European supranational or intergovernmental organizations, have required from the Republic of Cyprus to fill in the preexisting gap. It is this dichotomy applicable to the effectiveness of the European influence that must be assessed in the future in terms of additional steps to be taken for improving the status quo. It is indicative to mention the call by the **Environment Commissioner Charalampos Theopemptou[4] for a public interest disclosure legislation, which if in existence could have prevented the devasting explosion at the military base in Mari on the 11th July 2011 that killed 11 people and destroyed the main electricity supply station.**

At this stage two preliminary clarifications must be made, one conceptual and one methodological. From the conceptual perspective, a distinction must be drawn between internal and external whistleblowing. In the former instance, the person revealing sensitive information relating to wrongdoing in the legal sense is a member of the same organization. In the instances of external whistleblowing, the person in question is external to the organization under scrutiny. The preceding distinction is crucial, since in the case of internal situations the relationship is founded on the employment connection, thus triggering the protection mechanisms applicable for employees. In Cyprus, the distinction is paramount since there is considerable, yet in need of codification and improvement, protection for internal whistleblowers especially if those are employed in the public sector. There is weaker protection for private sector workers involved in internal whistleblowing and even weaker protection for external whistleblowers that are not satisfying the employee criterion.

[1] Committee on Legal Affairs and Human Rights, Council of Europe's Parliamentary Assembly, *The Protection of Whistleblowers*, (Doc.12006, 2009); See also Recommendation of Parliamentary Assembly 1916 (2010) *Protection of "whistle-blowers"*.

[2] B Rohde-Liebenau, *Whistleblowing Rules: Best Practice; Assessment and Revision of Rules Existing in EU Institutions* (2006), European Parliament, Directorate General Internal Policies of the Union, Budgetary Support Unit, Budgetary Affairs, available at www.europarl.europa.eu/document/activities/cont/200907/20090728ATT59162/20090728ATT59162EN.pdf.

[3] Council's Group of States Against Corruption (GRECO). See, e.g. the "Second Evaluation of Compliance Report on Cyprus" (2008) Recommendation 30 et seq., available at www.coe.int/t/dghl/monitoring/greco/evaluations/round2/GrecoRC2(2008)1_Cyprus_EN.pdf.

[4] P Pantelides, 'Time to Legalize Whistleblowing', *Cyprus Mail Interview* (Nicosia, 28 July 2011, available at www.thefreelibrary.com/'It's+time+to+legalise+whistleblowing'.-a0262673773, as at 10 December 2014).

From the methodological perspective, there is almost absolute lack of sources in Cyprus regarding whistleblowing, thus the research has been based on national reports and primary review and analysis of the legislative and juridical framework. Therefore, the desk review, the legal review and the analysis of the social perceptions and indicator relating to the concept of whistleblowing have taken place on the basis of all available material and after conducting primary level research into the legislative framework.

Moreover, the level of protection has been elevated in relation to civil servants, while in the private sector there has been lack of equivalent progress. There is, therefore, a combined protective effect for whistleblowers resulting from a plethora of legal sources[5] and its quality depending on the criterion of 'identity': more thorough protection for civil servants than for private sector employees. The applicable protection results from the *Unfair Dismissal Law, Law 24/67*, (as amended). Also, a potential source of protection lies under art 19 of the Constitution, safeguarding freedom of expression, which in conjunction with the decision of the Supreme Court in *Yiallouros v. Evgenios Nicolaou*,[6] human rights in general were found in certain instances to create horizontal effect between individuals. Accordingly, the public sector worker is in a better position to reveal important information relating to wrongdoings in the public sector, than an employee in the private sector. As will be explained, the protection for employees in the private sector is not crystal clear and needs to be supplemented.

Surmising, there is a hierarchy of protective intensity whereby the internal situations prevail over external situations, the public sector worker is protected in a more complete and comprehensive manner than an employee in the private sector, and the legal changes resulting from European influence that have been favoring whistleblowers have dominated over the social debate as to the need for furthering the phenomenon of whistleblowing.

Compilation, Description and Assessment of Whistleblowing Protection Laws

In terms of methodological approach, the present report is addressing the issues set out in the relevant part of the directions given and relating to the preceding heading, with a direct reference in parenthesis to the supplementing questions raised at the relevant questionnaire.

The legal framework lacks a specific legislation that offers independent standalone protection to whistleblowers. This legislative gap is the result of a choice made by the State as regards the method of compliance with its international and European legal obligations and undertakings. The preceding omission is being

[5] Public Service Law, Law 1/90, art 69A and Parts VI and VII. See also 369 Criminal Code and The Law on the General Principles of Administrative Law, Law 158/99.

[6] *Yiallouros v Evgenios Nicolaou* Civil Appeal No 9931, 8 May 2001.

partly compensated by the combined effect of different independent yet mutually impacting legislative acts. Needless to say, the lack of a *lex specialis* negates the need for analyzing whether there is universality of application or mere sectoral (public and private) scope of application.

The amalgam of legislative acts containing provisions relating directly or indirectly to the protection of whistleblowers is founded on the sector-related scope of application. Therefore, there is difference in scope of application of the existing legislative acts on the basis of the identity criterion, whereby the outcome is more thorough protection for civil servants than for private sector employees. In addition, the other crucial distinction is that made in the introductory part of the report and relating to internal and external aspects of whistleblowing. In the case of Cyprus, the existing legislative acts are exclusively focused on internal situations, whereas for external situations the protection in limited and untested. For example, if there is an instance of whistleblowing in the public sector and the person concerned is an employee of the State, then the protection granted is substantive. It stems from the *Public Service Law, Law 1/90* (as amended), art 69A and Parts VI and VII and also from art 369 of the *Criminal Code* (*cap 154*) and perhaps the *Law on the General Principles of Administrative Law, Law 158/99*. If the instance involves an employee of the private sector, the applicable legislation is the *Unfair Dismissal Law, Law 24/67* (as amended), with the protection afforded being indirect and of unclear nature. In cases of hybridity, where the whistleblower does not satisfy the substantive criterion of being an employee, the protection afforded could stem from art 19 of the Constitution safeguarding freedom of expression.

In detail, the *Public Service Law, Law 1/90* (as amended), art 69A and Parts VI–VII provide the point of reference for public sector employees. Art 69A was introduced in 2003 by the *Public Service* (*Amending*) (*no. 3*) *Law* (*Law 183* (*I*)/*2003*) and provides that:

> an employee that during the course of performing his duties becomes aware or has reasonable cause to believe that an act of corruption or bribery by another employee has taken place…*is obliged to report in writing* to the responsible authority to which he reports, providing all the necessary evidence in support of his claim (as translated by the author, emphasis added).

Therefore, art 69A creates an obligation to the civil servant to report in writing any instances of corruption, thus in the event that an employee complies then that person is to regarded as acting in accordance with the legal obligation resulting from art 69A and as a corollary can not be prosecuted. In a way, this provision offers a shield to the civil servant to safeguard from prosecution and/or disciplinary actions, by imposing an obligation to report to the responsible authority. Moreover, art 73 that lists the conditions for disciplinary action expressly provides (73 (1) (b)) the need for action or omission amounting to breach of duty or obligation of a civil servant. Therefore, a civil servant that is complying with the obligation arising from art 69A, can not be the subject of disciplinary investigation since the basic precondition of art 73 is not met. In addition the law introduced in 2004 to ratify the Civil law Convention on Corruption (*Law 7* (*III*)/*2004*) in art 7 provides that a person that has imposed an unjustified punishment on a whistleblower for reporting corruption, commits an offence that could lead to the imposition of prison sentence and/or pecuniary fine. Moreover, the possibility for civil law action is always possible for the victimized whistleblower.

In terms of supplementing legislative measures relating to the public service sector, reference must be made to art 369 of the *Criminal Code* (*cap 154*) stating:

> Every person who, knowing that a person designs to commit or is committing a felony, fails to use all reasonable means to prevent the commission or completion thereof, is guilty of a misdemeanor.

Therefore, the criminal code in effect imposes an obligation on civil servants and private sector workers equally, to report on individuals committing or designing to commit a felony, thus creating a solid defense against any prosecution based on their whistleblowing activities. It is apparent that the provision in the criminal code is predating the amended art 69A of the *Public Service Law* and is a provision of general scope that did not at the time had in mind the protection of whistleblowers. It can be stated that an amendment in the criminal code that would make express reference to whistleblowers could be beneficial and instrumental in creating a culture of transparency and accountability through the medium of active citizen reporting on crimes and corruptive practices. Such an amendment can be twofold: making it a criminal offense to prosecute or victimize whistleblowers and to make it a criminal offense if someone that becomes aware of the design to commit or actual committing of a *misdemeanor* fails to report it. The latter introduction will expand the range of criminal activity that will relate to whistleblowing obligation, while the former will strengthen the ethos of protecting those courageous individuals that decide to report on criminal activities. It is important to repeat that the *Criminal Code* provision of art 369 applies equally to private sector employees and also to hybrid cases, as those were defined supra, where the employee criterion is absent.

In relation to the Criminal Code, important is the provision in art 105 where it creates a criminal offense for the failure of a civil servant to report any attempt to influence him in the course of his duties. This provision does not relate to corruption and/or bribery but to attempts to influence the process of recruitment, promotion and evaluation of civil servants.

Finally, reference can be made to the *Law on the General Principles of Administrative Law*, *Law 158/99*, which provides a codification of the preexisting case law principles governing judicial review under art 146 Constitution. It is of indirect relevance to public sector employees that are whistleblowers in the sense that art 8 provides for legal boundaries that must guide administrative action and art 48 for the abuse of power by public authorities, thus creating a further preemptive shield against disciplinary action targeting civil service whistleblowers.

With reference to private sector workers, as stated previously, art 369 of the *Criminal Code* is relevant, as is the *Unfair Dismissal Law* (*Law 24/67* (as amended), with the protection afforded being indirect and of unclear nature. This is the case, since the legislation lists a number of grounds on which an employer can rely to dismiss an employee lawfully. In that list no express reference is being made to whistleblowers, but there is unfortunately room for such interpretation. In detail, the law lists among others as ground for lawful dismissal the behavior of the employee (art. 5 (f)) which is such that can no longer enable the relationship between employee and employer and also the disciplinary offenses of the employee in accordance with internal company rules. It would have preferable if an express provision is included whereby the dismissal of whistleblowers is prohibited, thus removing any room for interpretation. Nonetheless, the provisions of the *Unfair Dismissal Law, Law 24/67* (as amended), have to be construed in conjunction with art 369 of the *Criminal Code* thus creating a justifying basis for considering the whistleblowing activity as superior to any internal regulations of the company in the event that a felony is committed. Nonetheless, the overall protection is substantially weaker in comparison to that offered to civil servants.

The overview of the applicable legislation can not be complete if reference is not made to a very important and interesting decision of the Supreme Court that related to whistleblowing. That decision is *Yiallouros v. Evgenios Nicolaou*[7] the Supreme Court examined the issue of phone tapping between two individuals on the basis of suspicion of corruption in the public service and found for the horizontal effect of the constitutional provisions in art 15, 35 and 17 Constitution that create triangular relationships with the State and give rise to a right to sue for compensation despite of the lack of a legislative provision. That remarkable finding was supported by the analysis of *Klass v. FRG*.[8]

In the landmark decision *Yiallouros v. Evgenios Nicolaou*[9] it has been held "that a violation of human rights is an actionable right which can be pursued in civil courts against those perpetrating the violation, for recovering from them, *inter-alia*, just and reasonable compensation for pecuniary and non-pecuniary damage suffered as a result and or other appropriate civil law remedies for the violation".[10] Therefore, the right to pursue civil proceedings for human rights violations is as a corollary expanded in the horizontal sphere between individuals and is thus exercisable both against the State and private persons. The case therefore established that the violation of the plaintiff's right to the private life and the right to secrecy of correspondence and communications, as guaranteed by the Cypriot Constitution, provided him with an actionable right. Therefore, victims of human rights violations are entitled to rely directly on the provisions of the Constitution and the European Convention on Human Rights. The case concerned the action for compensation brought against Mr. Yiallouros for tapping telephone conversations made by complainant from his service phone, without the consent or the knowledge of the victim or the persons conversing with the latter over the telephone. The Court held that there was a direct

[7] *Yiallouros v Evgenios Nicolaou* Civil Appeal No 9931, 8 May 2001.

[8] *Klass v FRG*, A 28 para 64, (1979).

[9] *Yiallouros v Evgenios Nicolaou* Civil Appeal No 9931, 8 May 2001.

[10] Office of the Law Commissioner, "Answers to Issues/Questions submitted to the Government of Cyprus Regarding Fourth and Fifth Periodic Report (1998–2007) on the Implementation of the ICSECR" (March 2009), www.olc.gov.cy/olc/olc.nsf/0/0aa954e8aee4b23bc225758d001bf48b/$FILE/Answers%20to%20Issues%20-%20Questions.pdf (as at 10 December 2014).

breach of art 15 on privacy, irrespective of the fact that the motive of Mr Yiallouros was to reveal anomalies, omissions and/or improprieties resulting in unlawful enrichment of the victim. The Supreme Court held in the criminal trial[11] that took place firstly that Mr. Yiallouros' actions constituted first and foremost a criminal offence under *the Penal Code, Cap. 154*, as amended, as it amounted to an abuse of authority and that he was thus rightfully suspended and removed from his position and duties, respectively. In the subsequent 1992 criminal appeal,[12] where Mr. Yiallouros attempted to base his defence to criminal charges brought against him for the same set of circumstances, on the truth of the content of the magnetic tapes, the Supreme Court held that Mr. Yiallouros' actions constituted a gross breach of art 15 and the Executive Engineer's right to privacy under it and therefore the magnetic tapes, which were a by-product of such a breach, were rendered absolutely inadmissible as evidence. Evidence received or secured through the breach of fundamental rights and liberties of the person cannot be admissible for any reason whatsoever.

In the following civil action,[13] Mr. Yiallouros appealed to the Supreme Court against the first instance finding ordering the award CYP£5,000 to the victim in general damages for non-pecuniary damage or moral damage suffered. The appeal was dismissed by the Supreme Court that held that a plaintiff would be allowed to an award of general monetary damages, wherever there is a breach of a human right causing damage but where that breach does not also constitute a tort/civil wrong. The justification used by the Court was that of 'triangular situations i.e. tritenergia (in Greek)', whereby the Constitutional provision on the right to privacy becomes a third 'party' to a civil action that lacks legislative regulation, thus creating such a right of compensation simply because of the importance of the affected right. The case is potentially problematic for whistleblowers but only where they also violate the law in order to substantiate their accusations. The decision is far more important as a tool for protecting whistleblowers from persecution and unfair dismissal by their employers on grounds of whistleblowing activity. The possibility of actionable rights in horizontal relations where there is no express provision recognizing such an actionable right (as is the case with whistleblowing), creates an interesting protective option.

In relation to amendments and tabled legislation and regulations pending after 2007, it must be clarified that there has been no development despite calls for removing the requirement of art 69A *Public Service Law* (*Law 1/90*) for written submission of reports relating to corruption and bribery. The written form is possibly creating an obstacle for the reporting since it could be interpreted as requiring the whistleblower to reveal his identity. The fact that such reports must be made in

[11] (1990) 3 CLR 3532. See also, GN Apostolou, *Defamation & Privacy Laws in the Republic of Cyprus*, available at www.apostoloulaw.com/pdf_Defamation_Article.pdf (as at 10 December 2014).

[12] (1992) 2 CLR 147. See also, GN Apostolou, *Defamation & Privacy Laws in the Republic of Cyprus*, ibid.

[13] *Yiallouros v Evgenios Nicolaou* Civil Appeal No 9931, 8 May 2001.

written form was criticized in the GRECO Evaluation Report (paragraph 90)[14] and led to the adoption of recommendation vi.[15] The authorities had decided to maintain the requirement of written reporting as provided for in the law. However, they had also indicated that during training of public employees it would be highlighted that in urgent cases the written form would not be necessary. GRECO had stressed in the Compliance Report[16] that the measure taken was of an informal, administrative character and that the law remained the same. This constituted a contradiction that could generate problems in practice. GRECO was therefore not convinced that the measure taken would satisfy the objective of the recommendation, unless the law was amended accordingly. In conclusion, GRECO welcomed the decision to allow whistleblowers to report also orally where the circumstances so require. However, it invited the authorities of Cyprus to consider further the implementation of this recommendation, which was considered partly implemented.

In responding to the argument, the Cypriot authorities submitted that by virtue of the existing provisions of the Public Service Law, a person may give information about suspected corruption in writing without identifying himself/herself (anonymously), whereas in the absence of such a requirement, the identity of the whistleblower would be automatically revealed if such information were given orally. Moreover, the authorities claim that the system would be more open for misuse, if the requirement was abolished. Besides, the competent authorities have an obligation to act upon every report (whether written or oral). The authorities also stress that the General Audit Office has an obligation to investigate any written or oral complaint and/or report made to it and, furthermore, that the Police has introduced a direct phone line for the anonymous oral reporting of any suspected offence. Finally, the authorities reiterate that it is now the practice, during training seminars for public servants, to stress that in urgent cases they can avoid the written form of reporting, if they believe it is more appropriate under the particular circumstances to do so.

Regardless how reasonable the preceding argumentation may be, as the measure of encouraging oral submission of complaints has no legal basis and contradicts the legal provision contained in the *Public Service Law* (Art. 69A), the interpretation of section 81(2) of the *Public Service Law*, which according to the authorities, implies that a report, whether written or oral, shall immediately be investigated by the Public Service Committee, seems to be creating unnecessary confusion and mixed standards.

The Republic of Cyprus has no independent authority that receives and investigates complaints about whistleblowing, nor is there any exclusive jurisdiction for such a task. On the contrary, there is a variety of agencies dealing with such cases

---

[14] Council's Group of States Against Corruption (GRECO). See, eg the "Second Evaluation of Compliance Report on Cyprus" (2008) Recommendation 30 et seq., available at www.coe.int/t/dghl/monitoring/greco/evaluations/round2/GrecoRC2(2008)1_Cyprus_EN.pdf (as at 10 Dec 2014).

[15] ibid.

[16] ibid.

with the Public Service Commission being the point of reference for civil servants and the police for all other instances, while the General Audit Office is also responsible in cases relating to allegations of financial nature.

In the event of retaliation against whistleblowers, the civil action as expanded in the case of Yiallouros analysed *supra* is a possible remedy, while there is criminal liability under the law introduced in 2004 to ratify the Civil Law Convention on Corruption (*Law 7 (III)/2004*). In art 7 it provides that a person that has imposed an unjustified punishment on a whistleblower for reporting corruption, commits an offence that could lead to the imposition of prison sentence and/or pecuniary fine.

There has been no official assessment of the protective system to date, except in the form of the national reports submitted to GRECO where descriptive reference to the system is being made, yet with no actual assessment as to its efficacy and effectiveness. Unofficially, there have been calls for introducing a specific legislative provision by the **Environment Commissioner Charalampos Theopemptou**[17] **advocating for a public interest disclosure legislation, which if in existence could have prevented the devasting explosion at the military base in Mari on the 11th July 2011 that killed 11 people and destroyed the main electricity supply station**.

In terms of disclosures expressly covered under whistleblowing, those include corruption and bribery in accordance with art 69A of the *Public Service Law* (*Law 1/90*):

> an employee that during the course of performing his duties becomes aware or has reasonable cause to believe that an act of corruption or bribery by another employee has taken place…*is obliged to report in writing* to the responsible authority to which he reports, providing all the necessary evidence in support of his claim (as translated by the author, emphasis added).

Any other activities are possibly covered under the general provisions mentioned earlier (Criminal Code, Unfair Dismissal) but no express reference is made to whistleblowing therein.

In terms of individuals covered as whistleblowers, under the *Public Service Law 1/90*, the term employee includes anyone possessing a position permanently, temporarily or by way of substitution (art 2). This definition excludes non-traditional employees of the State, while in relation to the private sector the absence of specific legislation seems to render the issue obsolete.

In addition the law introduced in 2004 to ratify the Civil law Convention on Corruption (*Law 7 (III)/2004*) in art 7 provides that a person that has imposed an unjustified punishment on a whistleblower for reporting corruption, commits an offence that could lead to the imposition of prison sentence and/or pecuniary fine. The legislation does not explain the scope of unjustified punishment, but an interpretation can be made with art 79 of the *Public Service Law* (*Law 1/90*) that lists the possible sanctions that can be imposed against civil servants in disciplinary

[17] P Pantelides, 'Time to Legalize Whistleblowing' (2011 28 July), *Cyprus Mail Interview*, available at www.thefreelibrary.com/'It's+time+to+legalise+whistleblowing'.-a0262673773 (as at 10 Dec 2014).

proceedings. Those include demotion, firing, unwanted transfer, stripping of job duties or benefits, reduction of pay, financial penalty equal up to three monthly salaries and forced retirement. The threat for such action is not included in art 7 of *Law 7 (III)/2004*.

In terms of express protection granted to whistleblowers for good-faith disclosures found to be incorrect or inaccurate, there is no such provision. In relation to the burden of proof, in both public and private sectors (*Public Service Law 1/90 and Unfair Dismissals Law 1967*), that rests with the employer. As far as to whether the legislation includes any internal or external disclosure mechanisms, the legislative framework makes no such specific provision. The same unfortunate lack of reference applies in relation to hotlines, remedies available to whistleblowers, and to participation to follow-up reforms. As regards classification of information on the basis of confidentiality, there seems to be an unclear state of affairs since art 69A *Public Service Law 1/90* does not provide for a hierarchy of information and thus for the specific prohibition to disclose confidential information. Nonetheless, the same law provides in art 60 that any written or oral information that a civil servant possesses as a corollary of exercising his duties, is confidential and is prohibited to be communicated to any person but for the proper exercise of service duty or after the written approval of the relevant authority. Therefore, the communication of any information that relates to the obligation of the civil servant under art 69A "an employee that during the course of performing his duties becomes aware or has reasonable cause to believe that an act of corruption or bribery by another employee has taken place…*is obliged to report in writing* to the responsible authority to which he reports, *providing all the necessary evidence in support of his claim*" (emphasis added), is implying that there is no type of information that can be excluded from disclosing. Furthermore, the *Criminal Code* (*cap 154*) in art 50A provides that the disclosure of information relating to the defense of the State is a criminal offense, with the exception of where the recipient is duly authorized to handle such information. Therefore, the whistleblowing that has as a recipient an individual within the same service is likely to exclude any criminal liability, as the *Public Service Law 1990* excludes any disciplinary offense.

Nonetheless, special attention must be paid to the more specific provision of the *Criminal Code* (*cap 154*) relating to the disclosure of official secrets. Art 135 provides:

> Any person employed in the public service who publishes or communicates any fact which comes to his knowledge by virtue of his office, and which it is his duty to keep secret or any document which comes to his possession by virtue of his office and which it is his duty to keep secret, except to some person to whom he is bound to publish or communicate it is guilty of a misdemeanor. A prosecution for an offence under the provisions of this section shall not be commenced except by, or with the consent of, the Attorney General.

It is therefore apparent that the disclosure of even state secrets within the service that one is serving will not constitute a criminal offense, while the possibility of a prosecution for borderline cases is controlled by the Attorney General that has the sole responsibility for initiating criminal prosecution in this case. In the exercise of his duties the Attorney General is bound to take into account the broader public interests and the positive impact that the revelation of the information might have.

There is nonetheless limitation to the protection granted, since that extends only to case relating to corruption and bribery. With reference to the private sector, no similar protective provision is being mad and there is therefore a considerable gap in the protection afforded to whistleblowers.

Finally, there is clearly considerable legal protection granted to whistleblowers in the event of prosecution, on the basis of the right to a fair trial guaranteed fully under the Constitution (Art. 11, 12 an 30). In the event of disciplinary action, the decisions of the Public Service Commission are subject to appeal before the Supreme Court (Art. 73-86 *Public Service Law 1990*).

Surmising, the protection levels created by the complex and multi-sourced legislative framework are primarily limited to the public sector. The dichotomy of protection between public and private sector is stark and the private sector seems to be unnecessarily and unjustifiably overlooked. In addition, the protection in the public sector is limited to cases concerning bribery and corruption, thus excluding any other variations of illegal activity, while at the same time the emphasis of the system is placed on the employee quality. Moreover, the procedural aspects of protection to public sector whistleblowers are founded on the written submission of information, with the law requiring an amendment to expressly enable oral communications and unanimity. Finally, the system needs to be supported with auxiliary provisions relating to the status of whistleblowers and to mechanisms for faster communication with the authorities both internally and externally to the organization concerned.

Perceptions and Political Will

It must be clarifies from the outset that in the case of Cyprus there has been no study or statistics exploring the public or intra-institutional attitude towards whistleblowers, while at the same time the small size, population and closeness of the Cypriot society must be taken into account.

In terms of perceptions, the cases where whistleblowers were involved are normally kept from the public eye, with their anonymity being protected. There has been one notable recent instance where a civil servant posted at the Agriculture Ministry made written accusations against colleagues and the Minister for nepotism in relation to appointments of workers on hourly rate. The name of the civil servant (Mr. Dimitriou) was made public most likely by his own intention in order to attract the support of the press, which actually happened primarily because he was to face disciplinary proceedings. The press, the majority of the political parties and the Attorney General praised him for his action and a criminal investigation that resulted in prosecutions was the outcome. The saga was interesting also because the Minister was not prosecuted and was himself the institutionally responsible for dealing with the written information that Mr. Dimitriou provided while at the same time there was serious grounds for believing that the minister should have been aware of the nepotism.[18] From this case it becomes clear that when the media is involved, the whistleblower is perceived as an important person committed to fighting corruption. However, the press and the public tend to approach such cases with a rigid criterion of political affiliation, thus always questioning the motives of the whistleblower and frequently associating his actions with his political affiliation. In a small country and with a closed society such personal information is easy to obtain, thus placing the whistleblower amid the heated blaming debate of the political parties. This factor represents the main barrier to whistleblowing. In terms of 'labeling' the whistleblower, the perception is dependent on political affiliations and can range from the classical ends of the spectrum, namely 'snitch' (karfi in Greek) or 'hero'. The same applies equally to the political elite, which approaches the matter from the perspective of having potential for political gain or loss.[19]

Surmising, the political and public perceptions of whistleblowers are primarily politically influenced and there is frequent disclosure of information on the basis of anonymity. The whistleblower is seen favorably or negatively, depending on the political motivation associated with his actions, thus most often than not rendering the best available option being the maintenance of anonymity.

Strengths, Weaknesses and Recommendations

There is no move for legislative change relating directly to whistleblowers, although there are various initiatives taking place aiming to have an impact on corruption. These take the form of creating a system for declaring financial assets for public figures and individuals holding public office, yet those initiatives are not directly or indirectly related to enhancing the protection for whistleblowers.

The main strength of the Cypriot system is its willingness to correspond through implementation to calls for change coming from Europe. The creation of a European obligation that requires the strengthening of the support and protection for whistleblowers, will certainly impact on the Cypriot legislative framework. In terms of positive elements that can be traced in the Cypriot system, the point of reference has to be the introduction of art 69A *Public Service Law 1/90* that expressly addresses the issue of whistleblowing. Nonetheless, the positives end there since there is need for careful and structured reform rather than an unsystematic connection of whistleblowing with corruption. In other words, there needs to be an examination of the phenomenon of whistleblowing on its own right and not as a mere tool for reporting on corruption.

In terms of content, the protection levels created by the complex and multi-sourced legislative framework are primarily limited to the public sector. The need

---

[18] 'Οι Αθώοι και οι Θεματοφύλακες των Θεσμών', available at www.m4trix87.wordpress.com/οι-αθώοι-και-οι-θεματοφύλακες-των-θεσ/ (as at 10 Dec 2014).

[19] ibid.

for a *lex specialis* that would apply equally to the private sector is paramount. The dichotomy of protection between public and private sector is stark and the private sector seems to be unnecessarily and unjustifiably overlooked. In addition, the protection in the public sector is limited to cases concerning bribery and corruption, thus excluding any other variations of illegal activity, while at the same time the emphasis of the system is placed on the employee quality. Moreover, the procedural aspects of protection to public sector whistleblowers are founded on the written submission of information, with the law requiring an amendment to expressly enable oral communications and unanimity. Finally, the system needs to be supported with auxiliary provisions relating to the status of whistleblowers and to mechanisms for faster communication with the authorities both internally and externally to the organization concerned.

Therefore, the hierarchy of protective intensity whereby the internal situations prevail over external situations, the public sector worker is protected in a more complete and comprehensive manner than an employee in the private sector, need to be eradicated through centralization and streamlining of the legislation. The legal changes that would be resulting in favoring whistleblowers can find their source in the European influence (EU, Council of Europe) and will need to dominate over the social debate as to the need for furthering the phenomenon of whistleblowing.

Bibliography

Apostolou GN (1990) *Defamation & Privacy Laws in the Republic of Cyprus*. http://apostoloulaw.com/pdf_Defamation_Article.pdf. Accessed 10 December 2014

Apostolou GN (1992) *Defamation & Privacy Laws in the Republic of Cyprus*. http://apostoloulaw.com/pdf_Defamation_Article.pdf. Accessed 10 December 2014

Committee on Legal Affairs and Human Rights, Council of Europe's Parliamentary Assembly, The Protection of Whistleblowers, (Doc.12006, 2009); See also Recommendation of Parliamentary Assembly 1916 (2010) Protection of "whistle-blowers"

Council's Group of States Against Corruption (GRECO). See, eg the "Second Evaluation of Compliance Report on Cyprus" (2008) Recommendation 30 et seq., http://www.coe.int/t/dghl/monitoring/greco/evaluations/round2/GrecoRC2(2008)1_Cyprus_EN.pdf. Accessed 10 December 2014

Office of the Law Commissioner, "Answers to Issues/Questions submitted to the Government of Cyprus Regarding Fourth and Fifth Periodic Report (1998–2007) on the Implementation of the ICSECR", (March 2009). http://www.olc.gov.cy/olc/olc.nsf/0/0aa954e8aee4b23bc225758d001bf48b/$FILE/Answers%20to%20Issues%20-%20Questions.pdf. Accessed April 2015

Poly Pantelides, (2011, 28 July 2011) "Time to Legalize Whistleblowing", Cyprus Mail Interview. http://www.thefreelibrary.com/'It's+time+to+legalise+whistleblowing'.-a0262673773. Accessed 10 December 2014

Public Service Law, Law 1/90, art 69A and Parts VI and VII. See also 369 Criminal Code and The Law on the General Principles of Administrative Law, Law 158/99.

Rohde-Liebenau B (2006) *Whistleblowing Rules: Best Practice; Assessment and Revision of Rules Existing in EU Institutions,* European Parliament, Directorate General Internal Policies of the Union, Budgetary Support Unit, Budgetary Affairs. http://www.europarl.europa.eu/document/activities/cont/200907/20090728ATT59162/20090728ATT59162EN.pdf. Accessed 10 Dec 2014

Chapter 5
Whistleblowing: National Report for the Czech Republic

Jan Pichrt and Jakub Morávek

Abstract In the Czech Republic, there is no comprehensive special whistleblowing legislation. If the notification is made within industrial relations, more precisely within private-law relations, then protection of whistleblowers as well as the ones who are notified, provides direct support especially the legislation on protection of personal data and indirectly also the constitutional foundations of the Czech legal order. The Supreme Court of the Czech Republic and the Constitutional Court of the Czech Republic have commented, in the context of the principle of employee loyalty, on a practice which could be described as whistleblowing in the area of employment. The courts have in principle confirmed that even without an explicit legal basis it is possible in the legal order of the Czech Republic to found necessary normative basis for this practice.

The Concept of Whistleblowing in the Czech Legal System

We can view the issue of whistleblowing from different perspectives and in different breadth. In general (in a wider sense) this institution has an impact on (almost) all areas of law. Besides labour law and commercial law it is necessary to perceive its aspects in particular in the area of criminal law, constitutional, and civil law. Essential, is further the relation to personal data protection and bound to the transnational sources in the area of human rights and fundamental freedoms protection, etc.

In the legal order of the Czech Republic, there is not yet included a comprehensive regulation of whistleblowing, including the area of labour law. In the reality of everyday life, it is nevertheless possible to identify situations that can be subsumed under the general perception of whistleblowing, and in the Czech Republic these are seen through general regulations of the above-indicated areas of law.

Substantial influence on whistleblowing has been on (as a result of its cross-sectional character) especially legislation aimed at personal data protection in the

J. Pichrt (✉) • J. Morávek
University v Praze, Právincká Fakulta,
nám. Curieových 901/7, 11640 Praha 1, Czech Republic
e-mail: jan.pichrt@cmail.cz; MoravekJakub@seznam.cz

G. Thüsing, G. Forst (eds.), *Whistleblowing - A Comparative Study*,
Ius Comparatum - Global Studies in Comparative Law 16,
DOI 10.1007/978-3-319-25577-4_5

form of the Act No. 101/2000 Coll., personal data protection and amendment of certain laws in the Czech Republic.

The term whistleblowing is, in the Czech Republic, only directly mentioned in the Decree of the Czech National Bank No. 123/2007 Coll., on the rules on prudential undertakings of banks, credit cooperatives, and securities dealers; in this regulation this concept designates a mechanism of communication of major fears of employees regarding the functionality and effectiveness of the control system outside the normal flow of information. The concept of whistleblowing was supplemented into the mentioned Decree only with effect from 1 January 2011, and with no change in provisions laying down procedures in question. It was in fact a technical rather than substantive amendment of the relevant provision and this change was not directly legislatively justified. The decree thus can not be seen as a transparent regulation of whistleblowing, it is still rather a rare occurrence of this term in the Czech legal order. The concept of whistleblowing alone (without translation into Czech) has begun in the local legal environment to appear and began to be discussed about 5 years ago, following the practices of multinational corporations, which, as a result of application of legislation especially of the United States (especially of SOX), have started to implement also in the Czech Republic internal reporting systems for notification of malicious acts with a partial overlap towards external service providers.[1] These systems were (by their nature) associated with the procession of personal data and their transnational transfer.

Practical experience with sophisticated notification systems, as a result of this, have acquired vicariously also some public authorities of the Czech Republic especially the Office for Personal Data Protection.

From a terminological point of view it must be said that, as regards the concept of whistleblowing (neither in the wider nor in the narrower sense) there is no consensus so far in the Czech Republic even within the professional community. The professional community has begun a serious debate over this issue in the last 2 years.[2]

The Existing Legislative Proposals for Regulation of Whistleblowing in the Czech Republic

Stimuli which has opened professional debate over the issue of whistleblowing can be designated, as among others, two legislative proposals, "laws on whistleblowing" (debates over them culminated in particular in the first half of 2013), neither one of which has not been adopted.

---

[1] *cf.* for example J Pichrt, J Morávek, *Whistleblowing* (2009), Právo pro podnikání a zaměstnání. (Law for Business and Employment), sv. č. 7–8, pp. 19–25, J Morávek, *Whistleblowing – praktické otázky* (2009), Právo pro podnikání a zaměstnání, sv. č. 11, s. 12–20, J Morávek, *Whisteblowing – zákonná opora* (2009), Právo pro podnikání a zaměstnání, sv. č. 12, s. 12–17.

[2] *cf.* J Pichrt, *Whistleblowing* (Praha, Wolters Kluwer ČR, 2013).

The cause of their failure can be seen in the fact that the two proposals were essentially observed as primarily political aims. Both the formulation of legislative intent of the bill and drafting the paragraph text was not preceded by a professional discussion, which should have answered questions that naturally arise from the principle of subsidiarity of the law and subsidiarity in the law, and which actually are only a result of the development of the test that measures the goals and means.

These are the questions:

- What will we understand under the concept of whistleblowing? How widely will we perceive it (what all will be part of it and what is its aim)?
- Whether it is (in the context of potential benefits and consequences) suitable to strive to achieve the objective through the law and whether the legal description of this institution is the least invasive legal instrument to achieve the pursued objective.
- If yes, whether it is necessary to (among other things following the principle of legal certainty, etc.) to create special legislation regulating the institute, or whether there is sufficient existing legislation which as a result of its generality (and with contribution of legal principles and rules) allows the judicial power in this respect, to complete the law and cover social relations, on which the special regulation should fall.

The Government Proposal

In November 2012, the Czech government approved the outline of a bill to protect notifiers of criminal offenses (whistleblowing). The Proposal was submitted by the former Deputy Prime Minister, Chairman of the Legislative Council of the Government and the President of the Government Committee for the coordination of the fight against corruption Karolina Peak. Mrs. Peak in connection with the submitted proposal, said: "*The government today approved the outline of a bill <u>to protect notifiers of criminal offenses</u>* (*whistleblowing*). *Now I have to prepare an articulated version, which will consist of an <u>amendment of the Anti-discrimination Act</u>. An employee who <u>meets in his work with the offense, particularly corruption, should in future be protected against dismissal.</u> The articulated version will contain a list of offenses to which notification will relate the protection and also possibilities to defence of those who have been wrongly accused.*"

From the cited (in particular see underlined text) are evident the main points of the original intent, which can simultaneously be considered weaknesses and deficiencies of the proposed conception, when:

- The proposed regulation dealt only with notifications to authorities active in criminal proceedings (i.e. basically just develop some techniques that have been possible even without its adoption)
- The proposal did not consistently solve the protection of whistleblowers nor the one who was notified (data protection disregarded the proposal)

- The issue of internal investigation organs at the employer was not solved
- Whistleblower protection was limited to the creation of the new discriminatory reason

The aim of the proposal was in essence to constitute whistleblowing as a new discriminatory criterion, which was to be incorporated into the Act No. 198/2009 Coll., Antidiscrimination Act.

This tendency, which did not correspond to the resolution of the Parliamentary Assembly of the Council of Europe No. 1729, however, proved to be unsystematic and lifeless. Largely, among other things, because by its implementation the conception of the Antidiscrimination Act would be disruptive when besides discriminatory reasons (race, ethnicity, nationality, gender, sexual orientation, age, disability, religion, belief and world view) characterized with constancy and (mostly – with some reservations regarding religion, faith and belief) independence from a subjective choice, was ranked a reason temporary and completely dependent on the will, more precisely caused by the conduct of the "individual protected" by the Act. It is obvious that the individual is not born a whistleblower, and that he/she becomes a whistleblower.[3]

As a result of the fall of the government the proposal was not even heard in the Parliament of the Czech Republic.

Proposal of a Group of Senators

The second legislative proposal in this area was in July 2013. A proposal of an *act on some measures to increase the level of protection of whistleblowers, conduct that is not consistent with the public interest, and amendment of other laws*, was submitted by group of Senators.

Contrary to the government's proposal, a more challenging journey towards the adoption of a separate legal regulation was chosen that would regulate the issue of whistleblowing. Even this proposal, however, did not fully conform to the resolution of the Parliamentary Assembly of the Council of Europe No. 1729.

Senate debating print, "*returned to the proposer for completion*" after hearing, whereas the debate showed a large degree of non-sophistication of the proposal in the submitted form. An example is a partial immunity of a whistleblower regarding the crime of defamation, the merits of which is that the offender intentionally communicates false information about another person in order to damaged him/her significantly.

[3] *cf.* J Pichrt, 'Několik poznámek k whistleblowingu, loajalitě zaměstnance a k legislativním návrhům/Some remarks about whistleblowing, employee loyalty and legislative proposals', in J Pichrt (Ed.), *Whistleblowing* (Praha, Wolters Kluwer ČR, 2013), pp. 11–19.

Current Legislative Work

After the part concerning former legislative proposals now some notes to the current legislative work can be presented.

In the course of the year Act No. 234/2014 Coll., On State Service (hereinafter the "State Service Act"), was approved in the Czech Republic. The State Service Act empowers the government of the Czech Republic to issue decree (executive decree) based on which factually whistleblowing shall be implemented inside the state service.

In the concrete, by provision of section 205 letter (d) of the State Service Act, the Government of the Czech Republic is empowered to issue decree (executive decree) stating the rules for protection of state employees who make an claim regarding suspicion of illegal conduct of a superior employee or another state employee, another employee or person in the service relation established by a different legal act and stating suitable provisions for protection of these claimants; namely it should give conditions for the claimant's right to concealment of personal identity, the organization of anonymous claim of illegal conduct by a state employee, notification of the course and results of inquiry of the claim and terms for inquiry.

At this moment there is not even a preliminary proposal regarding the above mentioned executive decree. Hopefully in the process of its issuance the basic rules and principles of personal data protection stipulated in legislation will be followed – there is no doubt these rules and principles should be applied in the case.

In discussing legislative work concerning whistleblowing we should also mention that currently there is an expert working commission active within the Council of the Government of the Czech Republic for the Fight Against Corruption that is focused directly on the issue of whistleblowing. This commission, among others, researches possible legislative solutions in this respect. However, there are no concrete outputs up to the time of this publication.

Whistleblowing, Industrial Relations and Judicial Decisions

The realization of whistleblowing in industrial relations, especially if it is whistleblowing in the broader sense including also notification to the public authorities, is closely linked to the issue of employee loyalty to the employer. Positive expression of this principle can be found in Section 1 of the Labour Code, which, among others, indicates that among the basic principles of industrial relations falls proper work performance by employee in accordance with the legitimate interests of the employer.

The Supreme Court of the Czech Republic and the Constitutional Court of the Czech Republic have commented, in the context of the principle of employee loyalty, on a practice which could be described as whistleblowing in the area of employment. They have in principle confirmed that even without an explicit legal basis it is possible in the legal order of the Czech Republic to found a necessary normative basis for this practice.

The Constitutional Court in the case file No. III. ÚS 298/12 set aside the judgment of the Regional Court in Brno and the judgment of the Supreme Court which confirmed this judgment. This was the case where the Regional Court in Brno (in the year 2009) changed the judgment of the District Court in Břeclav, when it concluded that both of the plaintiffs (complainants in proceedings before Constitutional Court of the Czech Republic) violated labour discipline in a particularly gross manner when as employees of the employer operating a wastewater treatment plant informed in 2001, to the supervisory authorities concerned about violations of legal regulations while operating the wastewater treatment plant in the letter entitled "The disastrous state of wastewater treatment plant" (among others they pointed out that the water purifier was in a state not corresponding standards). The court concluded that the employer acted in accordance with labour legislation when he terminated the employment relationships of the employees immediately.

As a result of the defence of the employees concerned was the matter after the appeal and the appellate review submitted to the Constitutional Court of the Czech Republic. The Constitutional Court of the Czech Republic in the case file No. III. ÚS 298/12 (among others) said: "*The private-law demand for contractual compliance, the principle of pacta sunt servanda, more precisely contractual freedom and taken obligation of an employee to be loyal to his/her employer, can not a priori exclude other significant public interest, the interest in that employees also can turn to state authorities in situations when from the employer's side there is a serious threat to significant social interests, such as protection of health of citizens, environmental protection, or protection of the purity of water, or even when there is a breach of these public goods. The agreement between the employee and the employer can not interfere with public relations, interfere with the interest of society in ensuring that every citizen in a democratic legal state could assist the state in identifying deficiencies and, if necessary, to draw attention to the deficiencies.*"

Furthermore, the Constitutional Court stated the need to evaluate and compare in the relevant contentious matter, the public interest in protecting the environment and public health on the one hand with the interest on contractual compliance and loyalty to the employer on the other hand. The general courts failed to meet this need when in the judged case they "*…considered only one page, the interest in compliance with contracts, employee loyalty towards the employer and concluded that the employee must not break the loyalty by that he will 'snitch' on his/her employer, which they assessed as a gross breach of work discipline. But general courts have not paid sufficient attention to the fact, whether in this particular case, the employees' attempt to show the deficiencies and protect important social values does not justify their actions. General courts therefore in the judged case had to carefully weigh and consider which interest, whether public or private, is predominant.*"

Conclusion

The issue of whistleblowing is in the Czech Republic relatively actual and not only in the area of industrial relations. There are number of reasons. As a main reason may be designated on the one hand the above outlined unsuccessful legislative proposals seeking for a specific legal regulation of an Institute of Whistleblowing in the Czech Republic, worldwide growth of interest in this phenomenon, but also the fact that whistleblowing (with its conceptual fuzziness and non-inveteracy) represents in the Czech Republic, an ideal political slogan, under which can be subsumed or connected therewith many things, for example also permanent attempt of governments of the Czech Republic to take a position on the fight against corruption.

Besides the just mentioned efforts there also is a very practical and factual reason (speaking for the adoption of relevant legislation) which is the fact that some international corporations are already applying and implementing this practice in relation to their obligations ensuing for them indirectly from SOX. This fact then forces the professional public to deal with the issues concerning practices that are known as whistleblowing. Opponents of the adoption of specific legislation point to the fact that also without it the Constitutional Court was able to find in a particular case the proper constraints of employee loyalty to an employer in relation to the protection of the public interest.

In professional literature and other sources, however, has not been and is not in the Czech Republic paid adequate attention to whistleblowing. The exceptions are a few studies of non-profit organizations and the Parliamentary Institute, several articles in professional journals and currently this prepared collective monograph,[4] which came from a conference on the subject, which took place at the Law Faculty of Charles University in Prague in September 2013. In the future, however, may be expected developing of the professional debate.

As regards the assessment of legislative legal framework of whistleblowing in the Czech Republic, it can be in conclusion summarized what has already been indicated. In the Czech Republic, there is no comprehensive special whistleblowing legislation (byť se na příslušné legislative v různých podobách pracuje – viz bod 4 shora although now it is in various ways being worked on within respective legislation – see section “Whistleblowing, industrial relations and judicial decisions” above). If the notification is made within industrial relations, more precisely within private-law relations, then protection of whistleblowers as well as the ones who are notified, provides direct support especially legislation on protection of personal data and indirectly also the constitutional foundations of the Czech legal order (see the above-cited decision of the Constitutional Court in relation to the limits of application of the principle of loyalty in industrial relations).

Legislation on protection of personal data, which is based on the EU Directive 95/46/EC, has a cross-cutting nature and provides protection to the whistleblowers as well as the ones who are notified, also in cases of notifications outside industrial

[4] Pichrt, *Whistleblowing*, ibid., sub. 5.

relations (regardless of whether it is done in private-law or in public-law relations). In some cases, as for example in civil and criminal proceedings, specific legal regulations include additional special rules, typically in the context of criminal proceedings there is a special protection given to the accused, but also the victim (in both cases, it may be the whistleblower as well as the one who is notified).

In private-law relationships this is essential if there is collecting and processing of data without the consent of the person concerned (whistleblower or the one who is notified), that data can be processed and therefore whistleblowing in this direction realized only if it is to protect the rights and interests protected by law of administrator, receiver, or other persons concerned. Admissibility of processing is therefore tied to the successful implementation of the proportionality test.[5]

Existing, although general legislation, allows, while maintaining in particular the personal data protection and protection of personal rights, realization of an elaborate system of whistleblowing, which also could be utilized by external service providers; a system that is based on the rules laid down in the internal regulations and that allows, if necessary, also anonymous submissions, as well as allows to set channels towards public authorities or to media.

As regards the standard components of a whistleblowing system protective measures of deficiencies may be found in existing legislation, perhaps especially in the sense that there are missing special protective measures in relation to the one who is notified. To him protection is provided only in relation to the principle of non-enforcement of the law contrary to good morals and the prohibition of bullying and discrimination. Similarly, it is with direct motivational resources when there is not in any way determined any direct right to compensation or the like. Question of granting this now depends solely on the employer.

The article can be concluded with the fact that in the future there can be, among others from the above mentioned reasons, expected legislative proposals which will aim to regulate whistleblowing. Following the advanced professional debate and previous experience, these should certainly be better proposals than the previous legislative attempts.

Bibliography

Morávek J, Pichrt J (2009) *Whistleblowing,* Právo pro podnikání a zaměstnání. (Law for Business and Employment).

Morávek J (2009) *Whistleblowing – praktické otázky*, Právo pro podnikání a zaměstnání.

Morávek J (2009) *Whisteblowing – zákonná opora*, Právo pro podnikání a zaměstnání.

Pichrt J (2013) *Whistleblowing,* Praha, Wolters Kluwer ČR.

[5] *cf.* J Morávek, 'O whistleblowingu, jeho legitimitě a problémech mezinárodních přenosů osobních údajů /Whistleblowing, its legitimacy and international transfers of personal data problems' in J Pichrt (Ed.), *Whistleblowing* (Praha, Wolters Kluwer ČR, 2013), pp. 187–202.

Jan Pichrt is a Head of the Department of Labour Law and Social Security Law at the Faculty of Law, Charles University in Prague. He has lectured in labour law more than 20 years.

Jan Pichrt decides disputes as an arbitrator entered into the list of arbitrators of the Arbitration Court attached to the Economic Chamber of the Czech Republic and Agricultural Chamber of the Czech Republic. He works too as an advocate.

Jan Pichrt is an author or co-author of numerous monographs and articles in the field of labour law, a co-author of a prestigious commentary on the Czech Labour Code and some textbooks on labour law.

Jakub Morávek is a senior lecture of the Department of Labour Law and Social Security Law at the Faculty of Law, Charles University in Prague. He works too as an advocate.

Jakub Morávek is an author or co-author of numerous monographs and articles in the field of labour law.

Chapter 6
Whistleblowing: National Report for France

Katrin Deckert and Morgan Sweeney

As a false alert can raise a true panic, a false issue can provoke true complications (See G Lacroix, Les euphorismes de Grégoire (Paris, Max Milo, 2007))

Abstract Multinational companies implementing the US Sarbanes-Oxley Act of 2002 imported initially whistleblowing systems in France. At first, French public authorities were reluctant to welcome such systems as they recall the occupation time during the Second World War. Today, French law and authorities are less hostile to whistleblowing. In particular, three laws have been passed granting protection for whistleblowers in some specific areas (public health, environment, economic crimes).

French law has not only transposed the American whistleblowing model. Thus, first, the French authorities restricted indoor whistleblowing to a precise list of fields, which the legislator has extended little by little. French law also gave a new basis, which has completely changed the economy of those procedures. Indeed, basing the whistleblowing regulations on freedom of expression of the whistleblower, and not on internal control, opens the door to outdoor whistleblowing. There is no set hierarchy between both procedures. Consequently, the protection of whistleblowers lies in good faith, the non-abusive use of this freedom and the confidentiality of their identity. The restrictions which might be imposed on freedom of expression have to be strictly defined, as every exception to a principle of law.

The first part of this chapter was written by Morgan Sweeney the second by Katrin Deckert.

K. Deckert (✉)
Paris Ouest Nanterre University, Nanterre, France

93 rue de Varrene, 75007 Paris, France
e-mail: katrindeckert@hotmail.com

M. Sweeney
University of Paris Dauphine, Paris, France

45 rue de Présindent Wilson, 92300 Levallois Perret, France
e-mail: momodj@free.fr

G. Thüsing, G. Forst (eds.), *Whistleblowing - A Comparative Study*,
Ius Comparatum - Global Studies in Comparative Law 16,
DOI 10.1007/978-3-319-25577-4_6

Besides, the French legislator brought an original protection by sanctioning discrimination in some case of whistleblowing. By doing so, the legislator defines different regimes according to the object of whistleblowing, making the applicable law more complex and less understandable. The originality of the French system also and most importantly comes from the protection granted to the accused person. Employers are dissuaded from implementing systems, which might facilitate denunciation. The accused person must also have access to the elements of the whistleblowing, which allows them to prepare their defence. Indeed, the French model is grounded on a sense of mistrust towards whistleblowing, which has brought public authorities to search for a balance between the protection of the whistleblower and the protection of the accused person.

Giving an alert first aims at preventing an imminent danger. In the same way, whistleblowing aims to prevent wrongdoings, mainly inside companies. Even if whistleblowing systems' names vary – "Ethics Hotline", "dispositif d'intégrité professionnelle", "dispositif de ligne éthique", "alerte professionnelle" or "procédure de signalement" – the goal is the same: to encourage employees to indicate behaviour of others which is contrary to the rules which apply in the company. Whistleblowing systems are to prevent a serious and imminent danger: the company should be warned soon enough in order to avoid this danger to happen, or at least to act swiftly and to limit harmful consequences. Whistleblowing is raising an alert. Usually alerts concern a military attack, a fire or a crime. Nowadays alerts are raised when ethic regulations are broken also. In this respect company's, bank's and insurance's action are put more and more under scrutiny (accountability, health and safety, etc.). It enables to inform actors whenever they do not conform to those rules. Those controls are not realized by public authorities.[1] Therefore, there is an oversight responsibility, meaning that the ones in charge of control have the responsibility to make sure that those under their supervision are acting accordingly. The ones in charge have to end any violation.[2]

Oversight responsibility sometimes has shown to be inefficient. That's why whistleblowing systems are now mandatory for some corporations.[3] The whistleblowing systems[4] enable anybody to trigger an alert after witnessing a violation.

[1] For instance, Statutory auditors, see C. com., art. L. 820-7 et L. 823-12.

[2] See DF Thompson, 'À la recherche d'une responsabilité du contrôle', *Revue française de science politique*, 6/2008, p. 182.

[3] For a critic see J Delgas, 'De l'éthique d'entreprise et de son cynisme', *D.* 2004, p. 3126.

[4] National Commission on Computer Technology and Freedom (CNIL) has defined whistleblowing as "a scheme, complementing existing alert system, to encourage employees from the private or the public sector to report unethical or unlawfull behaviour and designed to monitor the alert"; See CNIL's deliberation n° 2005-305 adopted on 8 December 2005 relating to automatic authorization for data processing in a whistleblowing system. The most current definition of *whistleblowing* is: "The disclosure by organization members (former or current) of illegal, immoral or illegitimate practices under the control of their employers, to persons or organizations that may be

Whistleblower can turn to a designated person to receive such alerts. Those systems are open, not exclusive,[5] to employees. The whistleblower is now considered a modern hero who undermines authorities to publicly reveal dangers. The Chelsea (formerly Bradley) Manning leaking pieces of information to wikileaks and Edward Snowden revealing NSA actions are the most known cases.[6] But, whistleblowing can be more modest. However whistleblowing are met with considerable reticence in France. Actually, such systems recall occupation time during World War Two. In France, the word "whistleblowing" is carefully used to prevent confusion with those times.[7] Researchers rather use the word « denunciation » than « delation »,[8] as in French language the latter word implies despicable motives.

However, the European council gives whistleblowing the following definition: "*concerned individuals who sound an alarm in order to stop wrongdoings that place fellow human beings at risk*".[9] In the European perspective any whistleblower shall be protected against any harmful – either physical or moral – action. Revealing the wrongdoing is the first step. But it is not sufficient to put an end to it. To grant an effective protection to whistleblowers employees[10] shall take them off the hierarchy and confidentiality duty.[11] An equilibrium shall be found between the

able to effect action", See F de Bry, 'Salariés courageux oui, mais héros ou délateurs? Du Whistleblowing à l'alerte éthique', *Revue internationale de psychosociologie et de gestion des comportements organisationnels*, 34/2008, vol. XIV, p. 298.

[5] Some whistleblowing systems are opened to subcontractors and occasional collaborators.

[6] In France, Philippe Pichon, a police officer has revealed in a book the unlawfulness usage of the offense processing system (STIC). He has been sanctioned after he published his book. In France, Doctor Irène Frachon, revealed the mediator scandal against the Servier pharmaceutical labatory.

[7] See F. Chateauraynaud et D Torny, Les sombres précurseurs: une sociologie pragmatique de l'alerte et du risque, (Paris, éditions de l'EHESS, 1999).

[8] See D Lochak, 'La dénonciation, stade suprême ou perversion de la démocratie', in L'État de droit: *Mélanges en l'honneur de Guy Braibant* (Paris, Dalloz, 1996), p. 451.

[9] Résolution 1729, §1, Protection of whistleblowers, 2010. This definition is wider than the Cnil's. The CNIL do only recognise systems put in place by employers open to their employees. The NGO Transparence-International France grants another definition: "It is the action taken by an individual who witnessed during his professional activity an unlawful act and who civic minded decide to report it to the authorities in order to put an end to it"; see "Déclencher l'alerte – Un dispositif de prévention et de lutte contre la corruption", Présentation du rapport 2004 sur le whistleblowing, La lettre de Transparence, oct. 2004, p. 7. More recently, before Parliamentary debate, another definition has been given: "an individual or a group of personns who seek to make known the seriousness of a threat against the majority opinion"; see rapport AN, n° 650, relatif à l'indépendance de l'expertise en matière de santé et d'environnement et à la protection des lanceurs d'alerte, par J.-L. ROUMEGAS, 23 janv. 2013, p. 8.

[10] This study is focusing on private sector employees. The public sector employees do have a mandatory obligation to report any criminal offence to the public prosecutor.

[11] For studies in labour law, see O Leclerc, 'La protection du salarié lanceur d'alerte', in E Dockés (dir.), *Au cœur des combats juridiques* (Paris, LGDJ, 2007), p. 287. In favor of whistleblowing, PH Antonmattei et P Vivien, *Chartes éthiques, alerte professionnelle et droit du travail français: état des lieux et perspectives* (Rapport – La documentation française, 2007).

whistleblower's disobedient action[12] and the protection to the one who is accused. Actually a person shall not be too easily accused. The whistleblower shall not be authorized to insult. The whistleblower's protection shall be compatible with employer's true interest and with those of the one who is accused.

Whistleblowing systems have been introduced in France because some French companies acting on American soil had to met the Sarbanes Oxley's Act requirements[13]: all companies, even foreign ones, listed in the New York stock exchange[14] have to put in place a whistleblowing system. This Act has been taken to prevent likely ENRON and WORLDCOM scandals.[15] Both corporations had falsified their accountability to hide loss. Both cases have been revealed by (employee or senior manager) whistleblowers. It was clear in those cases that internal controls have failed, but whistleblowing have been efficient. Therefore, the Sarbanes Oxley Act made whistleblowing systems mandatory. This Act does not detail the kind of system and proceedings to put in place, but grants whistleblowers a protection. In the American perspective, the system is effective only if the whistleblower is granted a protection, especially he/she can remain anonymous. Such systems have not been welcomed easily in France.[16] The French regulation in this matter has been built against the American regulation. At first, the French authorities have been reluctant to apply the American law considering it too loose on whistleblowers – especially through anonymous or money-making whistleblowing. The French approach takes the situation of the accused one into consideration. However, since 2013, the French Parliament is more open and extended such whistleblowing systems to four new fields: public health, environment, economic crimes and conflict of interest.[17] We can reckon that whistleblowing is welcomed now in France.[18] From USA to France, transposing whistleblowing systems in France has been like a boat on the sea: from a rough sea to a steady situation.

[12] For a critical point of view on public servants situation, see JPh Foegle et A Slama, 'Refus de transmission d'une QPC sur la protection des fonctionnaires lanceurs d'alerte', *La Revue des droits de l'homme*, Actualités Droits- Libertés, mis en ligne le 14 mars 2014, available at www.revdh.revues.org/628.

[13] The Sarbanes-Oxley Act had been adopted on 31 July 2002. However, the legislator formerly passed the Whistleblower Protection Act of 1989, Bill text 101st Congress (1989–1990).

[14] At New York.

[15] ENRON was the energy trading number 1 and the seventh biggest company in the USA. Worldcom was a telecommunication company gone bankrupt after revelation on accounting discrepancies.

[16] See F Barrière, 'Le Whistleblowing – à propos de l'arrêt du 8 décembre 2009 de la Chambre sociale de la Cour de cassation', *Rev. soc.*, 2010, p. 483.

[17] See below.

[18] See FG Trébulle, 'L'efficacité comparée du droit et de l'obligation de dénoncer en droit du travail et de l'environnement' in M. Behar-Touchais (dir.), *La dénonciation en droit privé* (Paris, Économica, 2010), p. 31.

From USA to France: A Rough Sea Journey for Whistleblowing Systems

At first, French authorities threatened US whistleblowing systems applied on French soil: some worldwide companies' whistleblowing systems had been censored. Therefore, they had to modify their systems to comply with French requirements. In the French approach, a distinction has to be drawn between indoor whistleblowing and outdoor whistleblowing. In one hand, indoor whistleblowing imply a scheme set up by and for the company itself. It shall establish an early warning and response system. Those systems are put under stricter scrutiny. Such systems can be put in place only for specific topics and should comply with particular requirements. The French law is to protect the one who has been accused. On the other hand, outdoor whistleblowing is not about controlling the employer. As the whistleblower can turn to external body, the legal outcome is the freedom of speech.

Some recent legislations show a new trend. Whistleblowing is seen as a way for employees to protect the general interest against a company's current practice. Today, whistleblowing in France is not only a matter of internal governance.

From Constriction to Extension of the Indoor Whistleblowing

According to his oversight authority the employer can put in place an indoor whistleblowing system. The employer needs to check if orders are followed. However, whistleblowing systems are generally turned to legal and ethic compliance,[19] to prevent any condemnation coming from an employee's illegal or unethical action. The whistleblowing systems do represent a new pattern of control. As such, French authorities put them under strict requirements.

A New Pattern of Control

Traditionally, employers do ask supervisors to watch over the employees they are responsible for. Whistleblowing systems introduce a new way to exercise employer's oversight: employees themselves do report violations directly to the employer. Each employee is like a watchdog, able to report any violation they witnessed. Therefore, any person witnessing the violation can blow the whistle. Indoor whistleblowing systems aim at spotting the violation faster, enabling a more effective response.

Indoor whistleblowing systems put in place a way of control outside the supervisor's authority. Actually, the whistle is blown when the supervision failed to prevent

[19] Some authors do refer to « shared social values », see V Rebeyrol, 'La réception du « whistleblowing » par le droit français', *JCP E* n° 24, 14 juin 2012, 1386, p. 32.

the violation from happening. Indoor whistleblowing system works outside the hierarchy in the company: an employee can blow the whistle against his own supervisor. The main criterion to blow the whistle is to detain pieces of information regardless of the whistleblower's rank. Traditionally in French labour law whistleblowing were open only to some employees' representatives. For instance, the workers' delegates can raise an alert when a fundamental right violated.[20] The work council can trigger an alert any time is provided pieces of information liable to affect the company's economic situation.[21] Finally the health and safety committee can whistle the blow in case of imminent and serious threat to employees' health.[22] For each procedure the employer has to respond to the employees' representatives' concerns. The employer has whether to conduct an inquiry together with the employees' representatives or to respond arguably in a document to their concerns. Only after, if unsatisfied, the employees' representatives can go to court.

Concerning indoor whistleblowing, the employer is free to organize the warning and response system. They are not bound to drive an inquiry alongside with the whistleblower. They are not even in the obligation to keep them informed. The whistleblower has no say over the employer's managing the alert.

Indoor whistleblowing has two original features: it can be triggered outside the company's hierarchy and outside the employees' representatives' action. However, it is not those original features which put indoor whistleblowing systems into question. The public authority actually feared that such systems can be subverted.

Constriction of the Whistleblowing

French Labour law neither forbids nor authorises indoor whistleblowing systems. Therefore, employers are free to put in place such systems as long as they do not abuse of their right or infringe employee's fundamental rights.[23] Nonetheless, as whistleblowing systems imply personal data processing, they have to be declared to the French Data Protection Authority (CNIL). The CNIL set up a specific approach leading to forbid some indoor whistleblowing system. The CNIL approach has been backed up by the French judiciary Supreme Court (Cour de cassation).

---

[20] Art. L. 2313-2 of the Labour Code.

[21] Art. L. 2323-78 of the Labour Code.

[22] Art. L. 4132-2 of the Labour Code.

[23] Art. L. 1121-1 of the Labour Code. As speech is free, using whistleblowing scheme should not be mandatory for employees.

Limits Imposed by the CNIL

The CNIL settled the conditions for lawfully setting up an indoor whistleblowing system.[24] Firstly, such systems are authorised only for financial, banking and anti-corruption issues – matching the scope of the Sarbanes-Oxley Act.[25] The CNIL imposed stricter restrictions than the American Act. For instance, the CNIL discourages an anonymous whistleblowing. The CNIL provides that in principle the whistleblower should identify himself/herself and in counterpart the body receiving the alert shall keep his identity confidential. The body receiving the alert should not encourage an anonymous whistleblowing. By way of exception, an anonymous whistleblowing can be processed only if two requirements are met altogether: (1) The seriousness of the facts is established and the facts sufficiently detailed; (2) Processing such alert should be carefully done and for instance the one who received the alert should be able to choose whether or not to process the alert.[26]

On the contrary, in the American stock exchange law companies are to let the whistleblower choose to remain anonymous or not.[27] In the American approach, anonymity is a way to give protection to the whistleblower: if you cannot identify the whistleblower, you won't be able to sanction them. In the French system, anonymous whistleblowing are not forbidden per se but should not be encouraged.[28] Anonymous whistleblowing should remain the exception and can be processed only if the employer has a justified reason. The French position is supported by two reasons. Firstly, anonymous whistleblowing represents too many risks and could too easily undermine one's reputation.[29] Anonymous whistleblowing could enable alerts motivated by jealousy and resentment.[30] It could authorise slander without any risk of being sued. Secondly, open whistleblowing creates a sense of responsibility and ease processing the alert. For instance, open whistleblowing enables to

[24] CNIL's deliberation n° 2005-305 adopted on 8 December 2005 relating to automatic authorization for data processing in a whistleblowing system. This deliberation has been modified by both deliberations n° 2010-369 adopted on 14 October 2010 and n° 2014-042 adopted on 30 January 2014.

[25] Today, thanks to the different Acts of Parliament passed recently, whistleblowing system are now authorized in the fields of non-discrimination, anti-competitive practices, environment protection, health and safety at work.

[26] Art. 2 of Deliberation no. 2005-305.

[27] The whistleblower can be rewarded (generally in due proportion of the amount of the avoided sanction). Obviously the whistleblower must reveal his identity to be rewarded.

[28] See also TGI Libourne, 15 September 2005 (BSN Glasspack), Comm. com. électr.2005, comm. 191, note A. LEPAGE ; Comm. com. électr. 2005, comm. 194, note E. A.CAPRIOLLI. TGI Nanterre, 27 déc. 2006 (Dupont de Nemours): SSL, 15 January 2007, n° 1290.

[29] TGI de Caen, court's order on 5 November 2009 (Comité d'Entreprise Benoist Girard et autres/ Benoist Girard). The judges did consider the whistleblowing to be void as the whistleblower identification was not requested.

[30] D Danet, 'Misère de la corporate governance', *RIDE*, 4/2009, p. 407, et spéc. p. 428.

get back to the whistleblower to obtain more accurate information.[31] The CNIL is rather to protect the whistleblower by guarantying the confidentiality of his identity. The whistleblower's identity cannot be shared with the one who is the subject of the alert.[32]

Moreover, the CNIL set up a protection for the people reported by the whistleblower. The CNIL has also stated that whistleblowing schemes should preserve the right of defence of the person reported. That is to say, this person has to be aware of the accusation and should have access to the necessary information in order to organize his defence.[33] This person has the right to access its personal data and require any rectification or removal of any inaccurate, incomplete, equivoquial or expired information.[34] Unlike the stock exchange American law focusing only on the whistleblower's protection, the CNIL ensure a protection for the people reported by the whistleblower. This protection consists of avoiding slander alert and to enable this person to access its personal data. This person can though arrange for its defence.[35] Those two last aspects have been reinforced by the judiciary Supreme Court's case law.

The Judiciary Supreme Court Support

The French judiciary Supreme Court backed up and strengthened the CNIL's regulation. In this case, the Dassault system company put in place a "Code of Business conduct" in order to comply with the Sarbanes Oxley Act. This Code did apply to all subsidiary firms. The judiciary Supreme Court identifies two violations. Firstly, the company did not comply with the CNIL deliberation's requirements as whistleblowing was open in other fields than financial, banking and anti-corruption issues. Such opening could be authorized, according to the CNIL, only if the company's vital interest or the employees' physical or moral integrity are at stake. The code of business conduct enabled whistleblowing when the company's interests were at stake, for instance in case of intellectual property breach or if any confidential information are about to be revealed. In those cases the interest at stake are not vital. Whistleblowing was to largely open to employees. Therefore the company did not comply with the rules set up by the CNIL and should have asked for a different procedure to be granted authorization to set up its whistleblowing scheme in France.

---

[31] See CNIL's orientation guide issued on 10 November 2005 (modified in August 2004) on whistleblowing systems and data protections.

[32] See Art. 2 and 10 of CNIL's Deliberation no. 2005-305 above-cited. Confidentiality is a legislative requirement coming from art. 39 the Data protection Act no. 78-17 issued on 6 January 1978. Such protection should encourage and reassure whistleblowers, see F Barrière, 'Du contrôle interne à la dénonciation rémunérée?', *JCP E* n° 27, 7 July 2011, 1527, n° 19.

[33] Art. 9 of the CNIL's guidance no. 2010-369 issued on 14 October 2010.

[34] Art. 10 of the CNIL's guidance no. 2010-369 issued on 14 October 2010.

[35] See part 2.

A second reason led the judiciary Supreme Court to censor the company's scheme as it did not provide any protection for the one being reported to. Here lies the genuine French approach: the French law does not only protect the whistleblower it also provides protection to the one reported to by the whistleblower.[36]

Nevertheless, restrictions on whistleblowing fields set up by the CNIL and the French judge had been back draft by the Parliament.

Deployment?

Three Acts of Parliament[37] have been passed in 2013 to grant the whistleblower a protection in two fields: public health and environment in one hand and economic crimes and conflict of interest on the other hand.

Public Health and Environment

The law enacted on 16 April 2013 concerns experts independency in matters of public health and environment. Whistleblowers are granted a protection when they blow the whistle and reveal any pieces of information concerning a fact, an action, a data which may put at risk public health or the environment.[38] The whistleblower can choose either to use an indoor whistleblowing scheme or to go public. In case of an indoor whistleblowing the employer has the obligation to put in writing the alert.[39] The employer has to keep informed the whistleblower of any action taken in regard to the alert. Therefore companies have to put in place whistleblowing systems to manage alerts in public health and environment fields. Keeping the whistleblower informed of the action taken is a special feature of whistleblowing in those fields. There is no similar right in order fields, like finance, accountancy and corruption. In this prospect the whistleblower represents an oversight on the employer's action, as the employer will be accountable before the whistleblower. If the employer is doing nothing or not enough to respond to the alert, the whistleblower will be able to go further and turn towards public authority. The Act of Parliament put in place a new

---

[36] See part 2.

[37] See the law enacted on 11 October 2013 « relative à la transparence financière » (financial transparency), which is the continuation of the previous law enacted on 13 nov. 2007 « relative à la lutte contre la corruption » (fight against corruption).

[38] See the law enacted on 16 April 2013 « relative à l'indépendance de l'expertise en matière de santé et d'environnement et à la protection des lanceurs d'alerte » (for health and environnement Independent expertise and whistleblower's protection). In matter of environment, a former Act already set up an alert, but it could be activated only by some public authorities and environmental NGOs.

[39] Conditions for processing whistleblowing will be set by government regulation.

committee supervising ethics and whistleblowing in fields of public health and environment.[40]

This Act represents a great evolution. Beforehand, alerts regarding public health can only be triggered by specialized public authorities.[41] Now the whistle can be blown by individuals or groups of individuals, even if they have no scientific expertise. The whistle can be blown for any public health issues, meaning that employees can trigger an alert even if the risk does not concern them directly. Employees can blow the whistle when the companies neighbour or the consumers' health is at stake. However, whistleblowing is only possible in case of "serious risks".[42] The seriousness of the risk should be assessed regarding the number of the potential victims and the extent of the damages.[43]

In matter of environment,[44] whistleblowing is no more a reserved area for specialized public agencies composed of multidisciplinary and pluralist experts. Those agencies can now be ceased by anybody.

In other 2013 Acts of parliament, whistleblowing is less prominent.

Economic Crimes and Conflict of Interest

The law enacted on 11 October 2013 aims to foster more transparency in public life. It aims to prevent conflict of interests between persons in charge of the public interest, elected persons or member of the French government on one side and private interest on the other side. In this regard members of the French government have to fill in a form and communicate it to the public agency in charge of public life transparency. This act of Parliament concerns not only corruption but any conflict of interests. The purpose is to prevent favouritism. That is to say that the whistle can be blown to reveal any connections between someone in charge of a public interest and private interest. The law enacted on 6 December 2013 strengthens the prohibition regarding economic crimes.[45] Those two acts do not impose to the companies to set up indoor whistleblowing systems in those fields. However they both provide

[40] This « droit de suite » working like the workers' delegates process. However, whistleblowers seem to have a less strong « droit de suite »: The employer has the obligation to keep the whistleblower informed, not to respond to his concerns.

[41] For instance the national agency for medical safety of drugs (Agence nationale de sécurité du médicament et des produits de santé (ANSM had been put in place by the law enacted on 29 december 2011 « relative au renforcement de la sécurité sanitaire du médicament et des produits de santé » (drugs safety reinforcement).

[42] See Art. 1.

[43] See M Bacache, 'L'alerte: un instrument de prévention des risques sanitaires et environnementaux ', *RTD civ.* 2013, p. 689.

[44] See Art. 53 of the law enacted on 3 August 2009 « de programmation relative à la mise en oeuvre du Grenelle de l'environnement » (known as the program Law on implementation of the « Grenelle » environnement Round table).

[45] See the law enacted on 11 October 2013, « relative à la transparence de la vie publique (transparency in public life) the one enacted on 6 December 2013, « relative à la lutte contre la fraude fiscale

a protection for whistleblowers against any adverse actions. Such actions would be considered discriminatory.[46] Therefore, the whistleblower is free to turn towards their employer or outside the company. In both cases, they benefited from the same protection.

It seems that companies are free to set up indoor whistleblowing systems in matter of economic crimes or conflict of interests. Doing so, the companies have to comply with the CNIL and jurisprudence's requirements.

Both Acts of parliament set up two new public agencies to receive whistleblowing in their respective fields.

Outdoor Whistleblowing Expansion: A New Way to Protect the General Interest?

Thanks to outdoor whistleblowing the whistleblower employee can either publicly reveal a piece of information or turn to the competent authorities (tribunals, prosecutor, independent administrative authority, etc.). A great difference lies here with the American model. In the USA, the approach is to give priority to internal regulation over State's intervention. The Sarbanes Oxley act doesn't impose a federal control over company's practices but imposes to put in place indoor whistleblowing. Companies are free to determine procedures and terms of the whistleblowing systems. In the US approach problems shall first be solved inside the company. It is only when indoor procedures failed that an employee can legally turn to tribunals. On the contrary, in the French tradition there are no conditions to turn to public authorities. In France, indoor whistleblowing is not prioritised. Actually, in all three 2013 Acts of Parliament the whistleblower is considered has a defender of the public interest and public health, environment and a way to prevent conflicts of interests and economic crimes. The justification for outdoor whistleblowing is employees' freedom of speech, which is as strong inside and outside the company. An employee is therefore free to choose between indoor and outdoor whistleblowing. Moreover two 2013 acts set up a specific procedure for outdoor whistleblowing with new public agencies.

Freedom of Speech, the First Way for Outdoor Whistleblowing

Case law in both criminal and social provide maximum freedom to employees, which can freely turn to public authority or the media.

Since the "Pierre" case law on 14 December 1999, the social chamber of the judiciary Supreme Court states: "except in the case of manifest abuse, employee

et la grande délinquance économique et financière » (fight against tax evasion and serious economic and financial crime).

[46] See Art. 25.

enjoys freedom of speech inside an outside the company unless the employer set up justified and proportionate restrictions regarding the employee's position".[47] Therefore, even for employees freedom of speech remains a principle which can restricted only in exceptional circumstances. The employee is free to express his point of view and criticise managers' plan.[48] In the Dassault system case, even though the company compete in a highly sensitive industrial field it cannot impose to ask authorisation any time an employee is about to disclose pieces of information for "internal use". Such restriction is too vague and constitutes a disproportionate infringement of employees' freedom of speech.

Freedom of speech does apply to communication outside the company. In a former case, an employee strongly criticised in the media the company takeover. Once the takeover achieved the new owner required the employee to publicly take back his past criticism.[49] The employee refused and has been dismissed. The judiciary Supreme Court acknowledge that such requirement infringed the employee's freedom of speech. Employees are free to speak their mind and to criticise employer's plan or action. French judges do not make any distinction when employees express their point of view inside or outside the company. In both cases they enjoy the same guarantee.[50] For instance, an employee is not at fault when an employee uses reckless words during a public interview[51] or when a football player and manager expose their controversy in the media.[52]

Freedom of speech enables employee to whistle the blow outside the company. For instance to turn to the labour inspector to reveal abnormal facts does not constitute a fault, except if the employee knew those facts to be false – he/she lied – or he/she did act in a culpably thoughtless manner.[53] The employee can turn to the media. In the famously case law Clavaud, a Dunlop employee exposed mismanagement and incompetency among managers. French judges found the disciplinary dismissal unjustified as the employee exercised his freedom of speech and no abuse of rights has been proven by the employer. In principle, freedom of speech is not limited regarding topics or recipients. Therefore an employee can blow the whistle about any topic. However, employee's freedom is not absolute. Firstly, the employee should not abuse of his freedom. The employer can impose secrecy and confidentiality over identified pieces of information. The judiciary Supreme Court stated that

[47] See Cass. soc., 14 December 1999, no. 97-41.995.

[48] That was the case in *Pierre* case law (see above). The French judiciary Supreme Court also stated that an employee can respond to an open letter send to all personnel by the employer to respond to his alleged involvement in the company's malfunction (Cass. soc., 22 June 2004).

[49] See Cass. soc., 26 October 2005, no. 03-41.796.

[50] In some situations, employees do enjoy immunity. For instance, according to article L. 313-24 of the social work and family Code a social-healthcare institution employee can denounce any abuse without risking any sanction.

[51] See Cass. soc., 28 April 2011, no. 10-30.107. The employee can express himself/herself with a sarcastic or humours' tone, see Cass. soc., 2 February 2011, no. 09-69.351.

[52] See Cass. soc., 14 March 2000, no. 97-43.268.

[53] Except abuse, or secret and confidentiality infringement.

an employee is not entitled to reveal company's pieces of information, inside studies and decisions during a public meeting. It is worth noticing that the employee attended to this meeting outside his professional duties.[54] Therefore the professionals' duty of discretion can constitute a limit to outdoor whistleblowing anytime the information revealed is confidential. Judges will have to control if the confidentiality imposed was legitimate and justified. Judges will have to balance the public interest for the revelation with the company interest for secrecy.

The whistleblower's freedom of expression was at the centre of the parliamentary debate of the first two 2013 Acts. Those acts put in place a specific protection for whistleblowers.

The 2013 Acts

After several scandals concerning public health, environment, conflict of interest and economic crimes, parliamentary choose to reinforce the whistleblower's protection. Some members of Parliament (MP) wanted to reinforce the whistleblower's freedom of speech – to create some sort of a penal immunity. However, considering that the criminal jurisprudence was already protective, MPs decided not to change anything on this matter. Therefore the whistleblower has no particular protection regarding defamation and insults.

The genuine novelty lies in settling new proceedings for outdoor whistleblowing which can be addressed to public agencies.

The Opportunity of Outdoor Whistleblowing

The three 2013 Acts protect the whistleblowers against any discrimination.[55] Those Acts do not prioritised indoor whistleblowing over outdoor whistleblowing. The law enacted on 16 April 2013 grants people the right to reveal publicly or disseminate and in good faith a piece of information on a fact, a data or an action anytime it can generate a serious risk on public health and environment.[56] The Parliament put on the same level going publicly or to disseminate information which can be inside the company. However, Article L. 4133-1 of the labour code provides that employee should immediately alert the employer. This could imply that the employee has the obligation to alert the employer and has only the opportunity to blow the whistle outdoor. But the 2013 act does not impose the whistleblower to turn first to his employer before going public. Thus, the whistleblower can whistle the blow indoor

[54] See Cass. soc., 2 March 2011, no. 09-68.890.

[55] Above mentioned.

[56] Art. 1.

and outdoor at the same time.[57] The employee does not have to wait for the indoor whistleblowing to fail to use the outdoor whistleblowing.

In the law enacted on 11 October 2013 concerning conflict of interests, the Parliament considered indoor and outdoor whistleblowing altogether. This act only provides protection for whistleblowers against discrimination.[58] The whistleblower is protected anytime they revealed or testified in good faith to his employer or to the authority in charge of ethics or to an anti-corruption watchdog. Therefore, the whistleblower can either turn to his employer or to the competent authority or a watchdog NGO. MPs did not want to prioritise indoor whistleblowing over outdoor whistleblowing as the employer can be either complicit or benefit from the conflict of interest and therefore might do anything to avoid any revelation…

In the law enacted on 6 December 2013, the whistleblower can turn to public prosecutor or judges to reveal any economic crimes. This acts aims first at protecting public servants which have the duty to reveal any crime they encounter while working. Beforehand, public servants had no protection.

The three 2013 Acts do recognize outdoor whistleblowing. In no case indoor whistleblowing is prioritised. The first Act aims at public health and environment protection and therefore protects a greater interest than the company's interest. Conflict of interests' prevention concerns directly state's functioning. Economic crimes are against the public order. In the three cases the aim is to protect a public interest and justifies that the whistleblower can go public. Moreover two of those Acts put in place public agencies recipient for whistleblowing.

The Competent Authorities to Receive Alert

The first two 2013 Acts put in place new public authorities. But, each agency does not have the same power regarding outdoor whistleblowing. The one enacted on 16 April 2013 Act puts in place the French commission for public health and environment ethics and alerts. This commission establishes proceedings that any public authority intervening in fields of public health and environment has to set up to proceed with whistleblowing.[59] The commission can assess the admissibility and forward the alert to the competent minister. The commission monitors the alert as minister has to justify any action taken in consideration to the whistleblowing. The commission keeps the whistleblower informed of any action taken. The whistleblower has no obligation to turn to the commission. The outdoor whistleblowing can be done by other means, such as turning to the media.[60] To cease the commission

[57] For instance, the whistleblower can send an e-mail both to his/her employer and to the competent authority.

[58] See Art. 25.

[59] A unique registry might have been more efficient, see A Laude, 'Science et démocratie : garantir un juste équilibre. – À propos de la loi du 16 avril 2013' (10 June 2013), *JCP G*, doctr. 690.

[60] Therefore the whistleblower's protection falls into journalist's sources protection, see ECHR, *M. et a. c. France*, 12 April 2012, no. 30002/08. As long as the piece of information revealed falls in

is not the sole way. However when the whistleblower turns to the commission the added advantage for the whistleblower is to be kept informed of any action taken or not taken.

The outcome in the law issued on 11 October 2013 is different. The Parliament wanted to set up a preventive mechanism: elected persons and high-ranking public servants have to produce a detailed and sincere declaration of their patrimony. Those declarations are communicated to the High authority for public life transparency. Those authorities have to ensure transparency and prevent conflict of interests. Those authorities have no authority about whistleblowing proceedings. They can only be ceased by the persons involved for their own situations, by the French President, the prime minister, the president of the national assembly or the president of the senate and by any watchdog NGO.[61] Nonetheless, the high authority can examine cases *proprio motu*, implying that it can examine a case after a whistleblowing.[62]

Both Acts aim to protect the public interest. However the mechanisms are not the same. The first one sets up a proceeding and the whistleblower is kept informed of any actions taken thanks to them. On the contrary the 11 October 2013 Act sets up no proceeding and the whistleblower has no right to be kept informed. The only common point of those acts is to protect the whistleblowers against any discrimination. Those acts underline the French approach guided by balancing fundamental rights of both the whistleblower and the accused person.

The Berthing of Whistleblowing: An Enhanced Protection of the Person's Rights

The laws enacted in 2013 prove that the legislator now recognizes whistleblowing as a relevant instrument of risk prevention. This legislative acknowledgement is part of movement for a greater protection of the person's rights, not only of the whistleblower – which constitutes the originality of the whistleblowing frameworks – but also of the accused person – which constitutes the originality of the French approach. Hence, the transposition of whistleblowing mechanisms in France is continued by the protection of whistleblowers, which even encompasses protection against discrimination. In the same spirit, French law preserves the interests of the accused person. This way, the aim of whistleblowing in France resides in disclosing information rather than denouncing a person.[63]

---

the public interest, the journalist's source is protected. For instance, it is forbidden to search for the public servant's identity who revealed the content of a regional audit chamber report.

[61] See Art. 20.

[62] See the report « *Pour un renouveau démocratique* : *rapport de la Commission de rénovation et de déontologie de la vie publique* » (nov. 2012) – commission dite « Jospin » – recommandait pourtant l'instauration d'une alerte éthique de tout citoyen à destination des déontologues des institutions et administrations (proposition n°35).

[63] See V Rebeyrol, 'La réception du « whistleblowing » par le droit français' (14 June 2012), *JCP E* no. 24, 1386, no. 20.

The Protection of Whistleblowers

The efficiency of whistleblowing largely depends on the protection offered to whistleblowers. Thus, using the whistleblowing procedure should not, by itself, cause a prejudice to the whistleblower.[64] Since the CNIL was consulted on the issue of whistleblowing, French law deters the use of anonymous whistleblowing,[65] a major figure of the whistleblower's protection in American financial law. The protection of a whistleblower, viewed through the angle of personal data processing, is ensured by keeping their identity confidential- thereby prohibiting the accused person from retaliating against them. More generally, the protection of a whistleblower is ensured through the possibility given to them to disclose information. Such possibility is created by the whistleblower's freedom of expression. This freedom represents the main protection of the whistleblower. The 2013 laws, following the anti-corruption law enacted on 13 November 2007, ensure, in their respective fields, some original protection of whistleblowers: non-discrimination.

An Overall Protection Through the Whistleblower's Freedom of Expression

Freedom of expression is the main instrument for whistleblowers: by expressing themselves through oral or written means, the whistleblower reveals the information they detain to the person who manages the whistleblowing procedure. Whistleblowing, in every field, thus lies on freedom of expression. However, the use of this freedom must not be abusive. The European Court for Human Rights (ECHR) also provides protection for the whistleblower's freedom of expression, which, however, appears less liberal than the one developed by French case law.

The "Voice" of the Whistleblower

The employee's freedom of expression is a fundamental right, which the employer cannot "restrict without justifications from the nature of the task to be accomplished or from the proportionality of the restriction to its aim".[66] Any infringement upon the employee's freedom must be deemed void.[67] Thus, the rule is the employee's freedom, and the restrictions are only exceptions to the rule.[68] However, some

[64] See Cnil, Policy paper issued on 10 November 2005 for the implementation of whistleblowing procedure complying with Act no. 78-17 of 6 January 1978 on Data Processing, Data Files and Individual Liberties. See also M Bacache, 'L'alerte : un instrument de prévention des risques sanitaires et environnementaux' (2013), *RTD civ.*, p. 689.

[65] See above.

[66] Art. L. 1121-1 of the Labour Code.

[67] See above, the Clavaud case (Cass. soc., 28 April 1988).

[68] See above.

restrictions, which the employer is allowed to implement, may be in direct conflict with whistleblowing.

The employer may legitimately forbid employees to disclose secret or confidential information, even to their colleagues.[69] Contractual provisions on duty of confidentiality or secrecy allow, amongst others, to preserve the corporation's competitive advantage by avoiding disclosure of information to its competitors. The French Labour Code provides that, beyond such provisions, "the fact for a director or an employee to reveal or attempt to reveal a trade secret is punished by a 2-year imprisonment and a 30,000 Euros fine".[70] The duty of confidentiality, outside any contracts, is inherent to the contractual good faith of the employee.[71] Do such prohibitions, whether legal or contractual, prevent any outdoor whistleblowing on information covered by secrecy or confidentiality? Nothing is less certain.

Three considerations may come to support this doubt. First, the respect of secrecy or confidentiality, as restrictions to freedom of expression, must be justified: the employer must bring a reasonable justification. It is the employer, who has to determine, first of all, whether the information should be considered secret or confidential. However, the employer cannot use this faculty to dissimulate illegal things happening in the corporation. For example, an employer cannot decide that the fact that they disguise the corporation's finances is confidential; their decision to falsify accounts is illegal, it cannot be covered by confidentiality or secrecy.[72] Thereby, the employer cannot use their faculty to determine whether some information is secret or confidential to prevent disclosure and thus, whistleblowing. Furthermore, in the framework of indoor whistleblowing, the person who manages the whistleblowing procedure must be allowed to receive any kind of information: they cannot be prevented from receiving some specific type of information. Consequently, the person in charge of the whistleblowing procedure has the same duty of confidentiality or secrecy as the whistleblower. Confidentiality or secrecy must not constitute an obstacle to communication between the whistleblower and the person managing the procedure. Otherwise, the whistleblowing procedure would have a very limited interest. Lastly, confidentiality or secrecy cannot be considered an obstacle to judicial truth. That is why the Social Chamber of the judiciary Supreme Court has put aside the confidentiality attached to a transaction, in order to allow a third party to benefit from it.[73] The suspension of the duty of confidentiality provision is justified by the fact that the

[69] See O Leclerc, 'Sur la validité des clauses de confidentialité en droit du travail' (2005), *Dr. soc*, p. 173. When a whistleblowing procedure is implemented in a corporation, it must be agreed that the person in charge of the procedure may receive any type of information (secret, confidential or not), himself/herself not being compelled to respect the confidentiality or secrecy of those information.

[70] Art. L. 1227-1 of the Labour Code.

[71] The judiciary Supreme Court deducts an obligation of discretion for the employee, see Cass. soc., 25 March 1981, no. 79-40.976.

[72] On an employee's right to not abide by an illegal order, see, eg., Cass. soc., 6 April 2004, no. 01-45.227.

[73] See Cass. soc., 20 November 2013, no. 10-28.582.

third party was not able to defend themselves during trial,[74] and thus, the provision infringed on their right to defend themselves.[75] Thus, the right to receive evidence may justify putting aside confidentiality or secrecy. The whistleblower could be led to testify at trial, potentially against its corporation. The protection of the witness whistleblower is even ensured in case of harassment or discrimination: they benefit from the same protection as the victims themselves. The witness is thus protected against any retaliation by the employer.[76] A similar protection exists in case of a testimony about corruption facts before a judicial or administrative authority.[77] It is also to be noticed that the judiciary Supreme Court recognizes the fundamental right to testify before a court and guarantees its efficiency by sanctioning as void a dismissal based on the contents of a testimony given by an employee to the benefit of another.[78]

The French approach on whistleblowing, through the whistleblower's freedom of expression, explains why the use of whistleblowing procedure is only an option, and not an obligation.[79] Recognizing one's freedom gives this person the option to exercise it or not, but no one can be forced to exercise a freedom.[80] Thus, the person who detains information which could be disclosed through whistleblowing is not compelled to make it known. This person only has the option to do so,[81] if the whistleblower does not make an abusive use of their freedom.

[74] See B Ines, 'Clause de confidentialité : tiers privé d'un moyen d'assurer sa défense' (10 Dec 2013), *Dalloz Actualité* (www.dalloz-actualite.fr).

[75] A right now affirmed by the Fist Civil Chamber of the judiciary Supreme Court in a decision rendered on the basis of Art. 9 of the Civil Code and the Civil Procedure Code and Art. 6 and 8 of the European Convention on Human Rights: "by deciding as it did, without determining whether the production of evidence in cause was indispensable to the exercise of his/her right to evidence, and proportional to the antinomies rights in presence, the Court of Appeal's decision lacks legal basis", see Cass. civ. 1re, 5 April 2012, no. 11-14.177.

[76] Articles L. 1132-3 and L. 1153-3 of the Labour Code.

[77] Article L. 1161-1 of the Labour Code.

[78] Cass. soc., 29 October 2013, no. 12-22.447.

[79] It might have been possible to base the employees' whistleblowing on their duty of loyalty toward their employer. In this regard, it might have been possible to implement a compulsory whistleblowing, as soon as the employee gains knowledge of the information. If the employee does not exercise whistleblowing, he/she would be guilty and might be sanctioned. However, it seems more reasonable, and pragmatic, to base whistleblowing on freedom of expression, which as a fundamental liberty is above the contractual parties' duty of loyalty.

[80] We do not study here the specific duties of public agents. Some authors plead for a real duty to denounce any infringement in some economy sectors, see, eg., A Maurel, 'Le devoir d'alerte des chercheurs' in C Byk (dir.), *Les scientifiques doivent-ils être responsables ? Fondements, enjeux et évolution normative* (Bordeaux, Les Éditions hospitalières, 2013), p. 47. This obligation might, besides, come from a duty of vigilance, as recognized by the Conseil constitutionnel, on the basis of Art. 1 and 4 of the Chart, in a decision rendered on 8 April 2011: "Everyone has a duty of vigilance towards damages affecting the environment which may be a foreseeable consequence of one's activity", see Cons. const., 8 April 2011, no. 2011-116 QPC.

[81] There is a permissible doubt on whistleblowing in the field of public health and environment. The law enacted on April 16, 2014 seems to compel the employee to alert the employer. On the interpretation of Art. L. 4133-1 of the Labour Code, see above.

The Abuse of the Freedom of Expression: The Limit to Whistleblowing

The exercise of whistleblowing must not lead to abuses. Whistleblowers must be careful about the way they disclose information. Thus, an employee who works for a notary public and denounces their employer to the Board of Notary Public and to the Social Security and Family Allowance Contribution Collection Office (URSSAF) using "excessive and insulting terms" commits an abuse of their freedom of expression.[82] In this case, judges seem to focus on the employee's intention to cause deliberate harm and in particular, to discredit the notary public's management of office. A whistleblower, thus, must be careful on how they express their alert, because if the formulation is insulting, the employee would abuse their right.

Besides, the employee whistleblower must not commit defamation against or insult the accused person. Article 29 of the law on freedom of the press, enacted on 29 July 1881, prohibits insults, that is to say "any outrageous expressions, scornful terms or invectives which does not lead to the imputation of facts". Indeed, it is prohibited to express "any allegations or imputation of facts affecting one's honour or consideration". The prohibition of defamation is more problematic for the whistleblower. For example, an employee may not, in a letter addressed to a former corporate officer, question the morality of the corporation's agent based on facts of private life.[83] An employee may not either question, in e-mails addressed to the director of the mother corporation, the honesty and the loyalty of the subsidiary's director, through insinuations and insolent questions.[84] However, by revealing illegal facts committed by the accused person, the whistleblower necessarily affects this person's honour and consideration. Such a limit may dissuade employees from revealing illegal wrongdoings happening in the corporation. But in accordance with Article 35, paragraph 3 of the 29 July 1881 law, if the information revealed by the employee is true, defamation is excused and there is no ground for abuse of freedom of expression. Similarly, if the information turns out to be false, but is not disclosed in bad faith, there is no ground for abuse.[85] Considering this liberal approach, the legislator, in 2013, did not think necessary to implement derogations to insult or defamation to benefit whistleblowers.

Consequently, the whistleblower has to exercise their freedom of expression in good faith.[86] Such a condition does not make it necessary for violation, irregularity or malfunction to be true; the whistleblower has a right to be wrong. However, they must not use whistleblowing in bad faith. Bad faith cannot be qualified "by the only

[82] Cass. soc. 15 December 2009, no. 07-44.264.

[83] Cass. soc., 21 September 2011, no. 09-72.054.

[84] Cass. soc., 29 April 2009, no. 07-44.798.

[85] See eg. Cass. soc., 6 March 2012, no. 10-20.983.

[86] See esp., A Laude, 'Science et démocratie : garantir un juste équilibre. – À propos de la loi du 16 avril 2013' (10 June 2013) *JCP E* n° 24, doct. 690, no. 19; L Gamet, 'Éclairage – Le salarié lanceur d'alerte' (June 2013), *BJS*, no. 6, 198, p. 378, esp. p. 379.

fact that the denounced facts are not established as being true".[87] The judiciary Supreme Court has asserted that "bad faith may only result from the employee's knowledge that the facts they have revealed are false".[88] Bad faith of the whistleblower constitutes a wrongdoing which may be punished through internal discipline.[89] In a decision of the judiciary Supreme Court, rendered on 6 June 2012, an employee was dismissed on the ground of misconduct for having "revealed, by a lie, inexistent facts of moral harassment in order to destabilize the corporation and get rid of the manager of the financial department".[90] In their decision, judges took into account the intention of the whistleblower: If they aim at protecting the general interest (including the corporation's interest), or the social interest of the corporation, the whistleblower acts in good faith.[91] In some cases, bad faith may also constitute a misdemeanour of injurious denunciation, defamation or insult.[92] Nevertheless, proof that the whistleblowing was based on a lie, which comes from its author's inner thinking, is in practice difficult to establish. Protection of the whistleblower is thus all the greater.

Thus, the limits on the whistleblower's freedom of expression must be strictly defined. The approach of the ECHR appears more measured.

The Protection Offered by the ECHR

In the *Guja* case,[93] the ECHR was ceased for the first time on the question of a public agent's right to use whistleblowing to denounce corruption within their administration. The Court tried to solve the issue of whether restrictions might be imposed on a public agent's whistleblowing, in accordance with Art. 10, para. 2 of the European Convention on Human Rights. The Court, in this case, pleads for a compromise between the employee's freedom of expression and its duty of loyalty and discretion – or duty of confidentiality for public agents – toward their employer.[94] Considering this duty, the Court compels the employee[95] to proceed to an indoor whistleblowing in the first place. The Court affirms that "the disclosure to the public

[87] Cass. soc., 10 March 2009, no. 07-44.092 ; Cass. soc., 27 October 2010, no. 08-44.446.

[88] Cass. soc., 7 February 2012, no. 10-18.035.

[89] If the author is not an employee, such behaviour can constitute a breach of contract. The employee's civil liability may only be incurred in case of wilful misconduct.

[90] Cass. soc., 12 June 2006, no. 10-28.345.

[91] See, eg., CA Paris, 13 March 2013, no. 12/03679, in which the Court decided that the whistleblower did not abuse of his/her freedom of expression, but on the contrary, acted in the corporation's interests by signalling an attempted corruption.

[92] Injurious denunciation is punished by a 6 months' imprisonment and a 75,000 euros fine, see Art. 226-10, subpara. 1 of the Penal Code.

[93] ECHR, *Guja c. Moldova*, 12 February 2008, no. 14277/04.

[94] Section 70 of the decision.

[95] The Court seems to encompass all the employees and not only the public agents.

must be seen only as the last option".[96] In order to evaluate the proportionality of the restriction which might by imposed on freedom of expression, the ECHR takes into account four factors: the public's interest in the disclosure of the information; the author must not act in defamation or in bad faith and must investigate on the truthfulness of the information revealed; judges must balance the interest of the disclosure and the impact on public authority; the aim of the whistleblower must be taken into account.[97] The Court makes sure to protect the interests of the institution, the concerned public authority and not those of the individual in question. Would the ECHR vigilance be the same if a private corporation was put into question?

Considering the conditions imposed by the ECHR, outdoor whistleblowing must be only subsidiary. Outdoor whistleblowing could be exercised only when the person in charge, being alerted, wrongfully stays passive. Would the only fact that there is no hierarchy between indoor and outdoor whistleblowing be a violation of the Convention? Would the approach of French case law, clearly more liberal, making outdoor whistleblowing easier, be in contradiction with the European Convention on Human Rights?

Nevertheless, the potential contradiction between French and European case law could be nuanced, at least in some fields. Indeed, in the field of public health, the ECHR puts aside the duty of confidentiality to allow a general interest debate dealing "directly with an issue of public health and questioning not only the responsibility of pharmaceutical laboratories in charge of manufacturing and commercializing the vaccine against hepatitis B, but also the State's representatives in charge of health issues".[98] A similar protection, in the field of environment, was given to a journalist who "wanted to exercise whistleblowing and inform the inhabitants of the department [...] that the water was polluted by a corporation".[99] It seems that all the revelations regarding public health or environment are considered as part of public interest and thus, may be (more) easily disclosed. Nevertheless, in those two cases, the authors of the revelations have particular missions. In the first case, it is a lawyer who, during the pre-trial period, comments the information that journalists were about to publish. In the second case, the Court aims at protecting a journalist, which in the Court's point of view must play the role of a "watch dog".[100] The lawyer, as the journalist, must benefit, due to their functions, from an extended freedom of expression. In other words, the control exercised by the ECHR varies not only by field, but

[96] Section 73 of the decision.

[97] Sections 73–79.

[98] ECHR, *Mor v France*, 15 December 2011, no. 28198/09; see also L Burgorgue-Larsen, 'Actualité de la Convention européenne des droits de l'homme (juillet-décembre 2011)' (2012) *AJDA*, chron. p. 143; S Lavric (2012), D. obs. p. 667; ibid; T Wickers (2013), D. obs. p. 136; C Porteron (2012), *AJ pénal*, note p. 337; J-P Marguénaud (2012), *RSC*, obs. p. 260 ; B Pastre-Belda (2012), *JCP G*, p. 26.

[99] ECHR, *Tanasoaica c. Roumanie*, 19 June 2012, no. 3490/03. See also FG Trébulle, *D*. 2012, obs. p. 2557.

[100] See esp. section 50 of the decision.

also according to the functions exercised by the whistleblower: journalists and lawyers have a vocation to call out the public, which is not shared with the public agent. Thus, the limits imposed to whistleblowing by a public agent could not be imposed on a lawyer or a journalist.

The whistleblower's freedom of expression was a major point in the French parliamentary debates, which preceded the three 2013 laws. This freedom remains the general law applicable to whistleblowers. The 2013 laws also implement a specific protection, which is added to the one provided by freedom of expression.

A New Protection: Non-discrimination

The law enacted on 13 November 2007 is the first to provide a protection against any discrimination measure against whistleblowers.[101] Such a protection was extended to the situations envisaged by the three 2013 laws.[102] This way, the whistleblower's protection against discrimination is applied only within the frame of application of those four laws: fight against corruption, prevention of conflicts of interests, public health and environment, economic and financial misdemeanour. Outside those fields, the whistleblower only benefits from the protection inherent to the exercise of their freedom of expression.

The protection offered against non-discrimination aims at protecting the employee whistleblower against any retaliation measure by the employer.[103] Indeed, disclosing information on the risks inherent to the corporation's activity in those fields might affect the company's image, in particular through an outdoor whistleblowing. Some employers, in such conditions, may be tempted to retaliate against the whistleblower – whether the disclosed information is true or not. The employer is prohibited from taking into account the fact that the employee is the whistleblower. Any unfavourable measure[104] taken against the employee[105] in the fields of recruitment, internship, training, wage, reclassification, dispatch, qualification, classification, professional promotion, mutation or renewal of a contract is discriminatory. In other words, the protection is applied against any decision dealing with

[101] Now codified in Art. L. 1161-1 of the Labour Code.

[102] Non-discrimination in the field of public health and environment was codified in Art. L. 1351-1 of the Labour Code, see A. Laude, 'Science et démocratie : garantir un juste équilibre. À propos de la loi du 16 avril 2013' (10 June 2013), *JCP E* n° 24, doct. 690, no. 19. In the field of economic and financial misdemeanours, non-discrimination was codified in Art. L. 1132-3-2 of the Labour Code. In the field of conflict of interest, non-discrimination was not codified.

[103] The definition of non-discrimination is the same in all the four studied laws. Thus, we will study them together.

[104] However, it seems that the employer may take into account the whistleblowing for any measure favourable to the employee. A whistleblower could be promoted in consideration of the whistleblowing – which demonstrates a concern for the corporation's interests.

[105] The protection is extended to interns, applicants for jobs and trainees.

the professional relation between the employee and the employer. Thus, the only fact that the whistleblowing and the unfavourable decision are taken concomitantly may be sufficient to characterize a direct discrimination. The employee also benefits from protection against indirect discrimination, that is to say, measures neutral in themselves, but which have discriminatory effects. If the decision taken by the employer is qualified as discriminatory, the measure is void.[106]

The protection is offered in a large manner to the whistleblower: it is enough that they "talk or testify" about the information. There is no specific procedure. Thus, whistleblowing may be accomplished outside any procedure implemented by the employer or by the legislator. As long as the whistleblower expresses and externalizes the information, they benefit from that protection against discrimination. Nevertheless, the protection is valid only if the information is given to specific recipients: the employer or judicial or administrative authorities. Regarding conflicts of interest, the protection is also applicable in the case of a revelation to the authority in charge of ethics within the organization, to an approved association against corruption. However, the protection would not be applied in case of a revelation to a journalist. Moreover, as for freedom of expression, the whistleblower is protected only if that right was exercised in good faith.[107]

Finally, the whistleblower benefits from a change in the burden of proof. The whistleblower who claims they have been discriminated against must bring evidence of "facts which allow to presume that [they] talked or testified, in good faith, about information dealing" with the whistleblowing. In other words, they must demonstrate that they exercised their whistleblowing right and that the unfavourable treatment they suffered from was linked to their action.[108] Once this proof is established, it is the "defence who, in light of those facts, has to prove that its *decision is justified by objective elements, unrelated* to" the whistleblowing.[109] The employer then has to bring some justification to the unfavourable decision taken against the employee; if they decide to stay silent, they will be found guilty of discrimination.

Whistleblowers' protection must be applied together/reconciled with the protection of the natural or legal person accused.

---

[106] In consequences, in the field of dismissal for example, there is a right to the reintegration of the employee in the corporation, and the employer cannot oppose to this measure.

[107] See above. In the law enacted on 11 October 2013, contrary to the two others, the legislator deemed useful to remind that "any person who talks or testifies about facts linked a conflict of interest [...] in bad faith or with the intention to harm or with an at least partial knowledge that the disclosed facts are not accurate is punished by the sanctions provided in Art. 226-10, subpara. 1 of the Penal Code"- the misdemeanour of injurious denunciation.

[108] Such proof might be difficult to establish in case of an indoor whistleblowing: The information is received through a procedure established by the employer; hence the employer has all the material means of communication of the whistleblowing[...] The employer, if he/she is sued for discrimination toward the whistleblower, will be unwilling to communicate such elements.

[109] The judge might also order any investigation deemed useful to form his/her opinion.

The Protection of the Accused Person[110]

The accused person is not only protected against an abusive exercise or the bad faith of the whistleblower or against injurious denunciation.[111] The accused person must also be able to react to the whistleblowing against them. It is thus important that this person is granted the right to be informed of the whistleblowing dealing with them, in order to be able to organize their defence and to respond to it.[112]

The Protection of Personal Data

Whistleblowing procedure may entail automatic processing of personal data,[113] that is to say, collecting, recording, conserving and disseminating data on an individual, whether identified or identifiable.[114] The procedure is thus submitted to Act no. 78-17 of 6 January 1978 on Data Processing, Data Files and Individual Liberties.[115] In accordance with this Act, the person accused by the whistleblowing has the right to be "informed by the person in charge of the procedure as soon as data about them is recorded, whether through informatics or not, to enable them to refuse the processing of this data".[116] The aim is to prevent the risks of abuses linked to the automatic processing of personal data, and especially the risk of an illegal use of this sensitive data.[117] Of course, informing the accused person should not be immediate in case conservatory measures are necessary, especially to prevent destruction of proofs

[110] Guidance no. 1/99 on the level of protection of personal data in the United States and the ongoing discussions between the European Commission and the American government, adopted by the Group 29 – an European, independent advisory committee on the protection of data and private life – on January 26, 1999, confirmed the CNIL's position, estimating that "far from deterring" whistleblowing mechanisms, Directive 95/46/EC on the protection of personal data contributed to their good functioning, by giving a framework and reducing the risks.

[111] See above.

[112] In some situations, the accused person is even obliged to respond to it. It is the case when an institution representing the employees exercises its whistleblowing right, see above.

[113] A more detailed study see L Flament, 'Comment mettre en place un dispositif d'alerte professionnelle ?' (26 March 2013) *JCP S*, 1133.

[114] All of those measures must be applied loyally.

[115] The European Directive 95/46/EC of 24 October 1995 on the protection of individuals with regard to the processing of personal data and on the free movement of such data must also be respected. The European Commission currently works on a project reforming the protection of personal data that should lead to a Regulation which would replace the 1995 Directive: European Commission, "Safeguarding Privacy in a Connected World. A European Data Protection Framework for the 21st Century", Communication (COM(2012) 9 final), 25 January 2012.

[116] Art. 9 of the CNIL Deliberation, above-cited, taken in application of Art. 6 and 32 of the Act no. 78-17 of 6 January 1978 on Data Processing, Data Files and Individual Liberties.

[117] The above-cited law gives to the person the right to oppose to the processing of the data, if he/she invokes a legitimate motive. Such right is difficult to apply in the case of a whistleblowing: the accused person is normally not present when the whistleblowing is submitted and thus cannot exercise this right.

related to the whistleblowing. Once the accused person is informed of the procedure against them, they cannot exercise their access rights.[118] However, this access right does not confer the right to obtain information on other people. In particular, the accused person must not be allowed to know the identity of the whistleblower.[119] The accused person also has a right to rectify the data,[120] if the information turns out to be inaccurate, incomplete, ambiguous or dated.[121]

The CNIL, attached to the notion of private right, is very attentive and demanding on the matter. In addition, the CNIL ensures that the indoor whistleblowing does not constitute a system of denunciation. This is what comes out of its Guidance no. 2005-110 and 2005-111 adopted on 26 May 2005[122] on the question of the conformity of two "ethic lines" dealing with whistleblowing, established by McDonalds and Exide Technologies,[123] in particular to the Act no. 78-17 of 6 January 1978 on Data Processing, Data Files and Individual Liberties. In those two cases, the CNIL considers that "the implementation by an employer of a procedure which aims at organizing, among its employees, the collection whatever form it takes, of personal data on facts contrary to the corporation's rule or to laws, and which might be imputed to their colleagues, may only result in a reserve from the CNIL as it may lead to an organized system of corporate denunciation". The CNIL insists on the

---

[118] In accordance with Art. 39 and 40 of the Act no. 78-17 of 6 January 1978 on Data Processing, Data Files and Individual Liberties.

[119] Art. 10 of the above-cited CNIL Deliberation, and Art. 2 of Deliberation no. 2005-305 above-cited, as modified by Deliberation no. 2014-042 from January 30, 2014.

[120] See Art. 10 of Deliberation no. 2005-305 above-cited.

[121] Art. 6 of the above-cited Deliberation.

[122] CNIL, Deliberation no. 2005-11 adopted on 26 May 2005 on the approval of the Compagnie européenne d'accumulateurs towards the implementation of an "ethic guideline", and Deliberation no. 2005-110 adopted on 26 May 2005, on the application of approval of McDonald's France for the implementation of a professional integrity system.

[123] In order to conform itself to the provisions of the Sarbanes-Oxley Act, the McDonald's group wanted to implement, in its French subsidiary, a professional integrity system which would allow French employees of the group to alert the American mother company about behaviours "allegedly infringing on French legal rules and on the code of ethics". The American company Exide Technologies, as for it, wanted to implement in its European subsidiary, the Compagnie européenne d'accumulateurs (CEAC), a "hotline" for its employees. This procedure would have allowed employees of the group to "communicate with the audit committee of the board of directors of Exide Technologies about such topics as inaccuracies in the budget that might be encountered", and to alert directors of the group on alleged violations of the rules of the corporations or the enforceable laws. In both cases, the whistleblower had the choice to remain anonymous or to disclose his/her identity; he/she had to reveal the identity of the accused person and indicate the nature of the allegations. Those data were processed in a central report under the responsibility of the director in charge of ethics in the group, confidentially communicated to the director of the legal department of the group and sent to the accurate service, depending on the type of allegation made. This service was then to make the decision of whether to investigate, and if so, the investigation would take place under the control of the French director of the legal department. Exide Technologies' procedure also provided that any employee concerned by the whistleblowing would be informed "as soon as possible of the allegations against him, so that he is able to defend himself".

necessity of a strict supervision of the collection of personal data procedures, affirming that the procedures implemented by the McDonald group and the Exide technologies group are "disproportionate in regards to the objectives pursued" and may lead to injurious denunciations. Those whistleblowing procedures are consequently incompatible with the Act of 6 January 1978 on Data Processing, Data Files and Individual Liberties. The CNIL thus refused to authorize those two specifics "lines of ethics".

The accused person also has a right to oblivion. Indeed, in accordance with Art. 6, 5° of Act no. 78-17 of 6 January 1978 on Data Processing, Data Files and Individual Liberties, personal data are "conserved in a form which allows identification of the concerned people for a period of time not exceeding the period necessary for the aim for which the data were collected and processed". Not respecting this obligation would constitute a criminal offence.[124] The decision of the CNIL taken on 8 December 2005 provides in Art. 6 that the data will be kept for 2 months, provided that this information does not lead to a judicial or disciplinary procedure.[125]

The access right allows the accused person to know the facts they are accused of and the elements they are charged with. The exercise of the rectification right allows them to compel the person in charge of the procedure to discuss the truthfulness of those elements. Indeed, if the accused person demonstrates that those elements are inaccurate, they are allowed to demand the data to be erased. The respect of personal data constitutes a prior step to the defence right granted to the accused person.

The Defence's Rights

The defence's rights are a fundamental principle recognized by the laws of the Republic[126] and are part of the right to a fair trial of Art. 6 of the European Convention on Human Rights. Those rights are to be applied first for the citizen when being confronted by their judges and opponents. However, the requirements inherent to the defence's rights tend to integrate corporations, under the influence of the "proceduralization" of the law[127]: by implementing internal procedures and investigations, corporations must respect the rules inherent to those procedures, part of which are the rights of the defence. Implementing whistleblowing is one major illustration of this principle.

The accused person must know about the rights granted to them, amongst which the defence's rights. The first defence's right to know about is that one can defend

[124] Art. 226-20 of the Penal Code.

[125] Art. 6 of the above-cited deliberation, as modified by Deliberation no. 2010-369 adopted on 14 October 2010.

[126] Cons. const., 29 December 1989, no. 89-268.

[127] See eg. PH Coppens and J Lenoble (dir.), *Démocratie et procéduralisation du droit* (Bruxelles, Bruylant, Coppens and Lenoble J dir. 2001).

themselves, and the formalities to do so. Hence, those rights must be reminded in the internal rules[128] of the corporation and in the instrument which implements whistleblowing. The Social Chamber of the judiciary Supreme Court in the Dassault System case from 8 December 2009[129] reminds that the rules on the protection of the people targeted by the procedure – right to access and rectification – must be stated explicitly in the act instituting the whistleblowing procedure. In the present case, in the absence of such an statement, the code of conduct implementing whistleblowing in the Dassault group should have been voided. The French corporation, subsidiary of group which implemented whistleblowing on an international level, cannot just remind that the procedure will be used in accordance with the applicable regulation; the code of conduct implemented in the French subsidiary has to explicitly state all the information aiming at protecting the rights of the people targeted by the procedure.

In another case, the judge hearing applications for interim relief in the Tribunal de grande instance, the first instance civil court, in Libourne has ordered on 15 September 2005, the whistleblowing procedure to be put aside, and more precisely, the hotline implemented through two internal notes entitled "Ethics Hotline", in the BSN-Glasspack group, a French subsidiary of an American corporation.[130] The judge ordered the suppression of the procedure because the object of whistleblowing exceeded the scope of financial wrongdoings and appeared disproportionate. The judge then noted that the accused employees may be subjected to an investigation without benefiting from basic defence's rights. Indeed, according to the judge an anonymous whistleblowing does not allow the accused person to exercise their defence's rights.[131] Recording anonymous whistleblowing without condition would require that the accused person would need to bring the proof of their innocence, thus reversing the very idea of the presumption of innocence.

The right to a defence entails immediately informing the accused person about the whistleblowing against them. Only the necessity of conservatory measures, for investigations and preservation of evidence, might justify delaying this information.[132] In the whistleblowing procedure implemented by McDonalds,[133] it was provided that the accused employee would have to be informed of their right "of access,

---

[128] Pursuant to Art. L. 1321-2 of the Labour Code. The whistleblowing procedure, which might lead to a disciplinary sanction, falls into the scope of internal rules. Its implementation thus involves a consultation of the work council, a communication to the Labour inspector and to the secretariat of the Labour tribunal, and to display it in the corporation's offices.

[129] ibid.

[130] Above-cited.

[131] L Gamet, 'Le whistleblowing (ou le salarié mouchard)' (2006) *BJS*, p. 307.

[132] D Danet, 'Misère de la corporate governance' (2009) *RIDE*, p. 407.

[133] Above-cited.

rectification and opposition in a two working days delay". The CNIL ruled that such a delay of notification was not a loyal way to collect and record information.[134]

Lastly, if the accused person is an employee of the corporation and the employer considers the allegations of wrongdoing proven, the latter may initiate a disciplinary procedure. In the frame of this procedure, the employer must summon the employee to a preliminary interview, precising the object of the summons. This interview must take place in a reasonable delay, giving time to the employee to prepare for the interview and their defence.[135] During the interview, the employer must state the ground for the foreseen sanction and allow the employee to explain themselves. However, the Labour Code does not impose a contradictory debate: the employer does not have to detail their accusations, nor do they have to justify themselves.[136]

Thus the protection of personal data and the disciplinary labour law give to the accused person an opportunity to defend themselves. But the accused person still has to use those rights, and to challenge either the person in charge of the whistleblowing procedure to exercise their right of rectification, or the employer, to be informed of the treatment given to the whistleblowing by the latter.

To conclude, French law has not only transposed the American whistleblowing model.[137] Thus, first, the French authorities restricted indoor whistleblowing to a precise list of fields, which the legislator has extended little by little. French law also gave a new basis, which has completely changed the economy of those procedures. Indeed, basing the whistleblowing regulations on the whistleblower's freedom of expression, and not on internal control, opens the door to outdoor whistleblowing. There is no set hierarchy between both procedures.[138] Consequently, the protection of whistleblowers lies in good faith, the non-abusive use of this freedom and the confidentiality of their identity. The restrictions which might be imposed on freedom of expression have to be strictly defined, as every exception to a principle of law. Besides, the French legislator brought an original protection by sanctioning discrimination in some cases of whistleblowing. By doing so, the legislator defines different regimes according to the object of whistleblowing, making the applicable law more complex and less understandable. The originality of the French system also and most importantly comes from the protection granted to the accused person. Employers are dissuaded from implementing systems, which might facilitate denunciation. The accused person must also have access to the elements of the whistleblowing, which allows them to prepare their defence. Indeed, the French model is grounded on a sense of mistrust towards whistleblowing, which has brought public authorities to search for a balance between the protection of the whistleblower and the protection of the accused person.

---

[134] In accordance with Art. 6 of the Act no. 78-17 of 6 January 1978 on Data Processing, Data Files and Individual Liberties.

[135] The employee may be assisted by another employee of the corporation.

[136] The requirement of justification appears with the employer's decision after the interview.

[137] See also V Rebeyrol, 'La réception du « whistleblowing » par le droit français' (14 June 2012) *JCP E* 1386.

[138] Except within the 16 April 2013 Act (possibly) and the whistleblowing by institutions representing employees, see above.

Bibliography

Antonmattei P-H, Vivien P (2007) *Chartes éthiques, alerte professionnelle et droit du travail français: état des lieux et perspectives*, Rapport – La documentation française

Bacache M (2013) *L'alerte: un instrument de prévention des risques sanitaires et environnementaux*, Revue trimestrielle de droit civil, p. 689

Barrière F (2010) *Le Whistleblowing – à propos de l'arrêt du 8 décembre 2009 de la Chambre sociale de la Cour de cassation*, Revue des sociétés, p. 483

Bry F de (2008) *Salariés courageux oui, mais héros ou délateurs? Du Whistleblowing à l'alerte éthique, Revue internationale de psychosociologie et de gestion des comportements organisationnels*, 34, vol. XIV, p. 298

Burgorgue-Larsen L (2012) *Actualité de la Convention européenne des droits de l'homme* (juillet-décembre 2011), Actualité juridique de droit administratif, chron., p. 143

Chateauraynaud F, Torny D de (1999) *Les sombres précurseurs: une sociologie pragmatique de l'alerte et du risque*, éditions de l'EHESS

Commission de rénovation et de déontologie de la vie publique (Commission Jospin), (November 2012) Pour un renouveau démocratique, Rapport

Coppens Ph, Lenoble J (dir.) (2001) Démocratie et procéduralisation du droit, Bruylant

Danet D (2009) *Misère de la corporate governance*, Revue internationale de droit économique, 4, p. 407

Delgas J (2004) *De l'éthique d'entreprise et de son cynisme*, Dalloz, p. 3126

Flament L (26 March 2013) *Comment mettre en place un dispositif d'alerte professionnelle ?*, La Semaine Juridique – Édition sociale, no. 13, 1133

Flament L, Thomas P (2005) *Le Whistleblowing: à propos de la licéité des systèmes d'alerte éthique, Juris-classeur Périodique,* La Semaine Juridique, Édition Sociale 2005, n,° 17, 1227, pp. 15 et seq

Foegle J-Ph, Slama S (14 March 2014) Refus de transmission d'une QPC sur la protection des fonctionnaires lanceurs d'alerte, La Revue des droits de l'homme, Actualités Droits-Libertés, http://revdh.revues.org/628. Accessed: April 2015

Gamet L (June 2013) *Éclairage – Le salarié lanceur d'alerte*, Bulletin Joly Sociétés, no. 6, 198, p. 378

Gamet L (March 2006) *Le whistleblowing (ou le salarié mouchard),* Bulletin Joly Sociétés, no. 3, p. 307

Ines B (10 December 2013) Clause de confidentialité: tiers privé d'un moyen d'assurer sa défense, Dalloz Actualité, http://www.dalloz-actualite.fr. Accessed April 2015

Laude A (10 June 2013) Science et démocratie: garantir un juste équilibre. – À propos de la loi du 16 avril 2013, La Semaine Juridique – Édition générale, doctr. 690

Leclerc O (2007) La protection du salarié lanceur d'alerte, in Dockés E (dir.), Au cœur des combats juridiques, LGDJ, p. 287

Leclerc O (2005) Sur la validité des clauses de confidentialité en droit du travail, Droit social, p. 173

Lochak D (1996) La dénonciation, stade suprême ou perversion de la démocratie, in L'État de droit: Mélanges en l'honneur de Guy Braibant, p. 451

Marguénaud J-P (2012) Revue de sciences criminelle et de droit pénal comparé, obs., p. 260

Maurel A, Le devoir d'alerte des chercheurs, in Byk C (dir.) (2013) Les scientifiques doivent-ils être responsables? Fondements, enjeux et évolution normative, Les Éditions hospitalières, p. 47

Pastre-Belda B (2012) Violation du secret professionnel par un avocat et liberté d'expression, La Semaine Juridique – Édition générale, p. 26

Porteron C (2012) La liberté d'expression de l'avocat, la défense des intérêts de ses clients et la défense de l'intérêt général, AJ penal, note, p. 337

Rebeyrol V (14 June 2012) La réception du « whistleblowing » par le droit français, La Semaine Juridique – Édition générale, n° 24, 1386, p. 32

Roumegas J-L (23 January 2013) Rapport AN, n° 650, relatif à l'indépendance de l'expertise en matière de santé et d'environnement et à la protection des lanceurs d'alerte

Thompson DF (December 2008) À la recherche d'une responsabilité du contrôle, Revue française de science politique, no. 6, p. 933

Transparency Internationl France (Oct. 2004) Déclencher l'alerte – Un dispositif de prévention et de lutte contre la corruption, Présentation du rapport 2004 sur le whistleblowing, La lettre de Transparence

Trébulle F-G (2010) *L'efficacité comparée du droit et de l'obligation de dénoncer en droit du travail et de l'environnement*, in Behar-Touchais M (dir.), La dénonciation en droit privé, Economica, p. 31

Katrin Deckert Associate Professor at Paris Ouest Nanterre University, and former Deputy Secretary-General of the International Academy of Comparative Law. Studied law in different universities in France and Germany. Since 2009, holds a PhD in German and French law from Panthéon-Sorbonne University (Paris I, France) and the University of Hamburg (Germany). Research Fellow at Pantheon-Sorbonne University (2001–2004), research and teaching assistant at Panthéon-Assas University in Paris (2004–2006), Research Assistant at the Max Planck Institute for Comparative and International Private Law in Hamburg (2007–2009), Lecturer in German Law at Paris-Est Créteil University (2008–2010), and Senior Research Fellow at the Max Planck Institute for Comparative and International Private Law in Hamburg (2010–2011). Teaches and researches in German, French and European civil, corporate and capital markets law as well as in comparative law.

Morgan Sweeney Associate Professor at the University of Paris Dauphine, specialized in national and European labour law, especially in discrimination law, Contributes to bi-annual reports on the French judiciary supreme court's implementation of European law. Also published an article on the European strategy to fight child poverty (in ***La symphonie discordante de l'Europe Sociale***, L'aube, dir. N. KERSCHEN, M. LEGRAND, M.MESSU, 2013, p. 265).

Chapter 7
Duty to Loyalty, Fundamental Rights, and Public Policy: German Whistleblowing Law Between Conflicting Values

Rüdiger Krause

Abstract The phenomenon of whistleblowing is not new in German law but has attracted increasing attention in the past few years. The current German law on whistleblowing follows a two-channel-model, i.e. fragmentary legislation on the one side and case law on the other side which is a consequence of the lack of a general regulation on whistleblowing. Traditionally, the labour courts were reluctant to grant comprehensive protection to whistleblowers because they qualify every kind of whistleblowing in principle as a breach of the duty of the employee to loyalty which can constitute a reason for dismissal. However, in the course of time and influenced by decisions of the Federal Constitutional Court and the European Court of Human Rights the attitude of the labour courts towards whistleblowers became more open-minded. Nevertheless, the protection of whistleblowers remains primarily embedded in the terms of termination protection law with its focus on balancing the rights and interests of the parties to the employment contract and so running the risk of losing sight of public policy considerations.

Introduction

Talking about whistleblowing in German law means to talk about a phenomenon for which the German language has no clear equivalent. In particular, there is no definition in any German laws. A neutral German expression for whistleblower is the term "Hinweisgeber" ("hint-giver") which comprises – close to the definition of the International Labour Organisation (ILO)[1] – in a broad sense of all situations where

[1] Whistleblowing = The reporting by employees or former employees of illegal irregular, dangerous or unethical practices by employers, cf. Thesaurus (2011) International Labour Organisation, Geneva. Available via www.ilo.org/thesaurus/defaulten.asp. Accessed 1 May 2015. See also the definition of Transparency International: Whistleblowing = The disclosure of information related

R. Krause (✉)
Institut für Arbeitsrecht, Juristische Fakultät, Georg-August-Universität Göttingen,
Platz der Göttinger Sieben 5, 37073 Göttingen, Germany
e-mail: Lehrstuhl.Krause@jura.uni-goettingen.de

G. Thüsing, G. Forst (eds.), *Whistleblowing - A Comparative Study*,
Ius Comparatum - Global Studies in Comparative Law 16,
DOI 10.1007/978-3-319-25577-4_7

a (current or former) member of an organisation (enterprise or administration) reports any wrongdoing, i.e. illegal or unethical practices, occurring or having occurred within the organisation to responsible persons, bodies or authorities inside ("internal whistleblowing") or outside ("external whistleblowing")[2] of the organisation.[3]

Whistleblower cases are not new in German law. For over 100 years German courts had to decide on dismissals of employees who had reported a – real or supposed – illegal conduct of their employer and/or superiors or colleagues directly or indirectly (via the trade union) to public authorities[4] or to the media,[5] and legal literature has commented the issue as well.[6] However, as of the 1990s not only has

---

to corrupt, illegal, fraudulent or hazardous activities being committed in or by public or private sector organizations (including perceived or potential wrongdoing) – which are of concern to or threaten the public interest – to individuals or entities believed to be able to effect action, cf. Transparency International (2013), International principles for whistleblower legislation, p. 4. Available via www.transparency.org/whatwedo/publication/international_principles_for_whistle-blower_legislation. Accessed 1 May 2015.

[2] Intermediate forms between "internal" and "external" are possible, e.g. the appointment of an external ombudsman by the organisation.

[3] The Organisation for Economic Co-operation and Development (OECD) recommends a slightly narrower definition and has identified the following common characteristics of whistleblowing: (i) the disclosure of wrongdoings connected to the workplace; (ii) a public interest dimension, e.g. the reporting of criminal offences, unethical practices, etc., rather than a personal grievance; and, (iii) the reporting of wrongdoings through designated channels and/or to designated persons, in: OECD (Ed.), G20 Anti-Corruption Action Plan: Protection of Whistleblowers. Study on Whistleblower Protection. Frameworks, Compendium of Best Practices and Guiding Principles for Legislation, p. 9. Available via www.oecd.org/g20/topics/anti-corruption/48972967.pdf. Accessed 1 May 2015.

[4] cf. cases prior to 1990: Königliches Landgericht I zu Berlin 3.4.1901 – 26 S 17/01, KGBl. 1901, 121; Königliches Gewerbegericht Köln 5.12.1907, GewKfmG 1908, 167; RAG 1.11.1930 – RAG 192/30, ARS 10, 464; LAG Breslau 15.11.1934 – 15 S 46/34, ARS 23, 34; LAG Hamm 27.10.1949 – 2 Sa 415/49, AP 50 No. 172; LAG Düsseldorf 21.2.1953 – 1 Sa 74/52, BB 1953, 532; LAG Baden-Württemberg 25.10.1957 – VII Sa 39/57, AP BetrVG § 78 No. 2; BAG 5.2.1959 – 2 AZR 60/56, AP HGB § 70 No. 2; ArbG Krefeld 22.5.1959 – 1 Ca 315/59, AP GewO § 123 No. 23; LAG Düsseldorf 23.10.1959 – 5 Sa 358/58, BB 1960, 523; LAG Berlin 25.11.1960 – 3 Sa 88/60, DB 1961, 576; LAG Düsseldorf 18.1.1961 – 2 Sa 393/60, BB 1961, 532; ArbG Elmshorn 4.4.1963 – Ca 118/63, AP GewO § 124a No. 9; LAG Baden-Württemberg 29.6.1964 – 4 Sa 13/64, DB 1964, 1451; BAG 18.6.1970 – 2 AZR 369/69, AP KSchG § 1 No. 82; BAG 14.12.1972 – 2 AZR 115/72, AP KSchG § 1 Verhaltensbedingte Kündigung No. 82; LAG Düsseldorf 21.2.1974 – 7 Sa 122/73, DB 1974, 2164; LAG Baden-Württemberg 20.10.1976 – 6 Sa 51/76, EzA KSchG § 1 Verhaltensbedingte Kündigung No. 8; LAG Baden-Württemberg 3.2.1987 – 7 (13) Sa 95/86, NZA 1987, 756; LAG Frankfurt a. M. 12.2.1987 – 12 Sa 1249/86, LAGE BGB § 626 No. 28.

[5] ArbG Dortmund 8.1.1949 – Ca 104/49, BB 1950, 704; LAG Düsseldorf 4.11.1952 – 1 Sa 98/52, DB 1953, 24; see also BAG 11.8.1982 – 5 AZR 1089/79, BAGE 39, 289 (warning on the grounds of informing the media); related BAG 31.7.2014 - 2 AZR 505/13, NZA 2015, 245 (YouTube-Video).

[6] cf. P Dahns, 'Denunziation und Strafanzeige als Entlassungsgrund' (1949) *BB* 39-40; J Denck, 'Arbeitsschutz und Anzeigerecht des Arbeitnehmers' (1980) *DB* 2132–2139; W Hinrichs, 'Das Beschwerde- und Anzeigerecht des Arbeitnehmers', in: JbArbR 18 (1981), 35–52; U Preis and R Reinfeld, 'Schweigepflicht und Anzeigerecht im Arbeitsverhältnis' (1989) *AuR* 361–374.

the term "whistleblowing" been introduced into German employment law[7] but this topic has also attracted increasing attention in jurisdiction[8] and doctrine.[9]

Traditionally, whistleblowing evokes negative connotations in Germany and expressions like "Denunziant" ("denouncer"), "Petzer" ("squealer") and "Spitzel" ("snitcher") are ready at hand. Many commentators explain this appraisal with the bad historical experiences of informing the State of non-compliant behaviour of friends, neighbours, and colleagues with the prevailing ideology in order to bolster a totalitarian system first under the National-Socialist regime and later in the German Democratic Republic.[10] Indeed, the mental background of the perception of whistleblowing as denunciation is older and properly brought to the point in the

---

[7] cf. U Wendeling-Schröder, *Autonomie im Arbeitsrecht* (Frankfurt a. M., Klostermann, 1994), p. 35 ff., 163 ff.; B Gach and S Rützel, 'Verschwiegenheitspflicht und Behördenanzeigen von Arbeitnehmern' (1997) *BB* 1959–1963; D Graser, *Whistleblowing. Arbeitnehmeranzeigen im US-amerikanischen und deutschen Recht* (Bern, Lang, 2000); M Müller, 'Whistleblowing – Ein Kündigungsgrund?' (2002) *NZA* 424–437; B Rohde-Liebenau, *Whistleblowing*, edition der Hans-Böckler-Stiftung No. 159 (2005). Available via www.boeckler.de/pdf/p_edition_hbs_159.pdf. Accessed 1 May 2015; O Sauer, 'Whistleblowing – notwendiger Bestandteil moderner Personalpolitik?' (2005) *DÖD* 121–124; P Gänßle, 'Der Whistleblower im Spannungsfeld zwischen Korruptionsbekämpfung und arbeitsrechtlichen Pflichten' (2007) *Kritische Justiz* 265–277. The Federal Labour Court (Bundesarbeitsgericht) mentioned the term "whistleblowing" in its decisions for the first time as late as the 2000s: BAG 3.7.2003 – 2 AZR 235/02, BAGE 107, 36 (at II 3 b cc (1)); BAG 7.12.2006 – 2 AZR 400/05, AP KSchG 1969 § 1 Verhaltensbedingte Kündigung No. 55 (at 18).

[8] cf. BVerfG 2.7.2001 – 1 BvR 2049/00, AP BGB § 626 No. 170; BAG 3.7.2003 – 2 AZR 235/02, BAGE 107, 36; BAG 7.12.2006 – 2 AZR 400/05, AP KSchG 1969 § 1 Verhaltensbedingte Kündigung No. 55; ECtHR 21.7.2011 – 28274/08 – *Heinisch v Germany*, AP BGB § 626 No. 235.

[9] B Schmitt, Whistleblowing – "Verpfeifen" des Arbeitgebers (Hamburg, Kovac, 2003); C N Schulz, Whistleblowing in der Wissenschaft (Baden-Baden, Nomos, 2008); A Berthold, Whistleblowing in der Rechtsprechung des Bundesarbeitsgerichts (Frankfurt, Lang, 2010); A Neumann, Whistleblowing und die Frage nach dem rechtspolitischen Erfordernis einer gesetzlichen Schutzregelung (Berlin, Logos, 2010); R Groneberg, Whistleblowing (Berlin, Dunckler & Humblot, 2011); C Becker, Whistleblowing (Frankfurt, Lang, 2012).

[10] cf. C Buchert, 'Der Irrweg der EU-Kommission – Zu den Überlegungen über die Einführung einer staatlichen Whistleblower-Prämie' (2013) *CCZ* 144–149 (see 145, 147); H Fleischer, 'Zukunftsfragen der Corporate Governance in Deutschland und Europa: Aufsichtsräte, institutionelle Investoren, Proxy Advisors und Whistleblowers' (2011) *ZGR* 155–181 (see 177); T Mahnhold, '"Global Whistle" oder "deutsche Pfeife" – Whistleblowing-Systeme im Jurisdiktionskonflikt' (2008) *NZA* 737–743 (see 737); U H Schneider and C Nowak, 'Sind die Einrichtung einer Whistleblower-Stelle und der Schutz des Whistleblowers Teil guter Corporate Governance?', in: Festschrift für Peter Kreutz (Berlin, Luchterhand, 2010), p. 855–865 (at 856); R Sieg, 'Arbeitnehmer im Banne von Compliance-Programmen – zwischen Zivilcourage und Denunziantentum', in: Festschrift für Herbert Buchner (München, C. H. Beck, 2009), p. 859–874 (at 866); G Wisskirchen, A Körber, A Bissels, '"Whistleblowing" und "Ethikhotlines". Probleme des deutschen Arbeits- und Datenschutzrechts' (2006) *BB* 1567–1572 (see 1570–1571). See also W Vandekerckhove, T Uys, M Rehg, AJ Brown, 'Understandings of whistleblowing: Dilemmas of societal culture', in: AJ Brown, D Lewis, R Moberly, W Vandekerckhove (Ed.), *International Handbook on Whistleblowing Research* (Cheltenham, Edward Elgar Publishing, 2014), p. 37–70 (at 40). Remarkably, in the early period of the National-Socialist regime two Labour Courts have affirmed the dismissal of employees in cases of repugnant informing of public authorities; cf. LAG Breslau 10.8.1934 – 15a S 96/34, ARS 22, 20; LAG Frankfurt a. M. 18.10.1934 – 6 II S 82/34, ARS 22, 145.

satirical song "Der Denunziant" ("The informer") by *Max Kegel* (1850–1902), a social democratic writer and poet, in which he blamed the informer as "blemish of mankind" and "dastard".[11] According to this socio-cultural tradition, the State is not perceived as a community of citizens but as an antagonist of society who does not deserve any solidarity and thus must not be informed about incidents within society.[12] In the past two decades, the negative attitude towards employees who blow the whistle has partially changed and whistleblowing is linked increasingly to positive connotations like moral courage and the altruistic pursuing of public interests.[13] Finally, a growing number of authors emphasize that (internal) whistleblowing schemes are an appropriate instrument to ensure the compliance of corporations with legal norms in order to strengthen corporate governance.[14] Nevertheless, the image of whistleblowing is still controversial in Germany.[15]

The following report will focus on the question of the protection German employment law grants to whistleblowers while other parts of law are neglected or mentioned only briefly.

Current Legal Basis for the Protection of Whistleblowers

German law lacks a single regulation, which gives clear guidance for the protection of every kind of whistleblowing. A reason for this might be that Germany has not ratified ILO Convention No. 158 which expressly provides that the filing of a

[11] In: Der wahre Jakob, Illustrierte Zeitschrift für Satire, Humor und Unterhaltung, 1884, No. 8, p. 63. Available via www.digi.ub.uni-heidelberg.de/diglit/wj1884/0067. Accessed 1 May 2015.

[12] M Müller, 'Whistleblowing – Ein Kündigungsgrund?' (2002) *NZA* 424–437 (see 426). For an overview on the diverse dimensions of denunciation from a social science perspective see A Lütdke, G Fürmetz, 'Denunziation und Denunzianten: Politische Teilnahme oder Selbstüberwachung?', in: A Lüdtke, R Steiert, H Uhl, G Weißeno, G Wilke, G Hufnagel, *Sozialwissenschaftliche Informationen 27* (PZ PädagogicaZentrale GmbH, 1998) 80–86.

[13] cf. Deutscher Bundestag – Wissenschaftliche Dienste (German Parliament – Research Service), Whistleblower – Hinweisgeber mit Zivilcourage. Available via www.bundestag.de/blob/190436/2e01b3a139c2843f2d370f2f6a153323/whistleblower-data.pdf. Accessed 1 May 2015. Further D Deiseroth, 'Whistleblowing – Zivilcourage am Arbeitsplatz' (2000) *Betrifft Justiz* 266–272; D Deiseroth, 'Stärkung von Zivilcourage zur Verbesserung der Qualität der stationären Pflege' (2007) *ZRP* 25–28.

[14] cf. T Berndt, I Hoppler, 'Whistleblowing – ein integraler Bestandteil effektiver Corporate Governance' (2005) *BB* 2623–2629; D Weber-Rey, 'Whistleblowing zwischen Corporate Governance und Better Regulation' (2006) *AG* 406–411; M Casper, 'Whistleblowing zwischen Denunziantentum und integralem Bestandteil von Compliance-Systemen', in: M Hoffmann-Becking, U Hüffer, J Reichert, *Liber Amicorum für Martin Winter* (Köln, Schmidt, 2011), 77–98; H Fleischer, 'Zukunftsfragen der Corporate Governance in Deutschland und Europa: Aufsichtsräte, institutionelle Investoren, Proxy Advisors und Whistleblowers' (2011) *ZGR* 155–181 (see 174–180); K U Schmolke, 'Whistleblowing-Systeme als Corporate Governance-Instrument transnationaler Unternehmen' (2012) *RIW* 224–232.

[15] cf. LAG Düsseldorf 14.11.2005 – 10 TaBV 46/05, LAGE BetrVG 2001 § 87 Betriebliche Ordnung No. 2 (at B II 2 aa) which has qualified an internal whistleblower scheme as an incentive to "denounce" other colleagues.

complaint or the participation in proceedings against an employer or recourse to competent administrative bodies shall not constitute valid reasons for termination of an employment contract (Art. 5 (c) ILO Convention No. 158).[16] Several attempts in the past few years to introduce a general regulation on whistleblowing in Germany (2008,[17] 2011,[18] 2012[19] and 2014[20]) failed for political reasons: The resistance of lobby groups was apparently too strong. Instead, in regard to whistleblowing German law follows a two-track-model, i.e. fragmentary legislation on the one side and case law on the other side.

First Channel: Legislation

As regards the first channel, i.e. the legislation, the Works Constitution Act (Betriebsverfassungsgesetz – BetrVG) provides the right of each employee to bring a grievance before the competent bodies of the establishment if he feels that he has been placed at a disadvantage (Sec. 84 BetrVG). Furthermore, the employee has the right to complain to the works council to start a particular procedure for the settlement of the grievance (Sec. 85 BetrVG). The employee shall not suffer any prejudice as a result of having filed a grievance (Sec. 84 (3) BetrVG). Only untenable allegations against the employer or superiors are excluded from the protection.[21] However, these provisions are limited to issues which affect the employee personally. The reporting of other wrongdoings within the enterprise is not covered.[22] Thus, Sec. 84 and 85 BetrVG do not provide appropriate means for complaining

[16] The same is true in regard to the Civil Law Convention on Corruption of the Council of Europe which provides in its Art. 9 that each party shall provide in its internal law for appropriate protection against any unjustified sanction for employees who have reasonable grounds to suspect corruption and who report in good faith their suspicion to responsible persons or authorities. At least Germany has ratified in November 2014 the United Nations Convention Against Corruption (UNCAC). Available via www.unodc.org/unodc/en/treaties/CAC/signatories.html. Accessed 1 May 2015. This Convention prescribes in its Art. 33 that each State Party shall consider incorporating into its domestic legal system appropriate measures to provide protection against any unjustified treatment for any person who reports in good faith and on reasonable grounds to the competent authorities any facts concerning offences established in accordance with the Convention.

[17] Gemeinsamer Vorschlag von BMAS, BMELV und BMJ für eine gesetzliche Verankerung des Informantenschutzes für Arbeitnehmer im Bürgerlichen Gesetzbuch of 30.4.2008. Avalaible via www.webarchiv.bundestag.de/archive/2010/0304/bundestag/ausschuesse/a10/anhoerungen/a10_81/16_10_849.pdf. Accessed 1 May 2015.

[18] Bundesrats-Drucksache 534/11 of 6 Sept 2011.

[19] Bundestags-Drucksache 17/8567 of 7 May 2012 and Bundestags-Drucksache 17/9782 of 23 May 2012.

[20] Bundestags-Drucksache 18/3039 and Bundestags-Drucksache 18/3043 of 4 Nov 2014.

[21] cf. BAG 11.3.1982 – 2 AZR 798/79, Juris (at II 2 b); LAG Köln 20.1.1999 – 8 (10) Sa 1215/98, LAGE BGB § 626 Nr. 128.

[22] BAG 22.11.2005 – 1 ABR 50/04, AP BetrVG 1972 § 85 No. 2 (at B III 2 a cc (1) (a)); LAG Schleswig-Holstein 21.1.21989 – 4 TaBV 42/89, NZA 1989, 703.

about any misconduct. The same is true of grievances in antidiscrimination matters. According to the General Equal Treatment Act (Allgemeines Gleichbehandlungsgesetz – AGG) each employee is entitled to bring a grievance before the competent bodies of the establishment if he or she feels discriminated on the grounds of race, ethnic origin, sex, religion, belief, disability, age, or sexual orientation (Sec. 13 AGG). Aside from this internal complaint, the employee can address his complaint externally to a designated Federal Antidiscrimination Office too (Sec. 27 AGG). In implementing European antidiscrimination law[23] any kind of retaliation against the complainant is prohibited (Sec. 16 (1) S. 1 AGG). However, at the point of departure these rights are confined to personal grievances.[24]

A somewhat broader scope of protection exists in the field of occupational health and safety. Sec. 17 (2) S. 1 Employment Protection Act (Arbeitsschutzgesetz – ArbSchG) – in implementation of Art. 11 (6) Directive 89/391/EEC – grants the right to external whistleblowing to every employee, if there is some evidence that work place security standards are not upheld and the employer has not remedied the grievance of the worker. The employee is allowed to complain not only in his own interest but also in the interest of his colleagues.[25] There must not be any disadvantage for the employee who has exercised this right (Sec. 17 (2) S. 2 ArbSchG).

Another group of provisions has the main goal to pursue effective law enforcement and the detection and prevention of risks and violations of law. In this respect two types of statutory law can be distinguished. On the one hand, there are so-called officers at establishment level ("Betriebsbeauftragte"). These officers have to be appointed by the employer and given the task to cope with particular risks which can occur during the operation of the enterprise. In detail, there are – according to the respective regulations – officers for health and safety (Sec. 5 ff. Occupational Safety Act = Arbeitssicherheitsgesetz – ASiG and Sec. 22 Social Security Code Volume VII = Sozialgesetzbuch VII – SGB VII), for data protection (Sec. 4f Federal Data Protection Act = Bundesdatenschutzgesetz – BDSG), for emission monitoring (Sec. 53 ff. Federal Immission Protection Act = Bundesimmissionsschutzgesetz – BImSchG), for prevention and managing of incidences (Sec. 58a ff. Federal Immission Protection Act = Bundesimmissionsschutzgesetz – BImSchG), for radioactivity control (Sec. 31 ff. Radiation Protection Regulation = Strahlenschutzverordnung = StrlSchV), for water protection (Sec. 64 f. Water Resources Act = Wasserhaushaltsgesetz – WHG), and for waste (Sec. 59 f. Recycling Act = Kreislaufwirtschaftsgesetz – KrWG). While performing their tasks including internal whistleblowing this statutory law protects all of these officers, in parts expressly against dismissal. However, only Sec. 4 g BDSG provides a right to external whistleblowing.

On the other hand, there are some regulations which deal with the issue of whistleblowing in specific sectors of economy and administration in which financial matters are at stake and therefore a risk of moral hazard exists. According to this

[23] Art. 9 Directive 2000/43/EC, Art. 11 Directive 2000/78/EC, Art. 24 Directive 2006/54/EC.

[24] As to the protection of supporters and witnesses see below sub III.

[25] cf. B Wiebauer, 'Whistleblowing im Arbeitsschutz' (2015) *NZA* 22–27 (see 23) (controversial).

sectoral approach and in implementation of Art. 9 Directive 91/308/EC[26] Sec. 13 (1) Money Laundering Act (Geldwäschegesetz – GwG) provides an immunity for everybody who informs the competent public authorities about the suspect of money laundering unless the report is intentionally or grossly negligent false in order to enhance the willingness to report on suspicious transfers of money.[27] The same rule applies if an employee informs his superior or an internal competent body (Sec. 13 (2) GwG). Sec. 10 (3) Securities Trading Act (Wertpapierhandelsgesetz – WpHG) contains a comparable regulation in favor of whistleblowers on unlawful securities transactions, which aims to increase the readiness to report such transactions as well.[28] In implementation of Art. 70 (3) Directive 2013/36/EU,[29] Sec. 25a (1) S. 64 No. 3 Banking Act (Kreditwesengesetz – KWG) stipulates the duty of banks to establish a scheme for internal confidential whistleblowing of employees in regard to contraventions against Regulation (EU) No. 575/2013, the Act itself or other criminal conduct within the enterprise.[30] Art. 32 Regulation (EU) No. 596/2014, which intends to combat the abuse of the financial market and which has to be implemented by July 3, 2016, stipulates the duty of Member States to ensure that competent authorities establish effective mechanisms to enable reporting of actual or potential infringements of the Regulation to said authorities, i.e. inter alia specific procedures for acquiring reports of infringements and appropriate protection for persons working under a contract of employment, who report infringements, against retaliation, discrimination, or other types of unfair treatment. Further, Sec. 81a and 197a Social Security Code Volume V (Sozialgesetzbuch V – SGB V) as well as Sec. 47a Social Security Code Volume XI (Sozialgesetzbuch XI – SGB XI) intend to facilitate whistleblowing on misconduct in public health care.[31] Indeed, there exists no empirical data on the efficiency of any of these regulations.

Last not least, there are some particular provisions concerning persons employed by the State. As regards public servants (Beamte), the rules are laid down in the Federal Civil Service Act (Bundesbeamtengesetz – BBG), the Civil Service Status Act (Beamtenstatusgesetz – BeamtStG), and the corresponding Acts of the States of Germany (Länder). Firstly, public servants have the right to a complaint, but only step by step through the levels of their hierarchy (Sec. 125 BBG, Sec. 36

[26] Replaced by Art. 26 Directive 2005/60/EC. This Article provides that the disclosure in good faith as foreseen in Articles 22 (1) and 23 by an institution or person covered by this Directive or by an employee or director of such an institution or person of the information referred to in Articles 22 and 23 shall not constitute a breach of any restriction on disclosure of information imposed by contract or by any legislative, regulatory or administrative provision, and shall not involve the institution or person or its directors or employees in liability of any kind.

[27] 27 Cf. Bundestags-Drucksache 12/2704 of 29 May 1992 (see p. 18).

[28] Cf. Bundestags-Drucksache 15/3174 of 24 Jun 2004 (see p. 33).

[29] Art. 70 (3) Directive 2013/36/EU provides that Member States shall require institutions to have in place appropriate procedures for their employees to report breaches internally through a specific, independent and autonomous channel.

[30] Depicted in detail by H Renz, B Rohde-Liebenau, 'Die Hinweisgeber-Regelung des § 25a KWG' (2014) *BB* 692–697.

[31] Depicted in detail by G Forst, 'Whistleblowing im Gesundheitswesen' (2014) *SGb* 413–422.

(2) BeamtStG). Secondly, in principle they have to keep confidentiality on all information they had become aware of on the occasion of their official duties (Sec. 67 (1) BBG, Sec. 37 (1) BeamtStG). Thirdly, since 2009, there is an exemption in order to fight corruption. According to Sec. 67 (2) Nr. 3 BBG and Sec. 37 (2) Nr. 3 BeamtStG public servants are allowed to inform competent internal bodies or the prosecutor if there is a reasonable suspicion of bribery. Comparable rules apply to soldiers (Sec. 14 (1) S. 1 and 2 No. 3 Soldiers Act = Soldatengesetz – SG). Sec. 8 (1) Act on Parliamentary Monitoring of Federal Intelligence Agencies (Gesetz über die parlamentarische Kontrolle nachrichtendienstlicher Tätigkeit des Bundes – PKGrG) stipulates the right of every employee of any federal intelligence agency to inform a Parliamentary Control Panel regarding official matters, however not in the interest of the informant or his colleagues. Finally, every soldier is entitled to directly contact the Parliamentary Commissioner for the Armed Forces but not anonymously (Sec. 7 and 8 Parliamentary Commissioner for the Armed Forces Act = Wehrbeauftragtengesetz – WBeauftrG).

Second Channel: Case Law

The second channel consists of general rights and duties of the employee and their interpretation by the courts. In this respect the question of whistleblower protection has mostly been raised in cases in which an employee was dismissed because he has externally blown the whistle.[32] Consequently, whistleblower protection in German employment law is essentially embedded within the general structures of German termination protection law. Insofar, it is important to note two points at the outset: First, according to Sec. 626 German Civil Code (Bürgerliches Gesetzbuch – BGB)[33] a termination of an employment contract without notice requires a compelling reason. Second, according to Sec. 1 (1) and (2) S. 1 Protection Against Unfair Dismissal Act (Kündigungsschutzgesetz – KSchG) a termination of an employment contract with notice has to be "socially justified", i.e. it requires a just cause, if the employee falls under the scope of the Act.[34] Thus, in most cases the direct approach of the courts is not whether the whistleblower deserves a particular protection but whether the conduct of the employee constitutes a compelling reason or at least a just cause for a dismissal. Furthermore, a third general point must be mentioned which has gained much importance in coping with whistleblower cases. Namely

[32] Internal whistleblowing is often in accordance with the policy of the employer and thus does not raise the problem of protection of the whistleblower against retaliation. It is even questionable whether the term whistleblower should be limited to organisational dissent. Thus, internal whistleblowing (in the sense of defamation of superiors or colleagues) occurs only very rarely in case law; one example is BAG 27.9.2012 – 2 AZR 646/11, AP BGB § 626 No. 240.

[33] Respectively comparable previous regulations.

[34] The Protection Against Unfair Dismissal Act is applicable if the employment relationship has existed for more than 6 months without interruption at the time of dismissal and the establishment or administration regularly employs more than ten workers (Sec. 1 (1) and 23 (1) KSchG).

that according to a long tradition in German law, fundamental rights, which are enshrined in the German constitution (Basic Law = Grundgesetz – GG), do not only protect against state action, but have to be taken into account by the courts in private relationships as well when interpreting general clauses (so-called "indirect third party effect of fundamental rights").[35] This rule applies, for example, regarding the duty of each party of an obligation to respect the rights, legal interests, and other interests of the other party (Sec. 241 (2) BGB), and the duty of each obligor to perform in accordance with the requirements of good faith (Sec. 242 BGB).

However, in the beginning fundamental rights of the employee played only a minor role in whistleblower cases. Instead, as regards the lawfulness of the dismissal of a whistleblower, the labour courts traditionally held that the passing of information on unlawful or unethical conduct within the employers' organisation to public authorities or to the media can constitute a compelling reason and/or a just cause for the termination of an employment contract.[36] A commentator has assessed a latent distrust of German labour courts against whistleblowers.[37] Legal doctrine has unanimously endorsed that position.[38] This approach can be explained by the prevailing conception that the employment relationship is not a mere exchange of work and wage but depends on mutual trust and loyalty. Initially the duty to loyalty ("Treuepflicht") was based on the conception that the employment relationship is a "personal communitarian relationship" ("personenrechtliches Gemeinschaftsverhältnis"). Though this conception is outdated since the 1970s, the perception that the employee owes a high degree of loyalty to the employer is still common ground.[39] Thus, as point of departure each incident of external whistleblowing is qualified or at least can be qualified as a breach of that duty because the labour courts acknowledge in principle an interest of the employer to remain unoffended by public authorities even if he has committed any illegal activity.[40] Insofar harmonious and trustful relations within the enterprise enjoy obviously to a certain degree a higher status than lawful conduct of the enterprise and its representatives.[41] Indeed, in every case at the end of the day the labour courts balance the interests of the employer and the employee in order to decide whether a termination

[35] The landmark case was BVerfG 15.1.1958 – 1 BvR 400/51, BVerfGE 7, 198.

[36] The leading case was BAG 5.2.1959 – 2 AZR 60/56, AP HGB § 70 No. 2.

[37] C Reiter, 'Der Schutz des Whistleblowers nach dem Sarbanes-Oxley Act im Rechtsvergleich und im internationalen Arbeitsrecht' (2005) *RIW* 168–178 (see 172).

[38] cf. A Hueck, H C Nipperdey, *Lehrbuch des Arbeitsrecht*, 7th edn. (Berlin/Frankfurt, Vahlen, 1963), § 37 I, p. 242; A Nikisch, *Arbeitsrecht*, 3rd edn. (Tübingen, Mohr Siebeck, 1961), § 34 I 3 b, p. 448.

[39] As to the historical development see M Müller, 'Whistleblowing – Ein Kündigungsgrund?' (2002) *NZA* 424–437 (see 427–429).

[40] Insofar very clearly LAG Frankfurt a. M. 1.6.1967 – 5 Sa 211/67, BB 1967, 1168; further LAG Berlin 28.3.2006 – 7 Sa 1884/05, LAGE BGB 2002 § 626 No 7b (at 2.1.1); see also BAG 3.7.2003 – 2 AZR 235/02, BAGE 107, 36 (at 44–45).

[41] H Fleischer, 'Zukunftsfragen der Corporate Governance in Deutschland und Europa: Aufsichtsräte, institutionelle Investoren, Proxy Advisors und Whistleblowers', *ZGR* 155–181 (see 177); M Kort, 'Individualarbeitsrechtliche Fragen des Whistleblowing', in: G Hönn, H Oetker, T Raab, Festschrift für Peter Kreutz (Köln, Luchterhand, 2010), p. 247–262 (at 250).

of the employment contract is valid. However, despite a considerable number of decisions in favor of the employee in particular if the worker claims a violation of his own rights and not only of public interests,[42] the labour courts often have affirmed the dismissal of the whistleblower in the past.[43]

Since the 2000s, three important decisions have set new impulses for a more whistleblower-friendly approach in German employment law. First, in 2001 the Federal Constitutional Court (Bundesverfassungsgericht) underlined the constitutional law aspect of whistleblowing in the case of an employee who was dismissed because he had given testimony against his employer in criminal investigations.[44] Referring to a precedent that exercising the constitutional right to lodge a criminal complaint in good faith must not entail disadvantages in civil law,[45] the Court held that the fundamental right to free development of the personality (Art. 2 (1) GG) in connection with the constitutional principle of rule of law ("Rechtsstaatsprinzip", Art. 20 (3) GG) has to be taken into account by the labour courts when coping with whistleblower cases. This fundamental right would be violated if an employee could be dismissed only for having exercised his civil duty as a witness without reporting knowingly or frivolously incorrect information. According to the Federal Constitutional Court the same rule applies if an employee exercises a civil right and reports his employer on his own initiative to the prosecutor.

Second, following this decision of the Federal Constitutional Court in 2003 the Federal Labour Court (Bundesarbeitsgericht) developed guidelines for judging whistleblower cases.[46] As a point of departure the Court held that, according to Sec. 241 (2) BGB, the employee is in principle obliged to respect the rights and interests

[42] LAG Hamm 27.10.1949 – 2 Sa 415/49, AP 50 No. 172; LAG Baden-Württemberg 25.10.1957 – VII Sa 39/57, AP BetrVG § 78 No. 2; ArbG Elmshorn 4.4.1963 – Ca 118/63, AP GewO § 124a No. 9; LAG Baden-Württemberg 29.6.1964 – 4 Sa 13/64, DB 1964, 1451; BAG 18.6.1970 – 2 AZR 369/69, AP KSchG § 1 No. 82; BAG 14.12.1972 – 2 AZR 115/72, AP KSchG § 1 Verhaltensbedingte Kündigung No. 82; LAG Düsseldorf 21.2.1974 – 7 Sa 122/73, DB 1974, 2164; LAG Baden-Württemberg 3.2.1987 – 7 (13) Sa 95/86, NZA 1987, 756; LAG Frankfurt a. M. 12.2.1987 – 12 Sa 1249/86, LAGE BGB § 626 No. 28; LAG Hamm 12.11.1990 – 19 (16) Sa 6/90, LAGE BGB § 626 No. 54; LAG Köln 23.2.1996 – 11 (13) Sa 976/95, LAGE BGB § 626 No. 94; see also LAG Rheinland-Pfalz 22.12.1997 – 9 TaBV 38/97, Juris: dismissal invalid but only warning valid.

[43] For reporting to public authorities see ArbG Krefeld 22.5.1959 – 1 Ca 315/59, AP GewO § 123 No. 23; LAG Düsseldorf 23.10.1959 – 5 Sa 358/58, BB 1960, 523; LAG Berlin 25.11.1960 – 3 Sa 88/60, DB 1961, 576; LAG Düsseldorf 18.1.1961 – 2 Sa 393/60, BB 1961, 532; LAG Baden-Württemberg 20.10.1976 – 6 Sa 51/76, EzA KSchG § 1 Verhaltensbedingte Kündigung No. 8; ArbG Berlin 29.5.1990 – 18 Ca 47/90, EzA KSchG § 1 Verhaltensbedingte Kündigung No. 31; LAG Frankfurt a. M. 14.2.1991 – 12 Sa 846/90, LAGE KSchG § 1 Verhaltensbedingte Kündigung No. 31; BAG 4.7.1991 – 2 AZR 80/91, RzK I 6a No. 74; LAG Köln 10.6.1994 – 13 Sa 237/94, LAGE BGB § 626 No. 78; LAG Köln 7.1.2000 – 4 Sa 1273/99, RDV 2000, 226; LAG Köln 3.5.2000 – 2 Sa 78/00, ZTR 2001, 23; for reporting to the media see ArbG Dortmund 8.1.1949 – Ca 104/49, BB 1950, 704; LAG Düsseldorf 4.11.1952 – 1 Sa 98/52, DB 1953, 24; LAG Köln 3.5.2000 – 2 Sa 78/00, ZTR 2001, 43.

[44] BVerfG 2.7.2001 – 1 BvR 2049/00, AP BGB § 626 No. 170.

[45] BVerfG 25.2.1987 – 1 BvR 1086/85, BVerfGE 74, 257.

[46] BAG 3.7.2003 – 2 AZR 235/02, BAGE 107, 36. Affirmed by BAG 7.12.2006 – 2 AZR 400/05, AP KSchG 1969 § 1 Verhaltensbedingte Kündigung No. 55.

of the employer and thus has to keep internal matters of the enterprise secret. However, this general duty to loyalty is shaped by fundamental rights of both parties. Hence, on the one side the Court reiterated that there is a fundamental right of the employee to report a criminal offence of his employer to public bodies. Furthermore the Court stated that in these cases the employee can generally also rely on the right to freedom of expression (Art. 5 (1) GG). On the other side the Federal Labour Court watered down the strict approach of the Federal Constitutional Court. The Court expressly overruled the decision of the lower instance that only knowingly or frivolously false reporting can constitute a termination.[47] Instead, it held that all aspects have to be taken into account including the right of the employer to lead an enterprise and to cooperate only with those workers who protect the enterprise from harm as consequence of the fundamental right to occupational freedom (Art. 12 (1) GG). After all, according to the Federal Labour Court reporting of the employer constitutes a breach of the duty to loyalty if the report is a disproportionate reaction to the conduct of the employer or his representatives. In its decision the Court left open whether the employee can additionally invoke the general fundamental right to petition to the competent public bodies (Art. 17 GG) which is applicable alongside to the right to freedom of expression.[48] Actually, the right to petition is not employed in current case law though older decisions have referred to this fundamental right[49] and some authors suggest this approach as well.[50]

Third, in 2011 the European Court of Human Rights (ECtHR) had to decide a whistleblower case in which a geriatric nurse has lodged a criminal complaint against her (state-owned) employer and was dismissed for that reason.[51] The regional labour court had affirmed the dismissal as valid.[52] The Federal Labour Court and the Federal Constitutional Court had refused to reverse the decision without arguing on the merits. The ECtHR held that the German courts had failed to strike a fair balance between the need to protect the employer's reputation and rights on the one hand, and the need to protect the employee's right to freedom of expression, which is protected by Art. 10 European Human Rights Convention (EHRC), on the other hand. In particular, the ECtHR highlighted that the German courts had not suffi-

[47] LAG Hessen 27.11.2001 – 15 Sa 411/01, LAGE KSchG § 1 Verhaltensbedingte Kündigung No. 79.

[48] BVerfG 12.12.1990 – 1 BvR 839/90, NJW 1991, 1475 (at 1477).

[49] cf. BAG 18.6.1970 – 2 AZR 369/69, AP KSchG § 1 No. 82; LAG Düsseldorf 21.2.1974 – 7 Sa 122/73, DB 1974, 2164.

[50] G Binkert, 'Verfassungsgerichtliche Vorgaben für das Kündigungsschutzrecht – Grundrechtsschutz bei Anzeigen gegenüber der Staatsanwaltschaft' (2002) *AuR* 161–167 (see 166); N Colneric, Note to LAG Baden-Württemberg 3.2.1987 – 7 (13) Sa 95/86 (1987) *AiB* 261–266 (see 264); E Klasen, S Schaefer, 'Whistleblower, Zeuge und "Beschuldigter" – Informationsweitergabe im Spannungsfeld grundrechtlicher Positionen' (2012) *BB* 641–647 (see 643); L Rudkowski, 'Kernprobleme einer gesetzlichen Regelung zum Schutz von Whistleblowern' (2013) *CCZ* 204–209 (see 205); P Stein, 'Die rechtsmissbräuchliche Strafanzeige' (2004) *BB* 1961–1964 (see 1963).

[51] ECtHR 21.7.2011 – 28274/08 – *Heinisch v Germany*, AP BGB § 626 No. 235.

[52] LAG Berlin 28.3.2006 – 7 Sa 1884/05, LAGE BGB 2002 § 626 No 7b.

ciently taken the public interest in the disclosure of the information into account.[53] Indeed, in the past the German labour courts had focused mainly on the interests of the parties of the employment contract. Constrained by the "logic" of employment law, public policy considerations did not play a significant role. The labour courts regarded the employee not as defender of public interests but only of personal rights[54] though the Federal Civil Court (Bundesgerichtshof) had emphasized the relevance of such interests in an early case in which a previous freelancer was sued to cease the publication of dubious incidents at the editorial office of a tabloid.[55] Thus, some authors argue that the decision of the ECtHR drives the German courts generally to a more whistleblower-friendly attitude.[56] Others feel that the approach of the Federal Labour Court can be continued in principle and there is only a need for small adjustments.[57]

Up to now the Federal Labour Court had no opportunity to decide another whistleblower case. However, the Court will obviously maintain its own guidelines stating that they adhere to the case law of the ECtHR.[58] Recent decisions of regional labour courts show the same tendency.[59]

Last but not least Sec. 612a BGB shall be mentioned. This regulation provides that the employer may not discriminate against an employee in an agreement or a measure because the employee exercises a right in a permissible way. Contrary to the initial impression, this provision does not play an important role in whistleblower cases because it leaves the decisive question open under which conditions

---

[53] After the decision of the ECtHR the parties resumed their proceedings. However, in 2012 they agreed on a termination of the employment contract uponand a payment of a considerable compensation by the employer.

[54] cf. R Groneberg, *Whistleblowing* (Berlin, Dunckler & Humblot, 2011), p. 235, with citations; C N Schulz, *Whistleblowing in der Wissenschaft* (Baden-Baden, Nomos, 2008), p. 97. A rare exception is LAG Baden-Württemberg 3.2.1987 – 7 (13) Sa 95/86, NZA 1987, 756.

[55] BGH 20.1.1981 – VI ZR 162/79, BGHZ 80, 25 (at 30–41).

[56] C Becker, 'Das Urteil des EGMR zum Whistleblowing – Neuer Lösungsweg auch für deutsche Arbeitsgerichte?' (2011) *DB* 2202–2204 (see 2203–2204); C Kerwer, 'Zwischen Zivilcourage und Denunziantentum – Whistleblowing im Arbeitsrecht', in: E Hilgendorf, F Eckert, *Festgabe für Franz-Ludwig Knemeyer* (Würzburg, Ergon, 2012), p. 581–598 (at 595–597); A Seifert, 'Der EGMR zur Kündigung wegen Whistleblowing' (2012) *EuZA* 411–421 (see 417–420).

[57] G Forst, 'Strafanzeige gegen den Arbeitgeber – Grund zur Kündigung des Arbeitsvertrags?' (2011) *NJW* 3477–3482 (see 3479–3482); M Schlachter, 'Kündigung wegen "Whistleblowing"? - Der Schutz der Meinungsfreiheit vor dem EGMR' (2012) *RdA* 106-112 (see 112); C Schubert, 'Whistleblowing after *Heinisch v. Germany*: Much Ado About Nothing?' (2011) *GYIL* 753-763 (see 762); O Simon, J M Schilling, 'Kündigung wegen Whistleblowing?' (2011) *BB* 2421–2428 (see 2426–2427); D Ulber, 'Whistleblowing und der EGMR' (2011) *NZA* 962–964; M Wienbracke, 'Whistleblowing und Art. 5 Abs. 1 GG – Transposition eines EGMR-Themas', in: H-J Bontrup, T Korenke, M Wienbracke, *Festschrift für Peter Pulte* (Hamburg, Kovac, 2012), p. 21–40 (see 40).

[58] BAG 27.9.2012 – 2 AZR 646/11, AP BGB § 626 No. 240 (at 37); see also BAG 31.7.2014 – 2 AZR 505/13, BAGE 149, 1 (at 15–16).

[59] LAG Köln 2.2.2012 – 6 Sa 304/11, NZA-RR 2012, 298; LAG Köln 5.7.2012 – 6 Sa 71/12, Juris; LAG Düsseldorf 24.9.2012 – 9 Sa 1014/12, LAGE KSchG § 9 No. 45.

the employee has exercised his right in a permissible way. Thus, the labour courts very rarely refer to Sec. 612a BGB when deciding on the dismissal of a whistleblower.[60]

Personal Scope of the Protection

According to the legal basis for the protection of whistleblowers its personal scope varies. The regulations on the so-called officers at establishment level protect – of course – only those persons who are entrusted with the respective task. The Federal Civil Service Act and the Civil Service Status Act protect only public servants. The majority of the relevant Acts protects employees of the respective organisation but comprises partially of other groups as well. The Employment Protection Act which stipulates expressly the right to external whistleblowing if an internal compliant remains fruitless[61] is applicable to employees, to apprentices, public servants, judges, soldiers, and most importantly to so-called "employee-like" persons, i.e. persons who are legally independent but economically dependent and hence deserve protection similar to that of an employee (Sec. 2 (2) ArbSchG). The General Equal Treatment Act encompasses in principle more or less the same groups and includes expressly applicants and agency workers too (Sec. 6 (1) and (2) S. 2 AGG). In regard to the access to employment or professional advancement the Act is also applicable to self-employed persons and board members (Sec. 6 (3) AGG).[62] Sec. 13 (1) GwG and Sec. 10 (3) WpHG concerning external whistleblowing protect everybody whereas Sec. 13 (2) GwG and Sec. 25a (1) S. 6 No. 3 KWG concerning internal whistleblowing apply only to employees.[63]

As far as the protection provided by fundamental rights like the right to freedom of expression (Art. 5 (1) GG), the right to report a criminal wrongdoing to the prosecutor (Art. 2 (1) and 20 (3) GG) and the right to petition to the competent public bodies (Art. 17 GG) is concerned, in theory everybody is protected. However, in practice these rights will mainly become relevant in employment law when it comes to the question of whether a dismissal of an employee without or with notice is void. This is in particular true of cases in which the Protection Against Unfair Dismissal Act is at stake because this Act is applicable only to employees.

Interestingly, the General Equal Treatment Act enlarges its protection to supporters of the whistleblower and witnesses (Sec. 16 (1) S. 2 AGG). As case law does not exist, the concrete scope of this provision is unclear. In regard to witnesses legal doctrine tends to limit the protection to formal proceedings before courts and other

---

[60] One example is LAG Hamm 12.11.1990 – 19 (16) Sa 9/90, LAGE BGB § 626 No. 54 (at 1 c bb).

[61] See above sub II 1.

[62] The particular problems of whistleblowing concerning board members (and lawyers) are discussed in detail by H Fleischer, K U Schmolke, 'Whistleblowing und Corporate Governance' (2012) *WM* 1013–1021.

[63] See above sub II 1.

public authorities. Thus, a witness giving testimony in internal investigations would not be protected.[64]

Protected Behaviour

First of all, external whistleblowing is protected if there is a legal duty to report. Law would be inconsistent if it were to obligate an employee to blow the whistle on the one hand and accepts a dismissal for the same behaviour on the other.[65] Indeed, such a duty exists in criminal law but is limited to the situation that serious crimes like murder or robbery are just intended by others (Sec. 138 Criminal Act = Strafgesetzbuch – StGB). Other provisions require the employee to report internally without delay, e.g. if the employee detects an emergent risk for the safety or the health of other workers (Sec. 16 (1) ArbSchG).

Alongside special regulations which cover only particular sectors, a whistleblower can in principle report any wrongdoing concerning corruption, disregard of consumers or the environment, tax fraud etc. Even the information on unethical practices is not excluded from the protection at the outset though this case group is apparently irrelevant. This follows from the approach that every employee can in principle rely on the right to freedom of expression which is not limited to a particular kind of mistakes at the outset. The protection does not require that a specific wrongdoing within the organisation is in question. However, while assessing whether the (external) whistleblowing is disproportionate and thus the dismissal valid[66] the weight of the wrongdoing plays a decisive role.

As regards the question whether the allegations against the employer have to be true, a shift occurred in German case law. At the very beginning the courts tended to decide on the dismissal of the whistleblower according to the result: If the allegations were true the dismissal was void. If the allegations were objectively untrue the dismissal was valid.[67] Hence, the burden of proof regarding the trueness of the allegations lay with the whistleblower. In contradiction to this, the Federal Labour Court has developed another approach. On the one side, false accusations do not constitute as such a reason for the termination of the employment contract but rather only do so if the employee raises them knowingly[68] or frivolously.[69] So the whistleblower is protected if he has acted in good faith. On the other side, the motivation of the employee is one of the key criteria in assessing the proportionality

[64] More details at M Benecke, 'Umfang und Grenzen des Maßregelungsverbots und des Verbots der "Viktimisierung". Der Konflikt nach dem Konflikt' (2011) *NZA* 481–486 (see 485 with citations).

[65] cf. LAG Düsseldorf 21.2.1953 – 1 Sa 74/52, BB 1953, 532.

[66] See above sub II 2.

[67] Königliches Landgericht I zu Berlin 3.4.1901 – 26 S 17/01, KGBl. 1901, 121; RAG 1.11.1930 – RAG 192/30, ARS 10, 464 (at 468).

[68] This conduct is a criminal offence according to Sec. 164 StGB ("False accusation").

[69] cf. LAG Hamm 28.11.2003 – 10 Sa 1036/03, *NZA-RR* 2004, 475.

of the (external) whistleblowing.[70] Thus, the dismissal is valid if the accusations are true but the employee has lodged the complaint solely with the intention to cause damage to the employer or to "wear him down". In this context the Federal Labour Court expressly rebutted the argument that the interest of the employer to hide contraventions, is never protected by fundamental rights. Actually, the Court seems to qualify such contraventions as business secrets which are in principle protected by law against disclosure according to Sec. 17 Act Against Unfair Competition (Gesetz gegen den unlauteren Wettbewerb – UWG).[71] These rules apply as well if an employee reports a colleague to the police.[72] Some authors criticize that approach because it means that even an employer who has violated the law is potentially entitled to dismiss a whistleblower.[73]

Just as the employer, who has dismissed the employee without notice, has to prove that there is a compelling reason for the termination of the employment contract he must also prove that the whistleblower has acted in bad faith, that is to say he has knowingly or frivolously raised false accusations.[74] The same applies if the employer has dismissed the employee with notice and the Protection Against Unfair Dismissal Act is applicable (Sec. 1 (2) S. 4 KSchG). However, the labour courts regularly demand that the whistleblower provides an information basis for his allegations. If the employee fails to meet this requirement his behaviour is likely to be deemed frivolous.[75] Should the whistleblower fail to fall under the scope of the Protection Against Unfair Dismissal Act a termination of the employment contract can be invalid according to Sec. 138 (1) BGB which expressly provides that any legal transaction which is contrary to public policy is void. Nevertheless, in this case the burden of proof that the dismissal was meant as retaliation against the whistleblowing lies with the employee.

Anonymous whistleblowing is not prohibited although it raises several problems like the risk of misuse.[76] On the contrary, it is facilitated sometimes even by public

---

[70] cf. BAG 3.7.2003 – 2 AZR 235/02, BAGE 107, 36 (at 45); BAG 7.12.2006 – 2 AZR 400/05, AP KSchG 1969 § 1 Verhaltensbedingte Kündigung No. 55 (at 18). See already BAG 4.7.1991 – 2 AZR 80/91, RzK I 6a No. 74.

[71] BAG 3.7.2003 – 2 AZR 235/02, BAGE 107, 36 (at 44–45).

[72] LAG Frankfurt a. M. 14.2.1991 – 12 Sa 846/90, LAG KSchG Verhaltensbedingte Kündigung No. 31.

[73] G Forst, 'Whistleblowing im internationalen Vergleich – Was kann Deutschland von seinen Nachbarn lernen?' (2013) *EuZA* 37–82 (see 71); R Ogorek, 'Whistleblowing – oder vom Verpfeifen im Arbeitsrecht und anderswo', in: A Höland, C Hohmann-Dennhardt, M Schmidt, A Seifert, *Liber Amicorum für Manfred Weiss* (Berlin, Berliner Wissenschafts-Verlag, 2005), p. 539–555 (at 554–555).

[74] cf. LAG Düsseldorf 17.1.2002 – 11 Sa 1422/01, LAGE BGB § 626 No 138; see also LAG Hamm 3.11.2011 – 15 Sa 708/11, Juris; dissenting LAG Berlin 28.3.2006 – 7 Sa 1884/05, LAGE BGB 2002 § 626 No 7b.

[75] cf. G Binkert, 'Kündigungsrechtliche Aspekte bei Strafanzeigen gegenüber dem Arbeitgeber' (2007) *AuR* 195–197 (see 197).

[76] As to the pros and cons of anonymous whistlewblowing in detail Forst, 'Whistleblowing im internationalen Vergleich – Was kann Deutschland von seinen Nachbarn lernen?' (2012) *EuZA* 37–82 (see 72 f.).

authorities. For instance the Federal Cartel Office (Bundeskartellamt) has introduced an electronic system for anonymous whistleblowing as of June 1, 2012[77] whereas Sec. 25a (1) S. 6 No. 3 KWG requires only a scheme for internal confidential whistleblowing.[78] Admittedly, according to the Federal Labour Court anonymous whistleblowing is not protected by the right to freedom of expression if the whistleblower is unveiled afterwards and dismissed.[79] In this respect, the Court argued that a statement from an unknown party does not contribute to the intellectual dispute which is essential for democracy. However, this is not consistent with the opinion of the Federal Civil Court, which advocated for a broader understanding of Art. 5 (1) GG including anonymous statements.[80]

One of the most important questions is whether the employee is required to inform his employer before he reports to external public authorities or even the media. On the one hand, internal whistleblowing is regularly less costly[81] but can be less effective, on the other hand, external whistleblowing is frequently more effective but can raise incalculable costs for an enterprise in particular if the media are informed. This topic is linked with the general question which problem whistleblowing shall be sorted out. In principle, both internal and external whistleblowing can be regarded as an instrument to reduce informational asymmetries and thus it belongs to a modern risk management because whistleblowers provide the competent persons and/or bodies with the information they need to suppress contraventions and eliminate risks.[82] Internal whistleblowing localizes the informational asymmetries within an organisation while external whistleblowing assumes that the main problem are informational asymmetries between the inside and the outside of an organisation. Ultimately, the answer is influenced by the fact whether (large) private organisations are to be regarded as being (too) powerful and therefore need strict monitoring in order to avoid any harm to the public.

Sec. 17 (2) S. 1 ArbSchG stipulates that internal whistleblowing shall prevail. Some labour courts generalise that approach.[83] A similar opinion is held by the Federal Administrative Court (Bundesverwaltungsgericht).[84] However, in that respect the Federal Labour Court is less rigid and allows the employee to blow the

---

[77] cf. U Schnelle, A Kollmann, 'Bundeskartellamt führt anonymes elektronisches Hinweisgebersystem ein' (2012) *BB* 1559–1561.

[78] See above sub II 1.

[79] BAG 3.7.2003 – 2 AZR 235/02, BAGE 107, 36 (at 44).

[80] BGH 23.6.2009 – VI ZR 196/08, BGHZ 181, 328 (at 341–342); further OLG Köln 27.11.2007 – 15 U 142/07, NJW-RR 2008, 203 (see 204). Critical for this reason M Manger, *Kritik im Arbeitsverhältnis und ihre Grenzen* (Hamburg, Kovac, 2011) 160–161.

[81] Dissenting G Forst, 'Whistleblowing im Gesundheitswesen' (2014) *SGb* 413–422 (see 415) who argues that an external whistleblowing scheme is less costly because it can practice economies of scale.

[82] Cf. B Rohde-Liebenau, 'Gammelfleisch und anderer Ekel' (2006) *AuR* 377–379.

[83] ArbG Berlin 29.5.1990 – 18 Ca 47/90, EzA KSchG § 1 Verhaltensbedingte Kündigung No. 31; LAG Köln 3.5.2000 – 2 Sa 78/00, ZTR 2001, 43.

[84] cf. BVerwG 15.11.2000 – 1 D 65/98, Juris; BVerwG 13.12.2000 – 1 D 34/98, NJW 2001, 3280. This is in adherence with the right to freedom of expression: BVerfG 28.4.1970 – 1 BvR 690/655, BVerfGE 28, 191.

whistle externally from the outset, if there is a legal duty to report, if serious offences are in question, if the employer has committed the crimes himself, or if there is no reasonable expectation that an internal complaint will be sufficient in bringing wrongdoings to a halt.[85] This conception means on the one hand that a dismissal is not automatically valid if the whistleblower has failed to keep the information on illegal or unethical practices inside the organisation as the first step. On the other hand, informing public authorities or even the media as the first step can constitute a reason for the termination of an employment contract though the whistleblower has not knowingly or frivolously raised false accusations. So the approach of the Federal Labour Court oscillates between a conception of whistleblowing as tool to improve the ability of organisations to deal with wrongdoings autonomously and a conception in which whistleblowing is a tool to enhance the transparency of organisations.[86] Whether the passing of information to the trade union is a case of external whistleblowing is not yet clear.[87]

The same rules apply when the employee has not lodged a complaint but only threated to do so, in particular with the goal to achieve advantages for himself,[88] or if he has accused colleagues.[89]

Level of Protection

Several regulations prohibit expressly any reprisal by the employer in the case of whistleblowing or exercising a right to complaint. This is true of Sec. 16 (1) 1 AGG, Sec. 4f (3) S. 2 BDSG, and Sec. 17 (2) S. 2 ArbSchG. These provisions are amended by the general rule in Sec. 612a BGB that the employer may not discriminate against an employee who only has exercised his rights. So in theory there is a

[85] BAG 3.7.2003 – 2 AZR 235/02, BAGE 107, 36 (at 45–46); affirmative BAG 31.7.2014 – 2 AZR 505/13, BAGE 149, 1 (at 15–16). See also LAG Hamm 12.11.1990 – 19 (16) Sa 9/90, LAGE BGB § 626 No 54: no need for previous information to the employer if the accusations are true and the immediate report to external public bodies is the only way for the employee to avoid prosecution for tax fraud. In the case of informing external public authorities by works councils BAG 3.6.2003 - 1 ABR 19/02, BAGE 106, 188 (at 196) tends to favour internal whistleblowing as a rule.

[86] As to this aspect in detail G Forst, 'Whistleblowing im internationalen Vergleich – Was kann Deutschland von seinen Nachbarn lernen?' (2013) *EuZA* 37–82 (see 73–74).

[87] In this direction LAG Baden-Württemberg 20.10.1976 – 6 Sa 51/76, EzA KSchG § 1 Verhaltensbedingte Kündigung No. 8 with critical comment of M Weiss.

[88] cf. BAG 14.11.1984 – 7 AZR 133/83, AP BGB § 629 No. 89 (at II 3); BAG 11.3.1999 – 2 AZR 507/98, AP BGB § 626 No. 149 (at II 1); LAG Rheinland-Pfalz 17.11.2004 – 10 Sa 1329/03, Juris; LAG Brandenburg 21.12.2009 – 10 Sa 2193/09 u. a., Juris; LAG Sachsen 21.1.2011 – 3 Sa 181/10, NZA-RR 2011, 290; LAG Schleswig-Holstein 17.8.2011 – 3 Sa 196/11, LAGE BGB § 626 No. 35; LAG Hessen 26.10.2011 – 8 Sa 1554/10, Juris; LAG Hessen 5.4.2012 – 5 Sa 1117/11, Juris; LAG Hamm 13.11.2012 – 14 Sa 1178/12, LAGE BGB § 626 No. 38a; LAG Rheinland-Pfalz 15.5.2014 – 5 Sa 60/14, Juris.

[89] LAG Frankfurt a. M. 14.2.1991 – 12 Sa 846/90, LAGE KSchG § 1 Verhaltensbedingte Kündigung No. 31; LAG Nürnberg 16.9.2011 – 4 Sa 297/10, Juris; BAG 11.7.2013 – 2 AZR 994/12, AP KSchG § 1 Verhaltensbedingte Kündigung No. 69.

comprehensive protection against any kind of detriment like suspension, demotion, loss of promotion opportunities, punitive displacements, reduction in wages or harassment. However, the problem is often to prove that any measure taken by the employer is a direct reaction to justified whistleblowing. In certain situations a prima facie evidence is possible.[90] Furthermore, in antidiscrimination cases Sec. 22 AGG facilitates the burden of proof because the employee must only provide evidence for the assertion that he or she has been placed at a disadvantage based on forbidden grounds. If the employee is successful the employer must prove that antidiscrimination law was not violated. But this favorable regulation applies only to whistleblower cases with an antidiscrimination background and cannot be implemented in other whistleblower cases.

Hence, the focus is mainly on the protection against a termination of the employment contract. Insofar dismissals can be declared void if the courts find that there is no compelling reason or at least a sufficient reason for the termination of the contract. However, if a dismissal is declared with notice and the employer fails to show a sufficient reason it is in principle possible to avoid the consequence of the nullity of the dismissal since the labour court can rescind the employment contract if due to tensions between the employer and the employee a further collaboration seems not reasonable (Sec. 9 KSchG). In this case the employer has to pay an indemnity to the employee (Sec. 10 KSchG). Normally this regulation applies in cases in which the employee has "poured oil on the fire" during the litigation on the dismissal.[91] Nevertheless, one regional labour court has used this option in a whistleblower case,[92] whereas another regional labour court has strictly denied the possibility of applying that regulation in order to avoid diminishing of the protection of the whistleblower.[93] So there is legal uncertainty on that question and employees who have blown the whistle are at least exposed to the risk of losing their job even if the dismissal is void.

One particular dimension of protection concerns the question whether whistleblowers have a right to stay anonymous[94] or that confidentiality will be preserved. This issue concerns the protection of personal data of the whistleblower.[95] There are

[90] BAG 21.11.2000 – 9 AZR 665/99, BAGE 96, 274 (at 280).

[91] cf. LAG Düsseldorf 8.9.1978 – 6 Sa 927/78, DB 1979, 556 (employee has turned to the media in order to put pressure on the employer); LAG Bremen 12.4.2011 – 1 Sa 36/09, Juris (at A II 2) (criminal complaint against the employer during the court trial).

[92] LAG Schleswig-Holstein 20.3.2012 – 2 Sa 331/13, LAGE KSchG § 9 No. 44.

[93] LAG Hessen 27.11.2001 – 15 Sa 411/01, LAGE KSchG § 1 Verhaltensbedingte Kündigung No. 79.

[94] Anonymous whistleblowing causes other problems as well which shall not be tackled here. As to this topic see the so-called "Article 29 Data Protection Working Party" (an independent European advisory body on data protection and privacy set up under Art. 29 of Directive 95/46/EC), Opinion 1/2006 on the application of EU data protection rules to internal whistleblowing schemes in the fields of accounting, internal accounting controls, auditing matters, fight against bribery, banking and financial crime (at 10–11). Available via www.c.europa.eu/justice/policies/privacy/docs/wpdocs/2006/wp117_en.pdf. Accessed 1 May 2015. Further G Wisskirchen, A Körber, A Bissels, '"Whistleblowing" und "Ethikhotlines". Probleme des deutschen Arbeits- und Datenschutzrechts' (2006) *BB* 1567–1572 (see 1569).

[95] Whistleblowing raises a huge number of further data protection problems which are depicted in detail by A Breinlinger and G Krader, 'Whistleblowing – Chancen und Risiken bei der Umsetzung

some provisions which expressly address this problem (Sec. 81a (3a) and 197a (3a) SGB V, Sec. 47a (2) SGB XI) but mostly general rules apply. In the case of internal whistleblowing the employee is protected by the Federal Data Protection Act. This Act stipulates that the employer must not transfer data to others, in particular to colleagues who are accused, unless this is necessary for carrying out the employment contract (Sec. 32 (1) BDSG) or at least insofar as this is necessary to safeguard justified interests of the employer and there is no reason to assume that the employee has an overriding legitimate interest in his data being excluded from transfer (Sec. 28 (1) S. 1 No. 2 BDSG). As regards the personal data of the accused employee a notification of the data subject is not required if the data must be kept secret on account of an overriding legal interest of a third party (Sec. 33 (2) S. 1 No. 3 BDSG). In such a situation there is also no obligation to provide information on the source of the data (Sec. 34 (7) BDSG). In the case of external whistleblowing to public authorities the Freedom of Information Act (Informationsfreiheitsgesetz – IFG) applies. In general the Act stipulates that everyone is entitled to official information from the authorities of the Federal Government (Sec. 1 (1) S. 1 IFG). However, in order to protect special public interests the entitlement to access to information shall not apply inter alia in the case of information obtained or transferred in confidence, where the third party's interest in confidential treatment still applies at the time of the application for access to the information (Sec. 3 No. 7 IFG).[96] The reason for that regulation is clear: Citizens (including employees) will only give anonymous information to public bodies if they can be trusted to maintain the confidentiality of the information[97] and at the very least to prevent any retaliation. The same applies to the duty of banks to establish a scheme for internal confidential whistleblowing of employees according to Sec. 25a (1) S. 6 No. 3 KWG.[98]

The employer is not only required to refrain from any reprisal of his own but also to protect the whistleblower from any harassment by colleagues.[99] This duty is derived from the general duty of the employer to defend employees who are victims of a hostile attitude of other employees. For instance, the employer has to prompt the harassers to stop their conduct, to displace or even to dismiss them.

Regulations on the support of whistleblowers by collective organisations or specialized bodies do not exist. There is only a provision in the General Equal Treatment Act according to which antidiscrimination organisations are allowed to

---

von anonym nutzbaren Hinweisgebersystemen im Rahmen des Compliance-Managements von Unternehmen' (2006) *RDV* 60–70 (see 64–69); G Forst, 'Whistleblowing und Datenschutz – Brauchen wir eine spezielle Regelung?' (2013) *RDV* 122–131 (see 127–131); T Grau, 'Arbeits- und datenschutzrechtliche Rahmenbedingungen für Systeme zur Meldung von Missständen und Regelverstößen durch Arbeitnehmer' (2012) *KSzW* 66–76 (see 70–76); G von Zimmermann, 'Whistleblowing und Datenschutz' (2006) *RDV* 242–249 (see 243–248).

[96] Depicted in detail by H Greve, 'Korruptionsbekämpfung und Whistleblowing' (2014) *ZD* 346–342 (see 340).

[97] cf. Bundestags-Drucksache 15/4493 of 14 Dec 2004 (see p. 11).

[98] See above sub II 1.

[99] G Forst, 'Whistleblowing im internationalen Vergleich – Was kann Deutschland von seinen Nachbarn lernen?' (2013) *EuZA* 37–82 (see 76).

aid employees in court trials (Sec. 23 (2) S. 1 AGG). The same is true of trade unions for trade union members. Within the enterprise the whistleblower can gain support by the works council.

Financial incentives for whistleblowers do not yet exist.[100] However, in antitrust law the Federal Cartel Office (Bundeskartellamt) can reduce fines if a member of a cartel blows the whistle and acts in a cooperative manner.[101]

Conclusion

The image of whistleblowing in Germany is still ambiguous. According to a survey in 2010, a majority of large enterprises do not intend to implement an internal mechanism for whistleblowing because they fear to stimulate a culture of distrust and spying.[102] Indeed, the promotion of whistleblowing has to sail between Scylla and Charybdis: On the one side a "culture of keeping silence and looking away" has to be avoided and on the other a "culture of denouncing and sneaking".[103] Instead, a "culture of witnessing and intervening" should be introduced.

As regards employment law the legal framework is dominated by anti-retaliation protection. Other measures to provide a whistleblower-friendly environment play only a minor role. The protection of whistleblowers against reprisal is to some extent provided by special legislation. However, there is no system behind the rules which have only a fragmented character. Thus, the protection on the grounds of fundamental rights is much more important. On the one hand, this approach and particularly the reference to the right of freedom of expression has the advantage of embracing all situations in comparison to special provisions, which cover only particular situations and in doing so inevitably leave gaps. On the other hand, this approach means that the major burden to protect whistleblowers in particular against dismissals rests on the courts.

---

[100] A proposal from the 1990s to introduce financial incentives for whistleblowers on tax fraud failed; cf. M Müller, 'Whistleblowing – Ein Kündigungsgrund?' (2002) *NZA* 424–437 (see 425). Now Art. 32 (4) Regulation (EU) No. 596/2014, which has to be implemented by July 3, 2016, stipulates that Member States may provide for financial incentives to persons who offer relevant information about potential infringements of the Regulation. The proposal (Com (2011) 651 final of 20 Oct 2011) is discussed by H Fleischer and K U Schmolke, 'Finanzielle Anreize für Whistleblower im Europäischen Kapitalmarktrecht?' (2012) *NZG* 361–368; very critical C Buchert, 'Der Irrweg der EU-Kommission – Zu den Überlegungen über die Einführung einer staatlichen Whistleblower-Prämie' (2013) *CCZ* 144–149.

[101] cf. available via www.bundeskartellamt.de/SharedDocs/Publikation/DE/Bekanntmachungen/Bekanntmachung%20-%20Bonusregelung.pdf?__blob=publicationFile&v=7. Accessed 1 May 2015.

[102] PwC/Martin-Luther-Universität Halle-Wittenberg (Ed.), Compliance und Unternehmenskultur. Zur aktuellen Situation in deutschen Großunternehmen (2010) 32–33.

[103] The problem is nicely described by B Rohde-Liebenau, *Whistleblowing* (Düsseldorf, Hans-Böckler-Stiftung No. 159, 2005) 37–40. Available via www.boeckler.de/pdf/p_edition_hbs_159.pdf. Accessed 1 May 2015.

The existence of a high standard of protection against wrongful termination of the employment contract and the indirect third party effect of fundamental rights within the employment relationship deliver in principle the instruments for the courts to establish an appropriate level of protection. Insofar a particular normative framework for the protection of whistleblowers is less of a necessity than within an employment-at-will-system which regularly renders employees without protection against arbitrary dismissals by the employer.[104] All in all, the labour courts have used these tools at least since the 2000s mostly in a proper manner. There are only a few decisions that appear too rigid. Nevertheless, as the outcomes are not clear and certain the system of case law induces the danger to discourage potential whistleblowers.[105] For this reason, German law is far from having a comprehensive and coherent approach to facilitating public interest reports and disclosures as was recently recommended by the Committee of Ministers of the European Council.[106] Moreover, the incorporation of the protection of whistleblowers into the "logic" of termination protection law with its focus on the balancing of the rights and interests of the parties to the employment contract has contributed to the traditional negligence of public policy considerations.[107] In principle, the regulatory framework is flexible enough to integrate the "logic" of whistleblowing, i.e. public policy arguments[108] which are stressed by the ECtHR in the Heinisch-case[109] and in some further decisions.[110] However, this conception sticks inevitably to the axiom that each report of an employee to external bodies is basically a breach of the duty to loyalty. The alternative conception that the whistleblower acts as a monitor in the interest of the public and contributes to effective law enforcement will presumably only enter into German law together with an independent Whistleblower Protection Act.

---

[104] cf. B Fasterling, 'Whistleblower Protection: A comparative law perspective', in: A J Brown, D Lewis, R Moberly, W Vandekerckhove (Ed.), *International Handbook on Whistleblowing Research* (Cheltenham, Edward Elgar Publishing, 2014) 331–347 (at 333); B Fasterling, D Lewis, 'Leaks, legislation and freedom of speech: How can the law effectively promote public-interest whistleblowing' (2014), *ILR 153*, 71–92 (see 82, 89); C W Summers, 'Individualism, Collectivism and Autonomy in American Labor Law', in: D Simon, M Weiss, *Liber Amicorum Spiros Simitis* (Baden-Baden, Nomos, 2000) 413–436 (at 418–421).

[105] D Deiseroth, P Derleder, 'Whistleblower und Denunziatoren' (2008) *ZRP* 248–251 (see 249).

[106] Recommendation CM/Rec(2014)7 of the Committee of Ministers to member States on the protection of whistleblowers of 30 Apr 2014. Available via www.wcd.coe.int/ViewDoc.jsp?id=2188855&Site=CM. Accessed 1 May 2015.

[107] Critical R Ogorek, 'Whistleblowing – oder vom Verpfeifen im Arbeitsrecht und anderswo', in: A Höland, C Hohmann-Dennhardt, M Schmidt, A Seifert, *Liber Amicorum für Manfred Weiss* (Berlin, Berliner Wissenschafts-Verlag, 2005), 539–555 (at 552–554); similar S Simitis, 'Die verordnete Sprachlosigkeit: Das Arbeitsverhältnis als Kommunikationsbarriere', in: W Brandt, H Gollwitzer, J F Henschel, *Festschrift für Helmut Simon* (Baden-Baden, Nomos, 1987), 329–358 (at 346).

[108] As early as 1949 advocated by P Dahns, 'Denunziation und Strafanzeige als Entlassungsgrund' (1949) *BB* 39–40 (see 40).

[109] See above sub II 2.

[110] ECtHR 18.11.2011 – 102474/09 – *Sosinowska v Poland*; ECtHR 21.10.2014 – 73571/10 – *Matúz v Hungary*.

Certainly, one should not ignore that both ways of protecting whistleblowers rest on different approaches: A particular Act would express the approach that the protection of whistleblowers is a means to an end, namely to pursue the public interest in the compliance of organisations with legal and ethical standards. In contrast, protecting whistleblowers because they have exercised fundamental rights is a means in itself. Hence, the solution should not be "either-or" but rather "both" in order to cover all legitimate purposes of whistleblowing law.

Bibliography

Becker C (2011) *Das Urteil des EGMR zum Whistleblowing – Neuer Lösungsweg auch für deutsche Arbeitsgerichte?* Der Betrieb (DB) 64: 2202–2204

Becker C (2012) *Whistleblowing: Anzeigerecht und Anzeigepflicht des Arbeitnehmers in der Privatwirtschaft.* Lang, Frankfurt am Main

Benecke M (2011) *Umfang und Grenzen des Maßregelungsverbots und des Verbots der "Viktimisierung". Der Konflikt nach dem Konflikt.* Neue Zeitschrift für Arbeitsrecht (NZA) 28: 481–486

Berndt T, Hoppler I (2005) *Whistleblowing – ein integraler Bestandteil effektiver Corporate Governance.* Betriebs-Berater (BB) 60: 2623–2629

Berthold A (2010) *Whistleblowing in der Rechtsprechung des Bundesarbeitsgerichts.* Lang, Frankfurt am Main

Binkert G (2002) *Verfassungsgerichtliche Vorgaben für das Kündigungsschutzrecht – Grundrechtsschutz bei Anzeigen gegenüber der Staatsanwaltschaft.* Arbeit und Recht (AuR) 50: 161–167

Binkert G (2007) *Kündigungsrechtliche Aspekte bei Strafanzeigen gegenüber dem Arbeitgeber.* Arbeit und Recht (AuR) 55: 195–197

Breinlinger A, Krader G (2006) *Whistleblowing – Chancen und Risiken bei der Umsetzung von anonym nutzbaren Hinweisgebersystemen im Rahmen des Compliance-Managements von Unternehmen.* Recht der Datenverarbeitung (RDV) 22: 60–70

Buchert C (2013) *Der Irrweg der EU-Kommission – Zu den Überlegungen über die Einführung einer staatlichen Whistleblower-Prämie.* Corporate Compliance Zeitschrift (CCZ) 6: 144–149

Casper M (2011) *Whistleblowing zwischen Denunziantentum und integralem Bestandteil von Compliance-Systemen.* In: Hoffmann-Becking M, Hüffer U, Reichert J (eds) Liber amicorum für Martin Winter. Schmidt, Köln, pp 77–98

Colneric N (1987) Note to LAG Baden-Württemberg 3.2.1987 – 7 (13) Sa 95/86. Arbeitsrecht im Betrieb (AiB) 8: 261–266

Dahns P (1949) *Denunziation und Strafanzeige als Entlassungsgrund.* Betriebs-Berater (BB) 4: 39–40

Deiseroth D (2000) *Whistleblowing – Zivilcourage am Arbeitsplatz.* Betrifft Justiz 16: 266–272

Deiseroth D (2007) *Stärkung von Zivilcourage zur Verbesserung der Qualität der stationären Pflege.* Zeitschrift für Rechtspolitik (ZRP) 40: 25–28

Deiseroth D, Derleder P (2008) *Whistleblower und Denunziatoren.* Zeitschrift für Rechtspolitik (ZRP) 41: 248–251

Denck J (1980) *Arbeitsschutz und Anzeigerecht des Arbeitnehmers.* Der Betrieb (DB) 33: 2132–2139

Fasterling B (2014) *Whistleblower Protection: A comparative law perspective.* In: Brown A J, Lewis D, Moberly R E, Vandekerckhove W (eds) International Handbook on Whistleblowing Research. Edward Elgar Publishing, Cheltenham, pp 331–347

Fasterling B, Lewis D (2014) *Leaks, legislation and freedom of speech: How can the law effectively promote public-interest whistleblowing.* International Labour Review (ILR) 153: 71–92

Fleischer H (2011) *Zukunftsfragen der Corporate Governance in Deutschland und Europa: Aufsichtsräte, institutionelle Investoren*, Proxy Advisors und Whistleblowers. Zeitschrift für Unternehmens- und Gesellschaftsrecht (ZGR) 40: 155–181

Fleischer H, Schmolke K U (2012) *Finanzielle Anreize für Whistleblower im Europäischen Kapitalmarktrecht?* Neue Zeitschrift für Gesellschaftsrecht (NZG) 15: 361–368

Fleischer H, Schmolke K U (2012) *Whistleblowing und Corporate Governance*. Wertpapier-Mitteilungen (WM) 66: 1013–1021

Forst G (2011) *Strafanzeige gegen den Arbeitgeber – Grund zur Kündigung des Arbeitsvertrags?* Neue Juristische Wochenschrift (NJW) 64: 3477–3482

Forst G (2013) *Whistleblowing im internationalen Vergleich – Was kann Deutschland von seinen Nachbarn lernen?* Europäische Zeitschrift für Arbeitsrecht (EuZA) 6: 37–82

Forst G (2013) *Whistleblowing und Datenschutz – Brauchen wir eine spezielle Regelung?* Recht der Datenverarbeitung (RDV) 29: 122–131

Forst G (2014) Whistleblowing im Gesundheitswesen. Die Sozialgerichtsbarkeit (SGb) 61: 413–422

Gach B, Rützel S (1997) *Verschwiegenheitspflicht und Behördenanzeigen von Arbeitnehmern*. Betriebs-Berater (BB) 52: 1959–1963

Graser D (2000) *Whistleblowing. Arbeitnehmeranzeigen im US-amerikanischen und deutschen Recht*. Lang, Frankfurt am Main

Grau T (2012) *Arbeits- und datenschutzrechtliche Rahmenbedingungen für Systeme zur Meldung von Missständen und Regelverstößen durch Arbeitnehmer*. Kölner Schrift zum Wirtschaftsrecht (KSzW) 3: 66–76

Greve H (2014) *Korruptionsbekämpfung und Whistleblowing*. Zeitschrift für Datenschutz (ZD) 4: 346–342

Groneberg R (2011) *Whistleblowing: eine rechtsvergleichende Untersuchung des US-amerikanischen, englischen und deutschen Rechts unter besonderer Berücksichtigung des Entwurfs eines neuen § 612a BGB*. Duncker & Humblot, Berlin

Gänßle P (2007) *Der Whistleblower im Spannungsfeld zwischen Korruptionsbekämpfung und arbeitsrechtlichen Pflichten*. Kritische Justiz 40: 265–277

Hinrichs W (1981) Das *Beschwerde- und Anzeigerecht des Arbeitnehmers*. Jahrbuch des Arbeitsrechts (JbArbR) 18: 35–52

Hueck A, Nipperdey H (1963) *Lehrbuch des Arbeitsrechts*. Vol. 1, 7. Ed., Vahlen, Berlin

Kegel M (1884) *Der Denunziant. Der wahre Jakob, Illustrierte Zeitschrift für Satire, Humor und Unterhaltung:* 63. http://digi.ub.uni-heidelberg.de/diglit/wj1884/0067. Accessed May 2015

Kerwer C (2012) *Zwischen Zivilcourage und Denunziantentum – Whistleblowing im Arbeitsrecht*. In: Hilgendorf E, Eckert F (eds) Subsidiarität – Sicherheit – Solidarität. Festgabe für Franz-Ludwig Knemeyer (2012), p. 581–598

Klasen E, Schaefer S (2012) *Whistleblower, Zeuge und "Beschuldigter" – Informationsweitergabe im Spannungsfeld grundrechtlicher Positionen*. Betriebs-Berater (BB) 67: 641–647.

Kort M (2010) *Individualarbeitsrechtliche Fragen des Whistleblowing*. In: Hönn G, Oetker H, Raab T (eds) Festschrift für Peter Kreutz. Luchterhand, Köln, pp 247–262

Lütdke A, Fürmetz G (1998) *Denunziation und Denunzianten: Politische Teilnahme oder Selbstüberwachung?* Sozialwissenschaftliche Informationen 27: 80–86

Mahnhold T (2008) *"Global Whistle" oder "deutsche Pfeife" – Whistleblowing-Systeme im Jurisdiktionskonflikt*. Neue Zeitschrift für Arbeitsrecht (NZA) 25: 737–743

Manger M (2011) *Kritik im Arbeitsverhältnis und ihre Grenzen*. Kovač, Hamburg

Müller M (2002) *Whistleblowing - Ein Kündigungsgrund?* Neue Zeitschrift für Arbeitsrecht (NZA) 19: 424–437

Neumann A (2010) *Whistleblowing und die Frage nach dem rechtspolitischen Erfordernis einer gesetzlichen Schutzregelung*. Logos, Berlin

Nikisch A (1961) *Arbeitsrecht*. Vol. 1, 3. Ed., Mohr, Tübingen

OECD (ed), G20 Anti-Corruption Action Plan: Protection of Whistleblowers. Study on Whistleblower Protection. Frameworks, Compendium of Best Practices and Guiding Principles for Legislation. http://www.oecd.org/g20/topics/anti-corruption/48972967.pdf. Accessed May 2015

Ogorek R (2005), *Whistleblowing – oder vom Verpfeifen im Arbeitsrecht und anderswo.* In: Höland A, Hohmann-Dennhardt C, Schmidt M, Seifert A (eds) Arbeitnehmermitwirkung in einer sich globalisierenden Arbeitswelt/Employee Involvement in a Globalising World. Liber amicorum Manfred Weiss. Berliner Wissenschafts-Verlag, Berlin, pp 539–555

Preis U, Reinfeld R (1989) *Schweigepflicht und Anzeigerecht im Arbeitsverhältnis.* Arbeit und Recht (AuR) 37: 361–374

PricewaterhouseCoopers, Martin-Luther-Universität Halle-Wittenberg (eds) (2010) Compliance und Unternehmenskultur. Zur aktuellen Situation in deutschen Großunternehmen. Frankfurt am Main

Reiter C (2005) *Der Schutz des Whistleblowers nach dem Sarbanes-Oxley Act im Rechtsvergleich und im internationalen Arbeitsrecht. Recht der Internationalen Wirtschaft* (RIW) 51: 168–178

Renz H, Rohde-Liebenau B (2014) *Die Hinweisgeber-Regelung des § 25a KWG.* Betriebs-Berater (BB) 69: 692–697

Rohde-Liebenau B (2005) *Whistleblowing*, edition der Hans-Böckler-Stiftung No. 159

Rohde-Liebenau B (2006) *Gammelfleisch und anderer Ekel.* Arbeit und Recht (AuR) 54: 377–379

Rudkowski L (2013) *Kernprobleme einer gesetzlichen Regelung zum Schutz von Whistleblowern.* Corporate Compliance Zeitschrift (CCZ) 6: 204–209

Sauer O (2005) *Whistleblowing – notwendiger Bestandteil moderner Personalpolitik?* Der öffentliche Dienst (DÖD) 58: 121–124

Schlachter M (2012) Kündigung wegen "Whistleblowing"? – Der Schutz der Meinungsfreiheit vor dem EGMR. Recht der Arbeit (RdA) 65: 106–112

Schmitt B (2003) *Whistleblowing – "Verpfeifen" des Arbeitgebers.* Kovač, Hamburg

Schmolke K U (2012) *Whistleblowing-Systeme als Corporate Governance-Instrument transnationaler Unternehmen.* Recht der Internationalen Wirtschaft (RIW) 58: 224–232

Schneider U H, Nowak C (2010) *Sind die Einrichtung einer Whistleblower-Stelle und der Schutz des Whistleblowers Teil guter Corporate Governance?* In: Hönn G, Oetker H, Raab T (eds) Festschrift für Peter Kreutz. Luchterhand, Köln, pp 855–865

Schnelle U, Kollmann A (2012) *Bundeskartellamt führt anonymes elektronisches Hinweisgebersystem ein.* Betriebs-Berater (BB) 67: 1559–1561

Schubert C (2011) Whistle-Blowing after Heinisch v. Germany: Much Ado About Nothing?. German Yearbook of International Law (GYIL) 54: 753–763

Schulz C N (2008) Whistleblowing in der Wissenschaft. Nomos, Baden-Baden

Seifert A (2012) *Der EGMR zur Kündigung wegen Whistleblowing.* Europäische Zeitschrift für Arbeitsrecht (EuZA) 5: 411–421

Sieg R (2009) *Arbeitnehmer im Banne von Compliance-Programmen – zwischen Zivilcourage und Denunziantentum.* In: Bauer J-H, Kort M, Möllers T M J, Sandmann B (eds) Festschrift für Herbert Buchner. Beck, München, pp 859–874

Simitis S (1987) *Die verordnete Sprachlosigkeit: Das Arbeitsverhältnis als Kommunikationsbarriere.* In: Brandt W, Gollwitzer H, Henschel J F (eds) Ein Richter, ein Bürger, ein Christ. Festschrift für Helmut Simon. Nomos, Baden-Baden, pp 329–358

Simon O, Schilling J M (2011) *Kündigung wegen Whistleblowing?* Betriebs-Berater (BB) 66: 2421–2428

Stein P (2004) *Die rechtsmissbräuchliche Strafanzeige.* Betriebs-Berater (BB) 59: 1961–1964

Summers C W (2000) *Individualism, Collectivism and Autonomy in American Labor Law.* In: Simon D, Weiss M (eds) Zur Autonomie des Individuums. Liber Amicorum Spiros Simitis. Nomos, Baden-Baden, pp 413–436

Transparency International (2013) International principles for whistleblower legislation. http://www.transparency.org/whatwedo/publication/international_principles_for_whistleblower_legislation. Accessed May 2015.

Ulber D (2011) *Whistleblowing und der EGMR.* Neue Zeitschrift für Arbeitsrecht (NZA) 28: 962–964

United Nations Convention against Corruption, Official Gazette of RS – MP, No. 5/2008 of 4 March 2008

Vandekerckhove W, Uys T, Rehg M, Brown A J (2014) *Understandings of whistleblowing: Dilemmas of societal culture.* In: Brown A J, Lewis D, Moberly R E, Vandekerckhove W (eds), International Handbook on Whistleblowing Research. Edward Elgar Publishing, Cheltenham, pp 37–70

von Zimmermann G (2006) *Whistleblowing und Datenschutz.* Recht der Datenverarbeitung (RDV) 22: 242–249

Weber-Rey D (2006) *Whistleblowing zwischen Corporate Governance und Better Regulation.* Die Aktiengesellschaft (AG) 51: 406–411

Wendeling-Schröder U (1994) *Autonomie im Arbeitsrecht: Möglichkeiten und Grenzen eigenverantwortlichen Handelns in der abhängigen Arbeit.* Klostermann, Frankfurt am Main

Wiebauer B (2015) *Whistleblowing im Arbeitsschutz.* Neue Zeitschrift für Arbeitsrecht (NZA) 32: 22–27

Wienbracke M (2012) *Whistleblowing und Art. 5 Abs. 1 GG – Transposition eines EGMR-Themas.* In: Bontrup H-J, Korenke T, Wienbracke M (eds) Arbeit – Personal – Soziales. Festschrift für Peter Pulte. Kovač, Hamburg, pp 21–40

Wisskirchen G, Körber A, Bissels A (2006) *"Whistleblowing" und "Ethikhotlines". Probleme des deutschen Arbeits- und Datenschutzrechts.* Betriebs-Berater (BB) 61: 1567–1572

Chapter 8
Whistleblowing: National Report for Ireland

Michael Doherty and Desmond Ryan

Abstract The subject of whistleblowing has become one of very great significance in Irish employment law in recent years, a significance that is now reflected in the Protected Disclosures Act 2014 (hereafter referred to in this Report as the "2014 Act"), which came into force in Ireland in the summer of 2014. This new regime provides comprehensive protection for whistleblowers across all sectors of the economy, replacing what had hitherto been a piecemeal, sector-specific patchwork of protections that left significant lacunae in the legal regime. Accordingly, this Report offers analysis of the new legislative regime in Irish law and its implications for the development of an entirely new whistleblowing regime in this jurisdiction.

Overall Relevance of Whistleblowing in Irish Employment Law

The subject of whistleblowing has become one of very great significance in Irish employment law in recent years, a significance that is now reflected in the Protected Disclosures Act 2014 (hereafter referred to in this Report as the "2014 Act"), which came into force in Ireland in the summer of 2014.

Legislative reform on the subject of whistleblowing was a key component of the current Government's Programme for Government. Underpinning the legislation was the need to provide comprehensive protection for whistleblowers across all sectors of the economy, replacing what had hitherto been a piecemeal, sector-specific patchwork of protections that left significant lacunae in the legal regime.

A number of very prominent public controversies regarding whistleblowing, particularly in the context of An Garda Siochana (the national police force in Ireland) further increased the momentum for legislative change in this context.

M. Doherty (✉)
Department of Law, Maynooth University, Maynooth, Co. Kildare, Ireland
e-mail: Michael.B.Doherty@nuim.ie

D. Ryan
Trinity College Dublin, Law School, House 39, Dublin 2, Ireland
e-mail: dryan14@tcd.ie

G. Thüsing, G. Forst (eds.), *Whistleblowing - A Comparative Study*,
Ius Comparatum - Global Studies in Comparative Law 16,
DOI 10.1007/978-3-319-25577-4_8

To date, there is not an extensive body of either case law or academic literature on the subject in Ireland. This is likely to change in light of the introduction of the 2014 Act and the extensive protections contained therein.

The Legal Basis for the Protection of Whistleblowers in Ireland

The Protected Disclosures Act 2014 (the '2014 Act') has recently been enacted and transforms the legal position concerning whistleblower protection in this jurisdiction. One of the most significant features of the new legislation is the breadth of its coverage (set out in more detail below). This stands in marked contrast to the previous position in Irish employment law, where protection for whisteblowers had developed on an ad hoc sectoral-specific basis and was frequently linked to mandatory reporting obligations rather than being viewed as a substantive protection in its own right.

Thus, for example, section 8A of the Prevention of Corruption Act 2001 provides that a person shall not be not liable in damages in respect of communicating to an appropriate person his or her opinion that an offence under the Prevention of Corruption Acts 1889–2010 may have been or was being committed, unless the communication was made knowing it to be, or recklessly as to whether it was, false, misleading, frivolous or vexatious.

Similarly, section 59(3) of the Criminal Justice (Theft and Fraud Offences) Act 2001 provides that a mandatory report made in good faith by an auditor to the Garda Síochána where the accounts of the audited firm or person indicated that an offence under the 2001 Act may have been committed shall not be treated as a breach of any restriction imposed by statute or otherwise expose the person making the report to legal liability for so doing.

The precise legislative impact of the coming into force of the 2014 Act upon the existing piecemeal statutes concerning whistleblowing can be gleaned from Schedule 4 of the 2014 Act.

A range of other domestic statutes provide protection to employees against penalisation/victimisation in circumstances where an employee complains that a relevant legal obligation has not been complied with. These include:

- Employment Equality Acts 1998–2011
- National Minimum Wage Act 2000
- Carers' Leave Act 2001
- Protection of Employees (Part-Time Work) Act 2001
- Protection of Employees (Fixed-Term Work) Act 2003
- Safety, Health and Welfare at Work Act 2005
- Employees (Provision of Information and Consultation) Act 2006
- Protection of Employees (Temporary Agency Work) Act 2012

As can be seen from the foregoing, however, the legal framework in Ireland was, until 2014, severely lacking in being confined either to specific sectors or dealing only with certain types of wrongdoing intimately connected with the very purpose of the legislation enshrining the penalisation/victimisation provisions in the first place. The introduction of the 2014 Act therefore represents a watershed in Irish law in terms of the level of protection afforded to whistleblowers.

Although there is not as of yet any case law under this legislation, it is undoubtedly going to have a significant impact and it is anticipated that there will be a great many cases brought under this Act.

The Scope of Persons Protected Under the Whistleblowers Legislation in Ireland

A striking feature of the 2014 Act in Ireland is the very broad range of persons who enjoy protection. Unlike a great many pieces of protective employment legislation in Ireland, the 2014 Act affords its protections to "workers" rather than "employees" and the definition of worker contained in section 3 of the Act is extremely broad, being a person who is an employee; a person who entered into or works or worked under any other contract, whether express or implied and (if it is express) whether oral or in writing, whereby the individual undertook to do or perform (whether personally or otherwise) any work or services for another party to the contract for the purposes of that party's business; a person who works in circumstances in which the individual is introduced or supplied to do the work by a third person, and the terms on which the individual is engaged to do the work are or were in practice substantially determined not by the individual but by the person for whom the individual works or worked, by the third person or by both of them.

The range of persons afforded legal protection under the 2014 Act is further considerably widened by virtue of section 13 of the 2014 Act, which enshrines a new cause of action in tort for persons who have been adversely treated as a result of a protected disclosure made either by them or by another:

> "If a person causes detriment to another person because the other person or a third person made a protected disclosure, the person to whom the detriment is caused has a right of action in tort against the person by whom the detriment is caused."

This potentially very significant provision is another new protection for employees and non-employees alike and could be of potential relevance to, for example, persons who encourage or affirm the disclosures made by the whistleblower.

What Kind of Behaviour Is Protected Under the Irish Whistleblowers Legislation?

Under section 5 of the 2014 Act, a worker may make a protected disclosure of "relevant information". Information is relevant if, in the reasonable belief of the worker, it tends to show one or more "relevant wrongdoings", and it came to the attention of the worker in connection with the worker's employment. Very significantly, the protection for the whistleblower remains available even if the information disclosed, on examination, does not in fact reveal wrongdoing. This constitutes a very important illustration of the level of protection afforded in Ireland whistleblowers who are making allegations erroneously or in the face of an uncertainty of the relevant facts. It is important to note in this regard, however, that deliberate false reporting will fail the "reasonable belief" test and is not protected under the 2014 Act.

It is also noteworthy that under the Irish whistleblowing regime, the motivation for making a disclosure is irrelevant to whether or not it is a protected disclosure: section 5(7) of the 2014 Act.

The 2014 Act sets out, in section 5, a list of "relevant wrongdoings". These include the commission of an offence; failure to perform a legal obligation (other than one arising under a worker's contract of employment); a miscarriage of justice; endangerment of people's health and safety; environmental damage; improper use of public money; oppressive, discriminatory or grossly negligence or gross mismanagement in the context of a public body; and concealment of any of these wrongs.

The 2014 Act seeks to encourage the making of the vast majority of dislosures to the employer or another responsible person in the first instance. Under section 6 of the 2014 Act, the worker is permitted to disclose to a responsible person where the worker reasonably believes that this person has legal responsibility for the relevant wrongdoing or the wrongdoing does not relates solely or mainly to the worker's employer.

The 2014 Act provides (in section 6(2)) that a disclosure will be treated as a disclosure to an employer where it is done in accordance with a procedure authorised by the employer, such as, for example, an internal whistleblowing procedure.

Alternatively, section 7 of the 2014 Act provides that a worker may make a protected disclosure to a "prescribed person". The Minister for Public Expenditure and Reform may, by order and taking into account defined criteria, prescribe certain appropriate persons to be recipients of disclosures of relevant wrongdoings. Section 7(1)(b) of the 2014 Act provides that, in making the disclosure to the prescribed person, the worker must hold a reasonable belief that the wrongdoing falls within the description of matters over which the prescribed person has responsibility and the worker must also reasonably believe that the information disclosed and any allegations therein are substantially true.

Section 8 of the 2014 Act provides that, in the context of public bodies, a worker may make a protected disclosure to a Minister exercising any function relating to the public body.

A protected disclosure may be made by a worker in the course of obtaining legal advice from a barrister, solicitor or trade union official (or official of a statutorily identified body): section 9 of the 2014 Act.

Under section 10 the 2014 Act, a worker may make a protected disclosure in other circumstances if the worker "reasonably believes" that the information disclosed and any allegation contained in it are substantially true. The disclosure must not, however, be made for personal gain (although this excludes any reward payable under or by virtue of any enactment). In all the circumstances of the case, it must be reasonable for the worker to make the disclosure. One or more of the following conditions must also be satisfied:

- at the time the worker makes the disclosure, the worker reasonably believes that he or she will be subjected to penalisation by the employer if a disclosure is made in circumstances other than to a legal adviser;
- where no relevant person is prescribed in relation to the relevant wrongdoing, the worker reasonably believes that it is likely that evidence relating to the relevant wrongdoing will be concealed or destroyed if the worker makes a disclosure to an employer or responsible person;
- the worker has previously made a disclosure of substantially the same information other than to a legal adviser;
- the relevant wrongdoing is of an exceptionally serious nature.

Section 10(3) of the 2014 Act also sets out certain criteria which may be considered in determining whether it was reasonable in all of the circumstances of the case for the disclosure to be made.

These include:

- the identity of the recipient of the disclosure;
- the seriousness of the relevant wrongdoing;
- whether the wrongdoing is continuing or likely to occur again;
- any breach of confidentiality;
- in respect of a previous disclosure, any previous action taken or which might reasonably be expected to have been taken by the recipient of the disclosure, and
- whether a worker complied with any procedures authorised by an employer when making a disclosure to that employer or another responsible person.
- A subsequent disclosure may be regarded as a disclosure of substantially the same information as that disclosed by a previous disclosure even though the subsequent disclosure extends to information about action taken or not taken by any person as a result of the previous disclosure: section 10(4) of the 2014 Act.

Section 16 of the 2014 Act provides that a person to whom a protected disclosure is made, and any person to whom a protected disclosure is referred in the performance of that person's duties, shall not disclose to another person any information that might identify the person by whom the protected disclosure was made. There are various qualifications to this provision, but it does demonstrate an important identity protection for whistleblowers under Irish law.

What Is the Level of Protection Offered Under the Irish Whistleblowers Legislation?

The Irish Whistleblowers legislation affords a substantial range of redress options for employees who are adversely affected as a result of whistleblowing. An important feature of the 2014 Act is that amends the Unfair Dismissals legislation in Ireland (the Unfair Dismissals Acts 1977–2007), in three key respects. First, it expressly deems a dismissal to be unfair where that dismissal flows from the employee's having made a protected disclosure. As with regular unfair dismissal cases, the onus is on the employer to satisfy the relevant body (currently the Workplace Relations Commission) that it can justify the dismissal: the employee does not have any onus in this respect, save where the fact of dismissal is in issue.

Secondly, the 2014 Acts amends and significantly enhances the redress which could otherwise be awarded for unfair dismissal by allowing an employee who is dismissed for having made a protected disclosure to obtain compensation of up to a maximum of 5 years' remuneration. This is a striking development in the law on unfair dismissal and one that sits in marked contrast to other unfair dismissal cases in which the financial redress available is capped at 2 years' remuneration.

The third key change brought about by the 2014 Act to the existing Unfair Dismissals regime in Ireland is that the qualifying service requirement which applies to most unfair dismissal cases –whereby employees must have 1 year's continuous service before they may bring an Unfair Dismissal claim – is expressly waived in the context of protected disclosures.

Quite apart from the protection against dismissal, the employee who is a whistleblower in Ireland is also protected against penalisation. Penalisation is very broadly defined in section 3 of the 2014 Act and includes any act or omission that affects a worker to the worker's detriment (to include inter alia, suspension, lay-off, dismissal, demotion and loss of opportunity for promotion, transfer of duties or alteration of terms and conditions; unfair treatment; coercion, intimidation or harassment; discrimination, disadvantage, injury, damage or loss or threat of reprisal). Pursuant to Schedule 2 of the 2014 Act, the very strong redress of up to 5 years' remuneration is again possible here.

As already set out above, the 2014 Act (section 13) creates a new tort action open to a person who sustains 'detriment' as a result of whistleblowing, with detriment being defined to include coercion, intimidation, harassment, discrimination, disadvantage or adverse treatment in relation to employment (or prospective employment), injury, damage or loss, and threat of reprisal.

Whether Certain Interest Groups (e.g. Trade Unions, Consumer Protection Groups) Can Take Collective Action to Protect Whistleblowers

Claims for breaches of labour law must be pursued individually in Ireland (there is no 'class action' mechanism), meaning interest groups cannot pursue a legal action on behalf of an individual worker.

The circumstances in which trade unions could undertake industrial action in respect of individual whistleblowers are extremely limited; section 9(2) of the Industrial Relations Act 1990 allows this only when agreed procedures for the resolution of individual disputes have been exhausted. This would include the dispute being referred to the State's employment tribunals for resolution. As a result, any detriment at work suffered as a result of whistleblowing activities would ordinarily be dealt with as an individual matter.

Chapter 9
The Whistleblowing Dilemma in Malta Continues: A Personal View and Analysis

David Fabri

Abstract For many years, Malta did not have a law which specifically dealt with whistleblowing. No law acknowledged or defended whistleblowers. As in other countries, whistleblowers in Malta have generally faced great difficulties and suffered retaliation for their deeds. A few years ago, whistleblowing was acknowledged in a few provisions in employment law but these were rather incomplete and were not supported by any proper structure. After a number of false starts, the Maltese Parliament finally passed a 'Protection of Whistleblowers Act' in 2013. This was the first ever comprehensive law on the subject; but is it good enough and do whistleblowers feel safe now? The writer argues that the law does not protect all disclosures and various onerous conditions have been imposed in the law. A prospective whistleblower should seriously consider his position before reporting wrong-doing or corruption in his work place. This chapter concludes that in Malta, despite the recent 2013 Act, whistleblowing remains a very risky and thankless decision.

A Personal Introduction

My long-standing interest in whistleblowing and whistleblowers probably started with the startling discovery that the well-known whistleblower Stanley Adams was actually Maltese and that his original Maltese surname had been Formosa.[1]

I addressed the issue of whistleblowing for the first time in a public forum in 1997 at a Malta Bankers Union annual conference on issues in financial services.[2] It was well received. Re-invited the following year, I prepared a formal paper on

[1] He wrote a book on his misadventures, see S Adams, *Roche* versus *Adams* (London, Jonathan Cape, 1984).

[2] The financial services industry in Malta was then still taking off.

D. Fabri (✉)
Commercial Law Department, University of Malta,
Msida, MSD 2080, MALTA
e-mail: david.fabri@um.edu.mt

G. Thüsing, G. Forst (eds.), *Whistleblowing - A Comparative Study*,
Ius Comparatum - Global Studies in Comparative Law 16,
DOI 10.1007/978-3-319-25577-4_9

'White Collar Crime – a Regulator's Perspective'[3] which concluded that 'whistleblowers find little protection, let alone gratitude under our law' and that laws provided no comfort to persons who make disclosures, even where these may be in the public interest. Reference was made to scattered rules in the legislation which made certain reporting requirements to the authorities obligatory, describing them as 'useful provisions, but they are far from enough, and their scope is very limited.' The conclusion was that 'local reality with regard to whistleblowers is a negative one' and the paper suggested that 'The State should therefore accept responsibility for devising mechanisms and structures whereby employees and officials could – for the benefit of the public interest and without fear of reprisals or other risks – make disclosures relating to illegal activity.' This objective could be achieved by amending the various laws or by 'formulating a new law exclusively dedicated to regulating all the various aspects and implications of the matter in a comprehensive manner.' That was 1998, still very early days, but the media picked it up.[4]

Later that same year, and just before general political elections were to be held, the same theme was pursued in an article in Malta's leading Sunday paper concerning corruption and whistleblowing. This time I wrote:

> Briefly, our legal system has been largely unappreciative of *bona fide* whistle-blowers; it is inefficient by repeatedly ignoring them as a potential source of vital information, and it intimidates them with the risk of criminal or civil proceedings or other retaliatory measures such as dismissal for their unauthorized disclosure of secrets.[5]

The article concluded by re-iterating 'the duty of a democratic society to recognize a public interest in whistleblowing', and the doubt 'whether a determined political will exists to put in place efficient measures to uncover political corruption and fraud and to identify and punish the culprits.'[6]

For many years Malta did not have a law which dealt specifically with whistleblowing and no law acknowledged or defended whistleblowers. Some limited scattered attempts in various laws regulating particular activities sought to protect certain disclosures, but these were incomplete and rather patchy and did not remedy the general position of potential whistleblowers. In this scenario, it will come as no surprise that whistleblowers in Malta have over the years faced a tough time and have received little sympathy or recognition from the authorities.

---

[3] Malta Union Of Bank Employees Annual Conference held on the 22 July 1998.

[4] G Cini, 'White collar crime conference' (23 July 1998) *The Times* (*Malta*), p. 17.

[5] D Fabri, 'Political corruption, prescription and whistleblowing' (30 August 1998) *The Sunday Times* (*Malta*), p. 14.

[6] ibid.

The 2013 Law

Whistleblowing is today regulated specifically for the first time, thanks to the 'Protection of Whistleblowers Act' introduced in 2013.[7]

This law establishes a number of specific procedures in terms of which employees may disclose information regarding improper practices by their employers or other employees. It purports to protect employees who make such disclosures from what is termed as 'detrimental action'. This is the first comprehensive law on the subject in Malta. The law is very recent and is uncharted territory; years will have to elapse before one can assess whether the law has had a positive effect on whistleblowing and on the collection of information about wrongdoing in public offices. To date, there have been no actual published cases of whistleblowing and of people specifically seeking protection under this new law.

A previous attempt to pass a law was initiated in 2010 when a Bill, 'The Protection of the Whistleblower Act', 2010[8] was presented by Dr Tonio Borg, then still a Minister under the Nationalist administration. That Bill stalled and did not become law. It was eventually superseded and replaced by Act No. VIII of 2013 passed by the new Labour government elected to power that same year.[9]

The Act applies to employees in both the public and private employment sectors. Employees include former employees and persons conducting voluntary work. Although self-employed persons are not specifically referred to in the Act, the law applies to a 'contractor or sub-contractor who performs work or supplies a service'.[10] This would seem not to exclude self-employed persons from receiving protection under this law in the appropriate circumstances.

This paper highlights the provisions of the Act which may create the highest risks for whistleblowers. Before proceeding further, it would be useful to set out a summary of the provisions of the Act (Table 9.1).

---

[7] Act No. VIII of 2013, July 2013, Chapter 527 on the Laws of Malta. It was brought into force on 15th September 2013 and is available online at www.justiceservices.gov.mt/LOM.aspx?pageid=24.

[8] Bill No. 58 of 2010.

[9] J Ameen, 'Whistleblower Bill by end of the year: two electoral promises' (24 August 2009) *The Times*; N Grima, 'Whistleblower Bill presented' (1 October 2010) *The Malta Independent* (front page article); K Sansone, 'Draft law strives to protect whistleblowers' (1 October 2010) *The Times (Malta)* (front page article). See also brief review by Björn Rohde-Liebenau (Transparency International, November 2013, pp 63–65) section on Malta in *Whistleblowing in Europe*: *Legal protections for whistleblowers in the EU*. This refers to an earlier report by the same writer (Transparency International, November 2012) *Providing an Alternative to Silence*: *Towards Greater Protection and Support for Whistleblowers in the EU. Country Report*: *Malta*. These country reports preceded the enactment of the 2013 legislation, now in force.

[10] Art. 2 (1) definition of 'employee'.

Table 9.1 Protection of the Whistleblower Act 2013

Article 1	Title of the act and entry into force
Article 2	Definitions (25 terms covering four pages, including important definitions of 'detrimental action', 'employees', 'improper practice', 'occupational detriment', 'whistleblower')
Article 3	Prohibits detrimental action against whistleblowers
Article 4	Grants whistleblowers immunity from civil and criminal liability
Article 5	Withdraws immunity from a whistleblower who was an accomplice or perpetrator but allows a court to mitigate punishment or damages against him in certain cases, and establishes a procedure how the mitigation is managed and by whom
Article 6	Establishes the duty to protect the identity of the whistleblower
Article 7	Grants a whistleblower the right to sue for the removal of a detrimental action and obtain a remedy, including moral and other damages
Article 8	Recognizes the right of a whistleblower to compensation for any detrimental action he may have suffered
Article 9	Defines protected disclosures: requires that the disclosure be made in good faith and not made for personal gain, and that the alleged improper practice is substantially correct; false allegations are punishable as a criminal offence
Article 10	Law does not protect a breach of professional secrecy
Article 11	The law does not protect anonymous disclosures
Article 12	Employers are required to establish and to publish internal whistleblowing procedures to allow in-house disclosures
Article 13	Duty of whistleblowing officer to keep whistleblower updated
Article 14	Further regulates internal whistleblowing procedures
Article 15	Introduces the notion of 'external disclosures' – these are only protected where an internal disclosure has already been made
Article 16	Describes external disclosures and explains when they are justifiable. The length and complexity of this Article alone shows the risks that would be taken by the whistleblowing in these situations. This Article is far from whistleblower-friendly and may in practice prove to be potentially hostile
Article 17	All authorities to set up a whistleblowing unit to receive external disclosures
Article 18	One authority may transfer a disclosure to another authority more properly connected with the subject matter
Article 19	Threats and misconduct against a whistleblower may amount to a criminal offence
Article 20	This Article gives the Minister for Justice powers to issue regulations to better implement in detail the provisions of the act. The authorities may issue guidelines binding on the respective entities they regulate
Article 21	Private agreements cannot reduce whistleblower's rights under this act or discourage whistleblowing
Article 22	The Minister may exempt any persons from 'any' of the provisions of the act – exemption cannot be given retrospective effect
Article 23	Transitory provision – the act applies to disclosures after its coming into force
Article 24–25	Amendments to the Police Act
First schedule	Lists the authorities that can receive external disclosures
Second schedule	Lists the employers falling under Article 12 which are obliged to establish internal disclosure procedures

Preliminary Matters

Stylistic Deficiencies

The 2013 Act is constructed rather clumsily relying on no less than five pages of definition of terms which comprise Article 2. As a result, several important substantial rules are not stated by way of principle, but need to be extracted from the wording which describes one of the definitions listed in this Article. The drafting of some important articles too is rather unsatisfactory. Some provisions overlap or are actually repeated: for one example, article 9 (1) and (2) substantially replicate the provisions of article 4 (2).

A more substantial criticism of the Act is its readiness to exclude the immunity of the whistleblower on a number of grounds. Various factors may be employed to exclude or withdraw the law's protection even from well-meaning whistleblowers. Various provisions of the Act allow the authorities to second-guess the whistleblower's judgement and belittle or nullify his achievement. A prospective whistleblower might well find himself unable to safely predict whether or not he will benefit from immunity.

A rather confusing variety of public authorities have been somewhat incoherently roped into the new whistleblowing framework. Each plays a different role in examining whether and the extent to which a whistleblower will be protected. In the order of their appearance in article 5, they are: (1) the courts and tribunals; (2) the prosecution; (3) the President of the Republic; (4) the Attorney General; (5) the Commissioner of Police; (6) a judge.

Company and Employment Law

The Maltese Companies Act[11] does not require companies to have any whistleblowing procedure in place while under ordinary principles of employment law, an employee has a general obligation to safeguard his employer's secrets and information and owes him a general duty of loyalty.

The new law has an impact on general employment law in so far as a new dimension has been added to the relationship between the employer and his employees and the obligation by the latter to keep the employer's secrets confidential. An early whistleblowing provision had been inserted in the Maltese Employment Relations Act.[12] This prohibited the 'victimization' of employees who disclose wrongdoing in the work place. This law was passed in 2002, and the relevant provision, which is still on the statute book, reads as follows:

---

[11] Act No. XXV of 1995, Chapter 386 of the Laws of Malta.

[12] Chapter 452 of the Laws of Malta.

> 28. It shall not be lawful to victimise any person for having made a complaint to the lawful authorities or for having initiated or participated in proceedings for redress on grounds of alleged breach of the provisions of this Act, or for having disclosed information, confidential or otherwise, to a designated public regulating body, regarding alleged illegal or corrupt activities being committed by his employer or by persons acting in the employer's name and interests.

It is however surprising (and annoying) that the new law does not even make a passing reference to the above-quoted legal provision.

Disclosures and Protection from Retaliatory Action

The crucial concept introduced by the Act is that relating to 'protected disclosures'. 'Protected disclosure' is described in article 2 as 'an internal disclosure or an external disclosure of information, made in writing or on any format which may be prescribed'. Article 4 (1) adds that a whistleblower who makes a 'protected disclosure' is not liable to any civil or criminal proceedings or to a disciplinary proceeding. An 'external disclosure' to one of the designated authorities is only protected in a few prescribed circumstances.[13]

Two other significant related notions in the law are 'detrimental action' and 'occupational action'. Whistleblowers who satisfy the legal requirements enjoy protection from such retaliatory action. These concepts are defined in the law. The definition of 'detrimental action' includes:

- action causing injury, loss or damage; and, or
- victimisation, intimidation or harassment; and, or
- occupational detriment; and, or
- prosecution under the Criminal Code for calumnious accusations; and, or
- civil or criminal proceedings or discipline proceedings.[14]

The law also protects legal whistleblowers against 'occupational detriment', which includes:

- being subjected to any disciplinary action including for breach of ethics or confidentiality;
- being dismissed, suspended or demoted except where administratively or commercially justifiable for organisational reasons;
- being transferred against his will or being refused transfer or promotion except where administratively or commercially justifiable for organisational reasons;
- being subjected to a term or condition of employment or retirement which is altered or kept altered to his disadvantage;

---

[13] The Agencies authorized to receive prescribed external disclosures are listed in the First Schedule to the Act.

[14] Art. 2.

- being refused a reference or being provided with an adverse reference from his employer except where justifiable on the basis of performance;
- being denied appointment to any employment, profession or office; or
- being otherwise adversely affected in respect of his employment, profession or office, including employment opportunities and work secrecy.[15]

The nature of information that a whistleblower may 'safely' report under the Act is specifically listed and classified in the Act. The information disclosed will be protected only where it concerns an 'improper practice' within the definition found in article 2. This includes breaches of the law, corruption, bribery and other criminal acts, miscarriage of justice, environmental damage, health and safety concerns. Other possible categories of information are therefore implicitly excluded.

The burden of proving oneself to be a legitimate *bona fide* whistleblower is on the whistleblower himself. The normal rules of evidence would apply, namely that he who alleges something must be in a position to prove it, and no presumptions in his favour apply. This means that a whistleblower would face the burden of proving both his status as a whistleblower and that his actions are protected under the Act.

Exclusion

The law raises other circumstances where legal protection does not apply. These exclusions merit close attention as they delineate where protection applies and where it is withheld.

Complicity

Article 5 withdraws protection from a whistleblower who may have co-participated in an improper practice which constitutes a crime or a contravention. He would also lose his exemption from any disciplinary or civil proceedings or liability arising from his own conduct. In this context, the law does not distinguish between playing a minor part as an accomplice and playing a decisive or material role. While one may accept the logic behind withholding protection from what are termed in the Act as 'perpetrators',[16] no public interest exists to push away potentially vital and valuable information about corruption and abuse in high places simply because a potential whistleblower may have found himself marginally involved or been a minor accomplice.

This article places a whistleblower at the hands of public authorities which may be in a position to pin an accusation of complicity on him in relation to the improper

[15] ibid.

[16] The term remains undefined.

practices disclosed. In such circumstances, he would find himself legally exposed as his immunity may be lifted. The only minor concession, which is effectively of little help, is that his whistleblowing exploits could eventually be taken into account by a criminal court prosecuting him for complicity, or by a civil court if he is sued for damages, in connection with the improper practice disclosed.[17] This Article is quite convoluted and other dangers lurk behind the complicated drafting. As already stated above, the law does not distinguish between minor or significant complicity. Practice shows that it is easy for the authorities, with all their resources and access to information and power, to attribute a remote or indirect responsibility to the person disclosing the improper practice, or to sow doubts about his non-involvement, his good faith and integrity. Here the law would probably have done better to concede to accomplices, particularly those at the margins, full immunity. Such immunity would encourage accomplices to come forward and disclose the real perpetrators and could create a wedge between the wrong-doers.

Trivial Whistleblowing

Article 16 allows the authorities to determine ex post facto that the whistleblower had been unreasonable when he disclosed information, and consequently did not deserve protection. This can happen either because the alleged breach was not 'serious' enough, or because it involved a breach of confidentiality against a third party, or because the correct procedure was not followed. It is truly remarkable that the law should seek to penalize whistleblowers on the ground that his confidential disclosure related to an improper practice was, according to the judgement of the authorities, not serious enough. This strange exception confirms another regrettable rule found at the end of the definition of 'improper practice' in Article 2 which excludes the application of the Act where 'very minor and trivial matters' are involved. The question here as elsewhere is who is best placed to know a priori what is serious, trivial or minor, and what is instead major or serious. The law certainly gives no value to what the prospective whistleblower thought or how he prescribed the situation in circumstances which may have included haste, panic and uncertainty. Disclosures on 'trivial matters' do not enjoy legal protection, leaving the whistleblower defenceless.

Internal and External Disclosures

Article 3 makes it clear that, except in a few instances, a whistleblower cannot disclose information to a public authority directly, but he must first make an internal disclosure. Indeed, the joint effect of articles 3 and 4 is that, under normal

[17] This concession is not an automatic one but depends entirely on the discretion of the adjudicator and of the Attorney General as explained in art. 5 (4).

circumstances, a whistleblower should make a report internally within the organization which employs him. He cannot simply proceed to report outside his organization and make a direct external disclosure to a public authority. If he does so, he risks forfeiting all legal protection. In this context, one notes with concern that retaliatory measures or criminal or civil proceedings would be possible in terms of articles 15 and 16 against a whistleblower who failed to comply with all the requirements and procedures set out in the Act.[18] It is disturbingly evident from all these rules and restrictions that the law looks at external disclosures with great disfavour.

External disclosures may only be resorted to directly in the few instances described in article 16 (1). Briefly, these instances are: where the 'head' (again an undefined term) is involved in the malpractice; where the whistleblower 'will' face retaliatory action by his employer; where the disclosure is 'urgent'; where relevant documentation might be destroyed; where no action was taken following an earlier disclosure.

Equally ominously, Article 16 also specifically assigns to the authorities a discretion to decide that the whistleblower was wrong to make an external disclosure rather than an internal one. In such a circumstance, the authority in question 'must' within 45 days notify him 'that an internal disclosure … must be made and that it will not be dealing further with this disclosure'. If this sequence of procedure is not followed, the disclosure would not be protected, even though the public authority may have been given highly significant and useful information. There is no justification why disclosures should be kept strictly in-house and why whistleblowers should be discouraged and constrained from reporting at the outset to an external (and therefore nominally impartial) authority.[19]

The prohibition against external disclosures acts to the advantage of the organization or officials concerned and may help keep the malpractice in-house and hidden from the prying eyes of the relevant regulatory or enforcement authorities.

Good Faith and Personal Gain

Article 9(1) (a) only protects disclosures made in good faith. This requirement seems to be not merely superfluous but misguided. If the aim of the law is to help the State uncover serious wrongdoings, it should not be distracted or bothered by the possible internal motives of the whistleblower. Good faith is not defined in the law so this increases the uncertainties and risks for prospective whistleblowers. The enquiry into and possible contestation of motivations and intentions appear spurious.

[18] The rule that legal protection is only extended where an internal disclosure, or an attempted disclosure, has been made beforehand, is repeated in Art. 15.

[19] It seems that a recent new Bill on whistleblowing in Switzerland raises a similar impediment and has been criticized accordingly: 'White Collar Crime: Proposed legislation on whistleblowing – de facto ban on reporting to the public?' (1 December 2014) *International Law Office Newsletter*.

Art. 4(2) then states that:

> The protection afforded to a whistleblower shall not be prejudiced on the basis only that the whistleblower making the disclosure was, in good faith, mistaken about its import or that any perceived threat to the public interest on which the disclosure was based has not materialised or that the person making the disclosure has not fully respected the procedural requirements of this Act or of any regulations or guidelines made under this Act.

However, art. 9(2) states that: 'The protections conferred by this article do not apply to an employee who knowingly discloses information which he knows or ought to reasonably know is false…'. A whistleblower finds himself exposed to legal action and retaliatory action should it transpire that the information disclosed was false. Legal protection does not extend to an informant who either (a) knew that the information being relayed was false, or (b) ought reasonably to have known that it was false. Mistakes may be overlooked where the disclosing whistleblower proves that he had been in good faith.

Under Art. 9(1) (c), a disclosure is not protected if it is made for 'personal gain'. Personal gain too remains an uncertain concept. Does it extend to self-protection, to attempts not to find oneself further embedded in the mire of wrong-doing, to reduce the risk of being accused of complicity and to protect one's own personal safety and physical and moral security? Since when does the law punish someone for acting to protect and safeguard his own juridical interests?

The First and Second Schedules: Implications and Exclusions

The First Schedule lists seven public authorities empowered to receive external disclosures. It might have been simpler and more user-friendly for a potential whistleblower if just one easily identifiable specialized central authority assumed this role. As things stand, a prospective whistleblower has to work out for himself which of the seven entities is the correct one to approach with a view to making an external disclosure. This seems to be an unnecessary and risky complication for a person who decides to jeopardise himself and his career and his future by revealing serious wrongdoing in the public interest. The least the State can do in return is to keep procedures simple.

The Second Schedule might at first appear to be an innocuous list of entities to which the Act refers. What is startling is that by way of exclusion, most of Maltese private entities are excluded from the application of the law. In other words, the protection purportedly introduced by this Act will not apply to whistleblowers who uncover improper practices in one of the many entities excluded under this Schedule. Paragraph 2 excludes small and medium sized enterprises, which all would broadly employ less than 250 workers, have less than Euro 43 million balance sheet and less than Euro 50 million turnover. Few Maltese companies fulfil these very high parameters. The law also excludes voluntary organizations which raise less than Euros 500,000 in a year. Few organizations are that lucky. The signal which the law sends is that small and medium sized enterprises and entities need not bother with nuisance whistleblowers. By restricting the application of the legal protection so strictly, most whistleblowers in Malta will find that they have been left on the lurch.

These limitations make little sense in the local context as most Maltese enterprises do not fulfil these criteria. The net effect is that the law now actually serves as a serious discouragement of whistleblowing in the majority of Maltese private enterprises. The law only applies to a handful of companies and organizations.

Police and Army

Another particular limitation is found in Art. 2(3) which excludes the application of the Act to persons working with the Police, the Army, the Security Service or the diplomatic service. The Minister is given extraordinary powers to determine by way of regulations whether, when and how the primary Act will relate to these categories of persons and these regulations can dis-apply or modify any of the provisions of the Act. These law-making powers are to be exercised ‘as necessary for the purpose of the protection of national security, defence, intelligence, public order and the international relations of the State’. This provision is yet another proof that the law is anything but whistleblower-friendly and goes far to dis-allow or discourage whistleblowing especially where important State interests are involved.

Whistleblowers Who Turn to the Media and Others

The law does not specifically protect whistleblowers who resort to the media. Reports to the media do not amount to protected disclosures. The Press Act[20] allows journalists to protect their sources.[21] The role of the media as a potential channel for disclosure receives no mention or recognition in the 2013 Act.[22]

The restrictive nature of the law also means that legal protection is withheld from persons who report serious corruption and fraud to the press, to religious/church groups, to non-governmental organizations, or to political parties. The law does not

[20] Chapter 248 of the Laws of Malta.

[21] Art. 46: ‘46. No court shall require any person mentioned in Art. 23 to disclose, nor shall such person be guilty of contempt of court for refusing to disclose, the source of information contained in a newspaper or broadcast for which he is responsible unless it is established to the satisfaction of the court that such disclosure is necessary in the interests of national security, territorial integrity or public safety, or for the prevention of disorder or crime or for the protection of the interests of justice…’.

[22] This concern was identified in K Sansone,’ Whistleblowers who report to the media unprotected’ (19 October 2010) *The Times* (online version) and later K Aquilina, ‘A whistle-less whistleblower’ (9 April 2014) *Malta Today* (online version).

envisage or allow certain interested groups (e.g. trade unions, consumer protection groups) to take collective action for the protection of whistleblowers.

The law only protects the actual whistleblower. It offers no protection to persons who assist or encourage whistleblowers, and to those who come forward to confirm his disclosures, unless they qualify as whistleblowers in their own right.

Other Important Issues

Safeguarding a Whistleblower's Identity

The law sets out insufficient safeguards and deterrents against deliberate, accidental or careless disclosure of a whistleblower's identity. The law is weak in this regard and can easily be bypassed. Much harm may be committed by careless disclosures. Indeed, Stanley Adams' fate was sealed when EEC officials unwisely and carelessly blew his identity as their whistleblower to his former employers.[23]

The law does not protect and discourages anonymous whistleblowers. Through this specific exclusion, art. 11 limits further scope for potential whistleblowing where the identity of the informant would usually have no bearing on the benefits of having serious wrongdoing uncovered.

Although Article 11(2) grants a whistleblower reporting officer or a whistleblower reports unit the discretion to 'consider' anonymous disclosures, the onus lies on this latter officer/unit. Nonetheless, a 'whistleblower reporting officer' or a 'whistleblowing reports unit' may receive and process an anonymous disclosure and may take such a disclosure into account in determining whether an improper practice has occurred.[24]

Rewards and Compensation

Article 8 gives a right to compensation to whistleblowers who suffer 'detrimental action' following their disclosure, but only where this is validly made in terms of the Act. The Article does not define the type of compensation that may be awarded, and in the lack of a specific mention, moral compensation is excluded under general Maltese private law governing the award of damages. It would have been better for

---

[23] See the writer's 'The Price of Whistle-blowing: the flawed ECJ Decision in Stanley Adams vs Commission of the European Communities (1985)', Id-Dritt, Vol. XXII, 2012. More recent developments: 'FIFA whistleblower Pahedra Al-Majid fears for her safety' (20 November 2014) *BBC Sport* (online version) and 'Fifa whistleblowers submit formal complaint over blowing their cover' (17 November 2014) *The Guardian* (online version).

[24] Art. 11 (2).

the law to specifically allow whistleblowers to also receive moral damages by way of compensation for any loss or harm suffered, physical or psychological.

Maltese law does not introduce a system for rewarding whistleblowers. It is not essential for whistleblowing legislation to have rewards in place as is the case in the US. In principle such an approach might even undermine the true value of speaking up and acting against wrong-doing by adding what is a truly unnecessary mercenary element to it.

True whistleblowers do not ask for a reward, but they only ask for their disclosure to be kept secret and for their employment and personal safety to be adequately safeguarded. The notion that whistleblowing should be incentivized financially is abhorrent to true whistleblowing. Compensation for any loss suffered would be acceptable but actually profiting from whistleblowing is a different matter.[25]

Whistleblowing is not about making money, but about a person's moral right and duty to report wrongdoing, his right to remain detached from indirect involvement or complicity in such wrongdoing and his right to integrity and legality at his place of work.

Reports Received to Date

On the 12 October 2014, the Sunday Times[26] reported that the Justice Ministry had received 48 whistleblower helpline reports. Of these, 47 were ineligible as they fell outside the legal parameters. Details were provided as to the categories of reports received.[27] Finally the remarkable statement was made by the Justice Ministry that the government was considering amending the law so that 'all citizens could be treated as whistleblowers'.[28]

Some Final Considerations

Whistleblowing is but a small part of a broader fabric of how a transparent democratic society operates. In fact a proper workable whistleblowing framework can only function when a number of vital factors are present, including the satisfaction of certain basic surrounding assumptions. These include:

- that politicians and public officials accept themselves to be accountable and subject to scrutiny;

---

[25] M Goldstein, 'Whistle-Blower on Countrywide Mortgage Misdeeds to get $57 Million' (17 December 2014) *The New York Times*.

[26] K Micallef, 'Just 48 whistleblower reports sent to helpline' (12 October 2014) *The Times*.

[27] See also '48 whistleblowing reports lodged with Justice Ministry' (13 October 2014) *Malta Today*.

[28] ibid.

- that transparency is generally valued as an element of enlightened governance and not practiced exceptionally or selectively on the basis of convenience or advantage;
- that the Police and other public oversight agencies operate at arms' length from the government and receive no instructions, pressures or suggestions from its representatives;
- that citizens are free to comment and criticize those in power; and
- that human rights are respected.

In Malta the risk has therefore largely remained with the whistleblower who effectively can never be re-assured that no negative repercussions would follow his disclosures. The law does not protect all disclosures by whistleblowers, but only those which qualify as 'protected disclosures'. Whistleblowers should therefore be very wary of the unprotected disclosures. As the conditions for a protected disclosure are set rather high, they penalize whistleblowers who may be or who are shown[29] not to be in good faith or if they somehow make personal gain[30] from the disclosure. A whistleblower is doomed should any suggestion of bad faith[31] or of personal gain stick to him. The law also allows the authorities to hound a whistleblower by alleging that he 'ought to have reasonably known' that the information disclosed was false. Indeed the real focus of the law is made clear in sub-article 3 which reminds whistleblowers that it is an 'offence punishable in accordance with article 101 of the Criminal Code to knowingly provide false information in terms of this Act'. A whistleblower does not receive unconditional protection under the Act; far from it. Indeed, the Act raises a number of difficulties[32] that a prospective whistle-blower should seriously take into account before venturing with any disclosures of corruption or other wrongdoing.

Conclusion

Whistleblowing cannot be introduced in a vacuum and it is only effective and meaningful if adopted within a wider context where the state and its agencies follow, and are glad to follow, principles of good governance, where transparency reigns as a normal daily practice, where they feel accountable to the public and where they feel that the uncovering of public misdeeds is more important than keeping bad things hidden. Whistleblowing flourishes when it is integrated within a broader context of healthy and enlightened acceptance and consensus on high levels of transparency and accountability in the public sector.[33]

---

[29] It is not stated to whom this must be shown.

[30] 'Personal gain' is not defined.

[31] Or even the lack of good faith.

[32] Especially in articles 5 and 9.

[33] The writer has written more extensively on these aspects in 'Whistleblowing in Malta: a note on recent developments, proposals and missed opportunities' (2002) *The Company Lawyer* Vol. 23 No. 1, p. 30.

Laws may prove ineffective in practice if potential whistleblowers do not have sufficient faith and comfort that they will not be treated coldly or viciously by those to whom they report. Employers have yet to show that they will not react negatively and unkindly to employees who breach their normal confidentiality obligations and sneak on wrongdoing. This test has yet to come and has yet to be passed. In the meantime, whistleblowing in Malta shall remain a risky business.

The 2013 law arrived accompanied by much political posturing and self-praise. One wonders whether in reality the State and its entities and officials are that keen to find, and to allow others to find, that they are not so perfect and efficient after all. One may rightly doubt whether these entities, usually so sensitive and defensive about their internal workings, are now converted and have become receptive to the submission of their dirty linen to investigation and possible public scrutiny. The law fails to promote or encourage whistleblowing, but merely tolerates it and puts up with it.[34]

For the above considerations, in the opinion of the writer, the 2013 law is not a good law. Not all whistleblowers are protected. They find legal protection only in a restricted number of instances and then only if a specific procedure had been followed. Whistleblowers are not protected if they fail to first resort to internal reporting procedures or if they report to the press or other media. In essence, therefore, the law seeks more to restrict, control and restrain potential whistleblowers and it fails to open up innovative channels whereby they may be further encouraged to safely unearth wrongdoing, abuse and corruption. To facilitate the detection of fraud and corruption, the law should have, in the best public interest, unambiguously encouraged whistleblowing. Instead, by making whistleblowing less attractive, the law renders the pursuit of effective discovery of wrong-doing and successful prosecutions more difficult.

The conclusion here therefore has to be that this recent law of 2013 is not the final answer to the whistleblowing dilemma in the Maltese experience. It will take a very courageous man to brave the legal niceties and pitfalls of Act No. VIII of 2013. This flawed law still distrusts whistleblowers and is reluctant to extend the full protection of the law to them. Today whistleblowing in Malta remains a dangerous, risky, unrewarded and thankless vocation.

Bibliography

Ameen J (24 Aug 2009) Whistleblower Bill by end of the year: two electoral promises, The Times

Aquilina K (9 April 2014) *A whistle-less whistleblower*, Malta Today (online version)

Bencini C (15 May 2014) *Offering real protection to the whistleblower*, Malta Today (online version) // (2007) *Whistle Blowing in the Financial Services Sector: the position under Maltese Law*, Dissertation, Masters in Financial Services, University of Malta

Borg J (22 Dec 2014) *Whistleblowers Act not arbitrary go-ahead to leak information – Justice Minister*, The Malta Independent (online version)

[34] J Borg, 'Whistleblowers Act not arbitrary go-ahead to leak information - Justice Minister' (22 December 2014) *The Malta Independent* (online version).

Conway R (20 Nov 2014) *FIFA whistleblower Pahedra Al-Majid fears for her safety*, BBC Sport
Fabri D (30 Aug 1998) *Political corruption, prescription and whistleblowing*, The Sunday Times (Malta), p 14//*Whistleblowing in Malta: a note on recent developments, proposals and missed opportunities*, The Company Lawyer, Vol. 23 No 1, p30, 2002//*No more heroes any more? The whistle–blowing dilemma: recent developments and a fresh look at some conceptual and legal issues*, Id-Dritt, Vol. XX, September 2009 (and materials mentioned therein)//*The Price of Whistle-blowing: the flawed ECJ Decision in Stanley Adams vs Commission of the European Communities* (1985), Id-Dritt, Vol. XXII, 2012 (and materials mentioned therein)
Goldstein M (17 Dec 2014) *Whistle-Blower on Countrywide Mortgage Misdeeds to get $57 Million*, The New York Times
Grima N (1 Oct 2010*) Whistleblower Bill presented,* The Malta Independent (front page article)
International Law Office Newsletter (1 Dec 2014) *White Collar Crime: Proposed legislation on whistleblowing – de facto ban on reporting to the public*?
Rohde-Liebenau B (Transparency International, November 2013, section on Malta, pp 63–65) *Whistleblowing in Europe: Legal protections for whistleblowers in the EU/*(Transparency International, November 2012) *Providing an Alternative to Silence: Towards Greater Protection and Support for Whistleblowers in the EU. Country Report: Malta*
Sansone K (1 Oct 2010) *Draft law strives to protect whistleblowers*, The Times (Malta) (front page article)//(19 Oct 2010) *Whistleblowers who report to the media unprotected*, The Times (online version)
Vassallo H (13 Aug 2011) *Does Malta need a Whistleblower Act?,* Malta Today, p. 11
Vassallo R (16 March 2008) *Whistleblowin' in the wind*... Malta Today on Sunday, p. 15
Vella M, Sunday (20 Nov 2011) *Whistleblowers penalised for reporting abuse at Mount Carmel*, Malta Today on Sunday (online version)

Chapter 10
Country Report: The Kingdom of the Netherlands

Providing an Alternative to Silence: Toward Greater Protection and Support for Whistleblowers in the EU.

Björn Rohde-Liebenau

Abstract While the legal frame work for the protection of whistleblowers has continued to develop at a steady pace to its current above average effectiveness, the **Netherlands** stand out for their societal dialogue on whistleblowing, the broad consent beyond party line and above all: an independent, state financed **Advice Centre for Whistleblowers** and in all likelihood a **House for Whistleblowers** as a new institution with some protective functions and even the power to investigate.

Introduction

The Kingdom of the Netherlands with about 16 million inhabitants has been one of the first countries world-wide to introduce explicit whistleblowing legislation. Certainly since 2001, the Netherlands have witnessed an ongoing stakeholder debate and a comparatively quick sequence of further legislative steps.[1]

Nonetheless, from the perspective of these stakeholders, the landscape for whistleblowers may still lack comprehensive protection for whistleblowers, provisions for effective external whistleblowing, or the (truly?) independent centre for advice and protection. Within the consensus oriented Dutch culture, any past progress must be attributed to a serious, yet respectful and often open-minded wrestling between stakeholders, politics and administration. Any introduction and implementation of whistleblowing provisions was the result of a complex stakeholder dialogue,

[1] This country report was originally produced in 2012. It has been brought up to date in July 2015 with the generous support of Rik van Steenbergen, FNV – the legislative processes are still moving forward.

B. Rohde-Liebenau (✉)
Hochschule für Öffentliche Verwaltung, Bremen, Germany
e-mail: RCC@risk-communication.de

G. Thüsing, G. Forst (eds.), *Whistleblowing - A Comparative Study*, Ius Comparatum - Global Studies in Comparative Law 16,
DOI 10.1007/978-3-319-25577-4_10

each marking a step forward in societal consensus – albeit with parts of the administration, politics and industry stakeholders often remaining sceptical.

In the Netherlands, origin or chosen home to some internationally renowned whistleblowers,[2] such as Paul van Buitenen, and an active academic community, this must be seen as a work in progress, engaged in a public dialog with politics and administrations about the scope and the effectiveness of the existing regulations. For whatever the legislation does, the stakeholders will by necessity continuously monitor and question its effectiveness. As a truly ground breaking initiative we should commend 3 days in April 2000, when the Trade Unions (FNV) kept a whistleblowing advice line open which led them to the conclusion that whistleblowing guidelines (and risk assessments) were needed most.[3]

In a formal sense, the Netherlands already have a complete set of regulations, rules, and institutions. Yet, formal regulations are limited in their applicability to the public service. In 2001, when Art 125 quinquies 1.f. of the Ambtenarenwet (Public Service Officials Statute) introduced a new legal basis, these rules were merely laid out in an abstract, procedural manner, and limited to sections of the public service. The law suggested for the employers of the national public service to set up rules for the reporting of presumed irregularities. In the same year a model procedure was published (Voorbeeldregeling Klokkenluiders), and later updated and emulated for the different administrative branches beyond the national administration, such as the self-regulating political entities (towns, cities, provinces). In 2009 an up-dated version appeared for the Police and the Federal Administration,[4] and in 2010 an adapted version geared at the Military.[5] Under these rules civil servants should report to an internal Confidential Integrity Counsellor and to an external Committee for Government Integrity.[6]

From 2006 onward a decree had opened ways for civil servants to find advice and receive information at the Bureau Integriteitsbevordering Openbare Sector (BIOS, Office for the Promotion of Integrity in the Public Sector within the Interior Ministry – BZK).[7] Soon after, an Integrity Commission at the Interior Ministry was

---

[2] Renowned Whistleblowers (Bekende Klokkenluiders) listed at http://nl.wikipedia.org/wiki/Klokkenluider_%28melder_van_misstanden%29

[3] van Steenbergen, 2001, p. 3

[4] Decree of 15 Dec 2009 for the reporting of presumed irregularities in Government and Police (Besluit van 15 December 2009, houdende een regeling voor het melden van een vermoeden van een misstand bij de sectoren Rijk en Politie) Statsblad 2009, 572;

[5] Decree of 30 August 2010, with an amendment of the General Military Officers Law and the Civil Military Associates Law, as well as for the reporting of presumed irregularities, Statsblad 2010,706 (Besluit van 30 augustus 2010, houdende wijziging van het Algemeen militair ambtenarenreglement en het Burgerlijk ambtenarenreglement Defensie in verband met een regeling voor het melden van een vermoeden van een misstand)

[6] Commissie Integriteit Overheid

[7] The Bureau Integriteitsbevordering Openbare Sector, or BIOS (Dutch National Office for Promoting Ethics and Integrity in the Public Sector) is a section of CAOP, the Labour Management Consultancy Service of the Dutch Ministry of the Interior and Kingdom Relations (BZK), and was itself created in 2006.

tasked to investigate reports on presumed irregularities. Since January 1, 2010, whistleblowers who work for the central government and the police have received assistance in reporting malpractices of any kind under the Reporting of Suspected Malpractices Decree.[8] This decree emphasises the duty of management to ensure that whistleblowers shall not be hindered in any way to continue to perform in their functions. Decisions infringing the rights of the whistleblower "because of that person blowing the whistle" would be illegal. The decree defines infringement of whistleblower rights fairly widely and not exclusively as dismissal, ending a temporary employment contract or not renewing it, refusing to transform a temporary contract into a contract of continuous employment, transferring or relocating or refusing to do so, issuing a sanction, taking a disciplinary measure, withholding salary, withholding opportunities for promotion or refusing holiday leave. Since 1 January 2014 such provisions have been included in similar rules for other branches of the public service.[9]

From 2011 the Office of the National Ombudsman, who had from time to time acted upon request from whistleblowers, became involved as a general advice and information centre. Starting October 1, 2012, an Advice Centre for Whistleblowers (Commissie Adviespunt Klokkenluiders[10]) has been activated, with the former CEO of Siemens Netherlands at its helm.[11] This Advice Centre has been set up to serve both the public and the private sector. It is independent in its own affairs, and only for the purpose of appointments and discipline installed under the Dutch Minister of the Interior.

The Advice Centre for Whistleblowers received 32 reports in its first month

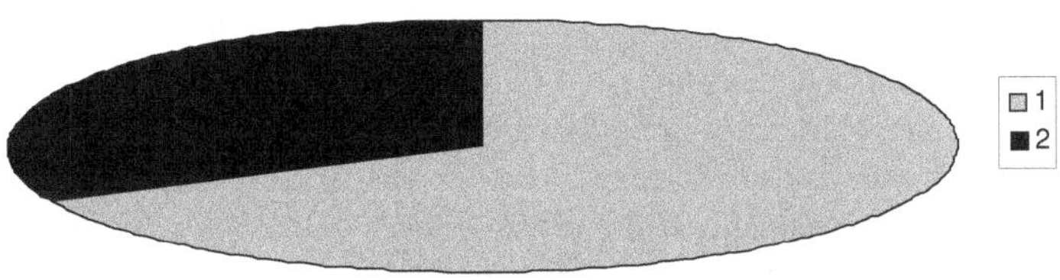

When the Advice Centre for Whistleblowers became operative and published its first monthly report 47 persons had contacted the Center, 32 of whom (slice 1) were actually looking for advice, while 15 others (slice 2) sought to share their previous experiences. Ten of those who were actually looking for advice came from the private sector, the rest from the public sector.[12]

[8] Besluit Melden vermoedens Misstanden Rijk en Politie.

[9] According to an unreviewed comment by van Steenbergen, 2015.

[10] Commissie advies- en verwijspunt klokkenluiden, active from 01 Oct 2012, introduced by Decree of 27 Sept. 2011, Statsblad 2011, 427.

[11] According to a release of 24 May 2012 by the Minister for BZK.

[12] "Klokkenluiders weten Adviespunt Klokkenluiders in eerste maand te vinden" (Whistleblowers know how to find the Advice Center in the first month), report on the Center's website at http://www.adviespuntklokkenluiders.nl/nieuws/klokkenluiders-weten-adviespunt-klokkenluiders-in-eerste-maand-te-vinden.

In the first quarter of 2015, 112 persons have contacted the Advice Centre. Eventually ten new cases have been marked as whistleblowing issues. One year earlier the respective numbers had been 117 contacts and 12 whistleblowing cases – the remainder typically falling in categories such as request for advice or clarifications regarding internal regulations.[13]

Beginning with its conception the Advice Centre had been comprehensively discussed, evaluated and legislative alternatives had been probed.[14] From a legal standpoint it has a life span until 01 July 2016[15] or until the coming "House for Whistleblowers Act" enters into force, whichever is earlier. While the Advice Centre has been given a fair chance to live up to its promise, it seems safe to assume that the Dutch search for further improvements will not stop with the creation of a House for Whistleblowers.

The private sector relies on an inter-industrial accord published as recommendations by the Stichting van de Arbeid (Labour Foundation consisting of Employer Federations and Employee Unions). According to the model rules[16] which came with these recommendations, under certain conditions, reporting to an external organisation (regulator, investigator) should be permitted. While these regulations are not legally binding, they set a certain standard which is honoured by Labour Courts.[17] Currently these recommendations may therefore be regarded like an expert opinion, or good labour practice. Wherever enterprise-wide whistleblowing regulations (codes of conduct, or the like) have been introduced, the recommendations will serve as their benchmark in Court. If a private enterprise has not even implemented its own rules on whistleblowing, in theory the recommendations ought to provide equal protection against the harassment of whistleblowers, because laws and labour practice make it clear enough that good employers should not let whistleblowers suffer a detriment.

The public follows the continuing debate which is normally left to experts and academics. There seems to be a general notion that both the reporting procedures and the protection mechanisms still merit considerable thoughts for improvement, whereas these improvements should be reached by small steps, regular monitoring and without entirely discarding whatever has been reached so far. Overall criticism focuses on the effectiveness of protections (or lack thereof), the independence of reporting recipients and investigators, as well as the quality of advice. Both government and critical experts take the UK PIDA legislation as well as the Public Concern at Work[18] advice centre as a reference point – yet, without fully agreeing as to con-

[13] https://www.adviespuntklokkenluiders.nl/nieuws/aantal-meldingen-bij-adviespunt-in-eerste-kwartaal-stabiel/

[14] From the proposed legislation van Raak, through a 2014 evaluation by an organizational consultancy to the present legislative developments.

[15] Originally terminating July 1, 2015 according to Art 14 of the Decree of 27 Sept. 2011, Statsblad 2011, 427, now extended by one year, Decree of May 22, 2015 https://zoek.officielebekendmakingen.nl/stb-2015–202.html.

[16] Statement on dealing with suspected malpractices in companies.

[17] according to a statement by the STAR.

[18] PcaW, the UK whistleblowing NGO.

sequences or conclusions. Reformers aspire for the efficiency they see rooted in the three tiered UK PIDA system. Those more content with the present Dutch status quo hold the PIDA model as already established in the Netherlands.

In 2012 a political alliance of six (later seven) parties led by the Socialist Party (SP) introduced a legislative proposal providing for a "House for Whistleblowers," as an option for making neutral legal advice more readily available. The Expert Group of Whistleblowers[19] unequivocally supported this proposal in its 2012 Black Book, a study advocating change addressed to the Interior Ministry.[20] Both the Labour Foundation and the Council for Public Sector Personnel Policy also supported the position of the Senate. In July 2014 the initiators of the bill and the Ministry of the Interior cooperated to finish the amending bill.

After early amendments the bill received Parliamentary approval.[21] The Senate then urged the initiators of the Bill to cooperate with the Ministry of the Interior for public sector issues and declared its willingness to accept a bill after a number of amendments to be made by the Parliament including what follows:

- The National Ombudsman should not serve as umbrella institution to the House for Whistleblowers;
- The House for Whistleblowers should not be tasked both to advise and to investigate reports.
- The Advice Centre for Whistleblowers should continue to exist independently from the House for Whistleblowers;
- The governance and rules of the House for Whistleblowers should reflect the differences between public and private sector;
- The relationship with the administration (regulators) should be clarified;
- Protection against retaliation should also be guaranteed if the whistleblower reports to a regulator other than the House for Whistleblowers;

After the amendments the Senate asked for, the National Ombudsman will be replaced by a new independent governing body. The existing Advice Centre for Whistleblowers will become an independent department of the House for Whistleblowers with 'advice' as its specific remit. The powers for investigations of the House for Whistleblowers will be different for the public and the private sector. In addition to the amendments the Senate asked for, the bill now provides for a standard of quality for the establishment of internal whistleblowing procedures, based on those of the model "*Statement on dealing with suspected malpractices in companies*." The employer is obliged to inform the workers about the situations in which a malpractice can be reported outside the organisation and about their protection. The Senate had gone into recess before the editorial deadline of this report – however prospects for a positive vote seem all positive.

[19] Made up of some of the renowned Dutch whistleblowers and some others, www.expertgroepklokkenluiders.nl.

[20] Zwartboek Klokkenluiders, 2012 (an evaluation of the status quo, how whistleblowers fare and which organisations might support them).

[21] House session of Dec. 13, 2013; Senate vote May 20, 2014.

Whistleblower Protection Laws

Typical Laws with Explicit Reference to Whistleblowing

While the Netherlands still lack a standalone act for the protection of whistleblowers, they do have a specific law – since 2001 integrated into the Civil Servants Act,[22] and they do have legal precedents relevant to whistleblowing.[23]

The referenced law, covering most of that part of the working population which is in the Civil Service, consists on the one hand of a formal prescription to implement codes of conduct in the administration,[24] and therein to include stipulations for whistleblowing.[25] These codes of conduct have been implemented and occasionally been updated, generally following a central template.[26] The model rules explicitly state what whistleblowing is, who whistleblowers are, and that they should not suffer detriments for their whistleblowing.[27] In addition to that official legal comments from the Government further define and explain these regulations.[28]

In order to merit reporting under the Dutch rules, the object of whistleblowing, the presumed irregularities (misstanden) have to concern

- A criminal act;
- An infraction of the rules of public service and government;
- Misleading of justice;
- A risk to public health, environmental safety; or
- Wilful withholding information on the above facts.

Since 2007 the existing official model rules for the branches of the public administration have been updated and identical ones for the Police and the Armed Forces

[22] Ambtenarenwet.

[23] The most recent one of importance arguably from the Amsterdam Superior Court: LJN: BR2582, Gerechtshof Amsterdam, 200.070.341/01 of 14 June 2011; The Supreme Court of the Netherlands (Hoge Raad) has explicitly been referring to whistleblowing (klokkenluiden) since 2003. Ever since that year the Hoge Raad has published at least one decision regarding this subject. The year 2011 even saw eight such instances.; www.rechtspraak.nl

[24] Art 125 quater 3rd paragraph "draagt zorg voor de totstandkoming van een gedragscode voor goed ambtelijk handelen;".

[25] Art 125 quinquies 1st paragraph f.) "een procedure voor het omgaan met bij een ambtenaar levende vermoedens van misstanden binnen de organisatie waar hij werkzaam is."

[26] The Province, Communities and Water Regulation Bodies each had their (largely identical) models published in Statsblad.

[27] Art 125 quinquies 3rd paragraph: De ambtenaar die te goeder trouw de bij hem levende vermoedens van misstanden meldt volgens de procedure, bedoeld in het eerste lid onder f, zal als gevolg van het melden van die vermoedens geen nadelige gevolgen voor zijn rechtspositie ondervinden tijdens en na het volgen van die procedure.

[28] Lately incorporated in the Decree: "Besluit van 15 December 2009, houdende een regeling voor het melden van een vermoeden van een misstand bij de sectoren Rijk en Politie" (Besluit melden vermoeden van misstand bij Rijk en Politie), Statsblad 2009, 572.

introduced. Suspicions can now be reported not only regarding ones own employing institution but also in regard to other branches of the public service.

Eligible reporters of irregularities are "ambtenaren" (public officials), only. This is a rather restricted definition oriented toward a formal status – and not e.g. toward the factual proximity to relevant sources of information.

The Dutch rules permit the internal reporting of a mere suspicion, if made in good faith. According to these rules, the reporting persons should not be prejudiced in their legal positions, or according to the newer model rules, "not in any way".[29] This level of protection (?) is accorded independent of material accuracy or veracity of the reported suspicion.

The exact meaning of "prejudice to legal positions" (nadelige gevolgen voor zijn rechtspositie) does not seem to have been tested in higher Courts. While it should be arguable that health and physical as well as psychological well-being are also protected legals positions, it may seems desirable to qualify protections. Currently the civil servant would have to prove

(a) A damage to his/her legal positions;
(b) The causation by the act of reporting a suspected irregularity;
(c) The unwarrantedness of these damages.

He or she would have a true day in Court. There are no particular stipulations under Dutch law granting potential whistleblowers extra rights, but reinstatement and provisional injunctions are potentially available – as for anyone else.

The model procedures do not provide for confidentiality let alone anonymous disclosures. However, there is a public hotline which accepts anonymous reports – obviously from anyone. The focus of this hotline seems to be more on violence, drugs and possibly organised crime – not so much the public service.[30] Its slogan is "Bel M" (Ring M.), with "M" standing for "Meld Misdaad anononiem." Its service number 0800 7000 has become popular,[31] and in 2009 an off-shoot was started as "De Vertrouwenslijn."[32] The purpose of this "Trust line" is to help politically exposed persons such as mayors and councillors resist unwarranted pressure or attempted extortion by offering advice, coaching and an experienced network. While "Bel M." is a "crime-stoppers" type of citizens' hotline for the reporting of misdeeds (misdaaden) rather than irregularities (misstanden), the latter may be intended as a backstop against denunciation (bad faith reporting). While anonymous calls are encouraged, the staffing of these services (at the Ministery for BZK or the

[29] e.g. Art 11.1. of the model procedures for the Provinces "De ambtenaar die met inachtneming van de bepalingen van deze regeling een vermoeden van een misstand heeft gemeld, wordt op geen enkele wijze in zijn positie benadeeld als gevolg van het melden."

[30] Stichting M, financed by National Police and Government, started in 2002, (www.meldmisdaadanoniem.nl).

[31] In 2008 it had received a total of 76.000 calls, which eventually led to 710 cases resolved and goods and moneys in the total value of 1,7 Mio. EUR confiscated, http://nl.wikipedia.org/wiki/Meld_Misdaad_Anoniem

[32] http://www.devertrouwenslijn.nl.

Police) also remains anonymous. Both services do not provide extra reporting channels in the typical whistleblowing situations.

The most recent model procedures for the public service explicitly provide for "external disclosures." External, in this case, means contacting the National Ombudsman, or a Commission for Help and Advice to Whistleblowers[33] at the office of the National Ombudsman. The purpose of this latter institution is to provide advice and support upon request

- To public officials who contemplate making an internal report on possible irregularities, and
- To the administrations and their managements.

The Commission may be approached before using the customary line of reporting – if there are good reasons. Eventually it is the "most external" potential recipient of whistleblowing information under Dutch Law. It has no duties or rights to make investigations or to provide specific protection.

The Office of the National Ombudsman, now host to this Commission, was introduced in 1982. Since 1999 it has been recognised as an independent body at the constitutional level. The first paragraph of Article 78a of the Dutch Constitution, reads as follows:

> The **National Ombudsman** shall **investigate**, on request or of his own account, actions taken by central government and other administrative authorities designated by or pursuant to Act of Parliament.

The Office of the National Ombudsman has indeed established three departments for the purpose of investigating those parts of the administration within its remit.[34] Undoubtedly the person of the incumbent National Ombudsman is respected across all sectors of society, and across the political spectrum. Both the above mentioned proposed legislation and the whistleblowing experts group, while intending to change procedures had wanted to keep their whistleblowing counsel and protection institutions attached to the National Ombudsman's office – which was clearly inacceptable at least to the Senate.

The Dutch laws stipulate that public officials should not suffer disadvantages in their legal positions, if they have made such a report correctly following the procedures. However, in case a whistleblower does experience such disadvantages, only the general rules would apply (e.g. provisions in criminal law and in the Civil Service Act), essentially leaving the whistleblower with the entire burden of proof, including causality. Understandably, there do not seem to be any reports on sanctions against anyone who may have retaliated against a whistleblower. In any case, the whistleblowing regulations lack explicit provision sanctioning those who might legally or factually inflict damage or suffering to persons making a report. At least,

[33] Commissie advies- en verwijspunt klokkenluiden, active from 01 Oct 2012, introduced by Decree of 27 Sept. 2011, Statsblad 2011, 427.

[34] The first round GRECO Evaluation Report NL, 2003, p. 18, ciph. 60, noted 115 staff at the office and a total of four investigation departments.

there for most cases of internal reporting, the rules set up an obligation, yet unsanctioned, to take up investigations without delay and eventually provide the whistleblower with some sort of conclusions.

There have been two major evaluations addressing the situation of whistleblowing in the Netherlands. One commissioned by the Ministry for BZK[35] and one self-commissioned by the Expert Group of Whistleblowers[36] these complement each other but come to similar conclusions:

- The existing regulations do not effectively promote internal communication about presumed irregularities;
- They do not protect whistleblowers;
- They should be developed – arguably radically – toward the UK model of whistleblowing in the public interest.

The Bovens study is continuously being quoted and is said to have vitalised the discussion amongst stakeholders and decision makers.[37] Another, smaller study on the (not always satisfactory) effects of self regulation pre-empted these findings in 2006, and underscored the need for at least a minimum of legislation.[38]

Laws with Indirect Effect on Whistleblowing

For some time, it had been propagated that imposing a *duty* to report could protect whistleblowers. The reasoning behind this was to have the activity of reporting more readily accepted – or at least legally excused. While the underlying assumptions seem worth debating on virtually all accounts, a strictly limited duty to report certain particularly serious crimes can be observed in most legal cultures. Thus failing to report plans or preparations for a war of aggression, for murder, or, more recently, for money laundering, will in most jurisdictions be a crime in itself.

Above that, the Netherlands have set up a duty in the Code of Criminal Procedure to support criminal proceedings and investigations through the provision of information – essentially by anyone. Article 160 of the Code of Criminal Procedure imposes a duty to report to a criminal investigator any knowledge of specific serious crimes.

If the crime is below this threshold of seriousness, according to Art. 161, anyone who has knowledge of an offence (such as corruption) that has been committed, *may* report it to said bodies. However, Art. 162 imposes a *duty* to report *any committed crime* on civil servants and on public bodies as such – if they are not charged with the investigations in the first place.

---

[35] Bovens et.al. Evaluatie klokkenluidersregelingen publieke sector 2008.

[36] Zwartboek Klokkenluiden, 2012.

[37] Sips, p. 64.

[38] Nauta and van Heel, 2006.

It would not surprise if reporting statistics under Art 162 were found to be rather low, because a mere suspicion is not sufficient for a duty to report. Often, it may be too challenging to know whether a crime has actually been committed, if the person to decide is not even charged with the investigations. And, while failure to comply with this duty will not be sanctioned, a breach of confidence, or a report in bad faith is quite likely to be sanctioned. However, these obligations were not entirely synchronised with the newer regulations and rules from and under Art 125 quienquies Ambtenarenwet.

Overall, it seems sufficient to note that the rules in the Criminal Procedure are unlikely to send a signal of support for whistleblowing either way. The First Round GRECO Evaluation Report nonetheless comes to a positive conclusion. Its recommendation to extend the original rules and clarify any possible tensions[39] had later been picked up by the improved model regulations of the Dutch Government.

Most Dutch Ministries seem to have their own complaints procedures. These may reflect on whistleblowing practice depending on their openness and communication culture. However as secondary legal materials, their texts and the administrative practice cannot be analysed within the confines of this report.

Self-Regulation (Private Sector)

The Dutch Private Sector has a longstanding, successful, internal and external lobbying instrument for self-regulation in labour relations. Founded in 1945 the Stichting van de Arbeid (Labour Foundation, StvdA, or recently most commonly STAR) brings together the larger part of employer foundations and trade unions. Seemingly, reacting to the Dutch construction fraud scandal in the late 1990s and early 2000s, the Ministry of Labour and Social Affairs had asked STAR to develop a (model) code of conduct, which could provide guidance to those confronted with an integrity violation. In a 2006 evaluation of whistleblowing procedures, again performed upon request by the Ministry, STAR advised its members to include whistleblowing procedures in all tariffs/collective bargaining agreements.[40] In reality, this appeal has been heeded in very few cases, only.[41]

The current version of the STAR recommendations[42] would have a number of distinct advantages over the model rules for the public sector. Most importantly, while the private sector parties are candid about their primordial interest of keeping the reporting internal, they have understood the UK model to the extent that this

---

[39] GRECO First evaluation report 2003 at N. 83.

[40] Zoon Nauta, Donker van Heel, Evaluatie zelfregulering klokkenluidersprocedures, rapport in opdracht van het ministerie van Social zaken en Werkgelegenheid, 2006.

[41] According to a written reply from the STAR.

[42] Annex 3 to this report.

interest will be served best, if they explicitly permit responsible outside reporting.[43] STAR explains this approach in words deserving a direct quotation:

> If reporting malpractice externally, the employee should approach the most relevant external party. He or she should consider how effectively that party can intervene and rectify or help to rectify the malpractice. The employee should also attempt to limit the loss or damage suffered by his or her employer as a result of such intervention. In other words, when an employee decides to report malpractice outside the company, he or she should first approach the competent authorities and not the media.
>
> The more serious the malpractice is, the more certain population groups are at risk and/or the more the malpractice persists despite repeated reports, the more justified the employee is in contacting the media. It will clearly not be easy for the whistleblower to argue plausibly that he or she was forced to call in the media to rectify the malpractice or prevent its recurrence.[44]

Perceptions and Political Will

It seems remarkable how the country had early on introduced a proprietary term for whistleblowing: klokkenluiden (bell ringing), which since then has regularly been used even in legislative materials. It seems that the metaphor of *klokkenluiden* refers to an external process: Ringing bells is meant to facilitate crossing thresholds. Accordingly, the Dutch klokkenluiden is a narrower or differing concept compared to what internationally is often called "whistleblowing." Klokkenluiden does not customarily include internal communication. By contrast and surprisingly, the existing Dutch legislation concerns merely the internal processes, regulates external whistleblowing only by way of omission – and therefore cannot be expected to make life much easier for whistleblowers: "melden" (internal reporting) is OK, even if it's only about a suspicion; "klokkenluiden" (external reporting) is what ought to be avoided.

The term klokkenluiden sounds to outsiders and foreigners as though one is talking about an accepted, certainly not tabooed or negatively connoted activity. However, even in 2009 some believed: "'Klokkenluiden' is too much contained with the negative connotations part of the conventional whistleblower framework. We should consider using also 'whistleblowing'."[45] This remark supports a view that "klokkenluiden" (and certainly external whistleblowing) may officially be used in the Netherlands to refer to an activity which the legislator would not want to condone. Language doesn't necessarily change attitudes, but it often valuable to pay close attention exactly how words are being used. So, if the connotation of klokkenluiden and the attitude towards have not yet been changed positively, a different

[43] Art 5 of the model (Annex 3).

[44] re. g), p. 11 in the English version.

[45] Evita Sips with further references, at footnote 364.

word might indeed be considered. However today, a majority is seen to consider 'klokkenluiden' as positive or neutral.[46]

Dutch laws, regulations and model rules usually refer to "vermoedens van misstanden" as object of such communication processes. This means a presumption or suspicion ("vermoeden") is enough to start the process. "Misstand" is a condition in which things are or "stand" other than desired, regardless of the underlying cause. This should be stressed, because in this case the legal phrasing may actually be more sensible than its everyday usage in the Netherlands. Beware: the common English translation of "misstand" as "abuse" seems potentially misleading, because "misstand" neither implies an actor or an act, nor a will behind it. Misstand is therefore a comparatively unemotional word, much less judgemental than e.g. "abuse." Any misstand is an object of (risk) identification and calls for further assessment, possibly a management decision and remediation; whereas an "abuse" is the result of assessments, may call to rally against the presumed responsibles, and to sanction them, be it for their inability, or their bad intentions. The label "abuse" raises defences ad personam, whereas a label "deficiencies" like a handicap might call for solidarity and co-operation. However, since deficiency also sounds a bit defective or even ideological, whereas the actual subject matter may even offer more or better than expected, for the purposes of this country report "misstand" will be translated as "irregularity." This is also supported by the nearly parallel use of the Dutch word "onregelmatigheden" in the (private sector governance) code Tabaksblatt. "Onregelmatigheden" is a word of Germanic origin literally meaning "irregularities."

However, what needs to be done about whistleblowing or risk communication has not always been clear. The Raad van State, the ancient organ through which every law has to pass before it may be presented to Parliament did not assume legal whistleblower protection to be necessary.[47] This body assumed the Dutch Civil Service to be managed in such a manner that it would react sensitively to any criticism and certainly not treat anyone unfairly, let alone loyal civil servants who in good faith gave internal reports according to the procedures. However, the reality was different, even in the Netherlands, and certainly in the years before the first model rules had come into force.

The first TI NIS Report mentioned how there was limited protection of whistleblowers.[48] Since then, there have been considerable improvements to the advice potential whistleblowers may request and receive, recently through the Advice Centre for Whistleblowers. In its 2012 updated report, Transparency NL remarks that whistleblower regulations are still considered to be ineffective by many, because too many issues are not reported or addressed; and whistleblowing in the private sector remained basically non-existent because existing procedures only apply to exchange-listed companies.[49] However, apart from the public sector, it is just these

[46] According to personal comments by Rik van Steenbergen, July 2015.

[47] Lissenberg, p. 12.

[48] NIS NL (2001), p. 33.

[49] National Integrity System, Report Netherlands 2012, p.31.

exchange listed corporations which have the most employees. Therefore it is probably a majority of Dutch private and public employees which may profit from internal whistleblowing regulations and processes having been installed.

It is noteworthy that only one in ten of those corporations, which have installed a whistleblowing regime, equally encourages their usage and internal criticism. In the last 5 years, only 1 company in 20 received at least 1 report on an irregularity from 1 of its employees.[50] And only about 1.6–3.5 % of all employees are to be considered (potential) whistleblowers.[51] About ten times as many (25 %) just know of the whistleblowing regulations.[52] Thousands of interviewed Dutch employees were overwhelmingly under the impression that reporting or not reporting is largely inconsequential for the resolution of irregularities.[53]

About half of this small number of employees who have internally reported an irregularity continue outside, because their internal reporting could not resolve the issue. Two thirds of the respondents named as most important reason for external reporting the idea that their internal reporting had not been taken seriously. Others expected more protection after external reporting. On the other hand, the reasons not to carry on outside are diverse: some don't expect benefits from third party activities, some fear a deterioration of work relations with colleagues, or received their discouraging advice, etc.[54]

In 2010 the old Commission received a total of 43 cases

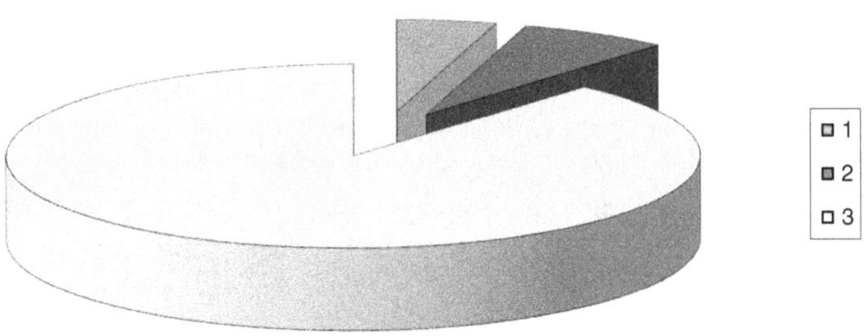

In 2010, the Commission Integriteit Overheid[55] received a total of 43 whistleblowing reports. Just two of these were taken up for further investigation (slice 1 in

---

[50] De weg van de klokkenluider p.12.

[51] De weg van de klokkenluider p.12.

[52] Zwartboek p. 13.

[53] De weg van de klokkenluider p.14.

[54] De weg van de klokkenluider p.14.

[55] Until Oct 2010 the only accessible semi-external body other than the so far non-specific National Ombudsman, renamed OIO (Onderzoeksraad Integriteit Overheid) and refurbished as of October 2012 http://www.onderzoeksraadintegriteitoverheid.nl and again together with the Advice Centre for Whistleblowers in 2014).

the image). Three persons withdrew their report (slice 2). Thirty-eight reports had been referred back because they were not covered by the rules of the procedure (slice 3).[56]

In 2014 both the Advice Centre and the Public Integrity Board have been evaluated by regulating bodies. Their report recommends to give the Advice Centre a permanent statutory basis whereas to reconsider the role and position of the Public Integrity Board.[57]

Cases

The pivotal whistleblowing case is arguably what is known as the construction fraud scandal of the late 1990s, early 2000s. The fate of that whistleblower (unfortunately coined a "slachtoffer"[58]) made it clear that regulation of the position of whistleblowers was more than just desirable.[59] Indeed introduction of the current legislation probably always had this victim or casualty in mind.

The case about the EU Commission and Paul van Buitenen certainly also preoccupied the Dutch public, though it is not exactly a 'Dutch case.'

In 2011 the Court of Amsterdam came to the conclusion that an employee had infringed upon the contractual confidentiality clause in giving confidential information of his employer to a third party (in this case a private banking client). The allegedly inflicted damage of around four million EUR to this client was not accepted as a sufficient justification. According to the Court, the employer had to inform his superior or other managers within the company – or else (even indirect) shareholders of the company – about the abuse of his employer before letting go the loyalty and discretion in relation to his employer. Only in case the employer did not react adequately, would it have been acceptable to make public the potentially serious abuse. However, in the latter case, this should have been carried out in a proportional way. Moreover this should be warranted by an important public interest.

In this case the conflict between the employee and his employer, according to the Court, did not meet these criteria.[60] The former banker lost, but carried his case on to the Supreme Court (Hoge Raad), which then decided[61] to send the case back to

[56] De weg van de klokkenluider p.14.

[57] Report "*Veilig misstanden melden op het werk* "http://www.vng.nl/files/vng/20140805-veilig-misstanden-melden-op-het-werk-eindrapport-2014.pdf.

[58] Slachtoffer is translated as "victim." Literally it is more than that: it tends toward the biblical human offering for slaughter … even more than the scapegoat of lore, but equally unsupportive imagery.

[59] NIS NL, 2012, p.283.

[60] LJN: BR2582, Gerechtshof Amsterdam, 200.070.341/01, proclaimed on 14 June 2011 and mentioned in NIS NL, 2012, p.276.

[61] LJN: BW9244, Hoge Raad, 11/04190, of 26 Oct 2012 and available at NJB 2012, 2254, RvdW 2012, 1341, and www.rechtspraak.nl.

the first instance for further contemplation. However, this time the Court of The Hague in lieu of the one in Amsterdam will serve as first instance.

The Hoge Raad followed the claimant's argument that the First Instance had not sufficiently respected his argument of a grave conflict of duties – duties which were all imposed on him by his employer. The duties overlooked or valued lowly by the First Instance was inscribed in the bank's compliance rules for private bankers: the account manager must treat customers with honesty and must inform them of a conflict of interest.[62] The Hoge Raad also concluded that the First Instance County Court had misinterpreted the criterion of a "serious" public concern so that it was outweighed by the interests of the employer, and did not assess fairly the arguments of the claimant how in fact he had informed his employer and why it would not have been reasonable to expect further reports.

In this case, an internal report in 2008 had proven that mistakes on the side of the bank had damaged the client. The banker had reasons to believe that neither the report nor its conclusions would be made known to the client, and that he (the account manager) had been targeted to become the scapegoat. Eventually, the Court through the Attorney General could not decide on its own whether the claimant had a right to be made whole (including a reference for his personal integrity and some immaterial damages). But the Court overturned the Amsterdam decision and pointed the Court in The Hague towards this conflict of duties.

Though explicitly pointing out the particularities of this case, the 26 Oct 2012 decision of the Hoge Raad will be a leading case for some time, because it confirmed a right or even a duty to report serious abuse "to whom it may concern," and because the interest of the employer to keep internal issues confidential did not overrule the duty of honesty and good trusteeship of the banking relationship which was honoured by the whistleblower.

The criteria applied by Dutch courts are essentially the same as the criteria the European Court of Human Rights applies in whistleblower cases (Guja v. Moldova, Heinisch v. Germany). However, compared to the Dutch lower courts, the European Court imposes less stringent requirements on the gravity of the public interest.[63]

A comprehensive study with the largest number of Dutch whistleblowers interviewed came to the conclusion, that most previous proceedings in Dutch Courts focussed on the troubled working relationship rather than the irregularities.[64] The underlying reasoning is that the relationship maybe so troubled that it cannot be upheld by the employer. This is a conventional but faulty argument, at least where the employer unduly strained the relationship by targeting a whistleblower, instead of honouring his or her valuable contributions. The 26 Oct 2012 decision rightly protects a whistleblower who followed some of the duties set up by the employer (honesty and fairness toward the client) but could not equally be held to follow other, conflicting ones (keeping irregularities or even illegal behaviour secret). As it happens, the Hoge Raad in this most recent judgement reverts to an old Common

[62] Point 4.11 on p. 12/13 of the Hoge Raad judgement.

[63] According to Rik van Steenbergen, July 2015.

[64] De weg van de klokkenluider p.86.

Law principle which is practically at the basis of the UK whistleblowing legislation. There is "no confidence as to the [non-] disclosure of iniquity"[65] (to appropriate institutions) – crime is not a legally protected trade secret.

Strengths, Weaknesses and Recommendations

Regarding the whistleblowing issue, the Dutch society may arguably rely on the best informed experts and specialists outside the Anglo-American or Common Law world. Its consensus oriented political system has managed to come up with a continuous stream of steps toward improved whistleblowing procedures.

The debate featured global core values, such as justice for the victims, loyalty, being a good employer/employee, and the protection of corporate confidentiality.

The model rules of the Labour Foundation (incorporating Employer Associations and Trade Unions) are praiseworthy for their reasoning as well as their clarity about opening an external communication channel.

The Dutch system seems to take pride in its consensus oriented Labour Foundation. So, it should be hoped that external whistleblowing as proposed by the Labour Foundation will soon become the law for everybody.

To this purpose, the Whistleblower Advice Centre as a dedicated advisory body for whistleblowers, according to a Bill which only awaits passage in the Senate, will form an independent part of a new 'House for Whistleblowers'. The House for Whistleblowers in turn will have investigative powers, now also accepted by the cooperative if sceptical Dutch employers.

Other stakeholders explicitly realise the value, benefit and necessity of systematically

- Assuring that everyone will get heard (a matter of justice and of responsibility in risk identification);
- Assuring that all risk information will flow were it is needed and were it will be processed responsibly, preferably internally, but better externally than not at all.

As of July 2015, it may safely be assumed that the amending bill for the House of Whistleblowers will soon come into force. In that case, the cooperative Dutch approach, as mentioned in the introduction, will have led to a body of rules and regulations, combined with case law, which renders an acceptable level of protection to individuals who in the context of their work report information on risks, or harm to the public interest. The public and private organisations on the other had will find better and timelier access to the information they need for responsible risk management.

---

[65] Gartside v. Outram (1856) 26 LJ Ch 113, 114, 116 per Wood VC, cit. by Anna Myers "Whistleblowing – The UK Experience" in Calland, Dehn (eds.) Whistleblowing around the World.

Bibliography

Bovens M (2006) et.al. *Evaluatie klokkenluidersregelingen publieke sector*, rapport in opdracht van het ministerie van BZK, 2006 2008

Bovens M, Pikker G (2010) (p.38–47), Binnenlands Bestuur (2011) Klokkenluiders kaltgestellt (qu. NIS NL 2012, fn. 305)

Calland R, Dehn G (2004) *Whistleblowing Around the World – Law, Culture and Practice*, ODAC and PCaW in partnership with the British Council Southern Africa, Cape Town

Demmke C, Moilanen T (Dec 2011) *Effectiveness of Good Governance and Ethics in Central Administration*: Evaluating Reform Outcomes in the Context of the Financial Crisis Study for the 57th Meeting of the Directors-General of Public Services of the Member States of the European Union, European Institute of Public Administration

Ecorys (2006; Coen Zoon, Mirjam Stuivenberg, Hans Nauta, Peter Donker van Heel), Evaluatie zelfregulering klokkenluidersprocedures – Eindrapport, Opdrachtgever Ministerie van Sociale Saken en Werkgelegenheid, Rotterdam. 15 mei 2006; http://docs.szw.nl/pdf/129/2006/129_2006_3_9270.pdf (Evaluation of self-regulation, commissioned by the Ministry for Social Affairs and Labour)

Expertgroep Klokkenluiders (Gerrit de Wit, Paul Schaap, Henk Laarman, Paul van Buitenen, Harrie Timmerman, Cees Schaap adv.), Zwartboek Klokkenluiders, 2012

Lissenberg E (2008*) KLOKKENLUIDERS EN VERKLIKKERS*, Rede uitgesproken door bij haar afscheid als hoogleraar criminologie aan de Universiteit van Amsterdam op 15 februari 2008

Sips E (2009*) Condemn Silence, Honour the Whistleblower?,* Erasmus University Rotterdam, Master Thesis in International and Comparative Criminology

Stichting van de Arbeid (Labour Foundation), Statement on Dealing With Suspected Malpractices in Companies, 3 March 2010(updated version), publication no. 1/10 (Translation, updated August 2012); earlier version: Statement concerning methods for dealing with malpractices in companies, publication 11/04, The Hague, 2004, translation of "Verklaring inzake het omgaan met vermoedens misstanden in ondernemingen" publication 6/03 of 24 June 2003, http://www.stvda.nl/en/~/media/Files/Stvda/Talen/Engels/2012/20120829_EN.ashx

Transparency International, National Integrity System, Netherlands, Berlin, 2nd, 2012; http://www.transparency.nl/wp-content/uploads/2012/05/TI-NL-NIS-report.pdf

van Steenbergen R, Vrijheid van meningsuiting van werknemers, FNV, Amsterdam, 2001, http://home.fnv.nl/bijlagen/2904/klokkenluiders.htm

van Steenbergen R, Help, ik vermoed een misstand, p. 247–266 in In Drescher, W.T.G. & e.a., (Eds.) *Langzaam maar zeker. Maar wel zeker*! Opstellen over onderwijs- en arbeidsrecht, (Liber Amicorum voor Frans Brekelmans), Algemene Onderwijsbond AOB, Utrecht, 2012, http://www.adviespuntklokkenluiders.nl/docs/bibliotheek/help-ik-vermoed-een-misstand!.pdf?sfvrsn=6

Verhulp E, Bij de geboorte van de eerste (ambtelijke) 'klokkenluidersregeling', SMA 2001, p. 196–203

Vermaas J, van der Linden R, Serail T, Klomps A, Jellinghaus S (KUB) en Krom J (NIPO), De weg van de klokkenluider: keuzes en dilemma's Onderzoek naar de klokkenluidersproblematiek in Nederland, IVA Tilburg 2001, http://docs.szw.nl/pdf/35/2002/35_2002_3_2107.pdf.

Chapter 11
Whistleblowing in Poland According to Legislation and Case Law

Dagmara Skupień

Abstract This chapter concerns the legal protection of whistleblowers in Poland. The author analyses the legislation and the case law concerning especially claims for the unfair dismissal and criminal proceedings for the defamation. The aim of this chapter is to present the current state of protection of persons who disclose irregularities in the organizations or companies and to detect the weaknesses of the present Polish legislation in order to recommend legal remedies helping to combat the malpractices with the aid of whistleblowers.

Legal Bases for the Protection of Whistleblowers

The legal situation of whistleblowers[1] (*sygnalista*) is not regulated in Poland in a separate legal act. The incentives to prepare a proposal of the law which would guarantee the legal protection to persons who 'blow the whistle' and inform about the irregularities in organizations come from public institutions and

This paper is based on the Polish report to the XIXth International Congress of Comparative Law, Vienne, 20–26 VII 2014. See also D. Skupień, *The legal protection of whistleblowers in Poland in Rapports polonais*, XIX Congrès international de droit comparé, Lodz University Press, Lodz 2014, pp. 257–267.

[1]The notion of '*whistleblowing*' is often used in the Polish writing, see i.a. W. Rogowski, Whistleblowing, czyli czego się nie robi dla pozyskania zaufania inwestorów (*Whistleblowing or anything that can be done to attract investors*), Przegląd Corporate Governance 2/2007, A. Wojciechowska-Nowak, *Whistleblowing* u pracodawcy – system wczesnego ostrzegania w organizacji (*Whistleblowing at the workplace – system of an early warning in the organization*), Przegląd Służby Cywilnej 2/12, p. 53 and ff. or M. Derlacz-Wawrowska, *Whistleblowing a ochrona informacji poufnych pracodawcy* (*Whistleblowing and the protection of the confidential information of the employer*) in Prawo pracy. Refleksje i poszukiwania (*Labour Law. Reflections and Searches*), ed. G. Uścińska, Warsaw 2013, pp. 390–403. However, a domestic term '*sygnalista*' (a signaller, a person who signals the irregularities) is proposed by experts.

D. Skupień (✉)
Faculty of Law and Administration, University of Lodz,
Kopcińskiego 8/12, 90-232 Łódź, Poland
e-mail: dstateczny@wp.pl; dagmara.skupien@wp.pl

G. Thüsing, G. Forst (eds.), *Whistleblowing - A Comparative Study*,
Ius Comparatum - Global Studies in Comparative Law 16,
DOI 10.1007/978-3-319-25577-4_11

non-governmental organizations. In 2009, Polish Ombudsman requested the Ministry of Labour and Social Affairs to launch the legislative initiative in order to guarantee the legal protection of whistleblowers.[2] The postulate to prepare a legal act on whistleblowers' legal protection as well as a consolidated system of information on the irregularities was included in the Governmental Programme to Counteract the Corruption of the Ministry of Internal Affairs and Administration.[3] As it concerns the citizens' activities, Stefan Batory Foundation's experts presented main features of the possible proposal of the legal act on whistleblowing in 2012.[4] Nonetheless these initiatives, no proposal of the law on whistleblowers has been lodged to the Parliament yet.

The protection of whistleblowers has its bases in different international conventions and national acts. Poland is bound by international anti-corruption conventions which i.a. guarantee protection for whistleblowers within its scope of application. Poland ratified the conventions on corruption of the Council of Europe adopted in 1999, namely Civil Law Convention on Corruption[5] and Criminal Law Convention on Corruption.[6] It is worth mentioning that Article 9 of the Civil Law Convention on Corruption refers directly to the employment relationships. This provision obliges parties to the Convention to provide in their internal law for an appropriate protection against any unjustified sanction for employees who have reasonable grounds to suspect corruption and who report in good faith their suspicion to responsible persons or authorities. As it concerns the Criminal Law Convention on Corruption, its Article 22 obliges the parties to adopt necessary measures to provide effective and appropriate protection for those who report the criminal offences covered by the scope of this convention or otherwise co-operate with the investigating or prosecuting authorities.

In 2000 Poland ratified The OECD Convention on Combating Bribery of Foreign Public Officials in International Business Transactions of 1999 (Anti-Bribery Convention). The 2009 OECD Anti-Bribery Recommendation recommends in particular that governments encourage their enterprises to develop and adopt adequate internal controls, ethics and compliance programmes or measures for the purpose of preventing and detecting foreign bribery and to provide channels for communication by, and protection of, persons not willing to violate professional standards or ethics under instructions or pressure from hierarchical superiors, as well as for persons willing to report breaches of the law or professional standards or ethics

[2] Ombudsman's letter of the 3rd March 2009, RPO-606960-III/09/RP/AF.

[3] Rządowy Program Przeciwdziałania Korupcji na lata 2012–2016 (*Governmental Programme of Combatting Corruption for the years 2012–2016*), Ministerstwo Spraw Wewnętrznych i Administracji (*Ministry of Internal Affairs and Administration*), Warsaw 2011, pp. 22–23.

[4] See A. Wojciechowska-Nowak, Założenia do ustawy o ochronie osób sygnalizujących nieprawidłowości w środowisku zawodowym. Jak polski ustawodawca może czerpać z doświadczeń państw obcych?, (Recommendations for the legal act on persons sygnalling irregularities in the professional environment. How Polish legislator may be inspired from the foreign countries' experiences, Warsaw 2012, see www.batory.org.pl/ (accessed on the 14th January 2015).

[5] Ratified by Poland 11/9/2002, entry into force 1/11/2003.

[6] Ratified by Poland 11/12/2002, entry into force 1/4/2003.

occurring within the company in good faith and on reasonable grounds, and should encourage companies to take appropriate action based on such reporting (pt X.C).

Poland also ratified (2006) the United Nations Convention against Corruption of 2003.[7] In relation to the protection of whistleblowers two provisions of this act should be mentioned. Firstly, Article 8 para. 4 encourages parties to establish in accordance with the fundamental principles of the domestic law, measures and systems to facilitate the reporting by public officials of acts of corruption to appropriate authorities, when such acts come to their notice in the performance of their functions. Then, according to its Article 33n, parties shall consider incorporating into its domestic legal system appropriate measures to provide protection against any unjustified treatment for any person who reports in good faith and on reasonable grounds to the competent authorities any facts concerning offences established in accordance with this Convention.

Poland is also bound by the European Convention on Human Rights. According to the case-law of the ECHR, Article 10 (Freedom of expression) of the above-mentioned Convention is applicable to the workplace. In case Wojtas-Kaleta vs. Poland,[8] the Court has decided that the infringement of Article 10 by Poland took place in a situation where the journalist – employee and at the same time a trade union official was given a reprimand by the employer, a public television company, for having criticized in public the employers' broadcasting policy.

The general principles concerning the protection of whistleblowers may be withdrawn from the Polish Constitution of 1997. Article 54 para. 1 of the Constitution guarantees the freedom of expression which within the scope of the employment relationship allows employees to express justified critical opinions about the employer.

In the light of Article 30 of the Constitution, the dignity of the person as an inherent and inalienable value shall constitute a source of freedoms and rights of persons and citizens. The human dignity is inviolable and the respect and protection thereof shall be the obligation of public authorities. The right to respect the dignity and other personal goods of the employee is one of the basic principles of labour law (Article 11^1 of the Labour Code).

In the public sector, Article 63 of the Constitution shall be applied to whistleblowers. According to this provision, everyone shall have the right to submit petitions, proposals and complaints in the public interest, in his own interest or in the interests of another person – with his consent – to organs of public authority, as well as to organizations and social institutions in connection with the performance of their prescribed duties within the field of public administration. The procedures for considering petitions, proposals and complaints shall be specified by statute.

Article 94 of the Labour Code enumerates the obligations of the employer versus the employee. It is worthy to draw attention among others to such employers'

[7] See also A. Wojciechowska-Nowak, Ochrona sygnalistów w Polsce. Stan obecny i rekomendacje zmian, *The protection of whistleblowers. 'The present state and the recommendations of changes'*, Instytut Spraw Publicznych, Warszawa 2012, p. 7.

[8] *Wojtas-Kaleta v Poland* (2009) ECHR *20436/02* (Fourth Section 16 July 2009).

obligations as: duty to evaluate the work of employees according to the impartial and just criteria as well as to enforce the principles of community life at the workplace. Article 94[3] of the Labour Code also obliges employers to combat mobbing. The breach of her/his obligations by the employer may be the fair cause for the termination of the employment relationship by the employee for the fault of the employer without notice (Article 55 § 1[1] of the Labour Code). In such a case the employee may demand the payment of damages by the employer (Article 55 § 1 of the Labour Code).

The employee who is a whistleblower may also rely on her/his obligation to protect the property of the establishment, to take care of the good state of the establishment, as well as to respect the principles of the community life at the workplace (Article 100 § 2 of the Labour Code). The employee is not bound by the orders of the employer if these orders are contrary to the legal provisions or to the employment contract (Article 100 § 1 of the Labour Code).

There are no legal provisions concerning the necessity to exploit the internal procedures of whistleblowing but such a sequence of whistleblowing may result from the internal regulations adopted by the employer. According to the legal writing, the internal reporting should have priority over the appeal to third parties.[9]

In the light of the public opinion poll of CBOS (2012) concerning whistleblowing,[10] the present legal protection of whistleblowers in Poland is not sufficient and there is a common expectation that the whistleblowers shall be guaranteed protection against dismissal, discrimination or other acts of retorsion from the employer. The above-mentioned survey showed a very high social approval for such employees' behavior as the disclosure to the prosecutors' office or to other public institutions of employers' acts like: the non-respect of safety norms which endangers life or health of employees, the illegal pollution of environment, the corruption of managers or members of the governing organs of the company, the financial abuses or the accountancy falsification. The survey also confirmed that a big number of the surveyed persons is afraid to disclose irregularities and declared that they would inform about the irregularities only anonymously. The majority of respondents are sure that whistleblowers would encounter negative consequences from the employer such as dismissal (56,1 %), mobbing, difficulties at work (12,9 %) or formal punishment by the employer (7,9 %). Only 4,1 % of respondents present an opinion that the knowledge or experience of the whistleblower would be used by the employer to avoid the irregularities in the future. 1,4 % of the respondents think that the whistleblower would be awarded by the employer.

---

[9] See M. Derlacz-Wawrowska, Whistleblowing a ochrona informacji poufnych pracodawcy (*Whistleblowing and the protection of the confidential information of the employer*), ibid., p. 401.

[10] See CBOS, "Bohaterowie czy donosiciele? Co Polacy myślą o osobach ujawniających nieprawidłowości w miejscu pracy? (*Heros or telltales? What do the Poles think about persons who denunciate irregularities at the workplace*?), Warsaw, April 2012.

Legal and Citizen's Duty to 'blow the whistle'

Whistleblowing may be spontaneous but may also result from legal duties of certain categories of employees' representatives. Firstly, trade unions are entitled to control the company's alignment with labour law provisions and health and safety norms by employers and to require the elimination of the disclosed irregularities by the competent public organs.[11]

The disclosure of irregularities by trade union officials is guaranteed a stronger protection. In case of discrimination based on the trade union membership, the burden of proof is reversed. Moreover, the trade union officials are also granted special protection against the dismissal.

Trade unions may undertake the collective dispute with the employer in order to defend i.a. trade union freedoms or to protect work conditions (Article 1 of the 1991 Act on the resolution of the collective disputes). It is thus possible that the collective dispute may aim at eliminating irregularities which are persistent at the workplace.

Moreover, according to Article 8 of the Code of the Civil Procedure, the organizations the statutory aim of which does not comprise commercial activities may, in cases provided for by the specific legal provisions, bring suit or take part in the judicial proceedings already initiated in order to protect the citizens' rights. In cases concerning labour law and social security, Article 462 of the Code of Civil Procedure allows the non-governmental organizations in the realm of their statutory tasks, to bring suit on behalf of the employee or to take part in the already launched proceedings if the employee who is party to these proceedings consents to it in writing. These provisions entitle thus among others trade unions to support in judicial proceedings an employee who encounters reprisals for having blown the whistle.

Social labour inspectors (*społeczny inspektor pracy*). are a second category of employees' representatives entitled to the 'institutional whistleblowing'. The social labour inspectors are elected by the staff from the workplace trade unions' members. Their competencies encompass i.a. the control of the alignment with the health and safety norms and with the environmental provisions as well as the respect of the labour law provisions by the employer.[12] Social labour inspectors are protected against dismissal with notice during their mandate and during 1 year after the expiry of the mandate. Their disciplinary dismissal requires the consent of the workplace trade union. They may require access to premises, demand to have a view into documents and give directives to the employer in case of found irregularities. The social labour inspectors cooperate strictly with public organs of control such as the State inspection of work (*Państwowa Inspekcja Pracy*) or the Office of the Technical Supervision (*Urząd Nadzoru Technicznego*).

---

[11] Art. 23 of the Polish Trade Unions' Act of 1991.

[12] See Art. 4 of the Law of the 24th June 1983 on the social labour inspection, Polish Journal of Laws (Dz. U.), 983.35.163.

The board-level employee representatives in the commercial companies[13] are also entitled to supervise and to control the activities of the company as they fulfill the duties conferred to them on the basis of the Code of the Commercial Companies. It should be noted however, that the employee participation in the supervisory or management boards of the commercial companies does not exist in the private sector in Poland.

Moreover, the general, citizen's duty to inform the Public Prosecutor's Office or the Police relies on any person who received an information about the criminal offence which is to be pursued by the public prosecutor (Article 304 § 1 of the Code of the Criminal Procedure). This duty is not legally enforceable, except for the duty to inform about the most serious crimes against peace, humanity and State defense etc.

The legally enforceable obligation to inform immediately the Police or the Public Prosecutor's Office and to undertake all necessary actions in order not to allow the traces and proofs of the infraction to be destroyed lies with the State and local administration institutions which take information about the commitment of the criminal infraction prosecuted by a public prosecutor in relation to their activities (Article 304 § 2 of the Code of the Criminal Procedure). However, not any employee of the institution has this duty to inform but only persons who have managerial or controlling functions. The non-fulfillment of this duty may result in the penal responsibility provided for the civil servants in Article 231 § 1 of the Criminal Code (sanction of maximum 3 years of imprisonment).[14]

On the other hand, an employee may be deterred from the denunciations to the Prosecutor's Office by the potential criminal responsibility for the disclosure of the confidential information of the employer (Article 265–267 of the Criminal Code) and the civil responsibility for the infringement of personal goods (Article 24 of the Civil Code). Polish legislation also provides for the legal professional privilege in relation to i.a. barristers or solicitors advising an organization or a company.

Polish legislation does not provide for any rewards or financial incentives for persons who disclose irregularities concerning the functioning of the institutions they work in. The employees who work in the internal control departments of enterprises do not benefit from any increased level of protection against unfair dismissal.[15]

---

[13] For details about the scope of the board-level representation in Poland see i. a. D. Skupień, *Board-level employee participation in Polish limited-liability companies*, in Arbeitnehmerbeteiligung in Unternehmensorganen im internationalen Vergleich, ed. G. Löschnigg, Wien 2011, pp. 139–161.

[14] See also M. Derlacz-Wawrowska, Whistleblowing a ochrona informacji poufnych pracodawcy (*Whistleblowing and the protection of the confidential information of the employer*) in Prawo pracy. Refleksje i poszukiwania (*Labour Law. Reflections and Searches*), ed. G. Uścińska, Warsaw 2013, pp. 397–398.

[15] See the Judgment of Supreme Court of the 9th December 1999, case I PKN 435/99.

Whistleblowing in the Case Law

The case law of Polish courts which concerns the whistleblowing mainly relates to disputes between employees and employers concerning the dismissal of the employee either with notice or without notice (disciplinary dismissal) by the employer. It should be underlined that the judicial control of valid grounds for the dismissal is possible only in case of an open-ended contract of employment. In case of fixed-term contracts, the labour court may only control the legality of notice. Moreover, in case of the fixed-term contracts, the dismissed employee may only demand the payment of damages in case of illegality of the dismissal with notice. In case of open-ended contracts, the employee may also demand the reinstatement in work, if she/he was dismissed with notice (Article 45 § 1 and 2 of the Labour Code). However, even in case of the open-ended contracts, the labour court adjudges only damages if the reinstatement in work is impossible or aimless. As the Polish Ombudsman pointed it, the whistleblower usually has no chances to be reinstated in work, as the labour courts estimate that the conflict between the employee and the employer makes it impossible or useless.[16]

According to the information delivered by the Ombudsman, the most common form of reprisals is the dismissal of the whistleblower with notice justified by the reason that his/her post of work is being liquidated. In such a case, labour courts have a narrow scope of appreciation if the dismissal is justified in reality. According to the Supreme Court,[17] the liquidation of the post of work in the scope of the real organizational changes justifies the dismissal of the employee. Decisions concerning the utility of maintaining of this post belong to the sphere of employers' prerogatives and shall not be subject to the control of the labour courts. This statement was confirmed in the more recent case-law. In the judgment of the Supreme Court of the 5th September 2001 (I PKN 613/00), the liquidation of the post of work as such is not a sufficient justification for the dismissal. The causal link between the liquidation and the given notice should be examined. However, according to the statement of the Supreme Court, if the causal link is established between the liquidation of the post and the dismissal, the liquidation constitutes the valid ground for the dismissal. The Supreme Court is not entitled to examine business or personal reasons of such liquidation.[18] Therefore, the control of the labor court is restricted to the analysis if the liquidation of the post of work really took place and if it was a truthful and not only an apparent reason for dismissal.

Then, the disclosure of irregularities by an employee may also lead to the disciplinary dismissal. According to the relatively recent judgment of the Supreme Court,[19] the aim of the employee to prevent the wages discrimination by the employer is not a fair ground to dismiss the employee without notice. In the circumstances of

---

[16] See the Ombudsman's letter of the 3rd March 2009, RPO-606960-III/09/RP/AF, p. 4.

[17] Judgment of Supreme Court of 23th May 1997, I PKN 176/97.

[18] Decision of the Supreme Court of the 2nd February 2012, II PK 252/11.

[19] Judgment of the Supreme Court of the 26th May 2011, II PK 304/10.

this case the employee discovered by a chance the unjustified disparities in wages between employees. The plaintiff had a coincidental access into documents which should have not been revealed (he received an e-mail containing confidential data by mistake). The plaintiff distributed the data among his colleagues in order to explain the inequality in remunerations. As a consequence, he was dismissed without notice for the breach of the duty of confidence. The Supreme Court stated that the transmission by the employee to other employees of data covered by the so-called clause of confidentiality of wages in order to prevent the unequal treatment and the wages' discrimination cannot constitute the valid ground for the disciplinary dismissal of the employee.

There is a plentiful case-law concerning the dismissals with notice or without notice for the fault of the employee justified by the critical opinions of the employee about the employer. This case-law gives indications for the limits of the legally acceptable criticism towards employer, the surpassing of which may justify the dismissal of the employee. It may be concluded from this case-law, that the acceptable criticism must be in conformity with the law, should serve the defense of the employees' interests, be done with *bona fide*. It also should be done in a manner which is adequate and proportional to the degree of the infringement of the employees' interests.[20] The Supreme Court stated that the critical opinions about the employer which are arrogant, malevolent, not based on any proofs should be treated as extending above the legally allowed limits of the criticism.[21] Similarly, the Supreme Court refused to give protection against unfair dismissal to an employee responsible for the internal control who was breaching the internal order of work, did not subordinate himself to the decisions of the superiors and was provoking unjustified conflicts while carrying out his controlling duties (case I PKN 435/99).

The Scope of Protection

The general provisions of law protect employees who are whistleblowers not only against dismissal but also against mobbing, infringement of personal goods or any unequal treatment concerning the conditions of work or remuneration. The whistleblowers who were punished with the reprimand by the employer, are entitled to lodge an appeal against this penalty to the labour court (Article 112 § 2 of the Labour Code). Employees who are helping or encouraging whistleblowers or affirming whistleblower's allegations may seek protection on the same basis as whistleblowers. There are no special provisions regulating their situation.

The burden of proof that the whistleblowing constituted the only reason for the dismissal is with the employee. The reversal of proof is only valid for the

[20] S. W. Ciupa, Niedozwolona krytyka pracodawcy ze strony pracownika jako przyczyna wypowiedzenia umowy o pracę, (*Unacceptable criticism of the employer by the employee as a reason for the dismissal with notice*), Monitor Prawniczy 20/2002.

[21] Judgment of the Supreme Court of the 17th December 1997, I PKN 433/97.

discrimination cases and the whistleblowing is not a criterion which may be included in the catalogue of the forbidden criteria. Article 18^{3a} § 1 of the Labour Code states that employees should be treated equally with regard to concluding and terminating employment contract, the terms of employment, promotion and access to vocational training aimed at upgrading their professional qualifications in particular independently of sex, age, disability, race, religion, nationality, political opinion, membership in a trade union, ethnic origin, belief, sexual orientation as well as employment for a fixed term or for an indefinite period of time or a part-time or full-time employment. Even though this catalogue is not a closed one, according to the judgment of the Supreme Court (Case II PK 82/12), discrimination shall be defined as a worse treatment of the employee which is not justified by the objective grounds for the reason of characteristics or properties which concern him/her personally and are relevant from the social point of view or for the reason of employment for determined or undetermined period or the fulltime or part-time employment. The disclosure of irregularities cannot be qualified as a personal feature of an employee in the meaning of this judgment. Also in cases concerning the mobbing,[22] it is the employee who is obliged to prove that all the legal elements of the mobbing[23] were fulfilled.

The realm of irregularities which may be disclosed is not limited. The whistleblowing may concern such irregularities as infringements of labour law provisions, dangers to health and safety or to the environment, malpractices related to the conduct of the business, accountancy irregularities or any criminal offences. The protection, especially in cases of criminal offences, is not dependent on the fact that reporting concerns only bygone incidents. Unfortunately, in Poland, there are no provisions in force which would enumerate the 'qualified disclosures' giving the right to the legal protection.

The drawback of the general protection of the whistleblowers on the basis of the Labour Code in Poland is that the Labour Code provisions do not protect the workers employed on the basis of civil law contracts. It is thus contrary to the newest recommendation of the Council of Europe[24] according to which the legal protection of whistleblowing should cover all individuals working in either the public or private sectors, irrespective of the nature of their working relationship and whether they are paid or not.

It should be mentioned that the number of workers employed on the basis of civil law contracts or on the basis of self-employment increased to an important scale in last years. This group is particularly vulnerable on the labour market and in practice deprived of means to seek legal protection in case of termination of a civil law contract by the opposite party. The available remedies consist only in claiming the

[22] See the judgment of the Supreme Court of the 5th December 2006, case II PK 112/06 or the judgment of the Supreme Court of the 5th October 2007, case II PK 31/07.

[23] See Art. 94^3 § 2 of the Polish Labour Code.

[24] Recommendation CM/Rec(2014)7 adopted by the Committee of Ministers of the Council of Europe on 30 April 2014 and explanatory memorandum, Protection of whistleblowers, point 3.

compensation for the damages resulted from the breach of the contract according to the civil law provisions and the contract's clauses.[25]

Problem of Anonymity

The anonymous whistleblowing is not a rule in Poland. The protection of the identity of the whistleblower is provided for in several situations.[26] In the realm of the controlling activities of the State Inspection of Labour (infringement of employment provisions or of environmental norms by the employer, etc.), the inspector of labour may deliver a decision concerning the non-disclosure of the identity of the whistleblower if the disclosure could be harmful or risky in any way for the employee or a self-employed person (Article 23 para. 2 of the Law on the State Inspection of Labour). It is thus a discretionary decision and the refusal to impose anonymity shall not be contested by the signaler. Moreover, the employer in such a situation may appeal from this decision to the Regional Inspector of Labour.

If the disclosed irregularities constitute criminal offences, the whistleblower may demand the status of the so-called *incognito* witness (Article 184 of the Code of the Criminal Procedure). The status of the *incognito* witness may be given if there is a justified risk of danger for life, health or property in the important amount for the witness or one of his/her closest relatives.

In the context of anonymity, a particular conflict between the disclosure of identity of a whistleblower and obligations of an employer concerning the protection of personal data is observed. Inspector General for the Personal Data Protection drew attention of the Labour Minister in the official letter of 2010 on the possible deterrent to whistleblowing consisting in obligation of the employer to inform the individual whose personal data are collected from a third party and not from him/her directly about the categories of the data and its source. This obligation is a result of the implementation of the Directive 95/46/EC of the EP and of the Council of 24 October 1995 on the protection of individuals with regard to the processing of personal data and on the free movement of such data (Articles 11 and 12). The Article 29 Data Protection Working Party set up by the above-mentioned directive partially clarified this problem enumerating the content of the information to be transmitted to the incriminated person[27] and allowing at the same time for the delay in its notification as long as there is a risk that such a notification would jeopardize the investigations. According to the Polish Inspector General for the Personal Data Protection, it is still difficult to define the precise time of notification in such cases.

---

[25] See also A. Wojciechowska-Nowak, Providing an Alternative to Silence. Towards Greater Protection and Support for Whistleblowers in the EU. Providing an Alternative to Silence, Country Report Poland, Transparency International 2013, p. 10.

[26] See also A. Wojciechowska-Nowak, Providing an Alternative to Silence. Towards Greater Protection and Support for Whistleblowers in the EU, ibid., p. 11.

[27] See Opinion 1/2006 (00195/06/EN) adopted on the 1st February 2006, p. 13.

As it concerns the anonymity, the Working Party stated that under no circumstances the incriminated person could obtain information about the identity of the whistleblower except where the whistleblower maliciously makes a false statement.[28]

Public Disclosure of Irregularities

Public disclosure of information may incur for the whistleblower the risk of the penal responsibility. The whistleblower who diffuses any information on irregularities at the workplace may be held responsible, according to Article 212 § 1 of the Criminal Code, for the defamation. The offence of defamation consists of accusing someone of a conduct or properties that may degrade him/her in public opinion or expose him/her to the loss of confidence necessary for a given position, occupation or type of activity. The proceedings are pursued on the request of the defamed person. In case of the condemnation for the offence of the defamation, the court may adjudge damages for the victim or for any social aim indicated by the victim. Penalties include a fine or a limitation of liberty (Article 212.1 of the Criminal Code). The penalty is more severe when the offense of defamation takes place through the media (Article 212.2 of the Criminal Code) and it includes a fine, a limitation of liberty but also an imprisonment for up to 1 year. It is also more difficult for the whistleblower to liberate her/him from the charge of defamation if the accusation is done through the media. In case of the non-public defamation, it is sufficient to prove that the accusation was true. In case of defamation through the media, there are two conditions to be met: firstly that the critical opinion was true and secondly that it served the socially justified interest (Article 213 § 2 point 2 of the Criminal Code).

According to the Supreme Court case-law,[29] the fulfillment of the latter condition requires that the person who commits the act of defamation pursues only the socially justified interest and is not motivated otherwise. According to the doctrine,[30] in order to estimate that the defamator acted in the pursuit of the socially justified aim, the following conditions have to be met: a social interest has to be put at risk by the addressee of the accusation, the accusator acts in order to defend this interest from the potential damage, the content of the accusation is such that its disclosure may in fact prevent the infringement of the interest put at risk.

It should be underlined that even if the freedom to express opinions, to acquire and to disseminate information is a constitutionally guaranteed right, this right does not allow for the dissemination of the untruthful or defamating information.

As it concerns the alleged offence of the defamation, only truthful allegations (in pursuit of the socially justified interest, in case of the defamation through the media)

[28] See Opinion 1/2006, p. 14.

[29] See e.g. the Supreme Court Resolution of the 17th April 2012, SNO 3/12, the judgment of the Supreme Court of the 30th September 2003, III KK 176/02.

[30] See W. Kulesza, Zniesławienie i zniewaga (*Defamation and insult*), Warsaw 1984, pp. 71–72.

exonerate from the criminal responsibility. In consequence, the Supreme Court (the judgment of the 4th September 2003, IV KKN 502/00) indicated that the condition of the socially justified interest is not fulfilled if the accusation is not confirmed (uncertain) even though later it would appear to be true. Moreover, the Supreme Court has judged that the defamation done with conscience that the information delivered and the alleged properties of another person are not truthful, never serves the socially justified aim.[31]

Moreover, the information about the criminal offence to the prosecuting organs with the conscience that this offence was not committed constitutes the criminal offence itself which is penalized with a fine, the limitation of freedom or the imprisonment up to 2 years (Article 238 of the Criminal Code).

As it concerns the labour courts' case-law, it is more favourable for the erroneous whistleblowing. According to the Supreme Court judgment of the 18th July 2012 (I PK 44/12), the critical statements about the employer and disclosure of the information to the owner of the establishment about the possible irregularities are not a flagrant infringement of the employee duties even if the charges will appear later to be unjustified. However, the allegations should be done in good faith with the belief that the irregularities exist at the workplace.

Concluding Remarks

The legal situation of whistleblowers in Poland is not regulated in one, separate legal act. The provisions concerning the protection of persons who disclose irregularities at the workplace are dispersed in different regulations. Such a situation is not in line with the above-mentioned Recommendations of the Council of Europe. According to point 8 of the Recommendations, the normative framework on whistleblowing should reflect a comprehensive and coherent approach to facilitating public interest reporting and disclosures. In the light if an OECD review, Poland's whistleblower regulations are largely ineffective and make it easy for employers to evade application of law.[32]

The case law of the Supreme Court protects the employees who disclosed irregularities against the reprisals from the employer consisting in unfair dismissal. However, this protection is mainly offered to employees employed on the basis of the open-ended contract. Moreover, in cases concerning mobbing or unequal treatment at the workplace, burden of proof lies with the employee. The adoption of the legal act concerning the whistleblowing is necessary in order to assure the bigger

---

[31] See the Supreme Court Decision of the 22nd June 2004, V KK 70/04.

[32] See OECD Working Group on Bribery, Phase 3, Report on Implementing the OECD Anti-Bribery Convention in Poland, June 2013, p. 42, www.oecd.org/daf/anti-bribery/Polandphase3 reportEN.pdf.Accessed 14.01.2015. For partially critical opinion on the Polish legislation see also Transparency International, Whistleblowing in Europe. Legal protections for whistleblowers in the EU, 2013, pp. 69–70, www.transparency-france.org/e_upload/pdf/eu_whistleblower_report_ final_web.pdf. Accessed 14.01.2015.

legal certainty concerning the consequences of disclosure of irregularities in the public interest. This act should regulate especially the personal scope of protection including not only employees but also workers employed on the basis of the civil law contracts and the self-employed persons as well as trainees or candidates to work. It is recommended that it establishes a catalogue of so-called 'qualified disclosures' such as for ex. criminal offences, dangers to health and safety or environment, corruption, breaches of law. In case of qualified disclosures the burden of proof that the disclosure was not the sole reason for dismissal or other acts of discrimination or harassment should lie with the employer. The new legal act should also provide for a general priority of the internal reporting and oblige the employers to set up procedures for internal reporting in cooperation with employees' representatives in the company, especially through collective labour agreements. Moreover, the penalties should be imposed on persons who are responsible of reprisals against the whistleblowers.[33]

According to the above-mentioned public opinion poll, the fear for the disclosure of the identity is the main deterrent for the potential whistleblowers. To eliminate the risk of retaliations the employer or the prescribed bodies to which the malpractices may be reported, such as Public Prosecutor's Office or the State Inspection of Work should guarantee confidentiality of the identity of the whistleblower for the time-being of respectively internal or external investigation procedure. The employers would be obliged to set in this respect special channels of reporting including persons selected in the organization (preferably in consultation with trade unions or other employee representatives) designated to receive reports in confidence and not to disclose it to third parties.[34]

However, if the disclosed information will be confirmed untruthful and not based on reasonable grounds, the maliciously incriminated person should have the right to get information about the identity of the whistleblower in order to launch criminal proceedings for defamation or claim damages according to the civil law provisions. Whistleblowing shall be protected and promoted insofar as it serves public interest and is done with sincere and honest intentions.

Bibliography

Ciupa SW (2002) *Niedozwolona krytyka pracodawcy ze strony pracownika jako przyczyna wypowiedzenia umowy o pracę,* (Unacceptable criticism of the employer by the employee as a reason for the dismissal with notice), Monitor Prawniczy 20/2002

Derlacz-Wawrowska M (2013) *Whistleblowing a ochrona informacji poufnych pracodawcy* (Whistleblowing and the protection of the confidential information of the employer) in Prawo pracy. Refleksje i poszukiwania (Labour Law. Reflections and Searches), ed. G. Uścińska

---

[33] For the postulates see also A. Wojciechowska-Nowak, Providing an Alternative to Silence. Towards Greater Protection and Support for Whistleblowers in the EU. Providing an Alternative to Silence, Country Report Poland, Transparency International 2013, p. 17 and M. Derlacz-Wawrowska, Whistleblowing a ochrona informacji poufnych pracodawcy (*Whistleblowing and the protection of the confidential information of the employer*), ibid., p. 402.

[34] Compare recommendations CM/Rec(2014)7, point 14.

Kulesza W (1984) Zniesławienie i zniewaga (Defamation and insult), Warsaw

Rogowski W (2007) *Whistleblowing, czyli czego się nie robi dla pozyskania zaufania inwestorów (Whistleblowing or anything that can be done to attract investors),* Przegląd Corporate Governance 2/2007

Sinzdak G (2008) *An Analysis of Current Whistleblower Laws: Defending a More Flexible Approach to Reporting Requirements*. California Law Review 96: 1633-68

Skupień D (2011) *Board-level employee participation in Polish limited-liability companies*, in Arbeitnehmerbeteiligung in Unternehmensorganen im internationalen Vergleich, ed. G. Löschnigg, OGB Verlag Wien

Smith JR (2011, June 22) *Classified Pentagon Report Upholds Thomas Drake's Complaints About NSA*. Washington Post. http://www.washingtonpost.com/national/national-security/classified-pentagon-report-upholds-thomas-drakes-complaints-about-nsa/2011/06/22/AG1VHTgH_story.html. Accessed April 2015

State Whistleblower Laws (November 2010) National Conference of State Legislatures http://www.ncsl.org/issues-research/labor/state-whistleblower-laws.aspx. Accessed April 2015.

Statement by President George W. Bush upon Signing H.R. 3763 (2002, July 30), reprinted in 2002 U.S.C.C.A.N. 543

Wojciechowska-Nowak A (2012) Ochrona sygnalistów w Polsce. Stan obecny i rekomendacje zmian, The protection of whistleblowers. 'The present state and the recommendations of changes', Warsaw: Instytut Spraw Publicznych.

Wojciechowska-Nowak A (2012) Założenia do ustawy o ochronie osób sygnalizujących nieprawidłowości w środowisku zawodowym. Jak polski ustawodawca może czerpać z doświadczeń państw obcych?, (Recommendations for the legal act on persons sygnalling irregularities in the professional environment. How Polish legislator may be inspired from the foreign countries' experiences), Warsaw. http://www.batory.org.pl/. Accessed 14 Jan 2015.

Wojciechowska-Nowak A (2013) Providing an Alternative to Silence. Towards Greater Protection and Support for Whistleblowers in the EU. Providing an Alternative to Silence, Country Report Poland, Transparency International.

Wojciechowska-Nowak A., *Whistleblowing u pracodawcy – system wczesnego ostrzegania w organizacji* (Whistleblowing at the workplace – system of an early warning in the organization), Przegląd Służby Cywilnej 2/12.

Chapter 12
Portugal: The Protection of the Whistleblower from the Perspective of a Country Without Specific Legislation

Júlio Gomes

Abstract Law may to some extent protect the whistleblower without a specific treatment of whistleblowing – even if that sounds as a paradox – and that is frequently the case in countries where the disciplinary dismissal requires a faulty breach of the employment contract by the employee, particularly if the employee is entitled to reinstatement if the dismissal is unlawful.

The issue of the legal protection of the whistleblower, at least in private employment relationships, can hardly be described as a contentious or important topic in Portugal. There is no doctrinal controversy and just a handful of court cases.[1] Nevertheless a few recent court rulings show that the problem exists and that whistleblowing remains a rather hazardous behaviour.

In one recent case[2] an employee of a butcher's shop made an anonymous complaint to the sanitary authorities concerning the lack of hygiene and the disrespect of health safety rules. As a result the authorities made a surprise inspection but were unable to detect any serious anomaly. The employer's lawyers had access to the complaint and were able to identify the whistleblower that was later subject to a disciplinary procedure and dismissed. The court ruled that the dismissal was justified. On the one hand, the court said, an employee has a duty of confidentiality that encompasses violations of the law by her/his employer, as long as they are not criminal offences. On the other hand the fact that the employee tried to conceal his identity was evaluated as further evidence of his awareness that he is acting in

[1] This scarcity of judicial cases is by no means restricted to Portugal. The same seems to be true, for instance, in Italy. See MARIA TERESA CARINCI, Whistleblowing in Italy: rights and protections for the employers, WPCSDLE "Massimo D'Antona". INT, n.° 106/2014 (http://csdle.lex.unict.it), p. 2. This writer explains the rarity of judicial cases concerning whistleblowing stating that the Italian citizen in average is not that much concerned with the common good.

[2] Acórdão Tribunal da Relação de Coimbra, 27/09/2012, 471/11.0T4 AGD.C1 (LUIS MIGUEL FERREIRA DE AZEVEDEO MENDES), available (in Portuguese) in www.dgsi.pt.

J. Gomes (✉)
Alameda Jardins da Arrábida 436, 3C, 4400-478 Vila Nova de Gaia, Portugal
e-mail: jgomes@porto.ucp.pt

G. Thüsing, G. Forst (eds.), *Whistleblowing - A Comparative Study*,
Ius Comparatum - Global Studies in Comparative Law 16,
DOI 10.1007/978-3-319-25577-4_12

breach of his contractual duties. In addition the employee was not able to give evidence showing that his accusations were truthful or, for that matter, that he had voiced his concerns within the enterprise previously to his complaint to the public authorities.

In another case[3] the employee filled a complaint with the public body charged with the enforcement of the legal rules on safety at work. This time however the complaint was not anonymous. Nevertheless the court decided that the dismissal was justified since the employee was unable to give sufficient evidence of the veracity of the charges.

These two court decisions show that there is a substantial risk of reprisals for a whistleblower in Portugal and even if it is true that the fear of reprisals by the employer is not necessarily the only reason[4] why people refrain from denouncing illegal behaviour, the introduction of some measure of legal protection would be beneficial.

My country has not adopted, so far, specific legal rules concerning the protection of Whistleblowers in labour law, particularly in private employment relationships. For the moment, the issue has not been the subject of a serious debate either. However, most Portuguese legal writers are not unaware of the debate that is raging on, in Europe and elsewhere.

What are then the reasons for this apparent lack of interest? In my opinion there are a number of motives for this state of affairs. Firstly, some suggest that whistleblowing is a common law concept, entirely superfluous in our legal culture.[5] Others have invoked a related argument: law is itself an expression of culture and there is a cultural divide[6] between Anglo-Saxon countries on one side and continental European countries on the other, concerning the social merits or demerits of the whistleblower. After all, in countries such as Portugal, Spain, Italy or Greece, but also Germany, that have endured dictatorships and authoritarian regimes, the practice of denouncing someone else's crimes or wrong doings may be reminiscent of the informers and is hardly seen as a public virtue.[7] There is a particularly strong rebuttal of anonymous reports. Another reason for this scepticism on the need for specific rules concerning whistleblowing lies in the fact that in my country, as in

[3] Acórdão Tribunal da Relação do Porto, 08/10/2012 (PAULA LEAL DE CARVALHO) available (in Portuguese) in www.dgsi.pt.

[4] Neither, perhaps, the main reason. See TERRY MOREHEAD DWORKIN, SOX and Whistleblowing, Michigan Law Review 2007, vol. 105, pp. 1757 et seq, pp. 1763–1764.

[5] GÜNTHER WIESE, Zur innerbetrieblichen und ausserbetrieblichen Kommunikation von Arbeitnehmern, Festschrift für Hansjörg Otto zum 70. Geburtstag, De Gruyter Recht, Berlin, 2008, pp. 621et seq, p. 634: "keine Veranlassung besteht, diesen Begriff zu übernehmen".

[6] See, for instance, LUCIEN FLAMENT/PHILIPPE THOMAS, Le *Whistleblowing*: à propos de la licéité des systèmes d'alerte éthique, JCP, La Semaine Juridique, Édition Sociale 2005, n,° 17, 1227, pp. 15 et seq, p. 17 and PATRICE ADAM, Le retour des sycophantes? (à propos du whistleblowing), Le Droit Ouvrier 2006, pp. 281 et seq.

[7] The legal discussion itself is at times somewhat emotive or even irrational, a danger pointed out by a number of writers. See ANDREI KIRÁLY, Whistleblower in Deutschland und Grossbritannien, RdA 2012, pp. 236 et seq, at p. 236 and RAMON RAGUÉS I VALLÈS, Whistleblowing, Una aproximación desde el Derecho Penal, Marcial Pons, Madrid, 2013, p. 23.

other continental European countries, there is no unemployment at will. Instead, the employer must be able to invoke a ground for the dismissal of the worker and, in cases of disciplinary dismissal, the employer must be able to assert and give evidence of a faulty behaviour of the employee with significant consequences, normally, a serious breach of the labour contract. As a result and although Portugal has ratified the ILO Convention 158, Portuguese scholars and courts seem mostly convinced that the necessary protection of the whistleblower is already provided by the general rules applicable to the termination of the labour contract.[8] One of the first criticisms that may be aimed at this kind of reasoning is, of course, that the protection of the whistleblowers, in order to be effective, should by no means be restricted to a protection against dismissal[9] and ought to encompass other persons and not just the whistleblower himself/herself.[10]

There is, therefore, a belief that the enforcement of the general rules concerning the labour contract and particularly termination, as well as the rights and duties of the parties of the labour contract are all that is required to a proper treatment of the whistleblowing cases.

On the one hand, whistleblowing is perceived as falling within the freedom of opinion and expression of the employee, guaranteed by our Constitution to any citizen and by the ordinary law to any employee. On the other hand, the whistleblower is normally an insider of an organization[11] and the labour contract is considered to be a fiduciary contract, creating a personal relationship between the parties. As a result the Portuguese courts will, in whistleblowing cases, take into account the conflict of rights, namely the right of expression of the employee and, on the other hand, the interest of the employer in a certain degree of confidentiality and secrecy,[12] as well as the need for a good working environment.

This belief that the general rules concerning the rights and duties that emerge from the labour contract are all that is needed to handle properly whistleblowing cases may be considered naïf.[13] Nevertheless another more serious ground may exist

---

[8] The same view was defended in Italy by ROBERTO LATTANZI, Prime Riflessioni sul c. d. Whistleblowing. Un Modello da Replicare “ad Occhi Chiusi”?, RIDL 2010, I, pp. 335, p. 344.

[9] As a matter of fact such protection should go beyond labour law, protecting the whistleblower, for instance, against civil liability, as correctly pointed out by, SEVERIN GLASER/PETER KOMENDA, Whistleblowing in Österreich – Gefahren, Probleme, und Lösungsmöglichkeiten, JRP (Journal fur Rechtspolitik), 2012, pp. 207 et seq, p. 221.

[10] As correctly pointed out by GREGOR THÜSING/GERRIT FORST, Whistleblowing around the World, A Comparative Analysis of Whistleblowing in 25 Countries, p. 13.

[11] MIKE SCHULZ, Compliance – Internes Whistleblowing, Betriebs-Berater 2011, pp. 629 et seq, p. 630.

[12] The same seems to be true in Italy: see FABRIZIA SANTINI, Il Diritto di Critica del Lavoratore alla Luce della Più Recente Ricostruzione dell’Obbligo di Fedeltà, RIDL 2009, parte II, pp. 921 et seq, p. 924.

[13] Some German writers, albeit possibly a minority, however, do not consider necessary to introduce specific legislation on whistleblowing in labour law. Compare MICHAEL SIMONET, Notwendigkeit eines Gesetzes zum Schutz von Whistleblowern?, RdA 2013, pp. 236 et seq (against such a need) and GERRIT FORST, Whistleblowing im internationalen Vergleich – Was kann Deutschland von seinen Nachbarn lernen?, EuZA 2013, pp. 37 et seq (in favour of such a legislation).

to justify a certain scepticism concerning the need of for specific legislation or, at least, to wonder if such a legislation is always coherent: if one considers the many, different, legislative solutions that have been enacted to deal with whistleblowers, it seems that there are two currents of though, two perceptions that may converge, but frequently collide and may lead to different results or outcomes.

On the one hand there is what might be called a moral or ethical perspective of whistleblowing. The whistleblower must be protected as someone that feels that his/her civic duty is to report a crime or a wrongdoing.[14] It is then something akin to a conscience objection: the same way an employee may refuse to perform an order by his/her employer if it amounts to a crime or simply, in certain cases to a wrongdoing or even an unethical behaviour, the employee must also have the freedom to express his/her concern and to denounce such practices. This ethical approach to whistleblowing seems to have a number of consequences: first of all, the motivation of the employee/whistleblower is of great importance. The whistleblower that is doing "the right thing" must not do it for the wrong reasons, like revenge, opportunism or a simple desire to cause harm. In addition the whistleblower who acts because he feels that it is hers/his duty as a citizen is not necessarily in bad faith, but invokes an allegiance stronger than the contractual bound. According to this view, the internal whistleblowing is to be preferred, with the exception only of very serious wrongdoings, namely crimes. After all, the whistleblower who is acting in good faith and who is not moved by the purpose of harming his/her employer will normally provide the employer with the opportunity to mend his/her ways. It is true that this ethical or moral perspective raises some difficult issues, for instance, to what extent should the whistleblowing be protected: it is clear that the whistleblower has the right to denounce serious crimes or wrongdoing done by his/her employer or colleagues, but less clear whether the legal protection of the whistleblower should be extended to cases where she/he reports, for instance, infringements or breaches of private contracts by his/her employer. The ethical approach seems also to endorse a stronger requirement for a good faith conduct by the whistleblower: she/he should, for instance, exercise a certain degree of care when making his/her report, namely, to public authorities. As a result he/she ought, not only to employ a proper language, but also to try to ascertain if her/his claims are truthful.

The pragmatic approach is quite different in its outcomes.[15] Now what is considered decisive seems to be the public interest and that interest dictates the requirements for the legal protection of the author of the disclosure. According to this perspective, the motivation of the whistleblower is of secondary importance or even irrelevant[16]: what really matters is that his/her disclosure was truthful and

[14] The protection of the whistleblower is seen as a result of the interdiction, as a rule, of private justice, by PETER GÄNSSLE, Der Whistleblower im Spannungsfeld zwischen Korruptionsbekämpfung und arbeitsrechtlichen Pflichten, Kritische Justiz 2007, pp. 265 et seq, p, 270.

[15] See also DAVID LEWIS, Whistleblowing at Work: on what Principles should Legislation be based?, Industrial Law Journal 2001, pp. 169 et seq.

[16] GERRIT FORST, *Strafanzeige gegen den Arbeitgeber – Grund zur Kündigung des Arbeitsvertrags*?, NJW 2011, pp. 3477, pp. 3480–3481, considers that the motives of the whistleblower ought to be irrelevant, at least whenever the whistleblowing refers to crimes. He reiterates this opinion in Whistleblowing im internationalen Vergleich – Was kann Deutschland von seinen

useful. On the other hand, this pragmatic approach emphasizes the preventive effect of the whistleblowing legal rules and one is left to wonder whether such preventive effect is not maximized with the so-called external whistleblowing.[17] The internal whistleblowing – the report or complaint within the frame of the organization – gives the actor of the wrongdoing the possibility to destroy evidence or to camouflage the practice and does not seem to be preferable in terms of protecting the public good. On the other hand, this pragmatic approach tends to have a different outcome concerning the matters that may be reported within the framework of the whistleblowing rules; there must be a strong public interest in the disclosure, an interest which may be present in fiscal, economic environmental crimes, but may be absent or at least weaker in cases such as breaches of private contracts by the employer (again with some exceptions whenever for instance consumer relations are at stake).

The debate on the need for a specific legislation concerning whistleblowing in private law employment relationships has become even more complex due to two related issues.

On the one hand the issue of anonymity of the whistleblower, forced upon many European countries by the American law, namely by SOX. That legislation has had the effect of forcing many American enterprises in Europe to introduce mechanisms – namely hotlines[18] – that allow for the anonymity of the whistleblower. In addition some of these enterprises have grasped the opportunity to go a step further than the requirements of the American law, establishing either a procedure that allows a wide range of unlawful or unethical behaviours to be denounced or even introducing a duty of the employees to denounce colleagues that they suspect to have committed infractions of the ethical codes of the enterprises.

As a result of these hotlines and of the so-called compliance a number of legal problems have arisen. The anonymity of the whistleblower does not fit well within the rules concerning data protection and is perceived by many European writers as promoting slander, allowing for cowardly attacks against persons who may find it difficult or impossible to defend them. From another point of view, a more pragmatic one, it has been suggested that anonymous information does not normally provide a reliable and sufficient ground for further enquiries. As a result some of the national authorities responsible for data protection have proposed systems that give

Nachbarn lernen?, EuZA 2013, pp. 37, p. 71. Similar remarks were made by PETER BOWAL, Malice and Whistleblowing, E-Journal of International and Comparative Labour Studies, 2013, vol. 2, n.° 3, pp. 94 et seq, p. 96.

[17] JAMES GOBERT / MAURICE PUNCH, Whistleblowers, the Public Interest and the Public Interest Disclosure Act 1998, The Modern Law Review 2000, vol. 63, pp. 25 et seq, p. 43.

[18] REYES CALDERÓN-CUADRADO/ JOSÉ LUIS ÁLVAREZ-ARCE/ISABEL RODRÍGUEZ-TEJEDO/SRELLA SALVATIERRA, "Ethics Hotlines" in Transnational Companies: A Comparative Study, Journal of Business Ethics 2009, vol. 88, pp. 199 et seq, draw a distinction between a "compliance approach" and a "value-based approach". The later preferred by many North-American multinational enterprises attempts to strengthen the internal cohesion of the enterprise around a set of values.

the whistleblower some measure of confidentiality but seem reluctant to allow for full anonymity.

Another troublesome tendency, as already stated, is the attempt of some employers to turn the right to whistleblowing in something which is quite different, if not the opposite: a duty to denounce misbehaviour by co-workers.[19] It is by no means clear to what extent an employee, who does not have supervising functions and is not responsible for someone else's performance, is bound to a duty vis-à-vis the employer to denounce the conduct of colleagues.[20] It is the general feeling, at least for a substantial body of doctrine, that such a duty does not exist, except in exceptional cases, namely when we are concerned with criminal offenses of a serious nature or threats to the safety of the working environment. The employee has a legitimate interest in keeping a good and functional relationship with his/her co-workers and that relationship might deteriorate substantially if he/she had to denounce any violation of the working rules. As a result, some writers have suggested that "ethical codes" that impose a duty on the employees to denounce to the employers infringements of those rules should not have legal relevance, namely for dismissal or other disciplinary sanctions.

Although it may look like a paradox it is, to some extent the generous legal protection granted to the employee in case of dismissal that explains the severity of the Portuguese courts in cases if whistleblowing. As a matter of fact the normal remedy in case of an unlawful dismissal remains, in Portugal, the reinstatement of the employee. In most cases of unlawful dismissal – and not just when the dismissal amounts to a discrimination – the employee has a choice between the reinstatement in the same undertaking or an indemnity. There are a few exceptions, cases where the reinstatement is not automatic: in very small enterprises (with up to ten workers) and whenever the dismissed employee has managerial and supervising functions the employer may oppose to the reinstatement and in such a case the reasons presented for this opposition will ultimately be assessed by the court that may or not decide in favour of reinstatement. If a whistleblower were to be reinstated in spite of being negligent and in cases where the accusation turned out to be false, the reinstatement of the whistleblower would be considered by some in Portugal as excessive. After all, the labour relationship is based upon trust and no one would like to work with an employee or a fellow co-worker always ready to denounce every shortcoming or wrongdoing.

Another concern seems to be that an increased protection of the whistleblower would have as an outcome a decrease in the flow of information within the enterprise itself. The representatives of the workers namely the shop stewards and the members of the workers' councils have a right to information concerning the man-

---

[19] MARIE-THESESTINNEFELD/JUDITHRAUHOFER, Whistleblower: Verantwortungsbewusste Mitarbeiter oder Denunzianten?, DuD (Datenschutz und Datensicherheit) 2008, pp. 717 et seq, p. 717.

[20] On this debate see SUSANNE MAYER, Anzeigepflicht des Arbeitnehmers, ZAS 2010, pp. 186–187 and JOHANNA NADERHIRN, Whistleblowing im Arbeitsrecht – Ausgewählte Aspekte, DRdA 2014, n.° 1, pp. 14 et seq, pp. 22–25.

agement of the enterprise. Whenever information of a confidential nature is provided to them they are under a special duty of confidentiality and secrecy that does not end even when they eventually cease to fulfil those functions. To protect them as whistleblowers – with the possible exception of very serious crimes – would undermine their special status and would probably mean that the employer would be far more reluctant than she/he already is, in providing them with sensitive information.

In short, the Portuguese reluctance in adopting a broader legal protection of whistleblowers, in the field of private employment law, seems to be based on the assumption that some measure of secrecy and mutual trust is necessary for the labour relationship to thrive and ought not to be endangered, unless in rather exceptional circumstances.

Bibliography

Adam P (2006) *Le retour des sycophantes? (à propos du whistleblowing)*, Le Droit Ouvrier, pp. 281 et seq

Bowal P (2013) *Malice and Whistleblowing*, E-Journal of International and Comparative Labour Studies, vol. 2, n.° 3, pp. 94 et seq

Calderón-Cuadrado R, Álvarez-Arce JL, Rodríguez-Tejedo I, Salvatierra S (2009) *"Ethics Hotlines" in Transnational Companies: A Comparative Study*, Journal of Business Ethics, vol. 88, pp. 199 et seq

Carinci MT (2014) *Whistleblowing in Italy: rights and protections for the employers*, WPCSDLE "Massimo D'Antona". INT, n.° 106, http://csdle.lex.unict.it, Accessed April 2015

Dworkin TM (2007) SOX and Whistleblowing, Michigan Law Review 2007, vol. 105, pp. 1757 et seq

Forst G (2011) *Strafanzeige gegen den Arbeitgeber – Grund zur Kündigung des Arbeitsvertrags?* Neue Juristische Wochenschrift (NJW) 64: 3477–3482

Forst G (2013) *Whistleblowing im internationalen Vergleich – Was kann Deutschland von seinen Nachbarn lernen?* Europäische Zeitschrift für Arbeitsrecht (EuZA) 6: 37–82

Glaser S, Komenda P (2012) *Whistleblowing in Österreich – Gefahren, Probleme, und Lösungsmöglichkeiten,* Journal für Rechtspolitik 2012, pp. 207 et seq

Gobert J, Punch M (1998) *Whistleblowers, the Public Interest and the Public Interest Disclosure Act 1998,* The Modern Law Review 2000, vol. 63, pp. 25 et seq

Gänßle P (2007) *Der Whistleblower im Spannungsfeld zwischen Korruptionsbekämpfung und arbeitsrechtlichen Pflichten.* Kritische Justiz 40: 265–277

Király A (2012) *Whistleblower in Deutschland und Grossbritannien*, Recht der Arbeit 2012, pp. 236 et seq

Lattanzi R (2010) Prime Riflessioni sul c. d. Whistleblowing. Un Modello da Replicare "ad Occhi Chiusi"?, Rivista Italiana di Diritto del Lavoro 2010, I, pp. 335 et seq

Lewis D (2001) Whistleblowing *at Work: on what Principles should Legislation be based?,* Industrial Law Journal 2001, pp. 169 et seq

Mayer S (2010) *Anzeigepflicht des Arbeitnehmers,* Zeitschrift für Arbeits- und Sozialrecht 2010, pp. 186 et seq

Moberly RE (2007) Unfulfilled Expectations: An Empirical Analysis of Why Sarbanes-Oxley Whistleblowers Rarely Win. 49 William & Mary Law Review 49: 65–155

Punch M – See Gobert J

Ragués i Vallés R (2013) *Whistleblowing, Una aproximación desde el Derecho Penal*, Marcial Pons, Madrid
Santini F (2009) *Il Diritto di Critica del Lavoratore alla Luce della Più Recente Ricostruzione dell'Obbligo di Fedeltà*, Rivista Italiana di Diritto del Lavoro, parte II, pp. 921 et seq
Schulz M (2011) *Compliance – Internes Whistleblowing*, Betriebs-Berater 2011, pp. 629 et seq
Simonet M (2013) *Notwendigkeit eines Gesetzes zum Schutz von Whistleblowern?*, Recht der Arbeit 2013, pp. 236 et seq
Tinnefeld MT, Rauhofer J (2008) *Whistleblower: Verantwortungsbewusste Mitarbeiter oder Denunzianten?*, Datenschutz und Datensicherheit 2008, pp. 717 et seq
Wiese G (2008) *Zur innerbetrieblichen und ausserbetrieblichen Kommunikation von Arbeitnehmern*, Festschrift für Hansjörg Otto zum 70. Geburtstag, De Gruyter Recht, Berlin,, pp. 621et seq

Júlio Gomes LLM (Columbia University), DPhil (Oxford), Invited Professor of Law at the Portuguese Catholic University, Member of the Católica Research Centre for the Future of Law, Judge at the Supremo Tribunal de Justiça (Portuguese Supreme Court).

Chapter 13
Romania: First Steps to Whistleblowers' Protection

Raluca Dimitriu

Abstract In Romania, the labour legislation applicable in private sector does not expressly regulate the protection of whistleblowers. The only normative act in this field is the Law no 571/2004 regarding the protection of the staff of the public authorities, public institutions and other units that notifies breaches of the law. Therefore, the only area where – in consensus between the public opinion and legal regulations – whistleblowing is encouraged is the public sector, where it focuses on denouncing corruption.

The paper aims to analyse the legal provisions in force and their consequences on legal practice, and to propose some steps to take further on in order to ensure wider and more efficient protection of whistleblowers in Romania.

Preliminaries. Who Are the Whistleblowers?

Whistleblowers – often seen as 'organizational dissidents'[1] – are persons that have a relation of subordination (labour relation or work relation) with the organization, and who inform the relevant bodies about allegedly illegalities committed by the organization or by its management.

Some authors define whistleblowing as: 'a deliberate non-obligatory act of disclosure, which gets onto public record and is made by a person who has or had privileged access to data or information of an organization, about non-trivial illegality or other wrongdoing whether actual, suspected or anticipated which implicates and is under the control of that organization, to an external entity having potential to rectify the wrongdoing.'[2] Others consider a whistleblower to be 'an employee or

---

[1] B. Martin, W. Rifkin (2004), *The Dynamics of Employee Dissent: Whistleblowers and Organizational Jiu-Jitsu*, "Public Organization Review", vol. 4, no 3, p. 221.

[2] P.B. Jubb (1999), *Whistle blowing: A restrictive definition and interpretation*, "Journal of Business Ethics", vol. 21, p. 78.

R. Dimitriu (✉)
Law Department Bucharest, Bucharest University of Economic Studies,
Romana P-ta no. 6, Bucharest, Romania
e-mail: Raluca.Dimitriu@cig.ase.ro; rdimitriu100@gmail.com

G. Thüsing, G. Forst (eds.), *Whistleblowing - A Comparative Study*,
Ius Comparatum - Global Studies in Comparative Law 16,
DOI 10.1007/978-3-319-25577-4_13

other person in a contractual relationship with a company who reports misconduct to outside firms or institutions, which in turn have the authority to impose sanctions or take other corrective action against the wrongdoers.'[3] The whistleblowers violate the 'unwritten code' of organizational relations so that they become very vulnerable to retaliation. Society in general is interested in disclosing such information, in order to remove potential damaging phenomena, so society should find mechanisms needed to encourage whistleblowers and ensure protection against potential retaliation.

The whistleblowers issue has come into the attention of the Romanian law system only relatively recently.

Being at the intersection of the labour law and administrative law, the protection of the whistleblowers seems to be rather a victim of a 'negative conflict of competence' in the Romanian law. Indeed, neither the labour law (as far as the employees are concerned), nor the administrative law (as far as the public servants are concerned) included the whistleblowers' protection as a field of study and regulation.

The only normative act in this field is the Law no 571/2004 regarding the protection of the staff of the public authorities, public institutions and other units that notifies breaches of the law,[4] which regulates certain measures regarding the protection of the persons who submit complaints or make allegations about breaches of the law in public authorities, public institutions and other units, done by individuals with management positions or executive positions in those authorities, public institutions and other public units. Romanian labour legislation, on the other hand, does not include any regulation in this field, so the employees of the private companies seem unprotected by the law if they choose to disclose to competent bodies any violations of the law or of the moral norms by their employer. Some authors state that 'apparently the actions of whistleblowing are blocked rather than stimulated by the national legislation'.[5]

Indeed, the whistleblowers' protection in the Romanian law has some characteristics, which may cause certain delays in study and regulation.

First, there is a current reluctance of people to denounce an illegal behaviour, because being a denouncer used to be encouraged by the former Communist regime and eventually the regime identified itself with this denouncement. Psychologically, informing the competent bodies about not following the rules is often regarded with cautiousness, and when the object of denouncement is the hiring company (of the employee who is under a legal confidentiality obligation), the denouncement generates aversion rather than admiration in the collective consciousness. There are therefore psychological and collective mind's motivations that justify the community's hesitation towards those who inform about potential illegalities.

---

[3] J.R. Macey, 2007, *Getting the Word Out About Fraud: A Theoretical Analysis of Whistleblowing and Insider Trading*, Faculty Scholarship Series. Paper 1383, p. 1903, available online at www.digitalcommons.law.yale.edu/fss_papers/1383, Accessed on the 1st October 2013.

[4] *Published in the Romanian Official Gazette* no. 1214 of 17th December 2004.

[5] R. Ogarca (2009) *Whistle Blowing In Romania*, "The Young Economists Journal", vol. 1, no 13, p. 108.

Besides, not only the institution or the company in which the whistleblower works has a negative attitude towards the whistleblower, but sometimes also his/her own colleagues (who can be collateral and innocent victims of the whistleblowing act that may jeopardize their jobs) are understandably reluctant. In fact, whistleblowers are those members of the organization who are willing to jeopardize their own career (and social life) for the public good.

Another characteristic of the Romanian system is that the first regulations on whistleblowing protection have been adopted in the public sector, in close correlation with corruption. Practically, currently, the only area where – in consensus between the public opinion and legal regulations – whistleblowing is encouraged is the public sector, where it focuses on denouncing corruption.

In other words, there is no general norm of whistleblowers' protection in Romania, but only special whistleblowers' protection norms for the public sector; there is no 'common law' when it comes to whistleblowing protection. There can be use as 'common law' in this field only the general law principles and the general labour law principles (such as the good-faith principle). This leads to a certain lack of balance: there is an oasis of detailed regulations in an ocean of uncertainty.

Indeed, the Romanian legislation does not refer to the employees of the private sector but only to the personnel (especially public servants) of public institutions. The option of the Romanian law-maker to regulate the whistleblowers in the public sector was justified in the context of the efforts to curb corruption. Both public opinion and the external pressure, especially from the EU – regarding corruption curbing – made the Romanian law-maker adopt a specific law on whistleblowers protection in the public sector. 'The law on whistleblower protection was formulated to respond to the gaps in the anticorruption policy framework, while blending with reform measures already implemented in the field of public administration. The law instituted a protection regime for public sector employees and also contained several strong provisions which discourage abuse of the mechanism'.[6]

The provisions of the Romanian law applies only to public authorities and institutions of the central public administration, local public administration, Parliament, Presidential Administration, Government, autonomous administrative authorities, cultural public institutions, education, health and social assistance, national companies, national and local autonomous régies and public national companies. The law applies also to persons who are appointed in scientific and consultative boards, specialized committees and other peer bodies within structures or attached to public authorities and institutions.

Therefore, the issue of the protection of whistleblowers appears especially in relation to corruption and covers exclusively the public space. The legislation of transparency – including Law no. 571/2004 and Law no. 365/2004 for the ratification of UN Convention against Corruption – covers exclusively the relations between the

[6]V. Alistar, *East-European practice in implementing whistleblowers' protection public policies – Romania's case*, p. 6, available online at www.venice.coe.int/webforms/documents/?pdf=CDL-UDT%282011%29015-e, Accessed on 23rd September 2013.

employee (especially public servant and less the contractual staff) and the public institution where he/she works.

From this point of view, a major attention enjoyed the case *Bucur and Toma v. Romania.*[7] The ECHR formulated some principles regarding the whistleblowers' protection, the notion of public interest and the conditions to ensure this protection.

But is the Romanian society ready to manage efficiently the fragile relations between private entities and their personnel, so that, without affecting the trust underlying the labour relation or the work relation, it should allow an efficient protection of whistleblowers?

This is a many-folded separate issue. While there is consensus in the Romanian public opinion regarding the need to curb corruption in the public sector, when it comes to whistleblowing in the private sector, the solutions are not equally clear.

The Range of the Whistleblowing Notion

Obviously, not all information disclosures can fall under protection. The concept of whistleblowing can be sometimes large, or vague or unclear. We may consider this concept to include:

- genuine information or information with a genuine appearance,
- having a confidential character,
- allowing a reasonable person to assume that an illegal or immoral act took place or is about to take place,
- information whose disclosure is done in good will and in the public interest,
- voluntarily,
- with the purpose of removing illegal or immoral effects or of preventing them,
- by a person in a work-related relationship
- who has no possibility to remove or prevent himself/herself these effects.

The respective person has a higher degree of vulnerability and needs special protection of the law only if all the above mentioned conditions are met.

We shall analyze these conditions by taking into account the way in which the whistleblowers' protection is articulated in the Romanian law: in detail – by a special law for the public sector, and by simply applying the general law principles for the private sector.

(a) The information disclosed shall be genuine, or at least, it shall have the appearance of being genuine, not only to the person who disclosed it, but to any other reasonable person (i.e., to an average individual, to a *bonus pater familias*).

A separate issue is the protection of whistleblowers that are making allegations erroneously or in the face of an uncertainty of the relevant facts. Other law systems

[7] *Bucur and Toma v. Romania*, no. 40238/02, 8th January 2013.

include express provisions of protection for whistleblowers who have made an error.

Theoretical, in Romanian law, according to the principle of good faith, the person working in a public authority or institution who submitted an allegation, being convinced of the reality of the facts or that the action is a breach of law, shall be protected. However, according to the *principle of responsibility*,[8] any person who makes allegations about braches of law shall support the allegations with data or information regarding the committed act.

Obviously, the extent to which an individual is indeed convinced about his/her statements – is a matter of fact, and it should be supported by evidence for each case. However, it is to take into account that the person who formulates charges has already violated the confidentiality obligation; if the accusations do not reflect reality, the person's protection may be very weak. The whistleblower may be obliged to provide evidence for the truthfulness of the statements.

However, the mere fact that the competent bodies informed by the whistleblower have found that the claimed fact does not constitute an offence or it should not be sanctioned as offence – shall not be in itself a ground to exclude the whistleblower from the legal protection. At least, this was the approach of the Romanian court in a relatively recent case.

The High Court of Cassation and Justice decided to annul a disciplinary sanction enforced on an employee of the Central Military Emergency Clinical Hospital.[9] The employee submitted a report (complaint) to the minister of defence to express his discontent regarding the managerial activity, the medical career, the teaching career as well as the behaviour of his hierarchical boss, the commander of the Central Military Emergency Clinical Hospital. Among other things, the employee claimed that the commander of the Hospital had been illegally promoted on the position of university lecturer as he hadn't the seniority needed to be promoted on such a position under the law. As a result of the employee's claim, the Minister's Control Body launched an investigation that didn't result into charges. The military prosecutor who was referred to the case about the alleged illegal acts committed by the commander of the Military Hospital decided not to launch a criminal investigation.

Next month, the employee was sanctioned, and he brought an action in court against this sanction. Following the decisions taken by the bodies which the matter was referred to, the Military Hospital felt entitled to enforce a disciplinary sanction upon the employee. The Military Hospital claimed in front of the High Court that the employee did not enjoy the provisions of Law no 571/2004 regarding the protection of the public authority staff, public institution staff and other staff who report about law violations, as the employee had ignored the principle of responsibility, under art. 4 letter c) in this law: all individuals who report about law violations should support their claim with evidence and data regarding the alleged fact.

[8] See below, section "Public sector".

[9] The High Court of Cassation and Justice, Administrative and Fiscal Contentious Section, Decision no 4743/2008, www.legeaz.net/spete-contencios-inalta-curte-iccj-2008/decizia-4743-2008.

According to the opinion of the Military Hospital, the claim of the respective employee was not supported by evidence.

However, the Court decided in this case the capacity of a good-faith whistle-blower of the plaintiff to be relevant, as the fairness of the evidence was partially proved to be true. The military prosecutor issued a decision not to launch criminal investigation, not because the alleged fact was not real (promotion in the position of university lecturer had been done based on an inappropriate seniority) but because the action was not serious enough to be seen as offence.

Consequently, the disciplinary sanction enforced on the employee was annulled by the court, although the complaint formulated by the employee of the Military Hospital did not result into criminal investigation against the commander of the hospital.

(b) The information already made public or information which is public to a certain degree cannot be subject of such disclosure.

Only confidential information shall be therefore considered, to which the whistleblower has access, by hypothesis. It is accepted that the employee's duty of fidelity ends when the interest of the employer to preserve confidentiality loses legitimacy. The employee shall be exonerated from liability in case of breach of the confidentiality obligation to the extent to which the disclosure of the information was done in order to remove or prevent a fact considered as illicit. Exoneration should be limited to the hypothesis where the disclosure of the information was done to the person or to the competent body (police, fiscal authority, environmental protection bodies, etc.).

In order to be licit, the disclosure of the information declared as confidential should be done to the public interest.

(c) According to the Law no 571/2004, informing about breaches of the law shall constitute allegations in the public interest to the extent to which it regards:

- corruption acts, offences assimilated to corruption acts, offences related to corruption acts, offences of false and offences related to the job;
- offences against the financial interests of the European Union;
- preferential or discriminatory practices or treatments in exercising attributions of public authorities and institutions;
- breaches of the provisions regarding incompatibilities and conflicts of interests;
- abusive use of material or human resources;
- political support in exercising the prerogatives of the position, except for the persons politically elected or appointed;
- braches of the law regarding access to information and decision-taking transparency;
- breaches of legal provisions regarding public procurement and non-reimbursable funding;
- incompetence or negligence at work;

- non-objective assessment of the staff during recruiting, selection, promotion, removal on a lower position;
- breaches of administrative procedures or enforcement of unlawful internal procedures;
- issuing of administrative or other documents that serve group or clientele interests;
- mismanagement or management leading to fraud of the public and private assets of public authorities and institutions;
- breach of other legal provisions imposing compliance with the principle of good management and protection of public interest.

Firstly, as we can notice, the law takes into account only the kind of acts for which the whistleblower made allegations and not the risk that the act may have a repetitive character. Consequently (unlike in other law systems) it is not relevant to what extent there is a possibility that the act for which the complaint was submitted may happen again in the future.

Secondly, we notice that the law includes a limitative list of acts that could be reported. One could consider this as a non-justified restriction that exposes whistleblowers to disadvantageous interpretation in case they report other acts than the acts listed in the law.

Thirdly, there are also taken into account, without justification, acts that are not actually violations of the law such as 'incompetence or negligence at work'. This list must be read in the context where the Law no 571/2004 was adopted, namely the national anti-corruption campaign. The scope of the law is limited on the one hand as not any violations of the law are taken into account, and broad on the other hand as it ensures the protection of those who disclose information not only about corruption, but also about the appearance of such act. In this context, incompetence to manage public assets may be the result of negligence indeed or it may hide certain illegal interests of the respective manager.

(d) Article 3 of Law no 571/2004 defines the disclosure in public interest as 'the disclosure made in good faith with regard to any action which involves a breach of the law, of the professional deontology or of the principles of good governance, efficiency, effectiveness, economy and transparency'.

Good faith is also one of the principles applicable in the matter, the law providing that the individual working for a public authority or institution shall be protected when he/she submits an allegation, as a result of the fact that he/she believes the fact is real and the act is a breach of law.

Moreover, the good-faith principle is also *a general principle of the Romanian law*. Consecrated in art. 14, para. (1): 'all physical and legal persons shall be entitled to exercise one's civil rights and obligations in good faith, according to public order and morals'.

But good faith is questionable, in case of anonymous whistleblowing. The whistleblower who does not assume one's allegations can be considered to be in violation of the principle of responsibility, expressly consecrated in the Law no 571/2004.

Besides, in the Romanian law, a problem in this case will be the efficiency of the disclosure act, because according to art. 7 of the Governmental Ordinance no 27/2002 regarding the regulations of the activity to solve petitions, 'anonymous petitions or petitions that do not include the identification data of the claimant shall not be taken into account and shall be archived'.

One could consider however that making public one's identity is the personal option of the whistleblower. To the extent to which he/she managed to make his/her complaint heard, and since the anonymity of the whistleblower ended, there is no reason why he/she should not enjoy protection against retaliation of the employer. In addition, we must mention the stipulation included in Labour Inspection's Law, according to which the labour inspectors shall keep the confidentiality of the identity of the person who submits the complaint about the non-compliance with the legal provisions and shall not disclose to the employer, to his representatives in charge or to other persons the fact that they perform the check as a result of a complaint. So the complaint is not anonymous, but the name of the whistleblower is only known by the labour inspectorate.

Besides, in certain cases of warning of public interest, a set of provisions of the Law no 682/2002 regarding the witness protection shall apply, for the protection of the identity data of the protected witness.

(e) The voluntary nature of the disclosure of such information implies that the person shall not have the duty, in one's job description, to make public that information.
(f) The purpose of the disclosure of the information needn't be proved separately. It is assumed to consist of removing the illegal or immoral act reported. However this assumption is relative (rebuttable presumption); consequently, the employer shall be able to prove that, for instance, the whistleblower served the interests of the competitor by his act.

In the Romanian legislation, Law 571/2004 does not include any reference to the motivations of the whistleblower. However, the Labour Code stipulates in art. 8 that 'labour relations shall be based on the principle of good faith', which implies that problem-making or illegitimate purposes could be considered an 'abuse of right'. As we mentioned, the principle of good faith is also consecrated in the Law no 571/2004, applicable in the public sector.

The Romanian law does not differentiate between cases where the illegal act may happen again or the whistleblower reports bygone incidents, which are unlikely to happen again. This may reinforce the conclusion that the Romanian legislation paid little attention to the real intentions of the whistleblower.

(g) The whistleblower shall be in a work-related relationship with the organization – object of the whistleblowing. It may be either a labour relation (if the whistleblower is an employee), or an administrative relation (if the whistleblower is a public servant), or even a de facto relation.[10]

[10] See Recommendation CM/Rec (2014)7 of the Committee of Ministers to member States on the protection of whistleblowers, Explanatory memorandum, para. 31: "It is the de facto working

In other law systems, this protection tends to cover the self-employed, who, although not in a relation pertaining to the labour law or to the administrative law but in a civil relation, may possess information regarding the possibility of their client to commit illegal or immoral acts.[11] However, here, the issue of the protection of the public interest confronts the issue of confidentiality that characterizes usually the relationship between the freelancer and his client. Besides, given the position of legal equality of the parties (not subordination, like in the case of the employment relations), the person who violated the confidentiality obligation and discloses such information regarding his client it is less probable to find himself in the vulnerable position. Such vulnerable position is typical for whistleblowers who are in relations pertaining to labour law or administrative law.

The Romanian legislation does not stipulate provisions regarding the protection of the self-employed; in order to enjoy protection, the whistleblower shall be a party in a labour relation (characterized by subordination). The para-subordinated work is not regulated in any way in the Romanian law.

Moreover, as we mentioned, there is a significant difference among employees as only the public employees are explicitly protected by the legislation.

The Romanian legislation in this field therefore covers exclusively public institutions; there are no such regulations in the private sector. However, we must say that even in private sector the general regulations on disciplinary sanctions and dismissal are extremely strict. For instance, disciplinary dismissal (without notice) can only take place if specific conditions are complied with, namely to expressly mention the disciplinary deviation committed and to make a disciplinary investigation procedure under the law. Consequently, although there is no express regulation to protect whistleblowers, abuses are somehow limited, since the Labour Code allows dismissal only if some strict norms are complied with.

In the case of public servants, the Law no 188/1999 stipulates that if the public servant considers that the measure received is unlawful, he/she shall justify in writing his/her refuse to comply with the respective measure. If the higher public servant, who took the respective measure, insists on its enforcement, he/she shall formulate his/her position in writing and only in this case the measure shall be obligatorily enforced.

Although we support the inclusion of the protection measures for whistleblowers employees in the Romanian legislation, as the reporting of relevant information regarding illegal or immoral acts committed by employers are useful for the public interest when they cover the private sector as well, we cannot omit that there is a difference from this point of view between public servants and employees. In the

---

relationship of the whistleblower, rather than his or her specific legal status (such as employee) that gives a person privileged access to knowledge about the threat or harm to the public interest".

[11] Or, even in a higher degree, the persons in a para-subordinated relation. *Idem*, para. 45: "In certain contexts and within an appropriate legal framework, member States might also wish to extend protection to consultants, free-lance and self-employed persons, and sub-contractors; the underlying principle of recommending protection to whistleblowers being their position of economic vulnerability vis-à-vis the person on whom they depend for work".

case of public servants, the whistleblowing acts are an element of their own ethical code. The public servant has indeed a loyalty duty towards his institution and towards the public.

(h) If the whistleblower has any other possibility to remove the effects of the reported irregularity, or to prevent it, he/she shall avoid the disclosure of the information outside the organization.

The matter has a different relevance in the case of persons who have managerial positions – who should have solved the problem within the organization, not outside the organization. As an example from practice, the information disclosure done by the new manager of the public institution regarding the previous manager is not a legitimate whistleblowing.[12]

To Whom Should Be Disclosed the Information?

The information about any misconduct should be normally disclosed to competent bodies to remove such misconduct. So, the recipient of the disclosure act is first of all the public body with competences in the field (labour inspector, environmental inspector, the Integrity Agency, etc.).

But is a whistleblower allowed to turn to the media? Is he/she somehow obliged to first submit the complaint internally? We will look a bit closer to these issues.

Disclosure to Media

The issue regarding the recipient of the disclosed information acquired significant relevance in the Romanian law because of the case *Bucur and Toma v. Romania*, on trial in the ECHR. Regarding the 'confidential' nature of the information that the plaintiff disclosed to the media, the national court decided on a condemnation because it took into account (among other things) the fact that the plaintiff did not denounce the alleged illegal acts of the director of the Romanian Intelligence Service (RIS) and did not inform the Parliamentary Commission for Oversight of the RIS activity, but – assuming that these bodies would not be efficient – turned straight to the media.

However, the ECHR found that the person had the behaviour of a whistleblower for public interest and the person became an object of protection.

The lawmaker has taken up this approach as well. According to art. 6 of Law no 571/2004, the allegation regarding the breach of law or of deontological and professional norms can be submitted alternatively or cumulatively:

[12] See also Ogarca, ibid., p. 113.

- to the hierarchical boss of the person who violated the legal provisions;
- to the head of the public authority or institution where the person who violated the legal provisions works, or where the illegal practice was found, even if the wrong-doer cannot be clearly identified;
- to the discipline commissions or other similar bodies within the public authority or institution where the person who violated the law works;
- to judicial bodies;
- to bodies responsible for finding and investigating conflicts of interests and incompatibilities;
- to parliamentary commissions;
- to the mass-media;
- to professional organizations, trade unions or entrepreneurs' associations;
- to non-governmental organizations.

So, art. 6 in the Law no 571/2004 stipulates that the allegation regarding the breach of law or of deontological and professional norms can be submitted among others to the mass-media.

But it should be noted here the limited scope of the law which has been adopted as a priority element in the campaign against corruption. Beyond this scope, the Law no 571/2004 no longer applies, but only the general law rules apply. And, given the lack of general regulations regarding the whistleblowers' protection, turning to the media to inform about law violations and not turning to bodies that are competent to solve them and / or sanction may imply the absence of good faith.

Internal Disclosure

Even thou there is no legal hierarchy of the recipients of the disclosure of information (provided in art. 6 in the Law no 571/2004), running out of internal solutions to the problem still seems to be an element indicative of the good will of the whistleblower.

This will give the entity the ability to report the wrong-doing and associated corrective action to appropriate authorities internally rather than suffering the embarrassment and potential legal penalties resulting from learning of the fraud through external channels.[13]

According to the law, the Work Rules can stipulate certain internal procedures to solve allegations and complaints, which sometimes differ depending on the violations found. Such norms included in the Works Rules could refer to whistleblowing policies and procedures. Thus, art. 242 letter d) in the Labour Code stipulates that the Work Rules shall include, among others, 'the procedure to solve individual requests or complaints of the employees'. This procedure can include forms of

[13] M.B. Curtis (2006) *Whistleblower Mechanism: A Study of the Perceptions of Users and Responders*, The IIA Research Foundation, p. 2.

mediation within the unit and solving the litigation with the whistleblower through alternative methods. Such procedures cannot be an obstacle for the employee's access to justice.

Also, some collective labour agreements include procedure to solve individual complaints of the employees. According to these collective agreements, all individual complaints shall be the object of an internal investigation done by a committee. After the check, the committee shall formulate an answer to the claimant employee. The employee who is not satisfied with the way this internal investigation takes place is free to go to court. The employee cannot be sanctioned in any way for having submitted the complaint.

And indeed, many Romanian companies stipulate in their Work Rules some specific procedures of internal reporting on potential abuses found by employees, as a solution to internally mitigate litigations. There are such internal norms, behavioural codes and ethical codes, applicable in companies and group of companies. However, 'multinationals active in the Romanian business environment have a clear propensity to import ethical codes from their origin countries by just translating them, without a detailed analysis of the local business conditions. This can be seen as a lack of intention to implement them'.

'Currently, the general trend is to implement internal behavioural codes, as a public message regarding the integrity of the company, but the lack of transparency regarding the contents of these codes indicates the low commitment to the promoted those values. Besides, the conformity structures allow no measures against high management such as the president of the company or the Board'.[14]

Regarding the alternative ways to solve conflicts, the Romanian legislation provides mediation. Thus, in 2009, after the Law no 192/2006 on mediation was amended, the professional mediator acquired the competence to solve labour conflicts. Before this modification, employment disputes were excluded from the possibility to be resolved by mediation. Currently, the mediation of such disputes can be done not only by mediation committee set up at the level of the unit, and by freelancers accredited as mediators.

However, practice is poor from this point of view. In fact, the very possibility to solve labour conflicts by mediation is controversial because according to art. 38 in the Romanian Labour Code, 'the employee cannot give up his/her rights'. As mutual concessions and giving up certain rights in exchange of others is the essence of mediation, it is difficult to accept, in the Romanian law, that such an option is viable and legal. From this perspective, the Romanian law system is less open to alternative ways to solve litigations which in other systems proved to be extremely useful in whistleblowing disputes.

Although the internal reporting seems to meet the interests of all interested parties, it is to note that there are limitations:

---

[14] Transparency International – Study on the Romanian National Integrity System (2012) available online at www.transparency.org.ro/politici_si_studii/studii/sistemul_national_de_integritate/NIS2012.pdf, p. 309, Accessed on the 12th May 2014.

- The internal reporting procedures can be difficult to conceive and enforce in small companies;
- There are few guarantees that the confidentiality of the reporting is always kept;
- The reporting does not entirely fulfil its purpose if the alleged act is highly dangerous.

Measures of Protection Under Romanian Law

Public Sector

According to the Law no 571/2004, the principles governing the whistleblowers protection for the public interest are the following:

- principle of legality, according to which public authorities and institutions shall respect the rights and liberties of the citizens, the procedural norms, the free competitiveness and the equal treatment to the beneficiaries of the public services, under the law;
- principle of supremacy of the public interest, according to which law order, integrity, impartiality and the efficiency of public authorities and institutions are protected and promoted by the law;
- principle of responsibility, according to which any individual who makes allegations about breaches of the law shall support the allegation with data or information regarding the act committed;
- principle of non-abusive sanction, according to which individuals who make allegations and submit complaints about breaches of the law shall not be sanctioned, either directly or indirectly, by enforcing unfair and more severe sanctions for other disciplinary deviations. In case of complaints for public interest, the deontological or professional norms susceptible to prevent the complaint for public interest shall not be applicable;
- principle of good management, according to which public authorities and institutions shall have the duty to perform their activity for the general interest, with high professionalism, efficiency, efficacy and economies of scale;
- principle of good conduct, according to which the act of submitting complaints about aspects of public integrity and good management, in order to enhance the administrative capabilities and the prestige of the public authorities and institutions, shall be protected and encouraged;
- principle of equilibrium, according to which no individual can take advantage of the provisions of this law to diminish the administrative or disciplinary sanction for a more serious act he committed;
- principle of good faith, according to which the individual working for a public authority or institution shall be protected when he/she submits an allegation, as a result of the fact that he/she believes the fact is real and the act is a breach of law.

These principles have had a weak practical usefulness during the 10 years when the law was in force. According to art. 11 of the law, public authorities and institutions were to harmonise their Work Rules with these principles but this did not happen in all cases.[15]

Law no 571/2004 stipulates that, in front of the disciplinary committee or other similar bodies, whistleblowers shall enjoy protection as follows:

- Whistleblowers in the public interest enjoy the good faith assumption, as long as contrary evidence does not exist (rebuttable presumption);
- Upon the request of the whistleblower who is subject to a disciplinary investigation as a result of an act of whistleblowing, the disciplinary committee or other similar bodies of the public authorities or institutions shall invite the press and a representative of the trade union or of the professional association. The information shall be made public by posting a notice on the Internet page of the public authority or institution or of the public unit at least 3 working days before the meeting, under the sanction of the nullity of the report;
- In case the person the allegation in the public interest is about is a superior in the hierarchy, either direct or indirect, or he has control, inspection and assessment attributions in relation to the whistleblower, the disciplinary committee or other similar body shall ensure the protection of the whistleblower and shall hide his identity;
- In labour litigations or litigations regarding work relations, the court can order the annulment of the disciplinary or administrative sanction enforced on a whistleblower, if the sanction was enforced as a result of an allegation in the public interest, in good faith.

Private Sector

The Romanian doctrine of labour law did not cover thoroughly the issue of whistleblowers, and general aspects of this issue can be found only in the context of anticorruption measures, namely in the sense of protecting of the staff that invokes such acts.

However, a special merit of the doctrine is to have consecrated the idea that it should be no disciplinary liability in case of inobservance of an unlawful order. It was considered that, if the unlawfulness of the order received is obvious, the refuse to execute the order shall be considered to be justified, shall be allowed and even compulsory.[16]

[15] See Alistar, ibid., p. 8.

[16] I.T. Stefanescu (2014) *Tratat teoretic şi practic de dreptul muncii*, Bucuresti, Universul Juridic Publishing House, p.772.

The protection of the whistleblower in the private sector is not ensured through specific means, but indirectly through general means provided by the law to sanction the employee.

The disciplinary sanctions applicable under the Romanian Labour Code are:

- written warning;
- demotion, accompanied by the corresponding wages, for a duration that cannot exceed 60 days;
- cut in the basic wages for a duration of 1–3 months of 5–10 %;
- cut in the basic wages and/or, as the case may be, of the management incentive for a duration of 1–3 months of 5–10 %;
- dismissal on disciplinary grounds.

On one hand, as already shown, in the private sector the protection of the employees who formulated complaints regarding their employer has rather a derived, secondary nature, arising from the general protection provided by the law to employees who are sanctioned on disciplinary grounds. On the other hand, the Romanian law on discipline at work is very strict, and it stipulates the nullity of any disciplinary sanction – even justified – if it was enforced in violation of procedural rules.

Thus, the validity of the disciplinary sanction depends on achieving the following stages:

- A report stating the disciplinary deviation;
- Summoning of the employee, in writing, for preliminary investigation. The employee shall be allowed a reasonable period of time to formulate his/her defence;
- Preliminary investigation.

During the preliminary investigation, the person charged with disciplinary deviation shall be able to defend himself/herself. The justification shall be written in the minutes of this preliminary procedure, accompanied by the modality used to deconstruct the justification. In other words, if the employee defends himself/herself by showing that the disciplinary procedure launched is retaliation resulted from a previous whistleblowing action, this shall be written in the minutes and the employer shall justify the modality used to reject this defence.

The issue of the employee's coming to the disciplinary investigation accompanied by a lawyer has been controversial so far. The issue was actually whether the disciplinary dismissal was null or not in cases where the employee was not allowed to be assisted by a lawyer during the disciplinary investigation.

The issue has been recently solved by the Law no 77/2014, that modified art. 251 para. (4) in the Labour Code with the following wording: 'During the preliminary disciplinary investigation, the employee shall be entitled to formulate and support defence and to provide to the person in charge with the investigation all evidence and justification seen as appropriate, and shall be entitled to be assisted, upon request, by a lawyer or by a representative of the union whose member he/she is'.

The employee therefore shall be entitled to appear in front of the disciplinary commission not only accompanied by the union's leader, but also – starting with the summer of 2014 – by a lawyer. This procedural modification is useful in terms of rendering the whistleblowers' protection policies more efficient; whistleblowers will be ensured qualified legal assistance during these preliminary procedures.[17]

The decision of disciplinary sanction shall be issued within 30 days since the moment when the preliminary investigation ended and within 6 months since the actual date when the act was committed.

The sanction decision shall be in written form and shall comply with some validity requirements stipulated by the law.

The main disadvantage deriving from the secondary nature of the protection of whistleblower in the private sector is that he/she can hardly defend himself/herself in case of a disciplinary sanction appropriately enforced from the procedural point of view for an actual deviation. But such a sanction could still hide retaliation for a previous reporting of an illegal act.

However, the court shall check the proportionality of the sanction enforced on the whistleblower for a disciplinary deviation, by comparing with the practice of sanctioning or with similar cases of the same company, in order to remove the possibility of an indirect sanction later on for the allegations made in the public interest.

Thus, if it finds that although the deviation is real, the sanction is not proportionate, the court shall be able to intervene and modify the disciplinary sanction. This is possible whenever the plaintiff can produce evidence that there are special causes – such as the employee's capacity of whistleblower – that caused the enforcement of a disproportionate sanction.

Regarding the onus in dismissal cases – as in all labour litigations – the burden of proof belongs to the employer and it shall produce evidence to defend itself before the first day in court (art. 272 in the Labour Code).

All these procedural aspects are modalities for the employee to protect himself/herself against managerial abuse. These are general rules applicable to all sanctioned employees, including those whose sanction was given for whistleblowing.

Dismissal of the whistleblower on another ground, such as professional inappropriateness, would also be difficult. Such a dismissal should be preceded by a preliminary assessment of the employee and only an unsatisfactory outcome may legitimate a dismissal decision. In other words, lack of discipline and lack of professional appropriateness cannot be arbitrarily invoked by the employer but carefully evidenced, to justify a valid dismissal. But there are no distinct provisions covering the protection of this category of employees against their employers' abuses.

We should notice, however, that also in the private sector, 'laws to protect whistleblowers could help organizations understand that it is in their interests to make it easier and safer for those who work for them to report their concerns and that the public should be alerted to serious wrongdoing or risk, particularly when it is not addressed. On the other hand, organizations that flout the law, engage in wrongdoing to boost profits, or whose leaders are corrupt will not want to encourage

[17] Other law systems, such as the French one, have stipulated for a long time the employees' right to be assisted by a lawyer during preliminary disciplinary procedures.

whistleblowing. In such instances, it is important that whistleblowers are legally protected for reporting information to the appropriate authorities and that they have access to appropriate remedies'.[18]

The Romanian jurisprudence regarding directly this topic is limited. The fact that a sanction or dismissal has occurred as a result of revenge is rarely invoked in courts (because it is difficult to prove the link between the act of the employer and the complaint or the allegation previously submitted by the employee). More often however the unlawfulness or the lack of justification for the measure is invoked by comparing the circumstances under which the measure was taken by the employer. Consequently, there is a rich jurisprudence in annulments of the disciplinary dismissals or of the disciplinary sanctions, and there is a very demanding legislation in this respect, even though cases where the latest cause of the abusive behaviour was the complaint previously submitted by the employee could not be easily found.

Future Prospects

In Romania, the protection of whistleblowers is only at the beginning. While the legislation covers exclusively the public institutions, it is not very effective.

As already shown, in the private sector, only the employees' general protection norms can be used by whistleblowers, and no special protection is stipulated.

The issue of the protection of whistleblowers is far from being entirely legal; it has a major moral component. Professional ethics is in fact professional morality,[19] and these 'saints of secular culture',[20] namely the whistleblowers, deserve a better image and higher social respect.[21] Some authors consider that 'being loyal to one's employer is not incompatible with blowing the whistle about their wrongdoing, because employee loyalty and the whistle-blowing serve the same goal, the moral good of the employer'.[22]

Others, in their effort to harmonize loyalty and public interest, introduced the concept of 'rational loyalty' as a learned attitude of the organization.[23]

---

[18] See 1198 Meeting, 30 April 2014, Recommendation CM/Rec(2014)7 of the Committee of Ministers to member States on the protection of whistleblowers, Explanatory memorandum, para. 8.

[19] M. Bouville (2007) Whistle-Blowing and Morality, Journal of Business Ethics, vol. 81, no 3, p. 584.

[20] C. Grant (2002), Whistle Blowers – saints of secular culture, *Journal of Business Ethics,* vol. 39, no. 4, p. 391).

[21] See also D. Balica, *Avertizorii, (încă) un instrument de luptă împotriva corupției nefolosit. Status quo, oportunități și posibile măsuri* (2011), available online at www.cogitus.ro/administratie/despre-cum-omul-poate-sa-sfinteasca-locul-avertizorii-oportunitati-si-posibile-masuri, Accessed on 8th September 2013.

[22] J. Varelius (2009) *Is Whistle-blowing Compatible with Employee Loyalty?*, "Journal of Business Ethics", vol. 85, no 2, p. 271.

[23] W. Vandekerckhove, M.S. Ronald Commers (2004), *Whistle Blowing and Rational Loyalty*, "Journal of Business Ethics", vol. 53, no 1, p. 223.

Given this complex ethical, moral and legal reality, we consider that some *de lege ferenda draft laws*, in the Romanian legislation of administrative law and labour law could be formulated. Here are some of the steps to take further on in order to ensure wider and more efficient protection of whistleblowers:

(a) The main legislative modification could be the adoption of a general protection law for whistleblowers, both in the public sector and private sector, thus transforming the already existing Law no 571/2004 in a special law (derogatory from 'common law'). The Law no 571/2004 is detailed and useful but it has a defined purpose and aims mainly at corruption, and it is not really interested in the protection of whistleblowers that report other illegal acts.

Therefore, it could be useful to adopt special provisions of protective measures for employees of the private sector who disclose information regarding illegalities committed by their employer. The issue of the protection of whistleblowers does not belong only to the public sector. Indeed, public interest can be served also by disclosing information by employees of the private sector; there are no Romanian regulations in this respect. There are large areas of public interest (such as the environmental protection) where the whistleblowers of the private sector may need the same encouragement and protection like those in public institutions.[24]

If the law in force is 'horizontally' limited, in terms of whistleblowers' protection, it goes deep when it comes to the level of their protection. In other words, only reporting on certain illegalities may entail protection, but this protection is significant.

The adoption of a law that may become 'common law' in this field may therefore establish a general protection standard, for a wider range of acts. Such a general law will not affect the Law no 571/2004;

(b) Transposition, in the Romanian legislation, of the principles formulated in the Recommendation CM/Rec(2014)7 of the Committee of Ministers to member States on the protection of whistleblowers, not enough taken into account yet by the Romanian law-makers;
(c) The express provisions regarding the possibility of trade unions to get involved in the protection of whistleblowers.
(d) Indeed, the Romanian legislation does not allow certain interest groups (e.g. trade unions, consumer protection groups) to take collective action to protect whistleblowers.

As we shown, according to art. 251 in the Labour Code, during the prior disciplinary investigation – which is compulsory before enforcement of any disciplinary sanction – the employee shall have the right to be assisted, upon request, by a representative of the trade union he is member of. Besides, according to art. 28 para. 2 in the Law on Social Dialogue no 62/2011 'in exercising their attributions,

[24] In the US, for instance, a National Whistleblower Centre was set up, a non-profit group dedicated to helping whistleblowers in their efforts 'to improve environmental protection, nuclear safety, and government and corporate accountability'. See Macey, ibid., p. 1902.

trade union organizations shall have the right to take any action under the law, including to take action in court on behalf of its members, under a written mandate from them. The action cannot be initiated or continued by the trade union organization if the person objects or expressly gives up the trial.'

Nevertheless, beyond this assistance, there is no distinct trade union right to protect the whistleblower employee, but only the general right to begin an action in court on behalf of the own members. In addition, the general role of the unions as messengers of their members was strongly diminished after the entering into force of the Law on social dialogue, which made even more difficult their representativeness in cases of whistleblowing;

(e) Increased role of mediation and other ways of alternative disputes resolution, which should allow solving the conflict without definitely affecting the image of those involved.

Indeed, these ways have the advantage of confidentiality, which is useful both for the employer and for the employee, who may believe that being visible as a whistleblower could inhibit his future job prospects;[25]

(f) Encouragement of public servants who disclose violations of the law in their institutions. A possibility is monetary incentives for whistleblowers (already existing in the US), at least in the public sector;
(g) Removal from the law of the limited list of acts that can be denounced (currently, art. 5 in the Law no 571/2004) and providing of a general protection that should cover whistleblowers who report about all violations of the law irrespective of their nature. Indirectly, such protection is currently ensured by corroborating the provisions of the Law no 571/2004, but it would be useful to leave open the list of acts that can be reported, under the law.

Bibliography

Alistar V (2013) East-European practice in implementing whistleblowers' protection public policies – Romania's case, p. 6. http://www.venice.coe.int/webforms/documents/?pdf=CDL-UDT%282011%29015-e. Accessed 23 Sept 2013

Balica D (2011) *Avertizorii, (încă) un instrument de luptă împotriva corupției nefolosit. Status quo, oportunități și posibile măsuri.* http://www.cogitus.ro/administratie/despre-cum-omul-poate-sa-sfinteasca-locul-avertizorii-oportunitati-si-posibile-masuri. Accessed 8 Sept 2013

Bouville M (2007) *Whistle-Blowing and Morality*, Journal of Business Ethics, vol. 81, no 3, p. 579–585

Curtis MB (2006) *Whistleblower Mechanism: A Study of the Perceptions of Users and Responders*, The IIA Research Foundation, available online at https://na.theiia.org/iiarf/Public%20Documents/Whistleblower%20Mechanisms%20-A%20Study%20of%20the%20Perceptions%20of%20Users%20and%20Responders%20-%20Dallas.pdf

[25] D. Lewis, (2013), *Resolving Whistleblowing Disputes in the Public Interest: Is Tribunal Adjudecation the Best that Can be Offered?*, "Industrial Law Journal", vol. 42, no 1, p. 37.

Grant C (2002) *Whistle Blowers – saints of secular culture*, Journal of Business Ethics, vol. 39, no. 4, p. 391–399

Jubb PB (1999) *Whistle blowing: A restrictive definition and interpretation,* "Journal of Business Ethics", vol. 21, p. 77–94

Lewis D (2013) *Resolving Whistleblowing Disputes in the Public Interest: Is Tribunal Adjudecation the Best that Can be Offered*?, "Industrial Law Journal", vol. 42, no 1, p. 35–53

Macey JR. (2007) Getting the Word Out About Fraud: A Theoretical Analysis of Whistleblowing and Insider Trading, Faculty Scholarship Series. Paper 1383. http://digitalcommons.law.yale.edu/fss_papers/1383. Accessed 1 Oct 2013

Martin B, Rifkin W (2004) *The Dynamics of Employee Dissent: Whistleblowers and Organizational Jiu-Jitsu,* "Public Organization Review", vol. 4, no 3, 221–238

Naderhirn J (2014) *Whistleblowing im Arbeitsrecht – Ausgewählte Aspekte,* Das Recht der Arbeit [Austrian] 2014, n.° 1, pp. 14 et seq

Ogarca R (2009) Whistle Blowing In Romania, "The Young Economists Journal", vol. 1, no 13, p. 105–114

Stefanescu IT (2014) *Tratat teoretic şi practic de dreptul muncii*, Bucuresti, Universul Juridic Publishing House

Vandekerckhove W, Ronald Commers M.S. (2004) *Whistle Blowing and Rational Loyalty,* "Journal of Business Ethics", vol. 53, no 1, p. 225–234

Varelius J (2009) *Is Whistle-blowing Compatible with Employee Loyalty?,* "Journal of Business Ethics", vol. 85, no 2, p. 263–276

Chapter 14
Protection of Persons Reporting Corruption and Other Whistleblowers in the Republic of Slovenia

Darja Senčur Peček

Abstract The article discusses the question of protection of employees and civil servants who report corruptive and other illegal and improper conduct of their employers or other persons in the Republic of Slovenia. While they are specifically protected by provisions of the Integrity and Prevention of Corruption Act in case they report corruption, they are only protected by general rules of labour law in case they report other improper conduct, for instance by rules referring to the protection against harassment and mobbing, illegal termination of employment contract and employer's liability for damages.

General

In the Republic of Slovenia, no special legal act exists which would comprehensively regulate the field of protection of employees and civil servants who have in the public interest revealed illegal, unethical, unprofessional, or otherwise improper conduct of their employer or at their workplace to competent authorities or to the public. Special protection for whistleblowers against consequences of disclosure of such information is likewise not provided by labour legislation, which nevertheless protects all the employees and civil servants from unlawful conduct by their employer (such as harassment and mobbing), as well as against unjustified termination of the employment contract.

A special regulation of protection of those whistleblowers who reported corruptive conduct is a part of Slovenian anti-corruption legislation, which follows requirements of international documents. This legislation entrusted an important role in ensuring the protection of persons reporting corruption to a special government body – the Commission for the Prevention of Corruption. As can be seen from annual reports on the work of the Commission for the Prevention of Corruption, the commission

D.S. Peček (✉)
Faculty of Law, University of Maribor, Mladinska 9, 2000 Maribor, Slovenija
e-mail: darja.sencur-pecek@um.si

G. Thüsing, G. Forst (eds.), *Whistleblowing - A Comparative Study*,
Ius Comparatum - Global Studies in Comparative Law 16,
DOI 10.1007/978-3-319-25577-4_14

has only acted in a few cases in the last 4 years since this legislation came into force.[1] The legislation, which ranks among the most adequate in the European Union,[2] is apparently not yet upheld in practice.[3]

This is also reflected by the fact that in publicly accessible case law,[4] which is in regard to the assessment of unlawful termination of the employment contract quite extensive, while it also includes court cases about harassment and mobbing, no connections with whistleblowing can be detected. Even in Slovenian labour-law theory, the issue of protection of whistleblowers has not yet been given special attention. Expert legal literature contains very few articles on this topic.[5] The commission played the most prominent role in raising public awareness and addressing issues related to the protection of whistleblowers,[6] while work of non-governmental organization was also important.[7]

Protection of Persons Reporting Corruption in Anti-corruption Legislation

General

The Republic of Slovenia has ratified Civil Law Convention on Corruption of the Council of Europe[8] and United Nations Convention against Corruption,[9] and adopted Integrity and Prevention of Corruption Act (*Zakon o integriteti in preprečevanju korupcije*, hereinafter referred to as ZIntPK)[10] in 2010. With this act, which "lays down measures and methods to strengthen integrity and transparency,

---

[1] See annual reports on the work of the Commission for the Prevention of Corruption for particular years. Available at www.kpk-rs.si/sl/komisija/letna-porocila.

[2] According to the report by Transparency International (Whistleblowing in Europe: Legal protection for whistleblowers in the EU (2013), p. 8), Slovenia, together with Luxembourg, Romania and the Great Britain, ranks in the group of countries with the most adequate legal protection.

[3] Conclusion about the need for adequate implementation of legislation in practice can also be derived from the report on the situation in Slovenia, included in the report Whistleblowing in Europe, pp. 77–78.

[4] In decisions of the Supreme Court of the RS and Higher Labour and Social Court.

[5] See for example Vuksanović I., Poziv za specialno zakonsko ureditev zaščite »žvižgačev«, Pravna praksa 45/2010, pp. 8–10.

[6] See the website of the Commission for the Prevention of Corruption, where papers, presented at conferences organized by the Commission, are published. Available at www.kpk-rs.si/sl/korupcija-integriteta-in-etika/integriteta-in-etika/eticno-in-zdravo-okolje.

[7] Society Transparency International Slovenia initiated a project Speak Up (*Spregovori*) and established the Advocacy and Legal Advice Centre for persons reporting corruption. See www.spregovori.transparency.si/sl/.

[8] Official Gazette of RS – MP, No. 8/2003 of 11th April 2003.

[9] Official Gazette of RS – MP, No. 5/2008 of 4th March 2008.

[10] Official Gazette of RS, No. 45/2010, 26/11.

to prevent corruption and to avoid and eliminate conflicts of interest«,[11] protection of persons reporting corruption is also regulated.[12] The importance of provision in the Chap. "3", which refer to protection of reporting persons, is also apparent considering their placement immediately after general principles, definition of terms and a chapter on the Commission for the Prevention of Corruption.[13]

In Chap. "3", the ZIntPK regulates reporting of corruption and protection of reporting person (Article 23), reporting unethical or illegal conduct (Article 24) and measures to protect the reporting person (Article 25).

Reporting Corruption

Art. 23 stipulates that any person may report to the Commission for the Prevention of Corruption[14] or to another competent authority cases of corrupt practice in a government body, local authority, holder of a public authorization or another legal person governed by public or private law, or of actions taken by individuals, which he believes show signs of corruption.

Protection of the Identity of the Reporting Person

One of protective measures regulated by the ZIntPK is the protection of the identity of the reporting person.[15] His identity shall not be established (if the report is anonymous) or disclosed, but only if it has been assessed by the Commission that the reporting person has filed a report in good faith or has reasonably believed that his information related to the report is true (paragraph 4 of Art. 23 of the ZIntPK).[16] In

[11] See Art. 1 of the ZIntPK.

[12] According to the first item of Art. 4 of the ZIntPK, a "corruption" means any violation of due conduct by officials and responsible persons in public or private sector, as well as conduct of persons initiating such violations or of persons benefiting from it, for the purpose of undue benefit promised, offered or given directly or indirectly, or for the purpose of undue benefit demanded, accepted or expected for one's own advantage or to the advantage of any other person.

[13] See also Kečanović B, *Zaščita posameznika, ogroženega zaradi razkrivanja korupcije*, p. 2, available at www.kpk-rs.si/sl/korupcija-integriteta-in-etika/integriteta-in-etika/eticno-in-zdravo-okolje.

[14] It is an autonomous and independent state body, which carries out tasks to prevent corruption, to enhance the rule of law, and to strengthen integrity and transparency in the society. See Article 5 of the ZintPK.

[15] In 2010, the Commission has protected the identity of the reporting person (with a pseudonym) in one case, in 2011 in 13 cases, in 2012 in 14 cases and in 2013 in 10 cases. See the Commission for the Prevention of Corruption, Annual report 2013, p. 80.

[16] For a situation when a malicious report has been filed and elements of criminal offence were not established, the ZIntPK imposes a fine for offence of between 1,000 and 2,000 EUR (first section of paragraph 2 of Art. 77 of the ZIntPK). During the period of the Commission for the Prevention of the Corruption's performance, four malicious reports were filed – two in year 2011 and two in year 2013 (Commission for the Prevention of Corruption, Annual report 2013, p. 80).

assessing whether the report has been filed in good or in bad faith, the Commission takes into account in particular the nature and gravity of the reported practice, threat of damage posed by that practice or the actual damage caused as a result, possible breach of the reporting person's duty to protect specific information, and status of the authority or person with whom the report has been filed.

Only a court may decide on disclosure of information or identity of the reporting person, if this is strictly necessary in order to safeguard the public interest or the rights of others (paragraph 8 of Art. 23 of the ZIntPK). The attempt to establish or disclose the identity contrary to these provisions is otherwise considered an offence and is punishable by a fine (third section of paragraph 1, and paragraphs 2 and 6 of Art. 77 of the ZIntPK).[17]

Along with the identity of the protected reporting person, which is secured even after the procedure has been concluded, a documentary material related to a procedure conducted by the Commission with regard to the reported suspicion of corruption is also protected. Until the procedure before the Commission or another competent authority has been concluded, this material (documents, files, evidences and other material) is not considered a public information.

Witness Protection

In cases when the reporting person and his family members are at risk due to having filed a report of corruption, they may be included in the program for the protection of witnesses and other persons who are endangered on account of their co-operation in criminal procedures, if the conditions under the Witness Protection Act (*Zakon o zaščiti prič*, hereinafter referred to as ZZPrič)[18] are met and they have given their consent (paragraph 6 of Art. 23 of the ZIntPK).

Under conditions specified in the ZZPrič, whistleblowers and their family members who are endangered due to having filed a report of some other criminal offence committed at a workplace or by the employer can also be included in the protection program.

---

[17] A fine for offence of between 400 and 1,200 EUR shall be imposed on an individual who in contravention of the provision of paragraph 4 of Art. 23 of the ZIntPK attempts to establish the identity of the reporting person; a fine of between 1,000 and 2,000 EUR shall be imposed on an individual who in contravention of the provision of paragraph 4 of Art. 23 of the ZIntPK discloses the identity, and a fine of between 400 and 4,000 EUR on a responsible person of a state body, local community body, holder of public authority, and legal person governed by public or private law which, in contravention of the provision of paragraph 4 of Art. 23 initiates a procedure for the establishment or disclosure of the identity of the reporting person due to the report being filed by this person (in the latter case, a fine for offence of between 400 and 100,000 EUR shall also be imposed on a holder of public authority or other legal peson governed by public or private law, with the exception of the Republic of Slovenia and local communities; as provided in Article 78 of the ZintPK).

[18] Official Gazette of RS, No. 113/2005, 61/06 and 110/2007.

Their inclusion in the program follows a proposal submitted by the Commission for the Prevention of Corruption (or other competent authority) and a decision of the Commission for the Protection of Witnesses Risk (composed of a Supreme Court Judge, the State Prosecutor General, a representative of the Ministry of Justice and a representative of the Ministry of Internal Affairs). The Commission for the Prevention of Corruption may also file a proposal with the State Prosecutor General to take urgent safeguarding measures (measures for protection of endangered persons before they are included in the witness protection program).

Taking into account evaluation of the type, degree and expected duration of the risk, the protection program offers a variety of measures to endangered persons, such as relocation of persons, altered documents, prevention of transmission of personal data and control of inquiries into records, concealment of identity in judicial proceedings, change of identity and economic and social support. The measure of economic and social support also relates to the field of employment regulations, since Art. 29 of the ZZPrič stipulates that protected persons shall be offered economic support until the moment of their economic independence, the latter being provided through employment with consent or assistance of the Endangered Persons Protection Unit (a special organizational unit of the police force). The Endangered Persons Protection Unit therefore helps protected person to find employment (to conclude an employment contract).[19]

Reporting Unethical or Illegal Conduct

Aside from reporting of corruption, the ZIntPK also regulates reporting of unethical or illegal conduct (Art. 24). An official person,[20] who has reasonable grounds to believe that he or she has been requested to engage in illegal or unethical conduct, or has been subject to psychological or physical violence to that end, may report such practice to the responsible person of the employer (superior or the person authorized by the superior). If there is no responsible person, or if the responsible person of the employer fails to respond to the report in writing within five working days, or if it is the responsible person of the employer himself who requests that the official should engage in illegal or unethical conduct, the report and the procedure shall fall within the competence of the Commission for the Prevention of Corruption. The responsible person of the employer or the Commission for the Prevention of Corruption shall assess the facts of the case on the basis of the report, if necessary issue appropriate instructions on further action to be taken, and take

[19] See Article 29 of the ZZPrič.

[20] Official persons are officials, high-ranking civil servants, and other public servants, as well as managers, and members of the management and supervisory boards of public sector entities. See Item 8 of Article 4 of the ZIntPK.

all the necessary steps to prevent any illegal or unethical requests and adverse consequences that may ensue.[21]

Protection of the Person Reporting Corruption (or Unethical or Illegal Conduct) Against Retaliatory Measures

If the reporting person (of corruption, unethical or illegal request) has been subjected to retaliatory measures by his employer which have resulted in damage, the ZIntPK provides basis for his right to claim compensation for the unlawfully caused damage by the employer (paragraph 1 of Art. 25 of the ZIntPK).[22]

The responsible person of the employer[23] who causes damage to the reporting person or subjects him or her to retaliatory measures is also punishable by a fine for offence of between 400 and 4,000 eur (paragraph 7 of Art. 77 of the ZIntPK), while the employer is punishable by a fine of between 400 and 100,000 eur.[24]

Considering the fact that the employers can subject employees and civil servants who have reported corruptive conduct[25] to various measures with adverse consequences (such as disciplinary measures, termination of employment, mobbing), while it can be difficult for the employees and civil servants to prove that these measures are connected to the report of corruption, a role of the Commission for the Prevention of Corruption is very important in this aspect. The Commission may offer assistance with establishing a causal link between retaliatory measures and damage to the reporting persons (paragraph 2 of Art. 25 of the ZIntPK).[26]

If during the course of this procedure the Commission establishes a causal link between the report and the retaliatory measures, it shall demand that the employer ensures immediate discontinuation of such conduct (paragraph 3 of Art. 25 of the ZIntPK).[27] If he should fail to comply, the ZIntPK imposes on the responsible person of the employer a fine for the offence of between 400 and 4,000 eur

---

[21] The Commission has provided protection for an official person in five cases (all in 2012). See the Commission for the Prevention of Corruption, Annual report 2013, p. 80.

[22] The employer's liability for damage caused by the employer to the employee due to infringement of employment rights, and especially the employer's liability for damages in the event of unequal treatment, harassment of employees or mobbing is also stipulated in labour legislation (see section "Protection of employees and civil servants against unfounded measures by their employer").

[23] This includes responsible persons of all employers (state body, local community body, holder of public authority, or other legal person governed by public or private law).

[24] Provision in Article 78 of the ZintPK applies to all the employers (holders of public authority or other legal persons governed by public or private law), with the exception of the Republic of Slovenia and local communities.

[25] Also official persons who have reported unethical or illegal conduct.

[26] The Commission has thus far provided such assistance in four cases (in year 2012). See the Commission for the Prevention of Corruption, Annual report 2013, p. 80.

[27] The Commission has so far only submitted one such request (in year 2011). See the Commission for the Prevention of Corruption, Annual report 2013, p. 80.

(paragraph 8 of Art. 77 of the ZIntPK), and on the employer a fine of between 400 and 100,000 eur (Art. 78 of the ZintPK).

A very important issue is regulation of burden of proof in a dispute initiated by a reporting person because of retaliatory measures. If a reporting person cites facts in a dispute that give grounds for the assumption that he has been subject to retaliation by the employer due to having filed a report, the burden of proof shall rest with the employer (paragraph 5 of Art. 25 of the ZIntPK). The employer can therefore only be exonerated if he can prove that measures were not retaliatory or that they were justified (e.g. existence of justified reasons for termination of employment).[28]

Continuation of work in his or her current work environment can very often become difficult for the reporting person; therefore, the most efficient protective measure is a change of work post. Legislation only offers this option to the reporting person who is a civil servant. He can request to be transferred to another equivalent work post.[29] Such a request may be made if he continues to be the focus of retaliation despite the Commission for the Prevention of Corruption's demand that such conduct is to be discontinued, making it impossible for him to continue work in his current work post. Civil servant shall request to be transferred to another workplace and inform the Commission of this request.[30] The employer has an obligation to ensure that civil servant's demand is met within 90 days at the latest, and to inform the Commission for the Prevention of Corruption of this fact (paragraphs 4 and 6 of Art. 25 of the ZIntPK). If the employer fails to transfer the civil servant without providing justified reasons, the ZIntPK imposes on the responsible person of the employer a fine for the offence of between 400 and 4,000 eur (paragraph 9 of Art. 77 of the ZIntPK), and on the employer a fine of between 400 and 100,000 eur (Art. 78 of the ZintPK).

Protection of Employees and Civil Servants Against Unfounded Measures by Their Employer

General

Retaliatory measures taken by employers against employees or civil servants reporting irregularities at their workplace can have different contents. A whistleblower may have to deal with threats, violence, harassment or mobbing by the employer or his other employees, as well as with termination of employment contract.

[28] Burden of proof that rests with the employer in cases of discrimination, harassment and mobbing, as well as termination of the employment contract, is also stipulated in labour legislation (see section "Protection of employees and civil servants against unfounded measures by their employer").

[29] Even though this is not explicitly stipulated by the law, mostly transfers to another body will be suitable (for example, from one ministry to another).

[30] Up to now, the Commission for the Prevention of Corruption has not yet been informed of any such requests. See the Commission for the Prevention of Corruption, Annual report 2013, p. 80.

Slovenian labour legislation does not explicitly protect whistleblowers against such practices and conduct by the employer, but they are nonetheless indirectly protected by provisions that prohibit harassment and mobbing in the workplace, which at the same time impose an obligation on the employer to protect employee's dignity at work, and by provisions protecting employees against unlawful termination of employment contract.[31] In labour legislation, some of these measures are also considered an offence, punishable by a fine, while the Criminal Code (*Kazenski zakonik*, hereinafter referred to as KZ-1)[32] regulates criminal offences against employment relationship and social security.

Individual employment relationships in the Republic of Slovenia are comprehensively regulated by the Employment Relationship Act (*Zakon o delovnih razmerjih*, hereinafter referred to as ZDR-1).[33] This act regulates both employment relationship of employees in a private sector, and employment relationship of civil servants (persons conducting employment contracts in a public sector), unless stipulated otherwise by a special act for civil servants. This special act, the Civil Servants Act (*Zakon o javnih uslužbencih*, hereinafter referred to as ZJU),[34] regulates some particularities of civil servants' employment (mainly those employed in state bodies or local communities).

Protection of Employees and Civil Servants from Harassment and Mobbing

The ZDR-1 lists obligation to protect the employee's integrity amongst obligations of the employer. The employer must protect and respect the employee's integrity and take into account and protect the employee's privacy (Art. 46). The cited provision is concretised with provisions related to various aspects of this obligation, including prohibition of harassment and mobbing.

Art. 7 of the ZDR-1 regulates prohibition of sexual and other harassment and workplace mobbing. Harassment is defined as any undesired behaviour associated with any personal circumstance with the effect or intent to adversely affect dignity of a person or to create intimidating, hateful, degrading, shaming or insulting environment. Workplace mobbing is any repeated or systematic, wrong or clearly negative and offensive treatment or behaviour directed at individual employees at the workplace or in connection with work. Employee who is a victim of harassment or mobbing, as well as persons who offer their assistance to the victim, must not be exposed to unfavourable consequences because of actions aimed at asserting the prohibition of harassment or workplace mobbing.

---

[31] Special provisions regarding the protection of employees who report irregularities are provided only by Banking Act (Zakon o bančništvu, Official Gazette of RS, No. 25/2015; ZBan-2), which requires banks to protect employees who internally (to the employer) report breaches of banking regulations and the bank's internal acts, or report breaches to the Bank of Slovenia. See Articles 140 and 239 of ZBan-2.

[32] Official Gazette of RS, No. 50/2012-UPB2.

[33] Official Gazette of RS, No. 21/2013.

[34] Official Gazette of RS, No. 63/2007 UPB-1, 65/2008.

The ZJU also defines a principle of prohibition of harassment in Art. 15.a, which prohibits any physical, verbal or non-verbal action or conduct by a civil servant that is based on any personal circumstance and results in intimidating, hateful, degrading, shaming or insulting environment for a person and offends their dignity. By classifying the prohibition of harassment amongst common principles of the civil servants system,[35] the ZJU emphasizes importance of this prohibition, but does not regulate it specifically for civil servants. Stipulations in the ZDR-1 therefore apply to both employees and civil servants.[36]

The employer has a duty to provide work environment where no employee is subjected to harassment or mobbing by the employer, a superior or by other employees. To this end, the employer must take appropriate steps to protect employees from harassment or mobbing in the workplace. The employer must inform the employees about adopted measures in writing, in a manner customary for the employer (Art. 47 of the ZDR-1).

Protection of employees against harassment, mobbing and similar conduct is also an aspect of the employer's obligation to provide employees with safe and healthy conditions (Art. 45 of the ZDR-1). Art. 24 of the main legal act in this field, the Occupational Health and Safety Act (*Zakon o varnosti in zdravju pri delu*, hereinafter referred to as ZVZD-1)[37] imposes a duty on the employer (in private and public sector) to adopt measures to prevent, eliminate and manage cases of violence, mobbing, harassment and other forms of psychosocial risks at the workplace which can pose a threat to employees' health.

The importance of this duty of the employer in the public sector is also specifically emphasized in the ZJU, which amongst the common principles of the civil servants system explicitly regulates principle of protection of professional interests. The provision of the first paragraph of Art. 15 thus imposes a duty on the employer to protect a civil servant against mobbing, threats and similar conduct, which can pose a threat to his work performance.

Art. 8 of the ZDR-1 determines that in the event of violation of the prohibition of harassment or workplace mobbing, the employer is liable to provide compensation to the employee under general rules of civil law. Non-pecuniary damage sustained by an employee also includes mental distress suffered due to failure to provide protection against harassment or workplace mobbing. When determining the amount of compensation for non-pecuniary damage, it must be taken into account that the compensation has to be effective and proportional to damage suffered by the employee, and that it also needs to discourage the employer from repeating the violation. The function of monetary compensation is therefore mainly deterrent and punitive.[38]

---

[35] These principles apply to all civil servants, both those who are employed in state bodies and local communities, and those who are employed in public institutions, public agencies, public funds, and other entities of public law that indirectly use state or local budgetary funds.

[36] Everything stated below with regard to the protection of employees against these conducts applies to both employees and civil servants.

[37] Official Gazette of RS, No. 43/2011.

[38] This is a new regulation of compensation in case of harassment and mobbing, by which provisions from the EU directives that refer to the prohibition of discrimination were implemented in

If, in the event of a dispute related to harassment or mobbing in the workplace, facts cited by an employee give grounds for suspicion that the employer has acted contrary to the first paragraph of Art. 47 (i.e. had failed to provide work environment where no employee is subjected to harassment or mobbing), the burden of proof shall rest with the employer.

The employee may extraordinarily terminate the employment contract if the employer has failed to ensure the protection against harassment or mobbing in the workplace in accordance with Art. 47 of the ZDR-1.[39] The employer shall pay severance (in the same amount that would be granted to the employee in the case of ordinary termination of the employment contract for business reasons by the employer) to the employee who has extraordinarily terminated the employment contract, and compensation amounting to no less than the amount of the lost remuneration during the notice period.

A fine for the offence can be imposed on an employer who fails to provide protection against harassment or mobbing in accordance with the first paragraph of Art. 47 of the ZDR (in accordance with paragraph 7 of Art. 217 of the ZDR-1), and on the responsible person of the employer.[40]

Furthermore, Art. 197 of the Criminal Code defines the criminal offence of "workplace mobbing", which also includes psychological violence and mobbing at the workplace or in relation to work, resulting in another employee's feelings of degradation or fear. The offender (another employee or supervisor) can be sentenced to imprisonment for not more than 2 years, or for not more than 3 years if the offence results in psychological, psychosomatic or physical illness or reduction of work productivity of the employee.

Protection of Employees and Civil Servants Against Unlawful Termination of Employment Contract

ZDR-1 and ZJU both stipulate that the employer may only terminate employee's or public servant's employment contract if there is a substantiated reason provided in these acts, and only in accordance with provisions of these acts (relating to

---

Slovenian legislation. For more, see Kresal, B., Kaj prinaša novi zakon o delovnih razmerjih, Delavci in delodajalci 1/2013, pp. 57, 58.

[39] Prior to extraordinary termination of the employment contract, the employee must remind the employer in writing to comply with his obligations and inform the Labor Inspectorate of the violation in writing. If within a period of three working days the employer fails to fulfil his obligations or fails to rectify the violation, the employee may terminate the employment contract within a 30-day period.

[40] The employer (a legal person, a sole proprietor or a self-employed person) shall be punished by a fine of between 3,000 and 20,000 EUR; smaller employer (with ten or less employees) by a fine of between 1,500 and 8,000 EUR; an individual employer by a fine of between 450 and 1,200 EUR; and a responsible person of the employer (of a legal person, but also in a state body or a local community) by a fine of between 450 and 2,000 EUR.

the employee's possibility of defence, to the role of employee representatives, to the form and content of termination and to the service of notice of termination). The burden of proof rests with the employer. These acts moreover determine circumstances or conduct that must not be considered a justified reason for the termination, for instance, trade union membership, participation in a strike, participation in trade union activities, as well as filing an action or participation in proceedings against the employer due to allegations of his violations of contractual or other obligations arising from the employment relationship before arbitration, court or administrative authorities, and others (Art. 90 of the ZDR-1).

If an employee is of opinion that the termination of the employment contract was unlawful (either because reasons were not justified or because of procedural reasons), he may request before the competent labour court to establish illegality of termination within 30 days from the day of the service. If the employer fails to prove the existence of reasons for termination, or if there are procedural reasons (e.g. if the employer fails to prove that the notice of termination has been served, or if the employee has not been granted a possibility of defence), the court shall establish that the termination of the employment contract is unlawful, and determine that the employee shall return to work, or under certain condition grant the employee adequate compensation instead of reintegration.[41]

A civil servant may file an appeal against the termination of the employment contract with the appellate commission, whereas a judicial review is only allowed if the civil servant has exhausted the right to appeal. Civil servant may request judicial review within 30 days after being served with the decision of the appellate commission or after the deadline for issuing the decision of the appellate commission has expired. If the unlawfulness of the termination of the employment contract is established, the civil servant shall also be ordered to return to work, or shall be under certain conditions granted compensation instead.

The KZ-1 defines criminal offence of violation of fundamental rights of employees in chapter on criminal offences against employment relationship and social security (in Art. 196). This criminal offence is also committed by whoever consciously acts contrary to regulations governing the termination of employment relationship, thereby restraining or depriving an employee of any of his rights, and is punishable by a fine or sentence to imprisonment for not more than 1 year. If this act results in unlawful termination of the employment relationship, the offender shall be sentences to imprisonment for not more than 3 years.

[41] The proposal can be made by either employee or employer, and the court may grant compensation instead of reintegration, if it has been established that with regard to all the circumstances and interests of both contracting parties, the continuation of the employment relationship would no longer be possible. See Art. 118 of the ZDR-1.

Protection of Whistleblowers in Slovenian Legal System

Who Is Protected as a Whistleblower?

General definition of whistleblowers and their protection against retaliatory measures of the employer is not provided in Slovenian legislation. Legal status of persons who report unlawful, unethical or otherwise inappropriate conduct of the employer or at the workplace depends on whether their report referred to the corruption (and in the case of official persons to unethical and illegal conduct) or to other types of conduct. In the first case, they are subject to protection provided by the ZintPK, while in the second case, they are generally protected against unjustified and illegal measures of the employer by labour legislation.[42]

Anyone can report corruption and thus be protected as a reporting person in accordance with the ZintPK. Art. 25 of the ZintPK, which provides measures that can be taken by the Commission for the Prevention of Corruption to protect the reporting person against retaliatory measures of the employer, however, can be understood to protect persons who are in employment relationship with the employer, i.e. employees and civil servants. Only civil servants, and not employees, are entitled to request a transfer to another work post.

ZDR-1 applies to both employees and civil servants regarding matters that are not otherwise regulated by the Civil Servants Act. Employees and civil servants who were victims of harassment or mobbing, as well as other employees and civil servants who have assisted the victims, all enjoy protection against harassment and mobbing. Employees and civil servants, as well as economically dependent persons[43] are also entitled to protection against termination of the employment contract due to unfounded reasons.

What Actions Are Defined or Protected as Whistleblowing?

Slovenian legislation does not stipulate general obligation of whistleblowing, neither does it provide for any rewards or financial incentives for whistleblowers.

---

[42] Only bank employees are also subject to special regulation in accordance with ZBan-2. Bank shall adopt measures to protect employees who report breaches of banking regulations via internal reporting lines to the bank or to the Bank of Slovenia against retaliatory acts, discrimination or other forms of inappropriate treatment.

[43] According to Art. 213 of the ZDR-1, an economically dependent person is a self-employed person who on the basis of a civil law contract performs work in person; for remuneration, independently and for a longer period of time in circumstances of economic dependency, and does not employ employees himself. Economic dependency means that a person obtains at least 80 % of his or her annual income from the same contracting partner (client).

In accordance with Article 145 of the Criminal Procedure Act (*Zakon o kazenskem postopku*, ZKP),[44] however, all state agencies and organisations having public authority are bound to report criminal offences liable to public prosecution of which they have been informed or which were brought to their notice in some other way.

The ZintPK only refers to the protection of employees and civil servants who report corruption (and to the protection of official persons who report unethical or illegal conduct).

The ZintPK allows for anonymous report of corruption to the Commission for the Prevention of Corruption, and in addition to that, it is also possible to anonymously report a criminal offence to the criminal law enforcement authorities.

The first paragraph of Art. 23 of the ZintPK, which regulates the reporting of corruption to the Commission for the Prevention of Corruption or to another competent authority, also does not affect the right of the reporting person to inform the public of the corrupt practice (unless the report contains information that is by law determined as classified information.[45]

The ZintPK does not require the person reporting corruption to inform first the employer or person authorised by the employer of the corrupt practice, before filing the report with the Commission for the Prevention of Corruption or other competent authority. This requirement is only stipulated in connection with report of unethical or illegal conduct by an official person (Art. 24 of the ZintPK).

The Commission for the Prevention of Corruption takes into account the good faith of the reporting person, and thus only protects the identity of the reporting person who has filed a report in good faith or has reasonably concluded that his information regarding the report is true. Furthermore, only a reporting person who has acted in good faith enjoys protection against his employer, while malicious filing of a report is also considered an offence punishable under provisions of the ZIntPK, or can even result in criminal charges if elements of a criminal offence have been established.

What Is the Level of Protection of Whistleblowers?

According to provisions in the ZintPK, employees or civil servants who have reported corrupt practices are protected against retaliatory measures of the employer. Since the act does not specify retaliatory measures, all the practices and conduct of the employer can be considered as such, including termination of the employment contract. Important is the role of the Commission for the Prevention of Corruption when establishing a causal link between the report and retaliatory measures (mobbing, termination of the employment contract) and authority of the Commission to demand immediate discontinuation of such conduct. Another important provision

[44] Official Gazette of RS, No. 31/2012 ZKP UPB8.

[45] In which case the reporting person can only inform the commission or criminal law enforcement authorities (paragraph 2 of Art. 23 of the ZIntPK).

states that in the event of a dispute (due to mobbing, due to unlawful termination of the employment contract), the burden of proof rests with the employer. The employer will thus have to prove that his conduct was not a retaliatory measure resulting from the report. Civil servants also have an option of transfer to another equivalent work post, which is often the most efficient measure.

In all the other cases (where there is no report of corruption), whistleblowers are protected from harassment and mobbing under general provisions of labour legislation.[46] These provisions stipulate that the burden of proof rests with the employer, who has to prove that he has not violated his duty to provide work environment free of harassment and mobbing. An employee is entitled to compensation, or may also extraordinarily terminate the employment contract.

Protection of whistleblowers against unlawful termination of employment contract also falls under the scope of general provisions of labour legislation. The employer will have to prove before the court that the reason for the termination was substantiated. Whistleblower will sensibly support his claims that the termination was unlawful because it was a consequence of disclosing improper conduct by the employer (which is an unfounded reason for termination) with Art. 90 of the ZDR-1, which lists participation in proceedings against employer (due to violations of contractual or other obligations arising from the employment relationship) amongst the unfounded reasons for termination of employment contract.

Conclusions

Slovenian ZintPK regulates measures to ensure protection of employees, and especially civil servants, who report corruptive practices. So far, there have only been a few cases of intervention by the Commission for the Prevention of Corruption in practice, suggesting that employees and civil servants are afraid to expose and reveal corruption.

This is even more true in cases of disclosure of other illegal and inappropriate conduct, when employees and civil servants are protected only by general rules of labour legislation. Even though Slovenian labour legislation and case law of specialized labour courts provide employees (and thus also whistleblowers) with adequate protection against harassment and mobbing and against unlawful termination of employment contract, the status of whistleblowers is not yet sufficiently protected. There is an obvious need to include special provisions related to the whistleblowing into labour legislation, or to regulate the protection of whistleblowers (not only of persons reporting corruption) with a special act.

---

[46] Only employees in banks are given a special protection. Banks shall protect the identity of employees who have reported breaches of banking regulations and the bank's internal acts, as well as adopt measures to prevent retaliatory acts, discrimination or other forms of inappropriate treatment of these employees, and measures to reverse the consequences of retaliatory acts, if inappropriate treatment has nevertheless occurred.

Bibliography

Commission for the Prevention of Corruption, Annual report 2013. https://www.kpk-rs.si/sl/komisija/letna-porocila. Accessed April 2015

Criminal Code (Kazenski zakonik, KZ-1), Official Gazette of RS, No. 50/2012-UPB2

Criminal Procedure Act (Zakon o kazenskem postopku, ZKP), Official Gazette of RS, No. 31/2012 ZKP UPB8

Employment Relationship Act (Zakon o delovnih razmerjih, ZDR-1), Official Gazette of RS, No. 21/2013

Integrity and Prevention of Corruption Act (Zakon o integriteti in preprečevanju korupcije, ZIntPK), Official Gazette of RS, No. 45/2010, 26/11 and 43/11

Banking Act (Zakon o bančništvu, ZBan-2), Official Gazette of RS, No. 25/2015

Bowers J, Fodder M, Lewis J, Mitchell J (2012) Whistleblowing: Law and practice, 2nd edn, OUP Oxford

Kečanović B, Zaščita posameznika, ogroženega zaradi razkrivanja korupcije, page 2. https://www.kpk-rs.si/sl/korupcija-integriteta-in-etika/integriteta-in-etika/eticno-in-zdravo-okolje. Accessed April 2015

Kresal B, Kaj prinaša novi zakon o delovnih razmerjih, Delavci in delodajalci 1/2013, pp. 55–75

Vuksanović I (2010) *Poziv za specialno zakonsko ureditev zaščite »žvižgačev«,* Pravna praksa 45/2010, pp. 8–10.

Darja Senčur Peček Associate Professor at the Faculty of Law, University of Maribor, where she is teaching Labour Law and Social Security Law. Head of the Labour Law Department and a head of the Institute for Employment Relations and Social Security at the Faculty.

Chapter 15
Financial Incentives and Truth-Telling: The Growth of Whistle-Blowing Legislation in the United States

Shawn Marie Boyne

Abstract Although government efforts to encourage whistleblowers to come forward date back to 1778, the United States has enjoyed a conflicted history with respect to whistleblowers. While some commentators pillory Edward Snowden, some privacy rights advocates praise his actions. Perhaps reflecting these conflicting sentiments, current protections in the U.S. are a patchwork collection of industry-specific legislation. The current slate of legislation is largely the result of the confluence of recurring waves of media publicity exposing government fraud, the growth in government spending and involvement, and Congress's attempts to respond to adverse publicity concerning government fraud. The succession of public crises running from Watergate to the wasteful spending in the Iraq War, to the collapse of the financial and securities industries have demonstrated that the government needs whistleblowers to help expose fraud and waste. As successive legislative attempts to extend whistleblower protections have demonstrated, reform "is usually precipitated by some crisis or new political movement that disrupts the preexisting status quo."

Introduction

> [I]t is the duty of all persons in the service of the United States to give the earliest information to Congress or any other proper authority of any misconduct, frauds or misdemeanors committed by any officers or persons in the service of these states, which may come to their knowledge. [Continental Congress-1778][1]

Although the history of whistleblowing in America predates the country's official birth, a whistleblower's path remains a difficult one. To be sure, truth-tellers

[1] Stephen M. Kohn, The Whistle-Blowers of 1777 *New York Times* (12 June 2011) www.nytimes.com/2011/06/13/opinion/13kohn.html.

S.M. Boyne (✉)
Indiana University Robert H. McKinney School of Law,
530 West. New York St., Indianapolis, IN 46202, USA
e-mail: smboyne@iupui.edu

G. Thüsing, G. Forst (eds.), *Whistleblowing - A Comparative Study*,
Ius Comparatum - Global Studies in Comparative Law 16,
DOI 10.1007/978-3-319-25577-4_15

who succeed in court may receive lucrative bounty payments. However, despite the benefits whistleblowers provide to society, whistleblower protections in the U.S. remain an inconsistent legislative patchwork. Rather than offer a dependable path to financial security, on both the federal and state levels, the protections have generated "inconsistent outcomes and incentives."[2] Despite these hurdles and inconsistencies, under the federal False Claim Act alone, whistleblowers had helped the government recover over $17 billion in public funds by September 2013.[3]

One unique comparative aspect of America's legislative scheme is the growing use of financial incentives on both the federal and state levels to encourage whistleblowers to come forward. For years, policymakers believed that first and foremost, prospective whistleblowers would come forward if legislators provided them with statutory protection. Although this policy choice resonates with the popular belief that most whistleblowers suffer severe retaliation, the proliferation of anti-retaliation statutes did not spur disclosures.[4] In contrast, when the Federal Claims Act was amended in 1986 to increase the likelihood that a whistleblower would receive a financial award, the number of FACA reports of false claims for government funds increased from an average of 6 per year to almost 2 per day in 1999.[5]

Amidst the widespread media coverage over the past year detailing the disclosure of top secret information by Bradley Manning and Edward Snowden, reporters chose to use the labels of "whistleblower" and "traitor" to describe both individuals. Indeed, the oft-repeated maxim that "one man's whistleblower is another man's traitor" seemed to ring particularly true with respect to the media's coverage of these particular cases. The decision regarding which label was appropriate varied depending on the speakers' view of the proper balance between government secrecy and transparency.[6] While top Congressional leaders condemned both disclosures, civil liberties advocates criticized government officials and even took aim at the President[7] and his Director of National Intelligence, James Clapper.[8] In the wake of the Snowden disclosures, it became evident that Clapper had lied to Congress during

[2] ND Bishara, ES Callahan, and TM Dworkin, The Mouth of Truth (2013) 10 *New York University Journal of Law & Business* 37, 43.

[3] Justice Department Recovers $3.8 Billion from False Claims Act Cases in Fiscal Year 2013 (*U.S. Department of Justice* 20 December 2013). Available at www.justice.gov/opa/pr/justice-department-recovers-38-billion-false-claims-act-cases-fiscal-year-2013.

[4] Bishara (n 2) 59–60.

[5] Bishara (n 2) 61.

[6] Brendan Sasso, 'Amash: Snowden is a Whistleblower'(*The Hill*, 4 August 2013). Available at www.thehill.com/blogs/blog-briefing-room/blog-summaries/315413-rep-amash-snowden-is-a-whistleblower11.

[7] Pema Levy, 'NSA FISA Surveillance: Is Obama's Latest Transparency Move A Trick?' *International Business Times* (30 August 2013). Available at www.ibtimes.com/nsa-fisa-surveillance-obamas-latest-transparency-move-trick-1401972.

[8] Fred Kaplan, 'Fire DNI James Clapper: The Director of National Intelligence lied to Congress about NSA surveillance' (*Slate* 13 June 2013). Available at www.slate.com/articles/news_and_politics/war_stories/2013/06/fire_dni_james_clapper_he_lied_to_congress_about_nsa_surveillance.html.

his previous testimony about the scope of the data collected by National Security Agency (NSA).[9]

American's views of Snowden himself have varied widely. While a Quinnipiac poll published on August 1st, 2013 found that 55 % of the population queried believed that he was a whistle-blower,[10] 53 % of individuals questioned in a July 2013 ABC News/Washington Post poll believed that the government should pursue criminal charges against Snowden.[11] These attitudinal variations reflect the complex nature of whistle-blowing itself.

The question of whether a whistleblower will be protected or pilloried depends on the interests of those in power. In a frenetic media environment in which media outlets rush to publish "leaked information" to sell copy, government officials often leak information to gain political advantage. For example, in the months leading up to the 2012 presidential election, Administration sources leaked information concerning the Bin Laden raid, the Stuxnet attacks on Iran's nuclear facilities, and even the President's hands-on involvement in drone attacks on foreign soil.[12] Of course, as the prosecution of former Vice President Dick Cheney's aide, Lewis Scooter Libby, revealed, the Obama Administration is not the first Administration to use leaks to achieve a political advantage.[13]

While the Obama Administration, like its predecessors, has selectively used leaks to gain political advantage, critics charge that the Administration's pursuit of public whistleblowers has grown vindictive.[14] A key case, which illustrates the Administration's persecution of national security whistleblowers, is the FBI's investigation of *New York Times* reporter James Risen. The government has subpoenaed Risen hoping to uncover the source of the intelligence disclosures published in his 2006 book, "State of War." The government is seeking to compel Risen to finger former CIA agent, Jeffrey Sterling, as the book's prime source. Ironically, Risen's book drew the Administration's ire because, rather than revealing the Administration's

---

[9] Kimberly Dozier, James Clapper: Answer On NSA Surveillance To Congress Was Clearly Erroneous (*Huffington Post* 2 July 2013) Available at www.huffingtonpost.com/2013/07/02/james-clapper-nsa_n_3536483.html.

[10] Quinnipiac University Poll, Snowden Is Whistle-Blower, Not Traitor, U.S. Voters Tell Quinnipiac University National Poll (*Quinnipiac University Poll*, 1st August 2013). Available at www.quinnipiac.edu/images/polling/us/us08012013.pdf.

[11] Gary Langer, 'Attitudes Shift Against Snowden; Fewer than Half Say NSA is Unjustified' (*ABC News*, 24 July 2013). Available at www.langerresearch.com/uploads/1150a3SnowdenandSecurity.pdf/.

[12] Peter Van Buren, Obama's War on Whistleblowers (*Mother Jones* 12 June 2012). Available at www.motherjones.com/politics/2012/06/obamas-whistleblowers-stuxnet-leaks-drones.

[13] US Officials 'betrayed' CIA Agent (*BBC News*, 14 July 2006). Available at www.news.bbc.co.uk/2/hi/americas/5180906.stm.

[14] Tim Shorrock, Obama's Crackdown on Whistleblowers (*Nation*, 5 April 2013). Available at www.thenation.com/article/173521/obamas-crackdown-whistleblowers#.

national security successes, it detailed the CIA's unsuccessful efforts to funnel defective weapons blueprints to Iran.[15]

Ironically, while many members of Congress chastised Edward Snowden for failing to work within the system to report government abuse, three career employees of the National Security Administration (NSA) employees who did just that found their lives destroyed and reputations tarnished. One recent NSA whistleblower, William Binney, described what happened when the three employees attempted to use internal channels to expose the fact that the government was illegally spying on its own citizens:

> We tried to stay for the better part of 7 years inside the government trying to get the government to recognize the unconstitutional, illegal activity that they were doing and openly admit that and devise certain ways that would be constitutionally and legally acceptable to achieve the ends they were really after. And that just failed totally because no one in Congress or — we couldn't get anybody in the courts, and certainly the Department of Justice and inspector general's office didn't pay any attention to it. And all of the efforts we made just produced no change whatsoever.[16]

When the trio used internal channels to complain, the Pentagon's inspector general responded, not by seeking to validate their claims, but rather by referring their names to the Department of Justice for prosecution under the Espionage Act.[17] In the Administration's eyes, the trio's allegations that NSA had wasted millions of dollars on a "technically flawed system for sifting through digital communications" did not further the public's interests.[18]

The U.S. government proceeded to prosecute one of the NSA whistleblowers, Thomas Drake. Drake was spared a possible life sentence when the government's case fell apart prior to trial after a federal judge ruled that the government could not proceed without publicly disclosing classified evidence. After accepting a plea offer to a misdemeanor charge, Drake received a sentence of 1 year of probation.[19] Still, the fact that Drake received a criminal sentence, rather than an award, may dissuade future national security whistleblowers from coming forward.

Outside the national security employment sector, the breadth and depth of whistleblower protections in the United States has grown exponentially since the Watergate era. The revelations of misconduct in that era led Americans to begin to

---

[15] Marc Pitzke, War on Whistleblowers: Has Obama Scrapped the First Amendment? (*Spiegel Online Int'l* 24 July 2013). Available at www.spiegel.de/international/world/obama-wages-war-on-whistleblowers-and-journalists-a-912852.html.

[16] Peter Eisler & Susan Page, '3 NSA Veterans Speak Out on Whistleblower: We Told You So' (*USA Today* 15 June 2013). Available at www.usatoday.com/story/news/politics/2013/06/16/snowden-whistleblower-nsa-officials-roundtable/2428809/.

[17] Eisler, *NSA* (2013).

[18] R. Jeffrey Smith, Classified Pentagon Report Upholds Thomas Drake's Complaints About NSA *Washington Post* 22 June 2011. Available at www.washingtonpost.com/national/national-security/classified-pentagon-report-upholds-thomas-drakes-complaints-about-nsa/2011/06/22/AG1VHTgH_story.html.

[19] Douglas Burke, Thomas Drake Sentenced in NSA Leaks Case *Huffington Post* (15 July 2011). Available at www.huffingtonpost.com/2011/07/15/thomas-drake-nsa-leak_n_900384.html.

openly question the traditional wisdom of loyally serving one's superiors. Over the past three decades, a series of sector-specific crises has led Congress to attempt to fight corporate fraud and government waste by gradually introducing more comprehensive whistleblower protections.

This article will review both the overarching and sector-specific whistle-blowing legislation currently on the books on the federal level in the United States today. In Part I, I describe the context behind the introduction of multiple pieces of sector-specific legislation on the federal level and briefly identify the limitations of that legislation. Part II introduces the general whistleblower protections that apply to federal workers. In this discussion, I will introduce the two main components of whistleblower provisions. The first type, which are designed to encourage whistleblowers to come forward, are provisions that monetarily reward whistleblowers with a portion of the recovered proceeds. The second type of legislative provision focuses on specific employment-related protections aimed at combating retaliation against the whistleblowers themselves. Finally in Part III, I briefly discuss the main variations in state-level whistleblower protections.

Sector Specific Legislation

Introduction

In the United States, Congress and state legislatures have adopted a piecemeal approach to establishing whistleblower protections by drafting industry-specific legislation. In some cases, these legislative efforts have followed adverse disclosures of industry fraud, while in others, legislators have tried to anticipate potential areas of need. One notable example of the later phenomenon is the Patient Protection and Affordable Care Act (PPACA).[20] As the government's involvement in the health care industry expands, legislators have attempted to anticipate and prevent opportunities for increased fraudulent activity. Since it is widely acknowledged that government auditors cannot hope to ferret out every case of fraud, the legislature has sought to encourage and protect employees who may be subject to retaliation for reporting potential violations of the law's consumer protections.

At both levels of government, legislators have tried to protect employees who publicize an employer's conduct in cases where that conduct may jeopardize the public's health, safety, or other legally protected interests. While these statutes are designed to encourage whistleblowers to bring unlawful activity to the government's attention, there are also significant areas of unprotected activity where little to no protection exists. In particular, the weak of protection extended to employees in the intelligence related sectors who seek to expose the government's unlawful behavior, challenges the extent of the government's commitment to the rule of law.

[20] Pub. L. No. 111-148, 124 Stat. 119 (2010) (codified in scattered sections of 42 U.S.C.).

Without a doubt, public concern about potential terrorist attacks has fueled the secret growth of the government's surveillance programs which the current prominent generation of whistleblowers has sought to expose. Ironically, while a large sector of the population currently supports the government's efforts to extend the reach of government power, the key building blocks of federal whistleblower legislation came to fruition during a period of social unrest and widespread distrust of government-notably, the post-Watergate era. In contrast to the polity's demand for increased security in the first two decades of the twenty-first century, it was the public's widespread disdain for the government's unlawful behavior during the Watergate era that spawned the initial legislative attempts to protect whistleblowers. In fact, it is unlikely that Congress would have taken up the mantle of protecting whistleblowers by enacting the Civil Service Reform Act of 1978 (CRSA) without the public bravery of several federal employees-some of whom were punished for their disclosures. While space does not permit an exhaustive list here, some of the pioneering whistleblowers of that era included:

- Ernest Fitzgerald, who while serving as the Deputy for Management Systems of the United States Air Force, informed the Senate in March 1968 about a two-billion-dollar cost overrun in the military transport program. After President Richard Nixon ordered Fitzgerald's supervisors to "get rid of the son of a bitch," the Air Force demoted him and assigned him to trivial duties.[21]
- Ron Ridenhour, a serviceman who participated in combat during the Vietnam War and subsequently disclosed the information regarding the execution of civilians by members of the U.S. Army at My Lai.[22]
- Daniel Ellsberg, a former Pentagon employee, who while working as an analyst at the RAND Corporation, disclosed "the Pentagon Papers" to the *New York Times*. The documents revealed that, early on in the Vietnam War effort, the government knew that the war could not be won.[23]

While those disclosures captured the public's attention, academics and consumer advocates viewed the disclosures, not as anomalies, but as symptomatic of a civil service mentality that rewarded conformity and loyalty. This theme was echoed in Senator Patrick Leahy's 1977 report to a U.S. Senate Committee entitled, "The Whistleblowers: A Report on Federal Employees Who Disclose Acts of Governmental Waste, Abuse, and Corruption."[24] One of the report's key findings reported that federal employees, who spotted waste or corruption and sought to fulfill their ethical obligations, faced resistance from management styles that stressed "team work and internal resolution of any concerns."[25] As a result of this

---

[21] Robert G. Vaughn, *The Successes and Failures of Whistleblower Laws* (Cheltonham UK, Edward Elgar, 2012) p. 60–63.

[22] Vaughn, *Successes* (2012) 25.

[23] Daniel Elsberg, Why the Pentagon Papers Matter Now Guardian (London, 13th June 2011). Available at www.theguardian.com/commentisfree/cifamerica/2011/jun/13/pentagon-papers-daniel-ellsberg.

[24] Senate Committee on Government Affairs, 95th Cong. 2nd Session (1978).

[25] Senate Committee (1978) 12, 28.

report, as well as a report by a staff lawyer employed by Ralph Nader named Robert Vaughn,[26] Congress attempted to overhaul the federal civil service system by enacting the Civil Service Reform Act of 1978.[27] Coupled with the Carter Administration's reorganization plan, the Act abolished the Civil Service Commission and created three separate agencies to implement the Act. The new agencies included the United States Merit Systems Protection Board, the Office of Personnel Management, and the Federal Labor Relations Authority. Additionally, the Act established special counsels' offices within individual federal agencies.

The Act has a key weakness. It did not grant federal employees the right to litigate their claims in federal court.[28] Prior to a 1994 Amendment, the Act stated that the procedures available under the Act "shall be the exclusive procedures for resolving grievances which fall within its coverage."[29] In 2006 however, the Supreme Court, in *Whitman v. Depart. of Transportation*, 547 U.S. 512 (2006), held that, while the CRSA blocks petitioners from using the CRSA's provisions in civil suits, it does not remove the jurisdiction that federal courts enjoy in employment matters under other statutes.

False Claims Reform Act

The one piece of federal legislation that has had the most significant impact on the protections and recoveries afforded to whistleblowers over the past two decades is the False Claims Reform Act of 1986.[30] The Act, as well as its subsequent amendments, has become the bedrock of whistle-blower protection. The Act, which itself amended the False Claim Act of 1864, opened the courtroom door to private citizens and entities that possess evidence of fraud involving federal programs or contracts.[31] Although we think of government fraud as a contemporary phenomenon associated with the country's increasing federalization, the law initially targeted Union contractors who defrauded the Lincoln Administration during the Civil War. The original FCA expressly applied to persons who filed false claims against the government and sought to punish anybody that knowingly submitted fraudulent claims to the federal government. The FCA provided that any person who knowingly submitted false claims could be held liable for double the government's dam-

[26] Robert G. Vaughn & Marion Weldon Brewer, *The Spoiled System: A Call for Civil Service Reform* (New York, Charterhouse 1975).

[27] Pub. L. No. 95-454, 92 Stat. 1111 (1978) (codified in scattered sections of 5 U.S.C.).

[28] Stephen Martin Kohn, The Whistleblower's Handbook: A Step by Step Guide to Doing What's Right and Protecting Yourself (Guilford, Lyons Press 2011) p. 49.

[29] The 1994 Amendment altered the language of Section 7121(a)(1) of the CRSA to state that "the [collective bargaining agreement grievance] procedures shall be the exclusive administrative procedures for resolving grievances which fall within its coverage."

[30] 31 U.S.C. §§ 3729-3733 (1986).

[31] ibid.

ages plus a penalty of $2000 for each false claim. In 1986, Congress increased those penalties to treble damages and raised the penalty levels from $2000 to a range of $5000 to $10,000. In recent years, the federal government's increased reliance on private contractors and use of economic development funds to spur the economy have opened the door to contractors who attempt to fraudulently exploit the system. Congress has responded by continuing to expand the scope of the Act's qui tam provisions as well as the level of potential damages.

To succeed in recovering under the FCA, the plaintiff must show that the defendant either: knowingly submitted a false claim to the government, caused another to submit a false claim, or knowingly made a false record or statement to get the government to pay a false claim.[32] The act defines the terms "knowing" and "knowingly" to mean that a person must: "(i) ha[ve] actual knowledge of the information; (ii) act(s) in deliberate ignorance of the truth or falsity of the information; or (iii) acts in reckless disregard of the truth or falsity of the information."[33] In the Act's reverse false claims section, the act creates liability for those person or persons who act improperly to avoid having to pay money to the government.[34] It is important to recognize that not every false claim submitted to the government will trigger liability under this statute. According to § 3729(b)(1) of the Act, to violate the FCA, a person must have knowingly submitted or caused the submission of a false claim. The 1986 amendments significantly strengthened the FCA by increasing the share of the pot that whistle blowers receive, granting employment protection to employees who file *qui tam* suits, and by reducing the level of proof required to support fraud to "actual knowledge," "deliberation ignorance", or "reckless disregard."[35]

The FCA grants private individuals the right to file actions alleging that a contractor who is doing business with the federal government is defrauding the government. Although a private individual must initiate a *qui tam* action, if the government chooses not to join the action, the private plaintiff may proceed on their own behalf.[36] Although, the private individual or relator[37] must first file suit on the government's behalf, the U.S. Attorney in that judicial district has the option to intervene. Under law, the relator must provide the government with a disclosure statement or a narrative detaining the evidence of the fraud.[38] The identity of the relator remains sealed for an initial 60 day period, which courts may subsequently extend.[39] The govern-

---

[32] ibid. at §§ 3729(a)(1)(A) & (B).

[33] ibid. at § 3729(b)(1).

[34] ibid. at § 3729(a)(1)(G). Individuals who conspire to violate the Act may be found liable under § 3729(a)(1)(C).

[35] DL Haron, MV Dordeski, and LD Lahman, Bad Mules: A Primer on the Federal and Michigan False Claims Act Claims (November 2009) Michigan Bar Journal 22–25, Available at: www.michbar.org/journal/pdf/pdf4article1590.pdf (*citing* 31 U.S.C. § 3729(b)(1)).

[36] 31 U.S.C. § 3730(c)(1).

[37] Under the provisions of the False Claim Act and related legislation a relator is the individual with direct knowledge of the fraud who files the civil action. *See* 31 U.S.C. § 3729–3730.

[38] Haron, Dordeski, and Lahman, *Bad Mules* (n 36) 24.

[39] See 31 U.S.C. § 3730(b)(2).

ment is required by law to investigate the allegations. However, the government may petition the presiding court for extensions of the seal period. Once the whistle-blower files suit, the Department of Justice will review the case and decide whether to intervene in the action. On average, the federal government joins about one-quarter of the suits filed by whistle-blowers.[40] If the government does intervene however, the whistle blower will lose a measure of control over the conduct of the case. As a Memorandum written by the U.S. Department of Justice summarizes the government's powers in a *qui tam* action[41]:

> It can dismiss the action, even over the objection of the relator, so long as the court gives the relator an opportunity for a hearing (§ 3730(c)(2)(A)) and it can settle the action even if the relator objects so long as the relator is given a hearing and the court determines that the settlement is fair. § 3730(c)(2)(B). If a relator seeks to settle or dismiss a *qui tam* action, it must obtain the consent of the government. § 3730(b)(1). When the case is proceeding, the government (§ 3730(c)(2)(C)) and the defendant (§ 3730(c)(2)(D)) can ask the court to limit the relator's participation in the litigation.[42]

If the government elects not to proceed with the claim, the individual who initiated the claim may proceed alone.[43] However, the government's refusal to intervene often results in the dismissal of the action by the court.[44] Indeed, employees have a financial incentive to proceed. The amendments create significant monetary incentives for private citizens to sue companies-as private citizens may retain between 15 and 30 % of the total monetary recovery even if the case is settled. Once a defendant is found to be liable, courts may hold the defendant liable for an amount equivalent to three times the dollar amount that company defrauded the government in addition to civil penalties that total between $5000 and $10,000 for each false claim. If the government joins an action brought by a *qui tam* plaintiff, the plaintiff must receive a minimum of 15 % of the action's proceeds or settlement up to a maximum of 25 %. How much money the whistleblower receives depends upon the extent of their contribution to the prosecution of the action.[45]

The federal government's increasing reliance on private contractors, coupled with the broadening reach of the FCA, have fueled the growth of *qui tam* actions.

---

[40] Pete Yost, *False Claims Act Leads To $5 Billion In Government Recoveries Over Past* Year Huffington Post (12 December 2012). Available at www.huffingtonpost.com/2012/12/04/false-claims-act_n_2238111.html.

[41] The term "qui tam" stems from the common law writ that allowed a private individual who assisted in the prosecution of a case to recover damages. The phrase itself stems comes from a Latin phrase meaning "he who brings a case on behalf of our lord the King, as well as for himself". See U.S. Department of Justice, False Claims Act Cases: Government Intervention in Qui Tam (Whistleblower) Cases (n.d). Available at www.doioig.gov/docs/falseclaimsact.pdf.

[42] U.S. Department of Justice, '*The False Claims Act*: *A Prim*er'(22 April 2011). Available at www.justice.gov/sites/default/files/civil/legacy/2011/04/22/C-FRAUDS_FCA_Primer.pdf.

[43] 31 U.S.C. § 3730(3)(c).

[44] U.S. Department of Justice, False Claims Act Cases: Government Intervention in Qui Tam (Whistleblower) Cases 2 (n.d.). Available at www.justice.gov/usao/pae/Documents/fcaprocess2.pdf.

[45] 31 U.S.C. § 3730(d)(1).

Because these *qui-tam* cases have successfully incentivized whistle-blowing, over 30 states have enacted legislation paralleling the FCA's remedies.[46] It also instituted whistleblower protections for employees who suffer employment discrimination as a result of their decision to participate in a *qui tam* action.[47] Those protections are necessary because, although the whistleblower's identity is initially kept under seal, an employer may be able to deduce the whistleblower's identity from the information revealed during the discovery stage. When the litigation reaches beyond the discovery stage, the court will unseal the complaint revealing the complainant's identity. Once an employer discerns the employee's identity, the whistleblower will inevitably face harassment on the job. The FCA however, seeks to block employers from retaliating against whistleblowers by prohibiting any subsequent discriminatory "action."[48] To make a retaliation case, the whistleblower must show that (1) he or she was engaged in activity protected by the FCA; (2) the employer knew about the *qui tam* action, and (3) the employer retaliated.[49] Although the requirements for establishing a claim of discrimination appear clear on their face, the federal courts are currently divided about the scope of whistleblower protection under Section 3730(h).

In recent decades the shortcomings of the extent of whistleblower protection under the FCA have become clearer. In particular, the FCA's provisions did not give plaintiffs a cause of action for several common forms of retaliation. The largest loopholes included: coverage for individuals who were planning to file a *qui tam* action, individuals who attempted to blow the whistle without filing an action, employees who refused to participate in the fraudulent practices, retaliation against the whistle-blower's family members and colleagues, and retaliation against contractors and agents employed by the defendant who did not fall under a strict construction of the word "employee."[50] In 2009, Congress attempted to close those loopholes in the Fraud Enforcement and Recovery Act (FERA) which is discussed below. In an effort to fight any potential liability, employers still found ways to fight *qui tam* suits. One of the chief impediments to an FCA suit was the act's "Public Disclosure Bar." In cases in which some of the information contained in the suit was

---

[46] According to the National Whistleblowers Center, the states of New York, California, and Virginia have enacted state versions of the False Claims Act which permit whistleblowers to recover a "finders' fee" for reporting fraud.

[47] 31 U.S.C. § 3730(h) (stating that any employee who is discharged, demoted, harassed or otherwise discriminated against because of the employee's lawful behavior under the Act is entitled to any relief necessary to make them whole including reinstatement, double back pay, compensation for other damages including litigation costs and reasonable attorneys' fees).

[48] "Any action" means demoting, suspending, terminating, or "in any other manner discriminat[ing] against [the employee] in the terms and conditions of employment ….", ibid.

[49] 31 U.S.C. § 3730(h).

[50] Nolan & Auerbach, 'Recent False Claims Act Amendments Fully Protect Whistleblowers' (*Qui Tam 101 Blog*, 9 August 2010). Available at www.false-claims-act.net/recent-false-claims-act-amendments-fully-protect-whistleblowers-2/.

based on information available to the public, employers moved courts to dismiss suits by alleging that the suits did not further the public interest. The U.S. Supreme Court attempted to weigh in on this issue in *Graham County Soil and Water Conservation District v. U.S. ex rel. Wilson*, 559 U.S. 280 (2010), when the Court held that relators could not proceed with an action when that action relied in part on information available from publicly available state and local administrative reports, audits, and investigations. However, that portion of the decision was moot before it was announced as, 1 week prior to the Court's decision, the President signed into law the Patient Protection and Affordable Care Act. This new legislation precluded courts from dismissing future cases under this section of the FCA. Until a 2010, the relator had to prove that he or she was the "original source" of the information and that the information provided by the whistleblower was not available from public sources to prevent courts from dismissing claims because they claimed to lack subject matter jurisdiction.[51]

The FCA also includes statute of limitations requirements. According to the Act, plaintiffs must file a *qui tam* action either within the date established by calculating a date 6 years from the date of violation is committed or 3 years after the date when government knows or should have known about "facts material to the right of action."[52] Under no circumstances may a suit be filed 10 years after the violation date.[53] To determine which time limit applies in a particular case, courts attempt to determine when the whistleblower or the government became aware of the violation. The 1986 reforms attempted to further clarify these time limits by specifying that plaintiffs may bring an action anytime up until 3 years after the date "when facts material to the right of action are known or reasonably should have been known by the official of the United States charged with responsibility to act."[54] Most courts have held that the "official" refers to the responsible official within the Department of Justice. Although courts are also split on the issue of whether a *qui tam* whistleblower is entitled to take advantage of the tolling provision in Section 3731(b)(2), the majority of courts have held that the tolling provision only applies to suits in which the government has elected to intervene.[55]

---

[51] BG Santo, 'The False Claims Act: Analysis of the Recently Expanded Legislation on Qui Tam Actions and Related Impact on Whistleblowers' (July 2010) American Bar Association Health E-Source, available at www.americanbar.org/content/newsletter/publications/aba_health_esource_home/Volume6_SE2_Santo.html.

[52] 31 U.S.C. § 3731(b). There is currently a disagreement between circuits regarding whether the tolling provision applies only to cases in which the government has decided to intervene.

[53] ibid.

[54] ibid.

[55] See, e.g., *Manning v. Utilities Mutual Insurance Co.*, 254 F.3d 387, 397 (2d Cir. 2001) (six year limit governs private claims).

Sarbanes-Oxley Act of 2002

After the economy collapsed during the Great Depression, the federal government began to wade into the regulation of the capital markets by establishing the Securities and Exchange Commission (SEC). Although the Commission enjoys broad rule-making authority today, the original legislation which created the SEC left the responsibility for setting financial disclosure standards in the hands of accounting professionals.[56] In the wake of the malfeasance committed by both ENRON and WORLDCOM, which was brought to the public's attention by whistleblowers,[57] Congress hurriedly enacted the Sarbanes-Oxley Act of 2002.[58] The Act responded to the public's increasing cynicism towards corporate officials and aimed to strengthen federal regulation of capital markets. The Act's final shape reflected the concerns expressed by the whistleblowers who had suffered retaliation after reporting accounting and securities-related malfeasance.[59] The Senate Report on the bill stated that the bill's whistleblower protections aimed to break the code of corporate silence and to encourage more individuals to report corporate wrongdoing.[60]

In keeping with the nation's largely industry-specific approach to whistleblowing, the Act's whistleblower protections initially focused only on employees of companies that sold stock on public exchanges or companies that were required to file certain reports with the Securities and Exchange Commission (SEC).[61] The Act required corporations to create channels that allowed whistleblowers to directly and anonymously report misconduct to the company's board of directors.[62] The Act also identified a specific type of wrongdoing reporting that would enjoy protection as it sought to protect employees who "reasonably believe[d]" that their employer had violated:

- any federal criminal law prohibiting mail, wire or bank fraud;
- any rule or regulation of the SEC; or
- any provision of federal law related to shareholder fraud.[63]

---

[56] JE Fisch, 'The New Federal Regulation of Corporate Governance' (2004) 28 Harvard Journal of Law and Public Policy 39, 40.

[57] The initial WORLDCOM report was made by WORLDCOM vice president, Cynthia Cooper. See N Schichor, 'Does Sarbanes-Oxley Force Whistleblowers to Sacrifice their Reputations?: An Argument for Granting Whistleblowers Non-Pecuniary Damages' (2008) 8 University of California at Davis Business Law Journal 272, 273. A key figure in the disclosures of ENRON's irregularities was ENRON Vice-President Sherron Watkins. See Shaheen Pasha, 'Enron's Whistle Blower Details Sinking Ship' (*CNNMoney.com*, 16 March 2006). Available at www.money.cnn.com/2006/03/15/news/newsmakers/enron/.

[58] Pub. L. No. 107-204, 116 Stat. 745 (2002) (codified in scattered sections of 15 U.S.C. & 18 U.S.C.).

[59] Vaughn (n 22) 152.

[60] Schichor (n 58) 276 (citing S. Rep. No. 107-46, at 5, 10 (2002)).

[61] Amendments to the SOX enacted in 2010 extended protection to employees of a public company's subsidiary if the subsidiary's finances are consolidated into the parent company's financial statements.

[62] 15 U.S.C. § 78j-1(m)(4)(A) (Supp. IV 2004).

[63] 18 U.S.C. §1514A (2002).

Despite problems that would later emerge with Act's application, one key goals of the Act was to provide broad whistle-blower protections across the land that would end employee's dependence on differing levels of state protection. By extending protection employees of publicly-traded companies, the Act attempted to ameliorate decades of disappointment with loophole-filled industry-specific protections.

One of the most innovative provisions of the Act was the Act's provisions that abandoned the use of administrative adjudication and appellate review as the sole reporting mechanism for whistleblowers.[64] It also criminalized retaliation against whistleblowers.[65] The Act granted whistleblowers the right to a jury trial in cases in which the Secretary of Labor had failed to issue a final decision on the whistle-blower's complaint within 180 days of its filing and there is no showing that "such delay is due to the bad faith of the claimant."[66] Predictably, employers responded to this provision by requiring employees to sign employment agreements, which mandated that they bring their complaints before arbitrators, rather than pursue a jury trial. In 2010, Congress declared those agreements null and void.[67] Employers may no longer "contractually require an employee to submit SOX retaliation claims to an arbitrator in place of a jury trial."[68]

By granting employees the option of a jury trial, the Act seemed to open the door to dispositions favorable to whistle-blowers. In reality, however, the administrative procedures that occur within the first 180 days following the filing of a complaint substantially narrow the number of claims that proceed. After Congress passed the Sarbanes-Oxley legislation, the Occupational Health and Safety Administration (OSHA) detailed the procedures for proceeding forward with a claim. Pursuant to those regulations, after an employee files a complaint, OSHA will then notify the respondents and the SEC of the allegation. The agency will dismiss any complaint that fails to make a prima facie showing of retaliation that: "(1) the employee engaged in protected activity; (2) the employer knew about the activity; (3) the employee suffered an unfavorable personnel action; and (4) the 'circumstances were sufficient to raise the inference that the protected activity was a contributing factor in the unfavorable action.'"[69] Even if the complainant survives that hurdle, OSHA may dismiss the case if the employer demonstrates, with clear and convincing evidence, hat the employment action would have been taken regardless of the

---

[64] Vaughn (n 22) 152.

[65] 18 U.S.C. § 1513 (e).

[66] 18 U.S.C. § 1514b(1)(b).

[67] That amendment was included within the Dodd–Frank Wall Street Reform and Consumer Protection Act of 2010, Pub. L. No. 111-203, 124 Stat. 1376 (2010) (codified in scattered sections of 5 U.S.C., 12 U.S.C., 15 U.S.C. & 18 U.S.C.). See discussion below, pt G.

[68] 'What is the Sarbanes-Oxley (SOX) Act?' (Katz, Marshall & Banks Blog (n.d.)). Available at www.kmblegal.com/practice-areas/whistleblower-law/sarbanes-oxley/.

[69] Richard E. Moberly, '*Unfulfilled Expectations*: *An Empirical Analysis of Why Sarbanes-Oxley Whistleblowers Rarely Win*' (2007) 49 William & Mary Law Review 65, 70(citing 29 C.F.R. § 1980.104(b)(1) (2006)).

protected activity.[70] If the complaint clears those hurdles, OSHA will commence an investigation. Within 60 days of the complaint's filing, OSHA must determine whether it finds reasonable cause to believe that retaliation in violation of the Act occurred and issue written findings.[71]

If OSHA issues a decision in the employee's favor, the Agency will issue a preliminary order of relief to the employee. Pursuant to 18 U.S.C.§1514C(1), "[a]n employee prevailing in any action under subsection (b)(1) shall be entitled to all relief necessary to make the employee whole."[72] In cases where the employer demonstrates with "reasonable cause" that the employee is a security risk, OSHA may elect not to order reinstatement. Unfortunately, it is unlikely that the litigation will end at that point. Both parties have 30 days to request that an administrative law judge (ALJ) review the ruling before the initial findings become a final order.[73] If either of the parties appeals, the ALJ will conduct a de novo hearing. A party who seeks to challenge the ALJ ruling must do so within 10 days of the decision.[74] The Department of Labor's Administrative Review Board sits above the ALJs and has the discretion to decline to review the ALJ's decision.[75] In those cases where the ARB elects to review the ALJ's decision, it must use a "substantial evidence" standard and issue a final decision within 120 days following the hearing.[76] The parties may then appeal that decision to the appropriate federal circuit court of appeals.[77]

Although the Sarbanes-Oxley Act initially appeared to offer whistleblowers an easy path to recover damages, empirical evidence suggests that the path was a particularly steep one. The fact that President Bush issued an executive signing statement immediately upon signing the Act, which narrowed the Act's whistleblower provisions, undoubtedly undercut the Act's effectiveness.[78] The two Senators, who were instrumental in the Act's passage- Patrick Leahy and Charles Grassley, complained to the President and alleged that his signing statement "threaten[ed] to

[70] See 29 C.F.R. §1980.104(c) (2006).

[71] Moberly (n 69) at 79 (citing 29 C.F.R.§1980.105 (2006)).

[72] The Act also defines the scope of compensatory damages permitted under the legislation. Those damages include: reinstatement to a position with the same seniority that the employee would have had, back pay with interest, and "compensation for any special damages sustained as a result of the discrimination, including litigation costs, expert witness fees, and reasonable attorney fees." See 18 U.S.C. §1514C(2)(a).

[73] See 29 C.F.R. §1980.107(b).

[74] ibid. § 1980.110.

[75] ibid. § 1980.110(b).

[76] ibid. § 1980.110(b)-(c).

[77] ibid. §§ 1980.112(a) & 1980.105(c).

[78] Statement by President George W. Bush upon Signing H.R. 3763 (July 30, 2002), *reprinted in* 2002 U.S.C.C.A.N. 543 ("The legislative purpose of section 1514A … is to protect against company retaliation for lawful cooperation with investigations and not to define the scope of investigative authority, therefore, the executive branch shall construe section 1514A(a)(1)(B) as referring to investigations authorized by the rules of the Senate or the House of Representatives and conducted for a proper legislative purpose.").

create unnecessary confusion and to discourage whistleblowers."[79] According to data collected by Richard Moberly, during the first 3 years following the Act's enactment, only 3.6 % of SOX whistleblowers secured relief through the Act's administrative procedures and only 6.5 % of whistleblowers were victorious in the appeals process.[80]

Although the new law appears straightforward on its face, employers employed numerous strategies to limit their liability. Additionally, the administrative law judges who heard the majority of the cases strictly interpreted the Act's legal requirements. As one example, the judges consistently determined that the protections did not extend to employees of privately-held subsidiaries or contractors of publicly held companies. By narrowly construing the Act, both OSHA examiners and the ALJ's declared that many claims failed as a matter of law. Many claimants, whose claims fell within the Act's legal parameters, saw their claims fail because they failed to adequately show that their employers took action against them because of their whistleblower activities.[81] To succeed in establishing the causation element, the employee must show that the employer knew that the whistleblower was engaged in protected activity and that activity was a "contributing factor" motivating the adverse employment event.[82]

Another barrier to effective enforcement lies in the fact that the Act delegates enforcement to the Department of Labor. At the time of the Act's enactment, the department was responsible for administering 25 other whistle-blower or anti-retaliation provisions. In an attempt to redistribute its workload, the department delegated responsibility for investigating the claims of 14 of these provisions to OSHA.[83] Adding to the hurdles faced by employees who blow the whistle under the Act, Moberly's study revealed that the administrative judges found few reasons to grant claimants relief from the Act's strict filing deadlines.[84] Finally, both the administrative law judges and federal judges continue to dismiss claims that appear to fall within the ambit of whistleblower activities but are not explicitly mentioned in the Act. For example, in 2010, a U.S. District Court in the State of Washington dismissed a claim filed by two former compliance auditors for the Boeing Company,

---

[79] *See* Kelly Wallace, 'Senators: Bush Could Undercut Whistleblowers' (*CNN*, 31 July 2002) (reporting that U.S. Senators Pat Leahy (D-Vermont) and Charles Grassley (R-Iowa) sent to President Bush on July 31, 2002, a letter expressing concerns with the signing statement). *See also* 152 Cong. Rec. S8189-90 (2006) (statement of Sen. Leahy). Available at www.fas.org/irp/////////// congress/2006_cr/s072506.html (stating that Bush's interpretation was at odds with the plain language of the statute, and the administration reluctantly relented on this view).

[80] Moberly (n 69) at 67.

[81] Moberly (n 69) at 90.

[82] Moberly (n 69) at 100.

[83] Moberly (n 69) at 146.

[84] According to 18 U.S.C. § 1514A(b)(2)(D) (Supp. IV 2004), the complaint must be filed within 90 days of the retaliation. Any appeal must be filed within 30 days of an OSHA decision. *See* 29 C.F.R. § 1980.105(c) (2006).

Inc.[85] Although the employees claimed that they had been dismissed for frequently complaining to their supervisors that Boeing was not complying with SOX, the court found that the employees were fired for leaking confidential information to the media-an act not protected by SOX.[86] This dismissal finding illustrates the difficulties that legislators face in attempting to delineate the full spectrum of potential whistleblower activity.

Consumer Products and Safety Improvement Act of 2008[87]

Given the significant influence that corporate interests exercise in the political process and on the race for the Presidency, it is not surprising that Presidents often appoint individuals to head regulatory agencies who have ties to the regulated industries. Where industry interests are protected by the White House, the fate of whistleblower protections and the extent of government assistance extended to whistleblowers may be in jeopardy. Such was the case in 2007, when the Bush Administration's acting Chairmen of the Consumer Products Safety Administration (CPSC), Nancy Nord, attempted to implement the Administration's deregulation agenda by condemning a Senate plan to increase the CPSC's budget. According to the *New York Times*, Nord objected to "provisions that would increase the maximum penalties for safety violations, make it easier for the government to make public reports of faulty products, protect industry whistleblowers and prosecute executives of companies that willfully violate laws."[88] As Stephen Labaton reported:

> Some of Ms. Nord's complaints were similar to the ones that business groups and manufacturers have raised, including that the legislation would be unnecessarily burdensome. But in other areas, such as whistleblower protection for company employees, her complaints went beyond those of industry.[89]

The public controversy over the CPSC's impotency prompted Congress to enact the Consumer Product Safety Improvement Act in 2008 (CPSIA). In addition to establishing product manufacturing and testing requirements, the Act created protections for industry whistleblowers. Under the Act, employees who have been the victim of discrimination or retaliation may file a complaint with the Department of

---

[85] Tides v. Boeing Co., Nos. C08-1601-JCC & C08-1736-JCC, 2010 WL 537639 (W.D. Wash. Feb. 2, 2010), *aff'd*, 644 F.3d 809 (9th Cir. 2011).

[86] Stephen Shiffman & Jonathan Rotenberg, "*District Court limits the Sarbanes-Oxley Act's Whistleblower Protections*" (*Lexology* 12 February 2010). Available at www.lexology.com/library/detail.aspx?g=c9fbf3d6-eefb-48c8-9cc2-95353d851d9c.

[87] 15 U.S.C. §§ 2051-2085 (2006) (CPSIA). The CPSIA amends the Consumer Product Safety Act of 1972, 15 U.S.C. §§2051-2089. (1972) (CPSA).

[88] Stephen Labaton, '*Strengthening of Consumer Agency Opposed by its Boss*' New York Times (30 October 2007). Available at www.nytimes.com/2007/10/30/washington/30cnd-consumer.html?_r=0.

[89] Labaton, *New York Times* (2007).

Labor.[90] Employees covered by the Act must work for a "manufacturer, private labeler, distributor, or retailer."[91] According to the procedures specified in the Act, employees must file a claim within 180 days of the alleged discriminatory action.[92] Similar to other administrative review provisions, the Act requires the Secretary of Labor to initiate an investigation to determine "whether there is reasonable cause to believe that the complaint has merit."[93] The Department of Labor must then follow a prescribed procedure, first issuing preliminary, and then, final findings. The Secretary has the power to order the employer to: (1) "abate the violation;" (2) reinstate the employee to his or her former position, and to pay compensatory damages.[94] Congress also offered whistleblowers access to the federal courthouse under the Act. If the Secretary does not reach a final decision within 120 days of the complaint or within 90 days of receiving a written determination, the whistleblower may "bring an action at law or equity for *de novo* review in federal district court." At the district court stage of the action, the employee may be (1) be reinstated with the "same seniority status that the employee would have had, but for the discharge or discrimination;" (2) entitled to back pay with interest; and (3) eligible to receive compensation for special damages including litigation costs, expert witness fees, and attorney's fees."[95]

While whistleblower protections play an important regulatory role, the government agency responsible for enforcing regulatory standards must not only have adequate legal power to fulfill its mission, but also adequate resources. While Congress and President Bush signed the CIPSA's new protection regime into law, behind the scenes, the ranks of the Commission itself were being gutted. As Scott McBride reported, although "the number of imported toys jumped by 597 % between 1980 and 2007. [T]he staff of the Commission was cut by 57 %. Partially as a result of the 'Reagan Revolution,' the staff of the Commission was decreased from 978 to 420 employees over a 28 year period."[96] It was not just the staff that was decimated, but also the agency's leadership. For almost a 2-year period at the end of the Bush Administration, the agency's five member commission was missing three members-hamstringing the Agency's ability to issue new rules or to impose penalties.[97] As the history of the Consumer Product Safety Improvement Act shows,

[90] See 15 U.S.C. §2087(b).

[91] id. §2087(a).

[92] id. §2087(b)(1).

[93] id. §2087(b)(2)(A).

[94] id. §2087(b)(3)(B).

[95] id. §2087(b)(4)(A)-(C).

[96] Scott D. McBride, 'Something Wicked This Way Comes: The United States Government's Response to Unsafe Imported Chinese Toys and Subsidized Chinese Exports' (2009) 45 Texas International Law Journal 233, 246 (citing Public Citizen, Closing Santa's Sweatshop: How to Deliver on Obama's and Congress' Toy-Safety and Fair Trade Promises 6, 24 (2008)), available at www.citizen.org/documents/SantasSweatshop08.pdf.

[97] David Lazarus, '*Obama needs to add consumer agency to his to-do list*' Los Angeles Times (19 August 2011). Available at www.articles.latimes.com/2011/aug/19/business/la-fi-lazarus-20110819.

standing alone, whistleblower protections cannot guarantee good governance especially when the federal government proceeds to decimate the ranks of the oversight agency.

Fraud Enforcement and Recovery Act of 2010

Two years after the Sarbanes-Oxley legislation, Congress continued its effort both to combat corporate fraud and to reduce the uncertainty of the financial markets. Following on the heels of collapse of the mortgage industry, the statute aimed to "increase accountability for the corporate and mortgage frauds that have contributed to the recent economic collapse."[98] For purposes of this Article, it is important to note that through this legislation, Congress considerably strengthened the False Claim Reform Act to make it easier for whistleblowers to file successful claims.[99] Speaking to this point, Senator Patrick Leahy of Vermont, one of the Act's co-sponsors, stated that the 2010 bill aimed to improve the country's efforts to prosecute individuals who defrauded the government and harmed the U.S. economy.[100] The Senate report accompanying the Act stated that Congress intended to remedy the judiciary's attempts to limit the FCA's scope.

The effectiveness of the FCA has recently been undermined by court decisions limiting the scope of the law and allowing subcontractors and non-governmental entities to escape responsibility for proven frauds. In order to respond to these decisions, certain provisions of the FCA must be corrected and clarified in order to protect Federal assistance and relief funds expended in response to our current economic crisis.[101]

The early results of these changes have been promising. As of December 2011, the Justice Department had recovered $8.7 million in False Claims Act recoveries during the first 3 years of the Obama Administration.[102]

The Act's key whistle-blowing related sections include provisions that widen the scope of protected conduct, broaden the types of individuals covered by the FCA, and expand the statute of limitations period. In addition to protecting employees against retaliation, the Act's new provisions applied to contractors and agents who had been:

---

[98] S. Rep. No. 111-10, at 2 (2009).

[99] Fraud Enforcement and Recovery Act of 2009, Pub. L. No. 111-21, 123 Stat. 1617 (2009) (codified in scattered sections of 18 U.S.C.).

[100] 155 Cong. Rec. S4774, S4775 (2009) (statement of Sen. Leahy).

[101] See Rep. No. 111-10, at 10 (2009), available at www.nacua.org/documents/SenateJudiciaryrReport_111_10.pdf#nameddest=EffectivenessFCA.

[102] Press Release, Senator Patrick Leahy, 'Comment of Senator Patrick Leahy on False Claims Act Settlements in 2011' (19 December 2011). Available at www.leahy.senate.gov/press/comment-of-senator-patrick-leahy-on-false-claims-act-settlements-in-2011.

> discharged, demoted, suspended, threatened, harassed, or in any other manner discriminated against in the terms and conditions of employment because of lawful acts done by the employee, contractor, or agent on behalf of the employee, contractor, or agent or associated others in furtherance of other efforts to stop 1 or more violations of this subchapter.[103]

This legislation also took action to protect employees who, in addition to pursuing a *qui tam* action, attempt to remedy corporate misconduct by reporting that misconduct through internal channels. In another key provision, FERA expanded the types of behavior that would trigger FCA liability. The list of prohibited acts now includes behavior such as conspiracy, making false statements, makes or delivers a receipt that the individual knows is untrue, and buys public property from a member of the government or Armed Forces who may not lawfully sell the property.[104]

The amendments also added language to Section 3730(h) to protect independent contractors.[105] While the complete language of Section 3730(h) seeks to protect employees from retaliation that occurs because of lawful acts made by the employee "in furtherance" of an actual or potential *qui tam* action, in the 2009 revisions to the FCA, Congress made clear that an employee need only have taken steps towards the exposure of the false claims. In effect, the Act extended protection to individuals who had only made an internal complaint or had just begun to investigate a claim when the retaliation occurred.[106]

Another key provision of the Act aimed to reverse the impact of the Supreme Court's decision in *Allison Engine Co.* v. *United States ex rel. Sanders*, 553 U.S. 662 (2008) where the Court had held that the Government must prove that "a defendant must intend that the Government itself pay the claim."[107] According to the Senate Report, the Court's interpretation blocked liability in cases where a subcontractor knowingly submitted a false claim to the general contractor and was paid with Government funds unless the subcontractor intended to defraud the Federal Government.[108] In the wake of the *Allison Engine* decision, the Department of Justice reported that the decision undercut efforts to enforce violations of the act with respect to a variety of government programs including Medicaid, student loans, and federal highway funds.[109] By enacting these changes Congress attempted to make the False Claims Act more amenable to whistleblower claims.

---

[103] 31 U.S.C. § 3730(h).

[104] id. § 3729(a).

[105] See id. § 3730(h).

[106] See, e.g., Guerro v. Total Renal Care, Inc., No. EP-11-CV-449-KC, 2012 U.S. Dist LEXIS 32615 (W.D. Tex. Mar. 12, 2012).

[107] 553 U.S. 662, 669 (2008).

[108] S. Rep. No. 111-10, at 10 (2009), available at www.nacua.org/documents/SenateJudiciaryrReport_111_10.pdf#nameddest=EffectivenessFCA.

[109] Letter from M. Faith Burton, Acting Assistant Att'y Gen., U.S. Dep't of Justice, to Sen. Patrick J. Leahy, Chairman, Senate Judiciary Committee (24 February 2009). Available at www.nacua.org/documents/LetterToSenLeahy_DoJ_Views_on_Section4_of_FERA_2.pdf.

Though the False Claim Act's whistleblower provisions continue to evolve, the amount of money recovered by federal and state authorities under the FCA set a new record in 2012. In that year federal and state government authorities recovered over $9 billion.[110] Approximately $5 billion of that amount stemmed from recoveries related to federal legislation with $3.3 billion of that total related to federal whistle-blower cases. The claims that led the way in fiscal year 2012 included fines collected from GlaxoSmithKline ($3 billion), Abbot Laboratories ($1.5 billion), Bank of America ($1 billion), and Merck ($950 million).[111] While whistleblowers do not have a smooth path to collecting damages through a *qui tam* suit, Congress continues to work on reducing the barriers to collection.

Patient Protection and Affordable Care Act of 2010

The health care sector stands out as one of the most significant economic sectors where *qui tam* lawsuits play a critical role in exposing industry attempts to defraud the government. Indeed a 2010 article in the *New England Journal of Medicine* asserted that *qui tam* lawsuits account for 90 % of health care fraud cases.[112] Acknowledging the important role played by whistle-blowers in the health care industry, in 2010, Congress included provisions in the Patient Protection and Affordable Care Act (PPACA)[113] designed to substantially strengthen whistleblower protections both within and beyond the health care sector.[114] Most importantly, the whistle-blower related provisions lowered the bar to *qui tam* suits in the health care industry According to several commentators, the legislative changes aimed to reverse the recent judicial trend towards limiting qui tam actions.[115] The key changes in the Act that directly affect the feasibility of *qui tam* actions include provisions that:

[110] 'False Claims Act Recoveries Double in One Year to $9 Billion' *Corporate Crime Reporter* (10 October 2012). Available at www.corporatecrimereporter.com/news/200/falseclaimsactrecoveries10102012/.

[111] False Claims Act (2012).

[112] A Kesselheim, D Studdert, and Mello, 'Whistle-Blowers' Experiences in Fraud Litigation Against Pharmaceutical Companies,' (2010) 362 New England Journal of Medicine 1832.

[113] Pub. L. No. 111-148, 124 Stat. 119 (2010) (codified in scattered sections of 42 U.S.C.).

[114] '2010 Mid-Year False Claims Act Update' (*GibsonDunn* 9 July 2010). Available at www.gibsondunn.com/publications/pages/2010mid-yearfalseclaimsactupdate.aspx.

[115] *See*, e.g., '*U.S. Health Care Reform Legislation Significantly Expands the False Claims Act*' (*GibsonDunn* 2 April 2010). Available at www.gibsondunn.com/publications/pages/HealthCareReformLegislationExpandstheFalseClaimsAct.aspx.

- Allow the Department of Justice to object to a dismissal of the action on "public disclosure" grounds that "substantially the same allegations or transactions alleged in the action or claim were publicly disclosed."[116]
- Eliminate the FCA's "direct knowledge" requirement and replaces it with a standard that favors the whistleblower by allowing *qui tam* actions based on "knowledge that is independent of and materially adds to the publicly disclosed allegations or transactions..."[117]
- Broadens the applicability of the FCA's Section 3729 to include health care transactions involving any "[p]ayments made by, through or in connection with a[n] [health care] Exchange" that includes public monies.[118]

In addition to making the FCA more whistle-blower friendly, the PPACA partially extended the protections for whistleblowers provided in the Fair Labors Standards Act of 1938 (FLSA). The PPACA strengthened provisions in the FLSA act that banned employers from discriminating against employees who provided information to the employer, the federal government, or a state attorney general "relating to the violation of, or any act or omission the employee reasonably believes to be a violation of, any provision of this title."[119] The scope of discriminatory actions addressed by the PPACA cover the employee's "compensation, terms, conditions, or other privileges of employment."[120] The PPACA prohibits employers from retaliating against any employee or either objected or refused to participate in any activity that the employee "reasonably believed" to violate any provision of Title I of the PPACA or the regulations promulgated under the Act. To be protected under these whistleblower provisions, an employee need only "reasonably believe" that their employer has violated the PPACA. This "reasonable belief" standard is likely to be one of the most troublesome aspects of the protections for employers as it protects whistleblower activity that may be based on an employee's reasonable, but inaccurate belief that the employer violated the law. This rule brings the PPACA's pleading requirement into line with the 2011 judicial opinion in *Sylvester v. Parexel Int'l LLC*.[121]

Emblematic of complex legislation, the federal agency charged with implementing the PPACA's whistleblower protections, the Occupational Safety and Health Administration (OSHA), issued interim rules "interpreting" the Act's protection provisions. One interesting aspect of the interim rule sheds light on the breadth of

[116] 31 U.S.C. 3730(e)(4)(A). The current version of the FCA reads "the Court shall dismiss an action or claim under this section, unless opposed by the Government, if substantially the same allegations or transactions alleged in the action or claim were publicly disclosed."

[117] id. § 3730(e)(4)(B).

[118] See PPACA §1313.

[119] See id. §1558.

[120] id.

[121] No. 07-123 (A.R.B. Dep't of Labor, May 25, 2011) (holding that, according to the SOX provisions, a whistleblower does not need to show that an actual SOX violation occurred, only that she had a subjective and objective "reasonable belief" that the conduct she complained about amounted to a SOX violation).

potential retaliatory actions that employees face if they speak out in the public interest. The rule states that any employee who receives a tax or cost sharing reduction in their health care insurance under the PPACA is entitled to whistleblower protection under the Fair Labor Standards Act.[122] This inclusion provision is designed to prevent employers, who face a potential tax penalty for not providing health care coverage, from acting in a retaliatory manner or discriminating against their employees.[123] Because the rule does not specify an endpoint for protection, according to one industry analyst, it is "conceivable that once an employee receives the cost sharing subsidy under section 1402 of PPACA, he or she is by virtue of that receipt in a protected class in perpetuity."[124] In essence, this interpretation of the PPACA could protect employees throughout the length of their lifetime.

Another positive development for whistleblower actions, which appeared in the interim rule, allows employees to use circumstantial evidence in their cases. In addition, the employee need not prove that the protected activity was the single reason that triggered the employer's retaliatory actions-merely only that it was "a" motivating factor.[125] *Finally, pursuant to the interim rule, beginning in 2014*, the protections provided by section 18C of the Act will extend "to cover retaliation with respect to an employee's compensation, terms, conditions or other privileges of employment by health insurance issuers offering group or individual health insurance coverage regardless of whether those issuers are the employer of the person retaliated against."[126]

Still, the PPACA is not a complete victory for potential whistleblowers as the Act only protects employees in one sector of the health care industry. While the employment protections cover employees who report medical care related violations relating in the conventional settings such as hospitals, physician offices, and clinics, they do not protect employees in some key health care sectors. Employees who report fraud, who work for entities outside those main health care access points, do not enjoy the same level of protection.[127] Given that the whistleblower protections currently on the books often do not fully protect whistleblowers,[128] this significant

---

[122] 29 C.F.R. § 1984.

[123] S. Tony Ling & Richard Joseph Zito, 'Occupational Safety & Health Administration extends broad whistleblower protections to employees complaining of violations of the Patient Protection and Affordable Care Act' (Lexology 18 March 2013). Available at www.lexology.com/library/detail.aspx?g=881218b5-4b23-4819-9b9d-45ae6aad58ea.

[124] id.

[125] 29 C.F.R. §1984.

[126] id.

[127] These include that individuals who administer the expansion of the Medicare and Children's Health Insurance (CHIP) programs; care for the elderly in nursing homes' "innovative treatment and therapies; payments and reimbursements outside the state exchanges; prescription drugs and preventative care; house-call visits; expansion of and increasing in training for the health care workforce; and grants for the expansion of health care to under-served populations." M Schutz, 'Whistleblower Protections in the Affordable Care Act,' (*Lexology* 20 April 2010). Available at www.lexology.com/library/detail.aspx?g=e5d83cf5-6f63-4390-8ade-f338587dea98.

[128] Kesselheim (n 113) 1838.

loophole in the PPACA's coverage is likely to deter potential individuals who work in the non-traditional sectors of the health care industry from coming forward and exposing fraud or illegal activity in those sectors.

Dodd-Frank Wall Street Reform and Consumer Protection Act

Congress's ongoing efforts to strengthen the FCA continued in the Dodd-Frank Wall Street Reform and Consumer Protection Act of 2010.[129] While the country's attempts to protect whistleblowers have caused employers to pause before taking action against whistleblowers, prior to Dodd-Frank, colleagues and family members of whistleblowers were often left unprotected. One key section of the Act amended Section 3730(h) of the FCA to protect the whistleblower's associates.[130] The Act also expands the whistleblower protections created by the Sarbanes-Oxley Act by widening the scope of employers covered in that legislation to include employees of non-publicly traded subsidiaries of publicly traded companies where the subsidiary's financial information is included in the parent company's consolidated financial statements.

In keeping with Congress's largely industry-specific and piecemeal approach to creating whistle-blowing protections, the whistleblower related provisions of the act apply to employees who provide information to their employers or to the government that they reasonably believe violates the Consumer Financial Protection Act of 2010 or any other provision of law subject to the jurisdiction of the Bureau of Consumer Financial Protection. A notable aspect of Dodd-Frank's provisions is that they allow whistleblowers to receive financial bounties if they report information that leads to successful securities enforcement actions. Unfortunately for whistleblowers, the legislation did not adopt the FCA's powerful *qui tam* litigation model which allows claimants to pursue litigation independent of agency action.[131] Instead, the whistleblowers' only hope of recovering monetary damages is in cases where the SEC recovers civil damages.[132] Ironically, some scholars have argued that, by failing to institute a *qui tam* system or to impose any costs on the whistleblower, the Act fails to provide an adequate screening mechanism to discourage frivolous tips.[133] In the first fiscal year after the Act's enactment, the SEC reported that more

---

[129] Pub. L. No. 111-203, 124 Stat. 1376 (2010) (codified in scattered sections of 5 U.S.C., 12 U.S.C., 15 U.S.C. & 18 U.S.C.).

[130] 31 U.S.C. § 3730(h).

[131] G Rapp, '*Mutiny by the Bounties? The Attempt to Reform Wall Street by the New Whistleblower Provisions of the Dodd-Frank Act*' (2012) Brigham Young University Law Review 73, 76.

[132] Rapp, Mutiny (2012) at 78.

[133] A Casey & A Niblett, '*Noise Reduction*: *The Screening Value of Qui* Tam' (2013). Available at www.ssrn.com/abstract=22376589.

than 3000 reports had been made to its hotline.[134] During the same period, there were only 143 enforcement judgments and orders issued that qualified as eligible for an award.

Although the Act allows whistleblowers to recover between 10 and 30 % of the proceeds from the enforcement action, those bounties are restricted to cases in which the monetary sanctions exceed one million dollars.[135] This restriction deviates from the recovery available to whistleblowers under the FCA, as under the FCA, whistleblowers may recover their share of the bounty regardless of how much the government recovers.[136]

The Act also significantly expands the statute of limitations that applies to cases filed directly in district court by giving whistleblowers engaged in SEC-related whistleblower conduct or other SOX-protected activity, 6 years from the date when the violation occurs or within 3 years after the date "facts material to the right of action are known or reasonably should have been known by the employee," to file a complaint.[137] In a break from the anti-retaliation provisions in the SOX, a Dodd-Frank claimant, who alleges retaliation for SOX-protected whistleblower activity, may file suit directly in federal court without exhausting administrative remedies. According to the rules issued by the SEC after the Act, an individual is a whistleblower if he or she "possess[es] a reasonable belief that the information [he or she is] providing relates to a possible securities law violation."[138]

Other Legislation

In addition to the legislation previously discussed, several other major pieces of federal legislation contain whistleblower protection provisions within a larger piece of legislation. There other legislative acts that protect whistleblowers through narrowly tailored responses include:

- The Military Whistleblower Protection Act of 1998 (protecting members of the armed services)[139];
- The Wendell H. Ford Aviation Investment and Reform Act for the 21st Century (AIR 21),[140]

[134] Samuel Rubenfeld, '*SEC Receives 3,000 tips in Last Year*,' (*Wall St. J. Corruption Currents* (15 November 2012)). Available at www.blogs.wsj.com/corruption-currents/2012/11/15/sec-receives-3000-tips-in-the-past-year/.

[135] See Dodd-Frank Act §§ 748, 922.

[136] Ben Kerschberg, 'The Dodd-Frank Act's Robust Whistleblowing Incentives' *Forbes* (18. April 2011). Available at www.forbes.com/sites/benkerschberg/2011/04/14/the-dodd-frank-acts-robust-whistleblowing-incentives/.

[137] 28 U.S.C. § 1658(a).

[138] 17 C.F.R § 240.21 F-2(b)(1).

[139] 10 U.S.C. § 1034.

[140] 49 U.S.C. § 42121 (creating the Federal Aviation Whistleblower Protection Program).

- The Surface Transportation Assistance Act (STAA)(covering private sector drivers and commercial motor carriers)[141]
- Consumer Product Safety Improvement Act (CPSIA) of 2008[142];
- Asbestos Hazard Emergency Response Act (AHERA)[143];
- Clean Air Act[144];
- FDA Food Safety Modernization Act[145];
- Energy Reorganization Act[146];
- Federal Railroad Safety Act[147];
- Moving Ahead for Progress in the 21st Century Act (MAP-21)[148];
- National Transit Systems Security Act (NTSSA)[149];
- Occupational Safety and Health Act (OSHA).[150]

Whistleblower Protection Act

The key piece of federal stand-alone legislation is the Whistleblower Protection Act of 1989 (WPA).[151] On the surface, the Whistleblower Protection Act of 1989 (WPA) effectively shields federal employees from retaliation when they disclose illegal or improper government activities. The WPA's protections extend to most federal executive branch employees with the notable exclusions of employees of the Central Intelligence Agency (CIA) and National Security Agency (NSA). Those employees, as well as all positions, which by law are excluded from the competitive federal service due their "confidential, policy-determining, policy-making, or policy-advocating character" are excluded from protection under the WPA.[152] Additionally,

[141] id. § 31105 (amended by The Implementing Recommendations of the 9/11 Commission Act of 2007, Pub. L. No. 110-53, 121 Stat. 266).

[142] 15 U.S.C. § 2087.

[143] id. § 265.1.

[144] 42 U.S.C. § 762. There are other whistleblower protection provisions embedded in other environmental acts, including: Comprehensive Environmental Response, Compensation and Liability Act (CERCLA), 42 U.S.C. § 9610; Federal Water Pollution Control Act, 33 U.S.C. § 1367; Safe Drinking Water Act, 42 U.S.C. §§ 300j-9(i); Solid Waste Disposal Act, 42 U.S.C. § 6971; Toxic Substances Control Act, 15 U.S.C. § 2622; and Pipeline Safety Improvement Act, 49 U.S.C. § 60129.

[145] 21 U.S.C. § 391 et seq.

[146] 42 U.S.C. § 5851.

[147] 49 U.S.C. § 20109.

[148] id. § 30171.

[149] 6 U.S.C. § 1142.

[150] 29 U.S.C. § 660.

[151] Pub. L. No. 101-12, 103 Stat. 16 (codified in scattered sections of 5 U.S.C.).

[152] 5 U.S.C. § 2302(a)(2)(B)(i).

any additional positions designated by the President which are necessary for the good administration of government are also excluded from protection.[153]

The statutory protections apply when "personnel action" has been taken against a "covered employee" because of a "protected disclosure."[154] In addition to current employees who do not fall under the above-referenced exception, employees who merit protection also include: former employees, or applicants for employment to positions in the executive branch in both the "competitive and excepted service and positions in the Senior Executive Service."[155] If an employee falls within one of the protected classes, the next requirement for protection pertains to the nature of the information disclosed by the employee. Pursuant to the statute, the statute protects "any disclosure of information by an employee or applicant which the employee or applicant *reasonably believes* evidences:

- any violation of any law, rule, or regulation, or
- gross mismanagement, a gross waste of funds, an abuse of authority, or a substantial and specific danger to public health or safety…"[156]

The WPA does not apply to disclosures that the President has specifically designated by Executive Order. The Act also applies to disclosures to the Special Counsel, the Inspector General of an agency or another employee designated by an agency head to receive such disclosures.

In order to receive the protection of the WPA, the employee must simply have a reasonable belief that the information is true. According to one commentator, this is essentially "a good faith requirement" as the information's actual veracity does not influence a determination of protection.[157] The employee's belief in the truth of the disclosure must be reasonable to a disinterested observer.[158] This makes intuitive sense as it might be too risky in some cases for any employee to disclose information if he or she believes that the disclosure would be unprotected if the information turned out to be inaccurate. Although the "reasonable belief" requirement tilts in the employee's favor, the WPA contains a key limit on the subject matter of the disclosed information. Specifically, when the disclosure applies to the mismanagement or waste of funds, that mismanagement or waste must rise to "gross" proportions. According to a Senate Committee report, which accompanied the WPA legislation,

---

[153] A full list of employees not covered by the WPA include employees of the Postal Service, Postal Rate Commission, Government Accountability Office, Federal Bureau of Investigation, Central Intelligence Agency, Defense Intelligence Agency, National Imagery and Mapping Agency, National Security Agency, and other agencies designated by the President that conduct foreign intelligence or counter-intelligence activities. *See* 5 U.S.C. § 2302(a)(2)(C).

[154] LP Whitaker, '*The Whistleblower Protection Act*: *An Overview*' (2007) Congressional Research Service 1. Available at www.fas.org/sgp/crs/natsec/RL33918.pdf.

[155] 5 U.S.C. § 2302(a)(2)(B).

[156] id. § 2302(a)(8)(A).

[157] Whitaker (n 155) at 4.

[158] Merit Systems Protection Board, 'Whistleblower Protections to Federal Employees: A Report to the President and the Congress' (2010). Available at www.mspb.gov/netsearch/viewdocs.aspx?docnumber=557972&version=559604&application=ACROBAT.

committee members voiced concern that the legislation might trigger a flood of "trivial" disclosures and they sought to limit the disclosures regarding the waste of funds to the most serious cases.[159] Pursuant to the WPA, employees are directed to invoke the provisions of the WPA in one of four forums which include:

> (1) employee appeals to the Merit Systems Protection Board of an agency's adverse action against an employee, known as "Chapter 77" appeals; (2) actions instituted by the Office of Special Counsel; (3) individually maintained rights of action before the Merit Systems Protection Board (known as an individual right of action, or IRA); and (4) grievances brought by the employee under negotiated grievance procedures.[160]

The final key part of the WPA delineated the list of personnel actions that received protection under the Act. The key prohibited actions include: an appointment, a promotion, any disciplinary action, a transfer and reassignment, and a decision concerning pay, benefits or decisions regarding training and education.[161] Unfortunately, the Act did not protect employees who disclosed wrongdoing to a supervisor who was the wrongdoer. Nor did it protect disclosures made in the course of a whistle-blower's job duties (i.e. inspectors, auditors). While the Act sought to protect a wide range of disclosures, subsequent Circuit Court decisions narrowed the scope of the protected conduct.[162]

In 2012, after a 13 year effort to strengthen the employment protections available to federal workers, Congress amended the WPA through the Whistleblower Enhancement Act (WEPA).[163] The legislation aimed to close several loopholes that managers and supervisors had exploited. It also extended protections to employees of the Transportation Safety Administration and required Inspectors General Offices to designate a whistleblower protection ombudsman to educate employees about whistleblower protections. Not only did the Act seek to reverse the tendency of Federal Circuit Court of Appeals judges to narrow the scope of the original Act's protection, the Act, for a 2-year trial period, explicitly suspended the court's exclusive jurisdiction on appellate review. The court had consistently narrowed the WPA's protections. Moreover, in cases where whistleblowers lose at the administrative hearing stage, the Act gives the Office of Special Counsel the authority to appear as amicus curiae at the appellate stage. Although the WEPA was a step forward for federal workers, two key sections of the proposed legislation did not make it into the

---

[159] 5 U.S.C. § 2302(c).

[160] Whitaker (n 155) Summary.

[161] 5 U.S.C. § 2302(a)(2)(A).

[162] Those decisions included: (1) *Horton v. Dep't of the Navy*, 66 F.3d 279, 282 (Fed. Cir. 1995) (holding that disclosures to the alleged wrongdoer are not protected); (2) *Willis v. Dep't of Agric.*, 141 F.3d 1139, 1144 (Fed. Cir. 1998) (excluding from protection a disclosure made as part of an employee's normal job duties) and (3) *Meuwissen v. Dep't of Interior*, 234 F.3d 9, 12–13 (Fed. Cir. 2000) (holding that disclosures of information already known are not protected). For an extensive discussion of the legislative changes, see 'Congress Strengthens Whistleblower Protections for Federal Employees' ABA Section of Labor and Employment Law, (*Flash* Nov.-Dec. 2012). Available at www.americanbar.org/content/newsletter/groups/labor.law/ll_flash/1212_abalel_flash/lel_flash12_2012spec.html.

[163] Pub. L. No. 112-199, 126 Stat. 1465 (2012).

final bill. Those provisions would have given employees the right to pursue a jury trial to enforce their protections and extended free-speech rights to national security workers making disclosures within agency channels.[164]

Statutes

On paper, all 50 states offer employees robust protection from retaliation. When one examines the extent of the protection and the prerequisites for invoking that protection, the situation is less optimistic. Indeed widespread disparities in the level and type of protection offered on the state level have led one commentator to criticize state-level protections as "murky, piecemeal, disorganized and [inconsistent] from jurisdiction to jurisdiction."[165] Many employees, who may be more likely to first report violations using internal reporting channels, are left unprotected from retaliation in states such as Texas. Indeed, most states only protect state and public employees, leaving employees of private entities unprotected under state law.[166] State whistleblower laws also vary widely with respect to the nature of available remedies.[167] However, in a number of states, employers who violate public policy, in the process of discharging an employee, may face common law wrongful termination claims. In a ground-breaking decision, in 1959, a California court held that an employer could not dismiss an employee for refusing to commit perjury at the employer's behest.[168] According to R. Scott Oswald and Michael Vogelsang, two decades after the *Petermann* decision, courts in Indiana, Illinois, Michigan, and Pennsylvania began to embrace this public policy exception to the at-will employment doctrine.[169]

---

[164] Joe Davidson, 'Congress Approves Stronger Whistleblower Protections' *Washington Post* (13 November 2012). Available at www.washingtonpost.com/blogs/federal-eye/wp/2012/11/13/congress-approves-stronger-whistleblower-protections/?clsrd.

[165] M A Cherry, 'Whistling in the Dark? Corporate Fraud, Whistleblowers and the Implications of the Sarbanes-Oxley Act for Employment Law' (2004) 79 Washington Law Review 1029, 1049.

[166] Examples of states that only protect public employees include: Alabama (State Employees Protection Act, Ala. Code § 13A-12-1); Colorado (Colo. Rev. Stat. § 24-50.5-101 et seq.); and Missouri (Mo. Rev. Stat. § 105.055). Examples of states with more comprehensive protection that extends to private employers include: Florida (Fla. Stat. § 448.102); Nebraska (Neb. Rev. Stat. §§ 48-1102 & 48-1114) (applying to all firms with more than 15 employees); and Rhode Island (R.I. Gen Laws § 28-50-4). For a summary of state whistleblower protections, see 'State Whistleblower Laws' National Conference of State Legislatures (Nov. 2010). Available at www.ncsl.org/issues-research/labor/state-whistleblower-laws.aspx.

[167] G Sinzdak, 'An Analysis of Current Whistleblower Laws: Defending a More Flexible Approach to Reporting Requirements' (2008) 96 California Law Review 1633, 1641–41.

[168] Petermann v. International Broth. of Teamsters, Chauffeurs, Warehousemen and Helpers of America, Local 396, 174 Cal. App. 2d 184 (Cal. Ct. App. 1959).

[169] RS Oswald and M Vogelsang, Jr. 'The ABCs of Common Law Wrongful Termination Claims In The Washington Metropolitan Region' (2013) 3 Labor & Employment Law Forum no. 2: 197–262.

While space limits prohibit a review of state whistle-blowing legislation, it is important to note that, in some cases, there are areas of overlap between federal and state protections. In some cases, such as reports of Medicaid fraud and abuse, federal law requires state agencies to conduct preliminary investigations upon receiving a report.[170] The Deficit Reduction Act of 2005 (DRA) included incentives for states to enact anti-fraud legislation modeled after the FCA.[171] Under the provisions of the Act, states may receive an additional 10 % of Medicaid recovers if the state's FCA contains provisions rewarding and facilitating *qui tam* actions that are similar to those in the United States Code.[172]

Conclusion

The current patchwork of whistleblower protection in the United States is largely the result of the confluence of recurring waves of media publicity exposing government fraud, the growth in government spending and involvement, and Congress's attempts to respond to adverse publicity concerning government fraud. The succession of public crises running from Watergate to the wasteful spending in the Iraq War, to the collapse of the financial and securities industries have demonstrated that the government needs whistleblowers to help expose fraud and waste. As successive legislative attempts to extend whistleblower protections have demonstrated, reform "is usually precipitated by some crisis or new political movement that disrupts the preexisting status quo."[173] Ironically, in this fight to extend protections, Congress has often found itself at odds with federal judges who have repeatedly narrowed the scope of whistleblower protections and raised numerous hurdles for whistleblowers.

Bibliography

Bishara ND, Callahan ES, Dworkin TM (2013) *The Mouth of Truth. New York University* Journal of Law & Business 10: 37–114

Burke D (2011, July 15) *Thomas Drake Sentenced in NSA Leaks Case*. Huffington Post. http://www.huffingtonpost.com/2011/07/15/thomas-drake-nsa-leak_n_900384.html. Accessed April 2015

---

[170] 42 C.F.R. § 455.14.

[171] Pub. L. No. 109-171, 120 Stat. 4 (2006).

[172] 'Incentivising State False Claim Acts' *National Conference of State Legislatures* (7 March 2013). Available at www.ncsl.org/issues-research/health/clarifying-requirements-for-a-state-false-claims-a.aspx.

[173] MK Ramirez, '*Blowing the Whistle on Whistleblower Protection*: *A Tale of Reform* Versus *Power*' (2007) 76 University of Cincinnati Law Review 183, 198.

Burton MF, Acting Assistant Att'y Gen., U.S. Dep't of Justice, to Sen. Patrick J. Leahy, Chairman, Senate Judiciary Committee (2009, February 4) http://www.nacua.org/documents/LetterToSenLeahy_DoJ_Views_on_Section4_of_FERA_2.pdf. Accessed April 2015

Casey A, Niblett A (2013) *Noise Reduction: The Screening Value of Qui Tam*. http://ssrn.com/abstract=22376589. Accessed April 2015

Cherry MA (2004) *Whistling in the Dark? Corporate Fraud, Whistleblowers and the Implications of the Sarbanes-Oxley Act for Employment Law*. Washington Law Review 79: 1029–1122

Davidson J (2012, November 13) *Congress Approves Stronger Whistleblower Protections*. Washington Post. http://www.washingtonpost.com/blogs/federal-eye/wp/2012/11/13/congress-approves-stronger-whistleblower-protections/?clsrd. Accessed April 2015

Dozier K (2013, July 2) *James Clapper: Answer On NSA Surveillance To Congress Was 'Clearly Erroneous*. Huffington Post. http://bigstory.ap.org/article/dni-chief-apologizes-erroneous-answer-nsa. Accessed April 2015

Eisler P, Page S (2013, June 15) 3 NSA Veterans Speak Out on Whistleblower: We Told You So USA Today. http://www.usatoday.com/story/news/politics/2013/06/16/snowden-whistleblower-nsa-officials-roundtable/2428809/. Accessed April 2015

Elsberg D (2011, June 13) Why the Pentagon Papers Matter Now. Guardian

False Claims Act Recoveries Double in One Year to $9 Billion (2012, October 10) Corporate Crime Reporter.http://www.corporatecrimereporter.com/news/200/falseclaimsactrecoveries10102012/. Accessed April 2015

Fisch JE (2004) *The New Federal Regulation of Corporate Governance*. Harvard Journal of Law and Public Policy 28: 39–50

Haron DL, Dordeski MV, Lahman LD (Nov. 2009) Bad Mules: A Primer on the Federal and Michigan False Claims Act Claims. Michigan Bar Journal 22–25. http://www.michbar.org/journal/pdf/pdf4article1590.pdf. Accessed April 2015

Incentivising State False Claim Acts (2013, March 7) National Conference of State Legislatures. http://www.ncsl.org/issues-research/health/clarifying-requirements-for-a-state-false-claims-a.aspx. Accessed April 2015

Kaplan F (2013, June 13) Fire DNI James Clapper: The Director of National Intelligence lied to Congress about NSA surveillance. Slate. http://www.slate.com/articles/news_and_politics/war_stories/2013/06/fire_dni_james_clapper_he_lied_to_congress_about_nsa_surveillance.html. Accessed April 2015

Kerschberg K (2011, April 18) The Dodd-Frank Act's Robust Whistleblowing Incentives. http://www.forbes.com/sites/benkerschberg/2011/04/14/the-dodd-frank-acts-robust-whistleblowing-incentives/. Accessed April 2015

Kesselheim A, Studdert D and Mello, M (2010) *Whistle-Blowers' Experiences in Fraud Litigation Against Pharmaceutical Companies*. New England Journal of Medicine 362: 1832–39

Kohn SM (2011) *The Whistleblower's Handbook: A Step by Step Guide to Doing What's Right and Protecting Yourself*. Lyons Press, Guilford

Kohn SM (2011, June 12) The Whistle-Blowers of 1777. New York Times. http://www.nytimes.com/2011/06/13/opinion/13kohn.html. Accessed April 2015

Labaton S (2007, October 30). Strengthening of Consumer Agency Opposed by its Boss. New York Times. http://www.nytimes.com/2007/10/30/washington/30cnd-consumer.html?_r=0. Accessed April 2015

Langer G (2013, July 24) Attitudes Shift Against Snowden; Fewer than Half Say NSA is Unjustified. ABC News. http://www.langerresearch.com/uploads/1150a3SnowdenandSecurity.pdf/. Accessed April 2015

Lazarus D (2011, August 19) Obama needs to add consumer agency to his to-do list. Los Angeles Times. http://articles.latimes.com/2011/aug/19/business/la-fi-lazarus-20110819. Accessed April 2015

Levy P (2013, August 30) NSA FISA Surveillance: Is Obama's Latest Transparency Move A Trick? International Business Times. http://www.ibtimes.com/nsa-fisa-surveillance-obamas-latest-transparency-move-trick-1401972. Accessed 30 Aug 2013

Ling ST, Zito RJ (2013, March 18) Occupational Safety & Health Administration extends broad whistleblower protections to employees complaining of violations of the Patient Protection and Affordable Care Act. Lexology. http://www.lexology.com/library/detail.aspx?g=881218b5-4b23-4819-9b9d-45ae6aad58ea. Accessed April 2015

McBride SD (2009) Something Wicked This Way Comes: The United States Government's Response to Unsafe Imported Chinese Toys and Subsidized Chinese Exports. Texas International Law Journal 45: 233–295

Merit Systems Protection Board (2010) Whistleblower Protections to Federal Employees: A Report to the President and the Congress. http://www.mspb.gov/netsearch/viewdocs.aspx?docnumber=557972&version=559604&application=ACROBAT. Accessed April 2015

Mid-Year False Claims Act Update (2010, July 9) GibsonDunn http://www.gibsondunn.com/publications/pages/2010mid-yearfalseclaimsactupdate.aspx. Accessed April 2015

Moberly, Richard E (2007) Unfulfilled Expectations: *An Empirical Analysis of Why Sarbanes-Oxley Whistleblowers Rarely Win*. William & Mary Law Review 49: 65–70

Nolan, Auerbach & White (2010, August 9) Recent False Claims Act Amendments Fully Protect Whistleblowers. Qui Tam 101 Blog. http://false-claims-act.net/recent-false-claims-act-amendments-fully-protect-whistleblowers-2/. Accessed April 2015

Oswald RS, Vogelsang, Jr. M (2013) *The ABCs of Common Law Wrongful Termination Claims In The Washington Metropolitan Region*. Labor & Employment Law Forum 3: 197-262

Pasha S (2006, March 16) Enron's Whistle Blower Details Sinking Ship. CNNMoney.com. http://money.cnn.com/2006/03/15/news/newsmakers/enron/. Accessed April 2015

Pitzke M (2013, July 24) *War on Whistleblowers: Has Obama Scrapped the First Amendment?* Spiegel Online International. http://www.spiegel.de/international/world/obama-wages-war-on-whistleblowers-and-journalists-a-912852.html. Accessed 24 July 2013

Press Release (2011, December 19) Senator Patrick Leahy. Comment of Senator Patrick Leahy on False Claims Act Settlements in 2011. http://www.leahy.senate.gov/press/comment-of-senator-patrick-leahy-on-false-claims-act-settlements-in-2011. Accessed April 2015

Quinnipiac University Poll (2013, August 1) Snowden Is Whistle-Blower, Not Traitor, U.S. Voters Tell Quinnipiac University National Poll. http://www.quinnipiac.edu/images/polling/us/us08012013.pdf. Accessed April 2015

Ramirez MK (2007) Blowing the Whistle on Whistleblower Protection: A Tale of Reform Versus Power. University of Cincinnati Law Review 76: 183–233

Rapp GC (2012)Mutiny by the Bounties? The Attempt to Reform Wall Street by the New Whistleblower Provisions of the Dodd-Frank Act. Brigham Young University Law Review 73–152

Rubenfeld S (2012, November 15) SEC Receives 3,000 tips in Last Year. Wall St. J. Corruption Currents. http://blogs.wsj.com/corruption-currents/2012/11/15/sec-receives-3000-tips-in-the-past-year/. Accessed April 2015

Santo BG (July 2010) *The False Claims Act: Analysis of the Recently Expanded Legislation on Qui Tam Actions and Related Impact on Whistleblowers*. American Bar Association Health E-SOURCE. https://www.americanbar.org/content/newsletter/publications/aba_health_esource_home/Volume6_SE2_Santo.html. Accessed April 2015

Sasso B (2013, August 3) Amash: *Snowden is a Whistleblower.* The Hill http://thehill.com/blogs/blog-briefing-room/blog-summaries/315413-rep-amash-snowden-is-a-whistleblower. Accessed April 2015

Schichor N (2008) *Does Sarbanes-Oxley Force Whistleblowers to Sacrifice their Reputations?: An Argument for Granting Whistleblowers Non-Pecuniary Damages*. University of California at Davis Business Law Journal 8: 272–297

Schulz M (2010, April 20) *Whistleblower Protections in the Affordable Care Act.* http://www.lexology.com/library/detail.aspx?g=e5d83cf5-6f63-4390-8ade-f338587dea98. Accessed April 2015

Shiffman S, Rotenberg J (2010, February 12) *District Court limits the Sarbanes-Oxley Act's Whistleblower Protections. Lexology*. http://www.lexology.com/library/detail.aspx?g=c9fbf3d6-eefb-48c8-9cc2-95353d851d9c. Accessed April 2015

Shorrock T (2013, April 5) *Obama's Crackdown on Whistleblowers*. Nation. http://www.thenation.com/article/173521/obamas-crackdown-whistleblowers. Accessed April 2015.

Sinzdak G (2008) *An Analysis of Current Whistleblower Laws: Defending a More Flexible Approach to Reporting Requirements* California Law Review 96: 1633-1668

U.S. Department of Justice (2011, April 22) *The False Claims Act: A Primer* http://www.justice.gov/sites/default/files/civil/legacy/2011/04/22/C-FRAUDS_FCA_Primer.pdf. Accessed April 2015.

U.S. Department of Justice (2013, December 20) Justice Department Recovers $3.8 Billion from False Claims Act Cases in Fiscal Year 2013. http://www.justice.gov/opa/pr/justice-department-recovers-38-billion-false-claims-act-cases-fiscal-year-2013. Accessed April 2015.

U.S. Department of Justice, False Claims Act Cases: Government Intervention in Qui Tam (Whistleblower) Cases' (n.d). https://www.doioig.gov/docs/falseclaimsact.pdf. Accessed April 2015.

U.S. Health Care Reform Legislation Significantly Expands the False Claims Act (2010, April 2) GibsonDunn. http://www.gibsondunn.com/publications/pages/HealthCareReformLegislationExpandstheFalseClaimsAct.aspx. Accessed April 2015.

US Officials 'betrayed' CIA Agent (2006, July 14) BBC News. http://news.bbc.co.uk/2/hi/americas/5180906.stm. Accessed April 2015

Van Buren P (2012, June 12) *Obama's War on Whistleblowers. Mother Jones*. http://www.motherjones.com/politics/2012/06/obamas-whistleblowers-stuxnet-leaks-drones. Accessed April 2015

Vaughn RG (2012) *The Successes and Failures of Whistleblower Laws*. Edward Elgar, Cheltonham UK

Vaughn RG, Brewer MW (1975) *The Spoiled System: A Call for Civil Service Reform*. Charterhouse, New York

Wallace K (2002, July 31) *Senators: Bush Could Undercut Whistleblowers*. CNN. http://edition.cnn.com/2002/ALLPOLITICS/07/31/bush.leahy.corporate/. Accessed April 2015

What is the Sarbanes-Oxley (SOX) Act? Katz, Marshall & Banks Blog (n.d.) http://kmblegal.com/practice-areas/whistleblower-law/sarbanes-oxley/. Accessed April 2015

Whitaker LP (2007) The Whistleblower Protection Act: An Overview. Congressional Research Service. http://www.fas.org/sgp/crs/natsec/RL33918.pdf. Accessed April 2015.

Yost P (2012, December 12) False Claims Act Leads To $5 Billion In Government Recoveries Over Past Year. Huffington Post. http://www.huffingtonpost.com/2012/12/04/false-claims-act_n_2238111.html. Accessed April 2015.

Part III
Synopsys of Whistleblowing in 23 Jurisdictions

	Austria	Belgium	Brazil	Canada	Croatia
What is the overall relevance of whistleblowing in your jurisdiction?					
How would you rate the overall relevance of this subject in the field of employment law?	Some relevance in the field of risk management and corporate governance Intensifying discussion since about 2009, although "whistleblowing" cases can be found decades ago already	Gaining importance	–	Some relevance	Little relevance
Are there many cases or is there extensive literature on this subject?	Some cases, some literature	Some cases, a lot of literature	–	About 60 cases, some literature	Little case-law or literature Important case: *Balenović vs. Croatia* (ECtHR)
What is the legal basis for the protection of whistleblowers in your jurisdiction?					
Are there any special statutes on the protection of whistleblowers in your jurisdiction?	Yes public sector environmental issues	Yes public sector (nationwide) private sector (regional)	No	Yes public sector (nationwide) private sector (regional)	No

(continued)

	Austria	Belgium	Brazil	Canada	Croatia
Are there any general statutes covering whistleblowing in your jurisdiction?	No	Labour law	Labour law	Labour law Criminal law	Labour law
Are whistleblowers protected by the case-law in your jurisdiction?	Yes, case-law on duty of care and loyalty in the employment relationship	Yes, but few cases	Few cases	Yes, case-law protected whistleblowers before special legislation entered into force	–
Who is protected?					
Does your jurisdiction protect everyone or employees only?	Employees	Public sector: Employees Private sector (regional): Employees	–	Public sector (nationwide): Employees Private sector (regional): Employees Region of Quebec: Everyone Criminal law (nationwide): Everyone	No provision, possibly employees only
Are self-employed persons also protected?	No	No	–	Not under nationwide laws, but under some regional laws	–
Does your jurisdiction protect people who are helping or encouraging whistleblowers?	No provision	Public sector: Yes Private sector: No provision, possibly yes	Yes, under general rules applicable	No provision, possibly yes	No
Does your jurisdiction protect persons who affirm a whistleblower's allegations?	No provision	Public sector: Yes. Private sector: No provision, possibly yes	Yes, under general rules applicable.	Yes Public sector (nationwide): Expressive rule Private sector (regional): Expressive rule Criminal law (nationwide): Implicit rule General laws applicable (nationwide): Testimony in court	No provision

(continued)

	Austria	Belgium	Brazil	Canada	Croatia
What kind of behaviour is protected?					
Does your jurisdiction allow for anonymous whistleblowing?	No provision, but used by public prosecutors since 2013	Prohibited in certain proceedings, unclear in other situations	Yes	No	No (unclear: anonymity is "guaranteed" in certain proceedings, which means that addressee must know identity)
Does your jurisdiction require the whistleblower to make use of internal reporting systems before he is allowed to appeal to third parties?	Yes, but exceptions apply	Public sector: Yes Private sector: Yes, but exceptions may apply	No provision, but "best practice"	Yes, at least in principle	Public sector: Yes
Is a whistleblower allowed to turn to the media in your jurisdiction, at least in severe cases?	No provision or case law, possibly not	Public sector: No Private sector: No provision, probably not	Yes	Yes	Yes
Does your jurisdiction protect whistleblowers who are making allegations erroneously or in the face of an uncertainty of the relevant facts?	Yes, good faith requirement	Public sector: Good faith requirement Private sector: No	Yes, good faith requirement	Yes, good faith requirement	No
Is the motivation of the whistleblower relevant in your jurisdiction?	No	Public sector: No Private sector: Yes, good faith requirement	No	Yes, good faith requirement	Yes, good faith requirement
What kind of facts may a whistleblower report in your jurisdiction?	–	Public sector: "Every violation of the duty of integrity"	Breaches of law	Breaches of law Danger to life, health or the environment Misuse of public funds Serious breaches of codes of conduct	Corruption, fraud, criminal offences

(continued)

	Austria	Belgium	Brazil	Canada	Croatia
Is a whistleblower protected if he reports bygone incidents which are unlikely to happen again?	Yes	–	Yes	Yes, but reports concerning a reprisal of an employee have to be made within 60 days after the event	No
Is there an obligation to blow the whistle in your jurisdiction?	Yes, e.g. for civil servants and to prevent money laundering	–	–	–	–
What is the level of protection offered?					
Are whistleblowers protected against any kind of detriment or against dismissal only?	Case-law covers dismissal protection only	Public sector: Any detriment	Any kind of detriment	Any kind of detriment	Dismissal only
	It is possible that whistleblowers are not even protected against ordinary dismissal	Private sector: In theory, any detriment, but in practice, dismissal protection is predominant			
Which party bears the onus in dismissal cases that a notice was given due to whistleblowing?	–	Variable	Whistleblower, but reverse of burden of proof is possible	Employer	Employer
Does your jurisdiction allow certain interested groups (e.g. trade unions, consumer protection groups) to take collective action to protect whistleblowers?	Yes, works councils may enter model case proceedings	Yes, in anti-discrimination cases	Yes, trade unions may take action	No provision	No
Does your jurisdiction allow financial incentives or rewards for whistleblowers?	Whistleblowers may be treated as key witnesses in certain proceedings	–	–	–	–

(continued)

	Cyprus	Czech Republic	Estonia	Finland	France
What is the overall relevance of whistleblowing in your jurisdiction?					
How would you rate the overall relevance of this subject in the field of employment law?	Gaining importance	Gaining importance	Little relevance	Little relevance	Met with reticence due to experience with Vichy-regime Gaining importance in the field of corporate governance
Are there many cases or is there extensive literature on this subject?	No	Some cases, increasing amount of literature	Few cases	Few cases	Few cases
What is the legal basis for the protection of whistleblowers in your jurisdiction?					
Are there any special statutes on the protection of whistleblowers in your jurisdiction?	No	No	No	No	No special act, but singular special rules Decisions of general applicability by data protection authority
Are there any general statutes covering whistleblowing in your jurisdiction?	Yes, labour law/law relating to public administration, criminal law	Labour law Data protection legislation	Freedom of expression vs. duty of trust and confidence	Labour law Data protection legislation	Freedom of expression Labour law Data protection legislation
Are whistleblowers protected by the case-law in your jurisdiction?	Yes	Yes	Yes (few cases)	Yes (few cases)	Yes
Who is protected?					
Does your jurisdiction protect everyone or employees only?	Public sector: Employees	–	Case-law: Employees Freedom of expression: Everyone	Labour law protects employees only	Freedom of expression: Everyone Labour law: Employees
Are self-employed persons also protected?	–	–	–	–	Directors could be protected (uncertain), "outsiders" rather not

(continued)

	Cyprus	Czech Republic	Estonia	Finland	France
Does your jurisdiction protect people who are helping or encouraging whistleblowers?	–	–	No provision	–	No provision
Does your jurisdiction protect persons who affirm a whistleblower's allegations?	–	–	No provision	–	Yes, if testimony is relating to Discrimination Environmental issues Corruption Health and safety at work
What kind of behaviour is protected?					
Does your jurisdiction allow for anonymous whistleblowing?	Public sector: Yes	Yes	No provision	–	Yes, but restrictions apply
Does your jurisdiction require the whistleblower to make use of internal reporting systems before he is allowed to appeal to third parties?	No provision, but probably yes	–	Yes	–	No provision
Is a whistleblower allowed to turn to the media in your jurisdiction, at least in severe cases?	No provision	–	No provision, but in practice, this happens	Yes	No provision
Does your jurisdiction protect whistleblowers who are making allegations erroneously or in the face of an uncertainty of the relevant facts?	No provision	–	No provision	–	Yes, good faith requirement
Is the motivation of the whistleblower relevant in your jurisdiction?	–	–	No provision	–	Yes, good faith requirement
What kind of facts may a whistleblower report in your jurisdiction?	Public sector: Corruption and bribery Other facts may be covered by general law	–	No provision	–	Freedom of expression is not restricted Statutes cover certain breaches of law and certain dangers (e.g. to life, health, environment) only

(continued)

	Cyprus	Czech Republic	Estonia	Finland	France
Is a whistleblower protected if he reports bygone incidents which are unlikely to happen again?	–	–	No provision	–	Yes, at least by freedom of expression
Is there an obligation to blow the whistle in your jurisdiction?	–	–	Yes serious crime health and safety at work corruption danger to the environment	–	–
What is the level of protection offered?					
Are whistleblowers protected against any kind of detriment or against dismissal only?	Public sector: Any kind of detriment Employers may commit a crime by sanctioning whistleblowers	–	No provision, case-law covers dismissals only	Any kind of detriment	Any kind of detriment
Which party bears the onus in dismissal cases that a notice was given due to whistleblowing?	Employer	–	Variable	Employer	Employer
Does your jurisdiction allow certain interested groups (e.g. trade unions, consumer protection groups) to take collective action to protect whistleblowers?	–	–	No provision	No provision	No, but legislator considers introduction of special legislation
Does your jurisdiction allow financial incentives or rewards for whistleblowers?	–	Yes, employer may set incentives	No provision	No	Yes, employer may set incentives

	Germany	Italy	Japan	Malta	Netherlands
What is the overall relevance of whistleblowing in your jurisdiction?					
How would you rate the overall relevance of this subject in the field of employment law?	Gaining importance, although met with reticence due to National Socialist (1933–1945) and communist (East Germany, until 1989) systems of denunciation	Little relevance	Gaining importance	Gaining importance after special legislation entered into force in 2013	Gaining importance

(continued)

	Germany	Italy	Japan	Malta	Netherlands
Are there many cases or is there extensive literature on this subject?	Some cases, growing body of literature	Few cases	Few cases and some literature	Some literature	Some case-law, some literature
What is the legal basis for the protection of whistleblowers in your jurisdiction?					
Are there any special statutes on the protection of whistleblowers in your jurisdiction?	No special act, but singular special rules	Yes, for the public sector	Yes	Yes	Yes, special statute for public sector Non-binding best practices exist in the private sector
Are there any general statutes covering whistleblowing in your jurisdiction?	Freedom of speech Labour law Antidiscrimination legislation Data protection legislation	Freedom of speech Labour law Data protection legislation	Labour law	Labour law	Labour law
Are whistleblowers protected by the case-law in your jurisdiction?	Yes Important case: *Heinisch vs. Germany* (ECtHR)	Yes, especially in the private sector	Yes, before entering into force of special legislation	Yes, before entering into force of special legislation No case-law on special legislation yet	Yes, case-law interpreting special legislation in the public sector Case-law is the basis of whistleblower protection in the private sector
Who is protected?					
Does your jurisdiction protect everyone or employees only?	Freedom of speech: Everyone Special rules: Variable (everyone/ employees) Labour law: Employees	Public sector: Employees and civil servants Private sector: Employees, apart from one specific case that includes "workers"	Employees, including agency workers	Employees, including former employees and volunteers	Public sector: Civil servants Private sector: Employees
Are self-employed persons also protected?	No	Possible (unclear)	No provision	Possible (unclear)	–

(continued)

	Germany	Italy	Japan	Malta	Netherlands
Does your jurisdiction protect people who are helping or encouraging whistleblowers?	Yes, under antidsicrimination legislation No provision outside that scope	No provision	No provision	No provision	–
Does your jurisdiction protect persons who affirm a whistleblower's allegations?	Yes, under antidsicrimination legislation No provision outside that scope	–	No provision	No provision	–
What kind of behaviour is protected?					
Does your jurisdiction allow for anonymous whistleblowing?	Yes, but according to case-law, freedom of expression does not protect anonymous whistleblowing	No provision, but anonymous whistleblowing is used in practice	No provision, but employers have to react to whistleblowing within 20 days which implies that they have to know the identity of the whistleblower	No	Not expressively, but sometimes accepted in practice
Does your jurisdiction require the whistleblower to make use of internal reporting systems before he is allowed to appeal to third parties?	Yes, but exceptions apply	No	No	Yes, but exceptions apply	Public sector: External reporting to certain institutions is permitted Private sector: Best practices allow for external whistleblowing in specific circumstances
Is a whistleblower allowed to turn to the media in your jurisdiction, at least in severe cases?	Yes	Yes	Yes	No	Yes, at least under the best practices applicable in the private sector, but restrictions apply
Does your jurisdiction protect whistleblowers who are making allegations erroneously or in the face of an uncertainty of the relevant facts?	Yes, good faith requirement	Yes, good faith requirement Expression of personal opinions, satire etc. protected to a wider extent	Yes, good faith requirement No protection if false information is spread via the media	Yes, good faith requirement	Yes, good faith requirement

(continued)

	Germany	Italy	Japan	Malta	Netherlands
Is the motivation of the whistleblower relevant in your jurisdiction?	Yes, good faith requirement According to case-law, the motivation is the predominant criterion	Yes, good faith requirement	Yes, good faith requirement	Yes, good faith requirement	–
What kind of facts may a whistleblower report in your jurisdiction?	Breaches of law	Breaches of law	Breaches of laws listed in an annex to special legislation (about 400 statutes at present)	No restrictions	Crime Infraction of the rules of public service Misleading of justice Danger to public health or the environment
Is a whistleblower protected if he reports bygone incidents which are unlikely to happen again?	No provision, possibly yes	Possibly yes	–	Yes	–
Is there an obligation to blow the whistle in your jurisdiction?	Yes Everyone is obliged to report serious crime (e.g. murder) that is yet just intended by others Obligations to report dangers exist in the fields of health and safety at work, protection of the environment and money laundering	–	Yes, civil servants have to report crime related to their office	–	Yes For everyone relating to serious crime For public servants relating to corruption
What is the level of protection offered?					
Are whistleblowers protected against any kind of detriment or against dismissal only?	Any kind of detriment	Any kind of detriment	Any kind of detriment	Any kind of detriment	Any kind of detriment

(continued)

	Germany	Italy	Japan	Malta	Netherlands
Which party bears the onus in dismissal cases that a notice was given due to whistleblowing?	Employer	Employer	Internal whistleblowing: Employer, whistleblower has to prove good faith only External whistleblowing: Whistleblower	Variable	Whistleblower
Does your jurisdiction allow certain interested groups (e.g. trade unions, consumer protection groups) to take collective action to protect whistleblowers?	No provision, general rights of trade unions and employee's representatives may be applicable	Yes, trade unions and antidiscrimination groups	No provision	No provision	No
Does your jurisdiction allow financial incentives or rewards for whistleblowers?	No provision	–	No provision	–	No

	Poland	Portugal	Romania	Singapore	Slovenia
What is the overall relevance of whistleblowing in your jurisdiction?					
How would you rate the overall relevance of this subject in the field of employment law?	Gaining importance	Little relevance	Relevant in public sector	Gaining importance Whistleblowing systems prescribed by law for purposes of corporate governance in listed companies since 2012	Little relevance
Are there many cases or is there extensive literature on this subject?	Some cases and some literature	Few cases	Few cases	Few cases	No cases, some literature
What is the legal basis for the protection of whistleblowers in your jurisdiction?					
Are there any special statutes on the protection of whistleblowers in your jurisdiction?	No	No	Yes, special statute for public sector	No special act, but at least 17 special rules	Yes, covering corruption

(continued)

	Poland	Portugal	Romania	Singapore	Slovenia
Are there any general statutes covering whistleblowing in your jurisdiction?	Freedom of expression	Freedom of expression	Labour law	No	Labour law
	Right to equal treatment	Labour law			
	Labour law				
	Criminal law				
Are whistleblowers protected by the case-law in your jurisdiction?	The case-law awards a whistleblower damages only, he may not hope for reinstatement usually	Yes (few cases)	–	Yes (few cases)	–
Who is protected?					
Does your jurisdiction protect everyone or employees only?	Fundamental rights: Everyone	–	Public sector: Employees and civil servants	Special rules: Everyone ("informers")	Special legislation: Everyone
	Labour law: Employees		Private sector: No provision		Labour law: Employees and civil servants
Are self-employed persons also protected?	Possible claim to damages (unclear)	–	No provision	See above	Labour law: Yes, if economically dependent
Does your jurisdiction protect people who are helping or encouraging whistleblowers?	Yes	No	No provision	No	–
Does your jurisdiction protect persons who affirm a whistleblower's allegations?	Yes	–	Yes	No	–
What kind of behaviour is protected?					
Does your jurisdiction allow for anonymous whistleblowing?	Yes, but uncommon	No, but stated in one case only	No provision, but presumably yes	Yes	Special legislation: Yes
Does your jurisdiction require the whistleblower to make use of internal reporting systems before he is allowed to appeal to third parties?	No provision	No provision, possibly yes (unclear)	Public sector: No provision, but possibly yes	Public sector: Yes	No, but exceptions apply under special legislation for officials
			Private sector: No provision, but work rules/ collective agreements may prescribe this	Private sector: No, but restrictions apply	

(continued)

	Poland	Portugal	Romania	Singapore	Slovenia
Is a whistleblower allowed to turn to the media in your jurisdiction, at least in severe cases?	No provision, but possibly not. At least, severe restrictions apply	No provision, possibly not (unclear)	Yes	Unclear	Yes, but restrictions apply
Does your jurisdiction protect whistleblowers who are making allegations erroneously or in the face of an uncertainty of the relevant facts?	Yes, good faith requirement	No	Yes, good faith requirement	No, whistleblower needs to establish that facts are true before reporting	Yes, good faith requirement
Is the motivation of the whistleblower relevant in your jurisdiction?	Yes, good faith requirement	Yes, good faith requirement	Yes, good faith requirement	Yes, good faith requirement	Yes, good faith requirement
What kind of facts may a whistleblower report in your jurisdiction?	Breaches of law	–	Breaches of law	Breaches of law Unethical conduct	Breaches of law Unethical conduct
Is a whistleblower protected if he reports bygone incidents which are unlikely to happen again?	–	–	–	Yes	–
Is there an obligation to blow the whistle in your jurisdiction?	Yes Everyone is obliged to report serious crime Certain employee representatives have to report dangers to health and safety	–	–	–	Yes, for civil servants concerning crime relating to their office
What is the level of protection offered?					
Are whistleblowers protected against any kind of detriment or against dismissal only?	Any kind of detriment	–	Any kind of detriment	Any kind of detriment	Special legislation: Any kind of detriment
Which party bears the onus in dismissal cases that a notice was given due to whistleblowing?	Whistleblower	Employer	Employer	Employer	Employer

(continued)

	Poland	Portugal	Romania	Singapore	Slovenia
Does your jurisdiction allow certain interested groups (e.g. trade unions, consumer protection groups) to take collective action to protect whistleblowers?	Yes, trade unions and non-commercial organisations	No	Yes, trade unions	Yes, trade unions	–
Does your jurisdiction allow financial incentives or rewards for whistleblowers?	No provision	–	Yes, employer may set incentives	No	No

	South Korea	UK	USA
What is the overall relevance of whistleblowing in your jurisdiction?			
How would you rate the overall relevance of this subject in the field of employment law?	Little relevance	Some relevance, but many cases do not seem to reach the courts	Important, relevance growing since "Watergate" scandal and again after Snowden disclosures
Are there many cases or is there extensive literature on this subject?	Few cases, some literature	Yes	Yes
What is the legal basis for the protection of whistleblowers in your jurisdiction?			
Are there any special statutes on the protection of whistleblowers in your jurisdiction?	Yes, special statute each for public and for private sector	Yes	Yes, many statutes for certain situations (nationwide and regional), but no general statute on the protection of whistleblowers
Are there any general statutes covering whistleblowing in your jurisdiction?	Yes, case-law interpreting statutes	Yes, antidiscrimination legislation	–
Are whistleblowers protected by the case-law in your jurisdiction?	Yes, case-law interpreting special legislation	Yes, case-law interpreting special legislation	Yes, case-law interpreting special legislation Case-law often interprets special legislation restrictively, lowering level of protection

(continued)

	South Korea	UK	USA
Who is protected?			
Does your jurisdiction protect everyone or employees only?	Everyone	"Workers", which has a broader scope than "employees"	Some statutes protect everyone
Are self-employed persons also protected?	See above	Yes	See above
Does your jurisdiction protect people who are helping or encouraging whistleblowers?	Yes	Yes, under antidiscrimination legislation, but only in relation to complaints of unlawful discrimination	–
Does your jurisdiction protect persons who affirm a whistleblower's allegations?	Yes	Yes	–
What kind of behaviour is protected?			
Does your jurisdiction allow for anonymous whistleblowing?	No	Yes	Yes
Does your jurisdiction require the whistleblower to make use of internal reporting systems before he is allowed to appeal to third parties?	No, but restrictions apply	Yes, but exceptions apply	Not in general
Is a whistleblower allowed to turn to the media in your jurisdiction, at least in severe cases?	Yes, but not covered by special legislation/by labour law only	Yes, but restrictions apply	Depends on the special legislation applicable
Does your jurisdiction protect whistleblowers who are making allegations erroneously or in the face of an uncertainty of the relevant facts?	Yes, good faith requirement	Yes, whistleblower must reasonably believe that disclosure is in the public interest	Yes, good faith requirement

(continued)

	South Korea	UK	USA
Is the motivation of the whistleblower relevant in your jurisdiction?	Yes, good faith requirement	Yes, whistleblower must reasonably believe that disclosure is in the public interest	–
What kind of facts may a whistleblower report in your jurisdiction?	–	Breaches of law Danger to life, health or the environment	Depends on the special legislation applicable, but they cover breaches of law, danger to life, health and public safety
Is a whistleblower protected if he reports bygone incidents which are unlikely to happen again?	Yes	Yes	–
Is there an obligation to blow the whistle in your jurisdiction?	Yes, in the public sector, corruption and a danger to the public need to be reported	–	–
What is the level of protection offered?			
Are whistleblowers protected against any kind of detriment or against dismissal only?	Any kind of detriment	Any kind of detriment	Any kind of detriment (may depend on the special legislation applicable)
Which party bears the onus in dismissal cases that a notice was given due to whistleblowing?	Employer	Employer	–
Does your jurisdiction allow certain interested groups (e.g. trade unions, consumer protection groups) to take collective action to protect whistleblowers?	No provision	No	–
Does your jurisdiction allow financial incentives or rewards for whistleblowers?	Yes, but only insofar as expressively provided for by special legislation (not by the employer)	Yes	Yes

(continued)

Civil service act and public service model rules

	Yes	No	Partial	Notes
Broad definition of whistleblowing[m18]	X			"Vermoeden Misstanden" as presumed deficiencies – an appropriately broad subject matter definition -
Broad definition of whistleblower[m19]		X		Only public servants in public service. In private sector recommendations, only – often unheeded.
Broad definition of retribution protection			X	The definition is a bit unclear: "No disadvantage of any sort to legal positions" – but only to legal positions ?! [m20]
Internal reporting mechanism[m21]	X			Yes, there the rules prescribe fairly clear internal reporting mechanisms within given public institutions.
External reporting mechanism			X	To National Ombudsman and Integrity Commission
Whistleblower participation		X		The public service whistleblower may ask for a conclusive answer within a given time frame – no actual participation in process.
Rewards System		X		
Protection of confidentiality			X	Only in the sense that the procedure is designed to have all information stay internal.
Anonymous reports accepted		X		Not under the official procedures
No sanctions for misguided reporting	X			As long as done in good faith.
Whistleblower complaints authority			X	National Ombudsman
Genuine day in court[m22]			X	There is no mechanism to debate "conclusive remarks" on internal whistleblowing. If whistleblowers suffer a detriment, they can challenge the administration in Court like anyone else.
Full range of remedies[m23]			X	Yes – as for anyone.
Penalties for retaliation[m24]			X	No special penalties on retaliated against whistleblowers, therefor only sanctions, if behaviour is generally prohibited.
Involvement of multiple actors		X		

STAR recommendations and model rules

	Yes	No	Partial	Notes
Broad definition of whistleblowing	X			
Broad definition of whistleblower			X	Employee, (…) whether or not under working contract
Broad definition of retribution protection			X	No disadvantage of any sort – to legal positions
Internal reporting mechanism	X			
External reporting mechanism	X			
Whistleblower participation			X	
Rewards System		X		
Protection of confidentiality		X		"not inform others in the company unnecessarily"
Anonymous reports accepted		X		
No sanctions for misguided reporting	X			
Whistleblower complaints authority			X	Now, also the Whistleblower Advice Center
Genuine day in court			X	As for anyone
Full range of remedies			X	As for anyone, however, since 2009 costs of proceedings could be partially reimbursed.
Penalties for retaliation			X	As for anyone
Involvement of multiple actors		X		

Legal Material

Ambtenarenwet

Artikel 125 quinquies

1. Voor zover deze onderwerpen niet bij of krachtens de wet zijn geregeld, **worden voor de ambtenaren**, door of vanwege het rijk aangesteld, bij of krachtens **algemene maatregel van bestuur voorschriften vastgesteld betreffende:**

   (a–e) (…) [conflicts of interest, outside employment; insider information;]

   (f) een procedure voor het **omgaan met bij een ambtenaar levende vermoedens van misstanden binnen de organisatie waar hij werkzaam is**.

2. (…)
3. De ambtenaar die te goeder trouw de bij hem levende **vermoedens van misstanden meldt** volgens de procedure, bedoeld in het eerste lid onder f, zal als gevolg van het melden van die vermoedens **geen nadelige gevolgen** voor zijn rechtspositie ondervinden tijdens en na het volgen van die procedure.

Model Procedures[1]

The three tiered procedure provided by the Labour Foundation has little resemblance of its UK role model:

Stichting Model Tier 1 [m25][only?] if the relevant hierarchical superior is involved, the whistleblower may address the immediate "superior authority";

[1] Stichting van de Arbeid, in Appendix: Sample procedure Procedural rules for dealing with suspected malpractice.

G. Thüsing, G. Forst (eds.), *Whistleblowing - A Comparative Study*,
Ius Comparatum - Global Studies in Comparative Law 16,
DOI 10.1007/978-3-319-25577-4

Stichting Model Tier 2 if the whistleblower has some doubts on whether and how to report, he/she may consult a confidential integrity counsellor designated by the employer[m26]; and

Stichting Model Tier 3 if the whistleblower disagrees with the decision of the hierarchical superior, or no information is provided in a reasonable period of time concerning the outcome of the relevant investigations of the reported suspicions, the whistleblower has the possibility to report to the Central Government Integrity Committee (as a second instance).

(Only] under special conditions – if significant risks are preventing the use of the normal internal channels from reporting suspicions (e.g., one or more senior officials are involved in

STAR Sample Procedure (2010)[2]

Procedural Rules for Dealing with Suspected Malpractice

The Labour Foundation believes it is important for employees to be able to report suspected malpractice within their companies by the most suitable means without putting themselves at risk. That requires a proper procedure to be put in place. The methods companies use to do this will depend in part on their size and the nature of their activities.

This annex presents a possible set of rules for dealing with suspected malpractice, based on the basic components of the "Statement on dealing with suspected malpractice in companies".

It is up to local parties to decide which of the following articles should be included – either as is or in amended form – in any procedural rules, given the size and nature of the company or companies concerned.

Section 1. Definitions

Article 1

In these rules, the following terms shall be understood to have the meanings assigned to them below:

employee: person working for the employer, whether or not under an employment contract;

external third party: an external third party as referred to in Article 6.1;

[2] dito.

G. Thüsing, G. Forst (eds.), *Whistleblowing - A Comparative Study*,
Ius Comparatum - Global Studies in Comparative Law 16,
DOI 10.1007/978-3-319-25577-4

advisor: the person referred to in Article 4;
senior corporate officer: the person who, either alone or in consultation with others, represents the highest level of authority in the employer's organisation;
accountable party: manager who is accountable, either directly or indirectly, for the unit of the organisation in which the employee works and/or in which suspected malpractice is taking place;
superior: the employee's direct superior;
counsellor: person appointed to act in that capacity for the employer's organisation;
suspected malpractice: a reasonable suspicion regarding facts or circumstances within the organisation in which the employee works that affect the public interest and involve:

(a) a criminal offence (or the threat of a criminal offence being committed);
(b) an infringement of rules (or the threat of an infringement taking place);
(c) a hazard to public health, public safety or the environment (or the threat of such a hazard arising);
(d) the deliberate misleading of public bodies (or the threat of such occurring);
(e) a waste of public monies (or the threat of such waste); or
(f) the deliberate concealment, destruction or manipulation of information concerning these facts (or the threat of such taking place).

Section 2. Internal Procedure

Article 2. Internal Report Made to a Superior, Accountable Party and/or Counsellor

1. Save in the exceptions referred to in Article 5.2, employees shall report suspected malpractice to their superiors or, if doing so is not considered desirable, to an accountable party or, if doing so is not considered desirable, to the counsellor. Employees may also report suspected malpractice to the counsellor in addition to their superior or an accountable party.
2. On request, the superior or the accountable party shall document the report in writing, recording the date on which it was received, and shall submit the document to the employee for him/her to sign. The employee shall receive a true copy of the document. The superior or the accountable party shall ensure that the senior corporate officer is notified immediately of the suspected malpractice and the date on which the report was received and ensure that the senior corporate officer receives a copy of the document. If the employee has reported his/her suspicions to the counsellor, the counsellor will also notify the senior corporate officer of the report and the date on which it was received, but doing so only at a time and in a manner agreed with the employee.
3. An investigation into the suspected malpractice shall commence without delay.

4. The senior corporate officer shall send confirmation to the employee who has reported suspected malpractice, referring to the original report made. Confirmation shall be sent even if the employee has told a counsellor of his/her suspicions rather than the superior or an accountable party.
5. The senior corporate officer shall decide whether an external third party as referred to in

   Article 6.1 should be notified of the internal report of suspected malpractice.

Article 3. Conclusions

1. The employee shall be notified in writing by or on behalf of the senior corporate officer of the latter's conclusions regarding the suspected malpractice, such notification being received within a period of 8 weeks of the internal report being made. The notification shall also indicate the steps taken following the employee's report.
2. If the senior corporate officer is unable to report his/her conclusions within 8 weeks, he/she or his/her representative will so notify the employee and indicate when the latter can expect to be informed about the conclusions.

Article 4. Advisor

1. The employee may report suspected malpractice to an advisor and request his/her advice in confidence.
2. An advisor may be any person whom the employee trusts and who is bound by professional or official secrecy.

Section 3. Reporting Suspected Malpractice to an External Third Party

Article 5

1. Subject to the provisions of Article 6, the employee may report suspected malpractice to an external third party as referred to in Article 6.1 in the event that:

   (a) he/she does not agree with the conclusions referred to in Article 3;
   (b) he/she has not received such conclusions within the required period of time referred to in Articles 3.1 and 3.2;

(c) the period referred to in Article 3.2 is unreasonably long given the circumstances involved and the employee has voiced his/her objections to the senior corporate officer; or
(d) an exception applies as referred to in the following paragraph.

2. An exception as referred to in Article 5.1.d. shall apply in the event that

   (a) an acute threat involving a serious and urgent public interest requires an immediate external report to be made;
   (b) the employee has good reason to fear reprisals if he/she reports the matter internally;
   (c) there is a clear risk that evidence will be concealed or destroyed;
   (d) a prior internal report of, essentially, the same malpractice made in accordance with the procedure has not led to the desired effect;
   (e) the employee is obliged or empowered by law to immediately report the matter externally

Article 6

1. Within the meaning of these rules, an external third party shall be any organisation or organisational representative, not including the counsellor or an advisor, to which the employee reports suspected malpractice because, in his/her considered opinion and given the circumstances of the case, the public interest being served by reporting the malpractice takes precedence over the employer's interest in maintaining confidentiality, and which, in the employee's considered opinion, can be regarded as capable of rectifying the malpractice or having it rectified, either directly or indirectly.
2. Subject to the provisions of Article 6.3, the employee may report suspected malpractice to an external third party as referred to in the preceding paragraph in one of the cases described in Article 5.
3. The employee shall report the suspected malpractice to the external third party that he/she deems most appropriate given the circumstances of the case, while duly considering how effectively that party can intervene as well as the employer's interest in minimising the loss or damage suffered as a result of such intervention, insofar as such loss or damage is not necessarily the result of measures taken to oppose the malpractice.
4. The greater the risk that reporting suspected malpractice to an external party will cause serious loss or damage to the employer, the stronger the employee's suspicions must be before doing so.

Section 4. Legal Protection

Article 7

1. An employee who has reported suspected malpractice in accordance with the provisions set out in these rules shall not suffer any detrimental effects in his/her job as a result.
2. An advisor as referred to in Article 4 or a counsellor as referred to in Article 1 who works under contract to the employer shall not suffer any detrimental effects in his/her job as a result of acting in such a capacity in accordance with these rules.

Section 5. Effective Date

Article 8

These rules shall take effect on 1 (month) (year).

Annex 1

Legal System Background

Decisions published by the Courts explicity refer to whistleblowing only in a limited number of cases [m27] However, not so much for this reason but rather because of the lesser importance of precedents under Dutch Law, the Courts have at most clarified some material standards for the conduct of employers or employees. Labour Court Judges would tend to search for norms with specific rights or obligations and in the lack thereof take recourse to general principles, such as the duty to be a good employer/employee. This approach may or may not render "sufficient" whistleblower protection. Before definitively assessing the situation,[3] it seems advisable to fully appreciate the Dutch Legal System, at least in regard to whistleblowing.

The legal tradition in the Netherlands is that of Roman or Civil Law country with a bottom layer, which may be termed "Saxo-Germanic." This means its legal ecosystem is not easily comparable with that of country in the Common Law tradition. On the Roman Law side, it is arguably a bit closer to France than to Germany. Looking at the legal valves and locks pertaining to "whistleblowing" communication, it is important to understand, especially from a Common Law perspective, that inherent regulation could be effective even without an explicit law and without reference to legal precedents. This is because in the absence of explicit regulations, the legal subjects as well as the Courts have to take recourse either to higher principles ("upward") or make up their own rules, usually by way of contracts or covenants (downward) which may not conflict with the higher principles. In our case, the latter is encouraged e.g. by offering templates for codes of conduct with whistleblowing procedures.[m28]

[3] As will be attempted in section 4 of this country report.

G. Thüsing, G. Forst (eds.), *Whistleblowing - A Comparative Study*,
Ius Comparatum - Global Studies in Comparative Law 16,
DOI 10.1007/978-3-319-25577-4

Courts have not been discovered to have referenced these codes of conduct in whistleblowing cases. Since many of these codes have been in force for more than five years, this observation might point out a lack of legal effectiveness and/or specific protection in these codes. On the other hand, this might show that very few whistleblowers see reasons to go to Court – or else, get a chance to do so. Another less speculative explanation: in the absence of a specific law spelling out rights, or exceptions to duties, the Courts could be hesitant to accept arguments regarding "whistleblowing" – unless "whistleblowing" is accepted as part of a higher principle, e.g. as an aspect of good employership/employeeship. Whistleblowing is necessary communication about risks.[4]

Therefore this type of communication could or even should be an accepted obligation of employees. For the same reasons it should also be facilitated by employers, and it should be an established element of good employership/employeeship relations.

Dutch Courts do make reference to good employership/employeeship, a legal institute codified in Civil Law.[5] In a case involving a whistleblowing situation, however, the Court let the privacy rights of the employer prevail, even though the facts that were to be kept private, qualified as illegal behaviour. This came about because the employee failed to convince the Court that he had taken the necessary steps to stop the fraud internally. Therefore, the Court was not tasked to discuss whistleblowing.[6] At least the Court clarified that only then, only in the public interest, and only in a "proportional" manner would the employee have been permitted to notify an outside party, e.g. indirect shareholders. This case reminds the reader of a large print testimonial by the Government Centre for Information and Training in Labour Management issues:[m29]

> **Een goede meldingsprocedure is onontbeerlijk!** [7]
> ("A good reporting procedure is indispensable!")

This slogan is literally the bottom line of a core information brochure from the Government to the benefit of Dutch public administrations. The leaflet has the title" Misstanden bespreekbaar maken is pure noodzaak" (a bit ambivalent and awkward to translate: It's pure necessity

- to lift the taboo of talking about deficiencies; or
- to put discussing deficiencies on the agenda; or
- to bring us in a position to speak about deficiencies; or plainly
- to make deficiencies discussable."

The Court did not need to refer to this leaflet, because it is not a legal source. However, the leaflet might have served in Court to indicate generally held values of

---

[4] See e.g. Björn Rohde-Liebenau (2006).

[5] Art. 7:611 Burgerlijk Wetbook.

[6] LJN: BR2582, Gerechtshof Amsterdam, 200.070.341/01.

[7] Information leaflet "Misstanden bespreekbaar maken is pure noodzaak" available for download from the CAOP at www.caop.nl (last access Sept 19).

what is expected of a good employer and a good employee. Especially, since the Labour Fund (Stichting van de Arbeid) makes exactly the same recommendations to its members. Deplorably, the Court saw no reason to ask the employer to prove a good reporting procedure or that there was no inhibition on venting deficiencies, let alone abuses at the workplace. The employer in this case was a private bank, not a public administration. But private banks should arguably be particularly sensitive to deficiencies or abuses to the detriment of their customers.

If one then takes into account the low aggregate numbers of registered internal or external whistleblower reports, the general scarcity of legal precedents, the missing recourse to basic and constitutional rights (e.g. freedom of expression) in balancing juridical arguments in the absence of explicit legislation, as well as the exclusion of effective internal reporting systems from the legal construct of "good employership," a suspicion that the Dutch legal system around whistleblowing may be ineffective and lacking important elements finds confirmation.[m30]

Dutch Courts do not yet perceive an effective reporting procedure or even an open risk communication culture as part of good employership. This in turn calls for measures to be taken to clarify and effectively include these features in the duty to be a good employer/employee. Since such standards in public life have failed to evolve to legal effect in more than ten years, this should now be achieved by a specific law effective for all public and private employers.

Annex 2

1998	Paul **van Buitenen**, Dutch National at the EU Commission becomes most visible European Whistleblower; **PIDA** is voted on in UK Parliament the Dutch Construction Fraud Affair becomes public. (Ad Bos)
1999	Van Buitenen publishes his first book "Strijd voor Europa;" first committee of experts confirms van Buitenen's reports; **OLAF** is installed at the EU Commission.
2000	**Art. 125 quinquies Ambtenarenwet** passed in TK, Decree of 7 Dec 2000; **European Parliament** officially makes itself available for whistleblowing.
2001	Dutch Whistleblowing rules activated, van Buitenen's reports fully confirmed by group of experts for EU Parliament (EP).
2002	Independent, anonymous reporting hotline "Meld Misdaad Anonoem" starts; EU Commission introduces new set of "whistleblower" rules in its standards for EU officials.
2003	Hoge Raad first concerned with klokkenluiden; rising peer pressure on the **private sector** through the US Sarbanes Oxley Act of 2002; STAR publishes an official declaration on how to deal with a suspected deficiencies.
2004	**Model rules for public administration branches;** van Buitenen founds Party "Europa Transparant" and is elected as Dutch Rep. to EP.
2005	Rules implemented in many Dutch administrations
2006	**BIOS** takes up work; first **STAR recommendations for private sector**. First expert report for European Parliament, declares EU Commission rules on whistleblowing low on standards and detrimental.
2007	Review of wb. Rules commissioned by Min. for BZK
2008	**Report on effectiveness of rules in public sector (Bovens et.al.)** published – Dutch rules miss their goal: few reports and NO protection.
2009	Decree on reporting suspicion of abuses in the Government and the Police published
2010	**WB rules in Central Gov. and Police activated,** those for the Military published
2011	Similar rules for Armed Forces; **National Ombudsman becomes involved**, SP offers alternative "**House for Whistleblowers concept [m31] "second expert report for European Parliament confirms EU Commission rules whistleblowing missing standard. [m32]**
2012	**Whistleblowing Advice Centre at the Office of the Nat. Ombudsman;** Dutch Expert Group of Whistleblowers presents **Zwartboek Klokkenluiden (black Book Whistleblowing)**

G. Thüsing, G. Forst (eds.), *Whistleblowing - A Comparative Study*,
Ius Comparatum - Global Studies in Comparative Law 16,
DOI 10.1007/978-3-319-25577-4

CPSIA information can be obtained
at www.ICGtesting.com
Printed in the USA
BVHW040151240419
546382BV00005B/22/P

9 783319 255750